RELIGION AFTER RELIGION

RELIGION AFTER RELIGION

GERSHOM SCHOLEM, MIRCEA ELIADE, AND HENRY CORBIN AT ERANOS

Steven M. Wasserstrom

PRINCETON UNIVERSITY PRESS   PRINCETON, NEW JERSEY

Library of Congress Cataloging-in-Publication Data

Wasserstrom, Steven M.
Religion after religion : Gershom Scholem, Mircea Eliade, and
Henry Corbin at Eranos / Steven M. Wasserstrom.
p.   cm.
Includes bibliographical references and index.
ISBN 0-691-00539-7 (cl : alk. paper). — ISBN 0-691-00540-0
(pb : alk. paper)
1. Religion—Philosophy—History—20th century.   2. Scholem,
Gershom Gerhard, 1897–   .   3. Eliade, Mircea, 1907–   .   4. Corbin,
Henry.   I. Title.
BL51.W225   1999
200′.7′2—dc21   99-24174

This book has been composed in Galliard

Hero-Gods, Prophets, Poets, Priests are forms of heroism that belong to the old ages, make their appearance in the remotest times; some of them have ceased to be possible long since, and cannot any more show themselves in this world. The Hero as *Man of Letters*, again, of which class we are to speak today, is altogether a product of these new ages; and so long as the wondrous art of *Writing*, or of Ready-writing which we call *Printing*, subsists, he may be expected to continue, as one of the main forms of Heroism in all future ages. He is, in various respects, a very singular phenomenon.
        —*Thomas Carlyle, 19 May 1840*

To give an author—and, in particular, an author who is a genius—the benefit of the doubt is a mark of our respect for his achievement; so respectful are we that we rightly tend to include his person in his achievement. . . . A genius lives in his work . . . [which] may help us see a reason why Socrates published nothing; he merely taught. Oral tradition is one thing; tradition and its individual talents, published, quite another. "Tradition" now exists to be broken through by the individual talent. This subversive activity gives its meaning to "creativity" and "originality."
        —*Philip Rieff, 26 March 1971*

Contents

Preface and Acknowledgments

THE IDEA of *religion after religion* has dominated my study of Gershom Scholem, Mircea Eliade, and Henry Corbin in the quarter century since they first attracted my attention. Like other readers, I wondered what kind of religion these awe-inspiring scholars represented. I asked myself whether they had experiential or even initiatic warrants for their authoritative expositions of esoteric and "secret" traditions. Later, when I routinely used their work as a teacher and scholar in the history of religions, I tended to push aside these curiosities, which seemed unduly probing. In postgraduate studies on Jewish and Muslim relations under early Islam, I regularly used many works by Corbin and Scholem. My scholarly identity, meanwhile, formed as a historian of religions; as such, I had necessarily also to engage Eliade. Whenever possible, I combined Judeo-Islamic research with my interest in the history of religions.[1]

Eventually, as I conceptualized the present project, it occurred to me that this could not be *only* a study in the history of "the History of Religions"—which it is first and primarily. The problem, I realized, was essentially the one I first worried about, though now in a modified form. That is, I realized that there was no way to take Corbin, Eliade, and Scholem seriously without understanding their writing as a whole. I could not "reduce" them to their psyches, their economic locations, or their societies. And so I sought, instead, to understand them integrally.[2] Accordingly, I do not present their lives on a technically biographical level—their marriages, tastes, adventures (almost nonexistent, so far as I know, for these sedentary scholars).[3] Nor do I provide an introduction to their work. Since I am neither writing an overview of their respective works nor undertaking biographies of them, I realized all the more that I could do what has not been done. And that is to elucidate, for the first time, their theory of religion. Readers like me have long sensed that the authority of their stance somehow transcended their control of languages, editions of texts, or even their masterful works of interpretation. My search for that "somehow" resulted in this book.

The overarching theory that they shared, I concluded, was a shared idea of *religion after religion*. A paradoxical idea on many levels—a nonreligious religiosity, a secular antimodernism, a metarationalism operating within academic discourse—*religion after religion* speaks for the mystical traditions they represented from within and without at the same time. *Religion after religion* speaks to this uncanny doubleness in their scholarship; it suggests that their stance toward the reader was Janus-faced.

On the one hand it alludes to some new form of religion after the expiration of traditional forms; on the other hand, it also refers to a project in comparative religion, a study of religions in the plural, a university-based study of one religion after another.

I want first to acknowledge Elliot R. Wolfson, who revealed himself to me as outside reader of this book for the Press. He provided detailed close readings of the entire manuscript and followed up with additional help when I asked for it. This help has been invaluable, and I appreciate it deeply. Invitations to lecture or write on aspects of this project came from Elliot R. Wolfson, S. Daniel Breslauer, Patrice Brodeur, Mercedes García-Arenal, Kambiz GhaneaBassiri, Jane Hathaway, Martin Jaffee, Jeffrey Kripal, Jane McAullife, Tamar Rudavsky, Guy G. Stroumsa, Richard Stein, and Brannon Wheeler. I owe each of them my appreciation. Others who provided helpful and insightful readings include Martha Balshem, Bruce Lincoln, Michael Ostling, Gustavo Benavides, and Hugh Urban. I am grateful to those who helped me find research materials, including Stefan Arvidsson, Leon Volovici, Horst Junginger, Peter Gordon, and Michele Rosenthal. My assistants at Reed included Eric Vandever and Anmol Nayyar. I want especially to mention the extraordinary efforts of Jeremy Walton. Andrea Speedie ushered the manuscript through its final days: she treated it with the solicitous care provided by a born physician. Help with translations from German came from Erica Weaver, Frederike Heuer, Sabine Frye, and Werner Brandl. Financial support has been generously and consistently provided by the deans at Reed College, Linda Mantel and Peter Steinberger. I want to thank the Graves Foundation for funding the semester that made much of the final composition possible. At Princeton University Press, Deborah Malmud took an early and sustained interest in this project. I want also to thank Ann Wald for her continuing support of my work.

I thank the editors and publishers of the following for permission to reprint revised versions of the following articles: "A Rustling in the Woods: The Turn to Myth in Weimar Jewish Thought," in *The Seductiveness of Jewish Myth. Challenge or Response?* edited by S. Daniel Breslauer (Albany, N.Y.: State University of New York Press, 1997): 97–123. "'Defeating Evil From Within: Comparative Perspectives on Gershom Scholem's 'Redemption through Sin,'" *Journal of Jewish Thought and Philosophy* 6 (1997): 37–57.

This book is dedicated to Reedies everywhere.

THE PRESENT volume is at most a preliminary foray into a highly complex area of research. The respective collected writings of each scholar alone occupies a bookshelf. Much of their work remains unpublished, if not inaccessible. Archives of these three scholars reside in three different countries on three different continents. Additional archival materials are scattered in at least six countries in their respective six languages (Germany, Romania, France, Israel, Iran, and the United States). I have chosen, generally, to concentrate on the published writings of these men, particularly their many English translations. As much use as possible has been made of materials in German, French, and Hebrew. The present volume, in any case, is not intended as an introduction to their work, nor does it pretend to be comprehensive. I provide neither introductory nor systematic reviews of their numerous contributions to so many varied areas of research. Such studies—some obviously superior to others—are readily available elsewhere. I have accordingly not attempted to engage these critiques, except when it has been necessary in the course of my exposition. In general, then, I will not argue with other ways of reading them.

The enormous scale of their production, and the intrinsic difficulty of much of their recondite materials, in the ideal situation, must be dealt with by any serious student of their work. In my case, I have tried to avoid extended discussion of the difficulties internal to their various expositions of theosophical, alchemical, hermetic, and other systems of symbols. My concern has not been with the technical adequacy of those expositions, but rather with the idea of religion which frames and undergirds them, and which they in turn seem obviously designed to support.

All three of these men eventually published autobiographical works—at some length, in the case of Eliade, of moderate dimensions for Scholem, and a few pages, in the case of Corbin.[1] Only a small percentage of their correspondence has been published.[2] That they did so provides another justification for the present work, at least to a certain degree.[3] That they themselves presented their own lives as worthy of study, in other words, invites us to do so, especially if we take them seriously.

The form of the present volume is, then, thematic and not systematic. I do not elucidate their ideas other than thematically. In doing so I have tried to establish authentic parallels on matters of substance.[4] I direct the reader who seeks introductions to their thought to look elsewhere.[5] Nor will I address all the themes possible for study in a work of this kind. The themes chosen here are a necessarily selective sample, though I would hope that they are both representative and central to their thinking. Cross-referencing is provided in my notes for the reader who is interested in moving from idea to idea.

Nothing like this project exists. There are many works on each of these thinkers, but none on all three of them. Only a handful of articles deal with the Eranos group, and these mostly deal superficially with the full range of its dozens of participants across all the years of its existence.[6] Given the scattered, difficult-to-access character of many of the texts cited, I decided to cite sometimes extensive sections of them. Since it is unlikely that many readers will be familiar with or even have access to all of these texts, I have tried to render the service of providing ample extracts. Obviously, I also hope that this choice will make this book clearer and more persuasive. I would just add that any perusal of the work of Eliade, Corbin, and Scholem will quickly reveal that they themselves likewise routinely cited copiously from their authorities. I do not hesitate—and not only in this connection—to associate myself with them.

RELIGION AFTER RELIGION

Introduction

. . . one must also learn to read books against
their declared intentions.
—*Gershom Scholem*

THE GREATEST SCHOLARS require the closest study. During the postwar
period, the critical study of religion in North America was significantly
altered under the impact of the discipline known as History of Religions,
especially as it was formulated by Romanian emigré comparativist Mircea
Eliade (1907–1986). Eliade was one of a group of scholars of religion
who met regularly at a chateau in Ascona, Switzerland. Beginning in
1933 these annual meetings, inspired by the Swiss psychotherapist Carl
G. Jung, were held under the designation of *Eranos*. The papers presented in Ascona (often two hours or more in length) were published in a
distinguished annual, the *Eranos-Jahrbuch*. Through this publication, and
through the general eminence of participating scholars, the approach to
religion that they epitomized infiltrated scholarship on religion throughout the world. These scholars were among the most influential in their
fields; many of them enjoyed an international readership and broad cultural impact during the peak years of the Cold War.

Between 1949 and 1976, the generalist Mircea Eliade, the Judaist Gershom Scholem (1898–1982), and the Islamicist Henry Corbin (1907–
1978) regularly lectured at Ascona and were eventually acclaimed as
being among the very most distinguished members of the Eranos group.
By 1961 they were three of the five members of the so-called guardian
committee of Eranos.[1] Although all three began their careers in the
1920s and 1930s, the synthetic works they delivered at Eranos brought
them each a new, vastly amplified international audience. Their lengthy
annual lectures were not only printed in the *Eranos-Jahrbuch*, but were
subsequently translated, collected, and reprinted in many forms and formats. The Bollingen Foundation, a patron of the Eranos meetings, also
provided fellowships to Scholem, Corbin, and Eliade, and their major
works were published by Princeton University Press's distinguished Bollingen Series.

The personal background of these three suggests, in many respects,
that they emerged from what, seen retrospectively, can permissibly be
characterized as a common milieu.[2] All three were born within a decade
of each other, and within a decade of the turn of the century (Scholem in

1898, Corbin in 1903, Eliade in 1907). They were each born into the prosperous middle classes of European capitals (Berlin, Paris, Bucharest). Each rejected the religious practice of his parents during or shortly after World War I. They each took Ph.D.s and became noted Orientalists at precocious ages. Each traveled widely in artistic, philosophical, and political circles in the 1920s and 1930s, forming friendships with some of the leading artists and philosophers not only of their own countries but throughout Europe. Each became passionately committed to what may be called "spiritual nationalism" (two of the three for adopted countries) and thereby consorted with and influenced future national leaders: Eliade for his native Romania, Scholem for Israel, and Corbin for Iran. Each eventually became highly influential as spiritual ideologues of those countries. They lived the bulk of their adult lives outside Europe. Two of the three lived most of their adult lives in the Middle East, and the third had visited the East and was a noted expert in so-called Eastern religions. By the 1950s each was world famous, and by the 1960s each had taken on international sage status. By this point, in fact, each was considered by many observers to be "the leading man" in his respective field of scholarship. Moreover, each was widely influential outside his chosen field.

This celebrity was accomplished partly by means of a common base of publication. Thus, for example, they each published in the Bollingen Series of Princeton University Press; the *Eranos-Jahrbuch*; UNESCO's *Diogenes*; Bibliothèque de l'Hermétisme series of the Paris publishing house Albin Michel; and *Revue de l'Histoire des Religions*. They even shared translators: Ralph Manheim translated Corbin and Scholem, while Willard Trask translated Eliade and Corbin. They served on editorial boards together: Eliade and Scholem served on the board of Ruth Nanda Anshen's "Religious Perspectives"; Eliade and Corbin served on the board of *Hermes*; and both Scholem and Eliade were published by Robert Hutchins's Center for the Study of Democratic Institutions.[3] Each of them cited the work of the others. And each contributed to the *Festschriften* for the others. Eliade published Corbin in his journal *Antaios,* and Corbin, reflecting a more profound level of esoteric intimacy, chose Eliade to "actively participate in the colloquia" of his Université Saint Jean de Jerusalem.[4]

Together, through such means, these three scholars transformed prevailing conceptions of monotheism. Perhaps most important, each devised a theory of religion, with monotheistic traditions as the primary concern of Scholem and Corbin and Christianity as a secondary (but still crucial) issue for the generalist Eliade. While many studies have been written concerning each of these individuals and his respective thought, no one has yet looked from a comparative perspective at their contribution to a general theory of religion. I hope to demonstrate that significant affinities, which they share, largely have been understudied, and that the equally important differences between them have often been misconstrued, when they have been noticed at all.

More specifically, I will assess their theories of religion, which each characterized both as a "phenomenology of religion" as well as a "History of Religions." Variously influenced by Jung's theory of "archetypes," these scholars isolated, described, and analyzed generic features of religion, with a focus on the centrality of mystical experience. In this theoretical revision, each scholar underplayed the importance of law, ritual, and social history. Instead, they primarily were concerned with myth and mysticism. With this striking reversal of the conventional emphases of adherents as well as of many scholars, they developed a monotheism without ethics. In addition to this theory of religion, I also will study their controversial views on history. Each was a practicing historian, but each espoused a theory of history quite counter to prevailing definitions of that term. The theory of language, including hermeneutics, symbolism, and myth, was likewise central to their work on religion, and therefore will be studied closely in this project. Variously influenced by such conceptions as Boehme's "theosophy," Schelling's "theogonic process," Nietzsche's "beyond good and evil," Jung's theory of "archetypes," and Rudolf Otto's "idea of the holy," their mythocentric and mystocentric approach posited generic features of religion, with an emphasis on the centrality of mystical experience, myth, gnosis, esoterism, and eschatology. Such German Romantics as Hamann and Goethe also influenced them markedly. The result of these shared influences may be considered an essentially aesthetic approach to religion insofar as it posited the epistemological centrality of symbols. They each tended to refer to symbolic complexes as "Ideas"—Scholem wrote *The Messianic Idea in Judaism*, Eliade wrote a three-volume *History of Religious Ideas*, and Corbin was a philosopher whose focus was what he called the *mundus idealis*, the world of visionary ideas. Each was a historian, in other words, with an explicitly metahistorical—if not idealist—agenda. Each explicitly positioned gnosis at the center of that program. And each, finally, placed as a mystery at the heart of that gnosis a *coincidentia oppositorum*, a godhead unifying opposites, transcendent but apprehensible through symbols.

I will consider both their widely studied books (dozens of which remain in print, in numerous languages) as well as lesser-known sources in order to set their theories of religion into appropriately integrated contexts. These contexts transcended the striking, unforeseen institutionalization of the critical study of religion in the international academy, of which they became prestigious superstars. Secondarily, I will reflect on the role they played in Judaism, Christianity, and Islam as such; that is, the ways in which they transcended the academic History of Religions and entered the active life of the religions that they studied. It will be necessary, in that connection, to investigate their various expressions of "spiritual nationalism"—Scholem's Zionism, Eliade's active and eventually official support (as a press and propaganda attaché) for a succession of Romanian regimes, and Corbin's Iranian romantic nationalism—to understand its relation to their theory of religion. All were European emigrants who lived outside Europe for most of their careers; all had personal access to heads of state; and all wrote influentially on the question of religion and nationalism.[5] They thus were importantly engaged in the nationalistic struggles of Iran, Romania, and Israel.

Their bodies of scholarship, in short, were interconnected in many respects. So too was the substance of their worldviews. Each resolutely opposed technology and sociology, reductionism and nihilism, orthodoxy and positivism. Against these targets they each were polemicists. Each was particularly acute on the inadequacies of contemporaneous studies of religion.[6] By contrast, they championed the autonomous reality of the "imaginal," or the "sacred," or "religious reality." Each nonetheless chose History of Religions as his profession, becoming a professor with the highest conceivable academic prestige while simultaneously crossing over to be seen as a "religious thinker" outside the academy. Finally, then, I will reflect on their impact on culture in general.[7] Their international and still-growing influence on literary critics, philosophers, theologians, poets, psychologists, novelists, politicians and clergy demands to be understood (and critiqued) for what it is: perhaps the most dynamic and innovative discourse on "religion" in the second half of the twentieth century.

EXILE

> Des caps ultime de l'exil—un homme encore dans
> le vent tenant conseil avec lui-même—j'élèverai
> une dernière fois la main.

> (From the very last headlands of exile—a man still
> in the wind holding counsel with himself—I will
> raise my hand one last time)
> —*St. John Perse*, Winds

The literary critic Elias Auerbach, a friend of Scholem's friend Walter Benjamin, spent the war years exiled in Istanbul, where Henry Corbin also lived in those years.[8] Auerbach's essay "Philology and *Weltliteratur*" illuminates the tension, unresolved if not unresolvable, between nationalistic programs and the universalistic character of general theories in religion. In Auerbach's concluding reflections, he observed that a certain dialectic must be brought into play if the philologist is effectively to transcend nationalism in quest of understanding "World Literature."

> In any event, our philological home is the earth: it can no longer be the nation. The most priceless and indispensable part of a philologist's heritage is still his own nation's culture and heritage. *Only when he is first separated from this heritage, however, and then transcends it does it become truly effective.*[9]

In other words, exile may stimulate a heightened awareness of universality.[10] I suggest that such a heightened awareness formed a significant backdrop for the scholars studied here. The second volume of Eliade's autobiography is titled *Exile's Odyssey*. Scholem wrote from a Zionist perspective, thus explicitly from a point of view concerned with the problem of Judaism in exile. His justly celebrated interpretation of Lurianic myth as itself being a myth both of Jewish exile and of a kind of exile within the godhead is well known.

> . . . the historical exile of the Jewish people is none other than the most striking symbol of that state of the universe in which there is no *tikkun* or harmony, and by which every thing is damaged and harmed. Exile and redemption are thereby transformed into powerful symbols, acquiring the background of a cosmic myth. This may explain the tremendous attraction of these ideas until the period of the Enlightenment.[11]

And Corbin made many analogous remarks from a gnostic perspective. "[The] sanctuary of the human microcosm [is] at present in exile, in the crypt of the celestial Temple. . . . Our measures are valid only for the world of exile, because they are provided by the very form of exile."[12] The world itself languishes in a kind of celestial exile, from this gnostic point of view.

Whether celestial or national, exile informed their approach to religion in at least two ways. On the one hand, exile accentuated the sense of professional marginality forced on them by circumstance. They not only moved to new countries as adults, they also worked in a fairly new discipline, generally in new universities, departments, or programs. On the other hand, as Auerbach suggested, exile stimulated their transnational, transcultural, or transreligious thinking as well. "Only when he is first separated from this heritage, however, and then transcends it does it become truly effective."[13] For each of them, a multinational perspective served them well, becoming effective in highlighting the universality of their ideas.

TRIUMPH

Although a heartfelt metaphysics of exile was integral to the thought of Eliade, Corbin, and Scholem, they surmounted personal exile as well. One could—inadequately, of course—claim that their extraordinary institutional successes marked a triumphant return from exile on the part of their thought if not of their lives. But, even if, as I do, one hesitates thus to assimilate the life with the work, it is still important to observe the enormous cultural significance of their success.

Not only did Scholem create the study of Jewish mysticism as we know it, he is also, more or less by consensus, the most influential, widely read, generally significant Judaist of the twentieth century. He was almost certainly the best-known Israeli professor in any field, elected president of the Israeli Academy of Arts and Sciences and winner of numerous prizes, including the Bialik Prize and the Rothschild Prize. Eliade founded what he personally named "the History of Religions," and he remains, even on the wane, almost certainly the most familiar name in the field. He likewise received many international honors, living to see both a chair and the leading encyclopedia in the field named for him. Henry Corbin was less feted than these colleagues of his, though he was certainly internationally celebrated. In the last decade of his life, Corbin founded l'Université Saint Jean de Jerusalem. This hermetic university more or less indisputably brought into the open his esoterism, which until then was, in any event, an open secret. The Templar dimension of l'Université Saint Jean de Jerusalem in turn seems to derive from a Martinist determination to "reconstitute" the Orders of the Knights Templars.[14] When Eliade discussed Martinism in his 1974 Freud Lecture, he mentioned just this point.[15] Corbin and Eliade seem to have shared some common affinities, if not initiatic affiliations, with illuminist orders that emphasize Christian Kabbalah. Corbin, it should be added, also lived long enough to a see a school of post-Jungian psychology, James Hillman's "Archetypal Psychology," substantially and explicitly influenced by his thought.

My account assumes—but does not provide the narrative for—the ascendance of the History of Religions as it marched from exile to triumph. The History of Religions itself, in the period of the Cold War, emerged from the wilderness of academic life to occupy, for a time, the center of Religious Studies. This remarkable rise of a new vocation was due in no small measure to such prolific, persuasive, and widely-read scholars as Mircea Eliade, Henry Corbin, and Gershom Scholem. In a sense, the success of the History of Religions reflected a kind of dialectic between power and powerlessness that worked itself out across their lifetimes.

THE "HISTORY OF RELIGIONS" IN HISTORICAL PERSPECTIVE

> I wonder if the wholesale transplantation of Euro-
> pean scholarship and science into an English-
> speaking environment in the middle of the twen-
> tieth-century will not seem a revolution compara-
> ble to the Renaissance itself.
> —*Fergus Millar*

After World War II, thanks to Talcott Parsons, Edwards Shils, and a handful of other sociologists, Max Weber's sociology of religion finally enjoyed its rightful impact in North America. With the belated reception of Weber came a renewal of interest in a *calling*, a *vocation* sufficient to surmount the alienation and anxiety then dominating cultural discussion. Weber's "Luther's Conception of the Calling" chapter in *The Protestant Ethic and the Spirit of Capitalism* was followed by Erik Erikson's daz-zling 1958 investigation of the same theme in *Young Man Luther*.[16] The following year, Norman O. Brown returned to this question in his widely discussed *Life Against Death*.[17] Into this cultural conversation the Eranos *Homo religiosus* exhibited his own calling (*Beruf*) to respond to postwar anxiety. It was into this conversation that Mircea Eliade contributed his French essay "Religious Symbolism and Modern Man's Anxiety," which appeared originally in 1953 and in English translation in 1960.[18]

The Historian of Religion as *Homo religiosus* had arrived on the scene. Against the anxieties of the time, and especially against the anxiety-pro-voking specter of professional specialization, this new vocation responded instead to the thirst for transcendence and totality. This exalted calling called not to a career-track but to life itself. In some respects it resembled the strong version of a philosophical calling. Count Yorck von Warten-burg, who was cited by Scholem in the epigraph to his *Sabbatai Sevi* (first published in Hebrew in 1957), once proclaimed that "[philosophy] is not science but life."[19] Edmund Husserl subsequently insisted that the *Beruf* of philosophy was nothing less than the "possibility of a radical transformation of humanity."[20] Such Jewish thinkers as Ernst Cassirer and Franz Rosenzweig, and of course Martin Heidegger among German phi-losophers, also addressed the question of a *Lebensphilosphie*, of the radical calling of philosophy as a call to Life as such.[21] Eliade's most dramatic treatment of the centrality of the theme of Life came in his debut work of large-scale, international scholarship, *Patterns in Comparative Religion*, published in English in 1963.[22]

A new kind of intellectual vitalism, this Life-centered idea of Religion came to be known as History of Religions. I am using the term "History of Religions" to refer jointly to the thought of Eliade, Corbin, and Scholem; others employ the term differently, then and now.[23] There were, to be sure, many significant differences between these three Historians of Religion—differences that I hope to illuminate throughout this book. But there also are a number of rather striking similarities. To sketch these similarities somewhat summarily by way of introduction, it may be said that Scholem occupied a position in relation to Jewish Studies closely analogous to that held by Corbin in Islamic Studies; Scholem shared his programmatic emphasis on antinomianism with Eliade; and Eliade shared his engagement with contemporaneous esoterism with Corbin.[24] These and other overlapping features, shared concerns, and parallel developments provide a purpose for this project.

A synoptic view of their composite intellectual biographies gives some sense of the depth of this common experience. The period with which this book is concerned, from 1949 to 1978, is roughly the length of a generation. These decades were chosen because they were the years in which Scholem, Corbin, and Eliade participated at Eranos, but they are significant for other reasons.[25] First, the Cold War began in 1949. While this book is not a political history, it is interested in the historical contexts of religious thought. These European men, who mastered "non-European" religious studies and who left the continent itself, were nonetheless still European in certain fundamental respects. They were men of the so-called Generation of 1914.[26] It is no little irony, furthermore, that perhaps their most enthusiastic professional acclaim stemmed neither from Europe nor from the "East" but rather from the United States, from which much of their funding and their book sales emanated during this period.

The story of their ascent to world fame is fraught with yet other ironies. The almost mythic drama of their intellectual biographies, on the one hand, largely derived from the encounter of European with extra-European sensibilities, especially religious sensibilities. On the other hand, they achieved their fame and influence at a time when religion, at least in its public manifestations and its private intellectual forms, seemed most on the wane. The year 1978 symbolizes this irony. This was the year of the first death among them, that of Henry Corbin. But this *annus mirabilis* also marked the first year of a new age, the age of the return of religion. This now familiar periodization is justified by, among other things, the world-historical import of the 1979 Iranian Revolution. Corbin, it has been observed, died only a few months before Ayatollah Khomeini returned from Paris to Tehran. These two champions of the soul of Iran, both of whom alternated in this period between these two cities, symbolize the tension of traditionalisms to be explored in this book. Similarly ironic world historical shifts likewise soon attended the final years of Scholem and Eliade. Scholem died in 1982, at a time when the theologico-political situation in Israel was about to shift dramatically. And Eliade's death in 1986 was followed in 1989 by the fall of the Ceauşescu regime in his native Romania. In short, the deaths of all three were shortly followed by astonishing changes in their spiritual homelands. These changes, it should be emphasized, each throw their respective careers into a quite unexpected new light. Most especially, these theologico-political changes brought large-scale changes regarding the position of religion in culture and society, changes that we are, even now, only barely beginning to comprehend.

The greatest scholars, whatever their contexts, demand the closest study. This truism, valid as it is, is only the point of departure for the present project. There are several intrinsically good reasons, I think, why this study is both necessary and important. I have chosen to study these great scholars not as specialists, as Orientalists, or as philologists, but rather as cultural giants. That I have done so is consistent with their holism, with their insistence that their thought be seen as a whole. They intended to be understood this way and they proclaimed that they should be read this way.[27] Still, however much they wanted to be studied organically in their totality, and not "reduced" to their constituitive parts, they each, variously, practiced what Leo Strauss famously termed "the art of writing."[28] This esoteric style of indirection resulted in fundamental difficulties in locating that totality. Accordingly, all the more, then, I have looked at them as "whole men," though, to be sure, men who were writing with a certain dissimulation.[29] None of this should be taken to imply that I am interested in any kind of conspiratorialism, and certainly not with any sort of retrospective prosecution. I claim neither to indict nor to uncover conspiracies.

Still, this group *was a group*, or at least a circle, that identified with the cultural project of Eranos. Eliade invoked this group identity in stirring historical images.[30] Though in each case they belonged to many other groups too, this group has not been discussed (at least not at any length) as a group. Although it would seem that few scholars today see them as a group, and they themselves at most sporadically and allusively identified themselves this way, the mutual reinforcement they provided each other at mid-career, in their Eranos years, naturally contributes to this perception. Most important for present purposes, the manifold points they shared in common—from technical terminology and formative influences to common venues of funding and publication—underwrites this perception. These seem a contemporary example of Goethe's *Wahlverwan-*

derschaften, Elective Affinities.[31] The foregoing, it seems to me, is warrant enough. The project in hand, then, concerns this affinity group as it formed and developed in the Eranos years.

It would appear that only Scholem might have participated in the event at the Annual Meeting of the American Academy of Religion in which a senior scholar is seated before an audience to discuss "How I Changed My Mind and Why." That is, Scholem alone of the three stated that he *had* changed his mind, that he was proud of it, and that such dynamism is a fundamental element in any scientific approach to one's subject.[32] By contrast, Corbin and Eliade espoused, both in form and in content, stasis, circular theories recirculated from a still point around which they turned. That is, they not only articulated theories of cycles, but they themselves repeated themselves, cycled through their theories, in long, slow, swooping repetitions. They never repudiated earlier ideas, but only continued to augment and elaborate a few basic ideas. This seems quite in keeping with Western esoteric traditions holding that various phenomena reveal singular truths. The many editions, translations, reprintings, that their work underwent—this holds true especially for Eliade, and less so for the others—therefore will not be sorted out here. Such a publishing history would be complicated indeed, and in any event would be unlikely to contribute much to the present effort.[33] Instead I have concentrated on the mature expresssion of their central ideas as they came to international attention between 1949 and 1976.

For the first time, *Religion after Religion* interprets the work of these three scholars with reference to the common discourse in which they participated. This book will analyze the thought of these three prolific writers utilizing the available range of their writings, which includes radio talks, poems, novels, novellas, short stories, letters, journals, autobiographies, correspondence, and interviews—in addition to every form of academic venue.[34] In short, for the first time, this book will analyze their conception of religion from a broadly integrated, comparative perspective. In so doing, my primary aim will be to set their distinctive thinking into appropriate historical and intellectual contexts. In that way, it may be possible to interpret the striking success of their approach, and, ultimately, to attempt to identify some of its inadequacies.

Such a study is warranted by their relatively recent deaths; is stimulated by the subsequent, rapidly expanding reconsiderations of their scholarship; and it is encouraged by the end of the Cold War, which now allows us to begin to understand how their mature work might have been a product of its historical era. Their bodies of thought, in short, can now be read as related responses to their common moment. These responses, reread in this light, still speak to us; perhaps, most important, they speak to the present transitional moment of our shared understanding of religion. I hope that the present effort will, in this more general sense, contribute to a critical reexamination of the approach to religion known as *History of Religions*.

SYMMETRY AND DIFFERENCE

There certainly were differences between them. Scholem was a master of primary historical research and a discoverer of the highest distinction; Eliade's work was largely derivative, most accomplished not at original research but rather at a kind of *haute vulgarisation*. Eliade succeeded as a gifted generalist and popularizer; Scholem generally balanced this task against his primary obligation to philological inquiry and historical discovery. Eliade and Corbin were overtly mystifying esoterists; Scholem was generally hardheaded in this respect, though he was not averse to playing an esoteric game. Eliade and Corbin obviated the centrality of historical change in their work; Scholem's historical and metahistorical work was preoccupied with the significance of historical change. Corbin and Scholem edited and translated vast quantities of difficult texts; Eliade never undertook such tasks.

One central asymmetry in this volume should be stressed at the outset. Gershom Scholem was a scholar spiritually unrelated to Eliade and Corbin, who were in fundamental respects esoteric blood brothers.[35] The impetus animating the labors undertaken here, then, is not to claim that Scholem was somehow to be understood as their third brother. Quite the opposite. Rather, in spite of deep differences dividing them, Scholem still chose to associate himself and his work with them and with their work—that is the interesting thing.

It is not enough to claim that Scholem attended the Eranos meetings merely out of professional expedience, because, as an isolated scholar in the Middle East, he had no other outlets.[36] To be sure, Scholem was, like Freud before him, an intellectual conquistador, and he certainly appreciated the professional advantages of operating annually out of Ascona.[37] Still—and this brings me to the substance of the present volume—he did so because there was simply much that he shared with his Eranos peers. Scholem, while not a Jungian, *did* identify with the Eranos enterprise.[38] To be sure, he appreciated it for the opportunities it provided him. As he put it in his acceptance speech for the Literary Prize of the Bavarian Academy of Arts, "I was given the opportunity [at Eranos] to arrive at a synthesis of things upon which I had worked for thirty years, without sacrificing historical criticism or philosophical thought."[39] This may seem lukewarm compared to the rather ecstatic encomia to Eranos repeatedly offered by Eliade and Corbin, but it also reflects much more than mere opportunism. Eranos was a place where, as he put it, Scholem could exercise synthesis without sacrifice.

Why, one might ask—unsatisfied with the merely trivial "explanation" of ambition—did Scholem struggle to convey his findings to a larger audience, and to continue to do so for the thirty years he was at the peak of his profession? Why, for that matter, had he chosen his international debut volume, *Major Trends in Jewish Mysticism*, to be published first in English? Why did this Zionist pioneer and early champion of Hebrew cultural literacy compose his magnificent, synthetic essays on Kabbalistic themes in German, a scant few years after the Holocaust? Why, at the peak of his career, lauded in Israel and venerated in the United States, did he return to the Europe he scornfully abandoned in 1923? What, in short, was the idiom of understanding religion to which he was drawn to express himself, the approach typified at Eranos that attracted him and retained him?

One obvious (if understudied) answer was that he was committed to understanding the phenomenon of religion. While he announced un-equivocally that "there is no such thing as mysticism as such," he also quite unmistakably was taken with the classical and general problems of understanding religion.[40] For more than a half century he studied Kab-balah not only in its parochial Jewish environment but also in its various relations with gnosticism, with Islam, with Christianity, with secularism, and so forth. And for all his overwhelming accomplishments as a philolo-gist, any reader of his knows that he was no mere technician. He was a humanist—a religious humanist, to be sure, but a humanist nonetheless. And Eranos allowed him to operate as a humanist—"without sacrificing historical criticism or philosophical thought."

His humanistic life's work was to articulate for the first time the world history of Kabbalah. What he discovered at Ascona was an environment in which he could locate Kabbalah inside both a spiritual and a critical history of humanity, however grandiose that may sound. The question then becomes, what was the idiom specifically available to Scholem at the Eranos events? A first effort toward that answer is found on the pages of this book. In a sense, then, this book is designed to probe the critical problem of universality versus particularity. That is, how is it that these three philologists and specialists came to be seen as sages with ele-vated understandings of religion in general? Were Scholem's Zionism or Eliade's Romanian patriotism or Corbin's Persophilia in tension with their attempts to understand religion in general? On the one hand, Scho-lem seemed to say that Kabbalah is identical only with its own (Jewish) history—but on the other hand he did go to Ascona in the heart of

Europe, where he could frame his *Judaistik* inside a universally comprehensible format. His Eranos lectures, as printed essays in the distinguished annual *Eranos-Jahrbuch*, served this purpose.

Still, Scholem carefully spoke and usually wrote only from the point of view of his specialization. When invited to contribute to a Swiss magazine honoring Eranos, Scholem submitted a piece modestly titled "Contributions of a Kabbalah-Researcher."[41] In fact, while Eliade regularly attacked specialization, Scholem felt it was both the bedrock of all insight and the propaedeutic to any advance upon that firm ground. In perhaps the most polemical piece he ever wrote—and one of the most moving apologies for philology ever put to paper—Scholem defended such attention to philological detail.

> We wished to immerse ourselves in the study of the finest detail. We were seized by a compulsion to deal with the dry details, the small things of the great things, so as to develop therein the closed well of turbulent vitality, for we knew that this was its place and there it was hidden, and that from there we could draw upon its waters and quench our thirst. We sought the great scientific idea which would illuminate the details like rays of the sun playing upon the surface of the water, yet we knew—and is there any serious man of science who has not experienced this eternal debate within his heart?—that it does not dwell save in the details themselves. . . . And we thereby became specialists, masters of one trade. And if we did not struggle with God, as in the words of the *aggadah*, we struggled with the Satan who danced among us. This was the Satan of irresponsible dilettantism, who does not know the secret of construction, because he does not know the secret of destruction.[42]

Corbin's assaults on historicism were thus in the most sharply pointed contrast to Scholem's consistent and emphatic defense of historical method and historical research. In the monumental essay on "Kabbalah" that he contributed to the *Encyclopedia Judaica*, an article that he must have known would be seen as a monumental centerpiece of his scholarly production, Scholem concluded with a review of scholarship on this subject. After World War I, he wrote, a "new attempt was made to understand, independently of all polemic or apologetic positions, the genesis, development, historical role, and social and intellectual influence of the Kabbalah within the total context of the internal and external forces that have determined the shape of Jewish history."[43] He then named himself—quite properly, of course—as one of the pioneers in this new attempt. And he again named himself, in conclusion, as the first of the "foremost representatives of the school of historical criticism" that subsequently developed at the Hebrew University.[44] Obviously and appropriately, he was proud to be a "foremost representative of the Jerusalem school of historical criticism."[45]

I would point to another important contrast. Scholem was a man of peace. I do not speak only of the trio's secular politics, though this difference is also biographically demonstrable. Even as a very young man, the budding Kabbalah scholar took the most unpopular stand of opposing German involvement in the World War I.[46] As an Israeli, Scholem was a member of the similarly unpopular early peace movement Brit Shalom; he was, in his words, "one of the first seven professors of the Hebrew University to publish, in August 1967, a declaration against the annexation of the West Bank"; and he felt, at the end of his life, that aside from Jerusalem and the Golan Heights, the State of Israel should give "everything else, back for peace."[47] One might even argue that his philosophical dialectics—in which, with convincing emotion and philosophical cogency, he could espouse both sides of a given case—revealed a fundamentally irenic world view.

By contrast, Corbin and Eliade were militants. Corbin, in particular, employed a militant vocabulary with surprising consistency, especially in the last decade of his life. In one of his final writings, a short piece in honor of Eliade, he proclaimed that this militancy was long shared with his Romanian friend.

> Nous avons fait connaissance et, d'émblée, nous avons su que nos conceptions scientifiques, nos projets, nos visées, nos conceptions de l'Homme, notre philosophie du destin de l'Homme, étaient vraiment semblables. *Nous nous sommes retrouvé frères d'armes*, et voyez, amité s'est confirmé. Nous nous sommes retrouvé chaque été, pendant des années mémorables, pour les conférences du cercle Eranos, à Ascona, en Suisse. Et nous avons toujours milité ensemble en philosophie des religions *du même côté d'un front invisible.*[48]

These "brothers in arms," in fact, did not merely utilize metaphors of militance. They also identified with secret militant orders. In particular, Eliade and Corbin wrote regularly, over many years, about the Fedeli d'Amore, a mysterious group whose historicity is impossible to ascertain. In Eliade's 1956 Haskell Lectures at the University of Chicago, he spoke of these Fedeli d'Amore in factual tones. "The Fedeli d'Amore constituted a secret and spiritual militia, devoted to the cult of the 'One Woman' and to initiation into the mystery of 'Love.' . . . We know nothing of their initiation rites; but they must have had such rites, for the *Fedeli d'Amore* constituted a militia and held secret meetings."[49] Antoine Faivre echoed this claim in his "Introduction" to *Modern Esoteric Spirituality*. "A veritable secret militia widespread in various countries of Europe, it expressed itself through a cryptic language."[50] Corbin's fullest discussion of the Fedeli d'Amore is found in *Creative Imagination in the Sufism of Ibn ʿArabi.*[51] Elsewhere Corbin, like Faivre, raised the specter of a *Militia hermetica.*[52] Julius Evola, a longtime colleague of Eliade, claimed to identify them as "a Ghibelline militia."[53] Historical research has, however, quite simply not borne out the assertions either that such a militia ever existed or that Dante adhered to such a group.[54] But Corbin, Eliade, Evola, and Faivre, all widely read authors, claimed its existence as historical reality, and each went so far as to call it a militia.[55]

The assertion that Dante adhered to some such militant secret society originally was championed in a series of Italian works, apparently culminating in Luigi Valli's *Il linguaggio segreto di Dante e dei Fedeli d'Amore.*[56] Valli was the author routinely cited by Corbin and Eliade when they conjured this so-called militia. More research is required on this subject, but for now it is important to note that René Guénon in fact published his own study, "Le langage secret de Dante et des 'Fedeles d'Amour'," almost a decade earlier, in 1919.[57] By the 1920s, this fictitious "militia" had gained a certain currency. Carl Jung, for example, cited a 1930 German translation of Valli in his essay "Dream Symbolism in Relation to Alchemy."[58] After a certain point, in other words, "traditionalist" writers came to take the historical existence of this "secret militia" as a matter of faith. One thus finds the Fedeli adduced as fact both by "classical" Traditionalists, like Guénon's one-time secretary Titus Burckhardt, and by more recent esoterists.[59] For Corbin and Eliade, this "militia" was the very paragon of the esoteric sodality. It constituted for them the model of "The Order." Overtly for Corbin, and obliquely for Eliade, this order, this Militia hermetica, was a military model they embraced and encouraged.

After the war, Eliade continued waging a kind of cultural war—in fact, what he called a religious war. In 1949 he counseled "fifteen or so Romanian intellectuals and students" in his hotel room that their "political mission" is "making culture," "the only efficacious form of politics open to exiles."[60] Years later, he clarified this advice: "I believe that at certain historical moments some kinds of cultural activity—literature and art especially—themselves constitute political *weapons.*"[61] Eliade thus unmistakably saw the action of culture-makers as being by definition political: "By wearing a mask he becomes what he is resolved to be: *homo religiosus* and *zoon politikon.* Such behavior has a good deal of bearing on the history of culture."[62] And this statement may shed light on reflections he made elsewhere. Recalling Julius Evola's meeting with him the same day that the Italian visitor had met the Iron Guard leader C. Z. Codreanu, Eliade noted that "Evola was still dazzled by [Codreanu]. I vaguely remember the remarks [Evola] made then on the disappearance of contemplative disciplines in *the political battle of the West.*"[63] For Eliade, then, it would seem that *Homo religiosus* and *zoon politikon* are to be identified as the culture-makers employing political weapons in a kind of cultural battle. These militant interpretations of the function of "making culture"—and thus of the History of Religions—seem especially illuminated by a statement Eliade issued to emigré Romanians in 1950. "In this historical moment of ours, we, on this side of the Iron Curtain, can do one thing alone: culture. . . . I have said this many times, but it is good to repeat: in the religious war we are engaged in, the political struggle has moved to the spiritual realm."[64]

The point at present, in short, is that the work of Corbin and Eliade is suffused with metaphorical violence in a way that Scholem's manifestly is not. Eliade celebrated what I have elsewhere detailed as his "violent rebirth" model of sacrality.[65] "Today we are beginning to realize that what is called 'initiation' coexists with the human condition, *that every existence* is made up of an unbroken series of 'ordeals,' 'deaths,' and 'resurrections,' whatever be the terms that modern language uses to express these originally religious experiences."[66] Corbin, for his part, grew increasingly explicit in the violence of his rhetoric as he aged. He convoked the final session that he led of his Université Saint Jean de Jérusalem on a topic of his choosing, the "Combat for the Soul of the World," (Le combat pour l'ame du monde. Urgence de la sophiologie).[67] In their public activities, their choices of topics, and their rhetorical stance, Scholem showed himself a peacable man, in opposition to his comparatively aggressive Eranos companions Corbin and Eliade.[68] This is no small point, though it lies beyond my purview here to develop it in detail.

Other similarities and differences will be detailed in the following pages. I mark only one other difference at this point, and that concerns their attitude toward universality. Corbin and Eliade, quite unlike Scholem, wrote from the perspective of the Universal Man. Eliade's disciple Culianu could write a tribute titled "Mircea Eliade et l'Idéal de l'Homme Universel,"and Corbin's admirer Hoyveda could name an essay on his hero "Architect of the Invisible," but no such accolades are possible for Scholem, however much one admires the global dimensions of his life's work.[69] This is hardly to say that Scholem lacked a philosophical anthropology. But his conception of "humanity" differed from that of his two friends. Corbin could praise Eliade in the following fashion.

> Nous lui avons dû une rénovation complète de la conception de la science des religions. Nous étions tombés pendant plusiers générations dans les ornières de l'historicisme, du sociologisme, quels soient les noms que l'on donne à ces prises de position qui aboutissent à une impasse. Grâce a lui, nous avons vu éclore une manière de comprendre, d'interprêter l'*Homo religiosus*, non plus comme si nous étions face à face, avec des concepts sur lesquels on délibère, mais en laissant resurgir du fond de nous-mêmes le sens permanent des choses qui sont son mode d'existence, qui expriment son mode d'être.[70]

Scholem, in sharp contrast, did not pronounce, as Corbin did about Eliade, "conceptions de l'Homme, notre philosophie de l'Homme" and the like. Even in his correspondence, engaged with such important philosophers as Walter Benjamin, Leo Strauss, Hans Jonas, and many others, he did not speak of humanity in such terms. In other words: yes, Scholem was a humanist, but his conception of humanity, his philosophical anthropology, was quite distinct from that of the other two Historians of Religions under study here.[71] While Eliade famously called for a New Humanism, Scholem wrote always explicitly from a particularist position—as a Kabbalah researcher, as a Jew, as a Zionist. Eliade's writerly perspective was from everywhere and nowhere at once, from a kind of timeless and spaceless elevation. Corbin's vivacious passion, apparent in virtually everything he wrote, made his universality still somehow intensely personal. But he too was writing, like Eliade, and unlike Scholem, in the voice of the Universal Man.

And yet, even given all the foregoing differences—and others could be tallied, as I will show, for example, with regard to Corbin in chapter 3 "Tautegorical Sublime"—Scholem was not a man entirely apart. Like Corbin, his "twin" in this sense, he was the leading student of the mystical tradition of one of the two great nomocentric monotheisms. I have not included in this volume a contrasting chapter devoted to the relationship of Scholem and Eliade, in part because too much of the documentation remains inaccessible to me. But even with Eliade, Scholem retained a respectful tone, eventually contributing to Eliade's *Festschrift*.[72] Eliade, from his side, claimed that Scholem had read all of his books.[73] What I am emphasizing, in any case, is that I will not indiscriminately assimilate to one another the disparate ideas of these men. Nevertheless the Eranos project was one they all embraced; they did so for many years, and they did so with their good reasons. However many critical differences there were between them, in the end they did share important, even fundamental features of their theory of religion. Their shared ideas of religion were neither passing nor incidental. This significant commonality has not been studied as such. I set out to begin this work in the following pages.

Part I

RELIGION AFTER RELIGION

CHAPTER 1

Eranos and the "History of Religions"

> The historian of religions is in a better position
> than anyone else to promote the knowledge of
> symbols, his documents being at once more com-
> prehensive and more coherent than those at the
> disposal of the psychologist or the literary critic;
> they are drawn from the very sources of symboli-
> cal thinking. It is in the history of religions that
> we meet with the "archetypes," of which only ap-
> proximate variants are dealt with by psychologists
> and literary critics.
> —*Mircea Eliade*

SCHAFPELZ DES PHILOLOGEN: BETWEEN MYSTICISM AND SCHOLARSHIP

> Le paradoxe d'Eranos!
> —*Henry Corbin*

Joseph Dan, a student and colleague of Gershom Scholem and the first
Gershom Scholem Professor of Jewish Mysticism at the Hebrew University, recently noted:

> The crucial context for understanding Scholem's concept of mysticism in
> general and the position of Jewish mysticism within the wider framework of
> the humanities, as well as his methodological approach to the study of the
> subject, is that of *his long-standing, though submerged and, to a very large
> extent, hidden confrontation with the Jung-Eliade school of thought*, which
> culminated in the 1950s and 1960s. This chapter in Scholem's life is also
> meaningful for the understanding of his intricate and complex relationship
> with Germany and its culture.[1]

The "Jung-Eliade school of thought" exhibited a peculiarly equivocal
attitude towards religion. On the one hand, its members were physicians
and professors, doctors of religions who insisted on the scientific stature
of their endeavor. On the other hand, they were also, more or less explicitly, engaged and even passionate religious intellectuals. Scholem alluded
repeatedly to his own concerns with this conflict between intellectual

distance and spiritual intimacy: "Will I, so to speak, suffer a 'professorial death'? But the necessity of historical criticism and critical history cannot be replaced by anything else, even where it demands sacrifices."[2] Corbin, similarly, was ambivalent about the profession of scholarship as practiced in the contemporary university.

> [It] is impossible to construct an investigation of this nature without furnishing what are commonly called "notes" and which are, in fact, the commentaries without which the whole structure would remain hanging in the air. Nevertheless, we wished to write a book that would be of general interest—that is, to the prepared seeker, who will find in it many themes to study in depth, was well as to him who in eighteenth-century France was called "honnête homme," the open-minded man to whom the scholar owes consideration, the more so in that his kind is perhaps doomed, owing to contemporary conditions, to disappear.[3]

Eliade confessed a fear of being seen as a dilletante.[4] And so he transformed himself into a prodigiously prolific scholar. Yet, even as he too cast his lot with university teaching and publishing, he derogated scathingly most forms of thought with which he disagreed, including almost the entirety of the social sciences.[5] The romantic passion with which he wrote on questions of transcendence seemed to condescend, almost grudgingly, to the ordinary tolerations of scholarly life. The very profession seemed inadequate to the task of transcendence (if one is permitted to put it this way). And yet academic scholarship was his chosen path regarding transcendence too—at least as it was performed in public.

"THE MYSTICAL VALUE OF PHILOLOGY"?
OR "PROFESSORIAL DEATH"?

At the end of World War II, the distinguished student of ancient religions Erwin R. Goodenough published a now forgotten essay titled "The Mystical Value of Scholarship."[6] This theme was revisited a generation later by another Yale scholar, Jaroslav Pelikan, in his "Scholarship: A Sacred Vocation."[7] Neither, however, addressed what may be called an "illuminist" sense of scholarship as theosophy embraced by the three scholars under study here. This radical approach to the academy was (literally) underwritten by a Yale graduate, the philanthropist Paul Mellon. This last version, I submit, is the distinctive contribution of Eranos: its "strong construction" of the mystical value of scholarship.

The Historians of Religion under discussion here, who benefited from Mellon's Bollingen Foundation, used the tools of philology, edition, and interpretation in a way that seemed somehow subordinated to a muted metatheory—if not to a covert theology. Of the three, Scholem alone gave historical research as such his full respect.[8] Only Scholem plumbed the depths of scholarly inquiry as an activity valued in its own right. Only Scholem, of these three, could write an essay concerning his respective specialty called "Kabbalah and Historical Criticism."[9] While Eliade's use of his sources has been called into question, and Scholem, by contrast was outstandingly scrupulous and precise, I want nonetheless to suggest in what follows that these men shared a common animus: a lasting suspicion of mere academicism.[10] Corbin thus could characterize Eranos as "the meeting of acting, autonomous, individualities, each in complete freedom revealing and expressing his original and personal way of thinking and being *outside of all dogmatism and all academicism.*"[11] And, indeed, even Scholem, whose fervor for what he called "historical consciousness" was as fully developed as it could conceivably become, still recognized the limitations of philological research. He made this point candidly before a German audience in 1974 when he referred to "[a] person such as myself, who throughout these years of his life devoted to scholarship was a philologist, *at times serious and at times ironic.*"[12]

"THE PHENOMENOLOGY OF RELIGIONS"

> Our science is phenomenology.
> —*C. G. Jung*

The interwar European turn to myth and symbol, with its concomitant spurning of academicism, ran the risk of aesthetization. An answer to this serious dilemma seemed, for a time, to have been provided by what came to be called "phenomenology of religions."[13] In the 1950s, Mircea Eliade, Henry Corbin, and Gershom Scholem were calling themselves "phenomenologists," though Eliade did so rather less so than did the others. Eliade's new "History of Religions," however, was explicitly designed to subsume "phenomenology of religion." In 1961, he opened his new journal, *History of Religions*, with a manifesto, "History of Religions and a New Humanism."[14] Here, in one of his most explicit methodological statements, he called for an approach to religion that transcended phenomenology and history, "to reach a broader perspective in which these two intellectual operations can be applied together."[15]

Gershom Scholem encountered Edmund Husserl's phenomenological "intuition of essences" (*Reine Wesenschau*) during his 1917–1918 college studies in Jena. It was, he later wrote, "suspect" to him.[16] By 1919, "I came to reject the phenomenology of Husserl, though I had been greatly in sympathy with it for a few years."[17] Still, Husserl was for Scholem "perhaps the keenest mind to emerge from German Jewry."[18] A half century later, on 14 July 1968, Gershom Scholem presented the opening address to a conference on the theme of redemption held by the International Association for the History of Religions in Jerusalem. Here he provided perhaps his most sustained discussion of "the History of Religions" and the "phenomenology of religions." After raising a long series of rhetorical questions, he held himself in reserve regarding their answers. Most especially, he acknowledged the legitimate differences that distinguished the field from theology. Whatever those differences, he continued, by invoking the "bracketing" practiced in phenomenology of religion—"as *Religionswissenschaftler*, to use the commonly accepted term, they practise the great virtue of reserving their judgment."[19]

> But, entering the sphere of scholarly research in the phenomena of religion, we all agree that statements regarding ultimate truths or the value of a given system or series of facts are not of our concern. Trying to describe or to understand the phenomena of religion may be a very modest thing compared to the ambiguous aspirations of those who claim to have a message, be it as theologians or as witnesses to the Truth. But this is what historical scholarship stands for, and to achieve it, an immense effort of disciplined minds and the cooperation of many scholars from the four corners of the earth are required.[20]

In the introduction to his first collection of Eranos lectures, he cited phenomenology as essential for understanding symbolic systems. "A proper understanding of them requires both a 'phenomenological' aptitude for seeing things as a whole and a gift for historical analysis."[21] Alexander Altmann's obituary note for Gershom Scholem thus seems accurate when he speaks of Scholem's "phenomenological approach at Eranos."[22] On the identification of Scholem as "phenomenologist," Altmann's student Elliot Wolfson agrees.[23] Moshe Idel, another leading successor to Scholem, has remarked at length on Scholem's conceptions of the "scholarly state of religious phenomenon" and especially on the close relations between his notions of "History of Religions, phenomenology of religion, and comparative religion."[24] In short, like Eliade, Scholem attempted to be not only a historian but also a phenomenologist. "Nihilismus als religiöse Phänomen," Scholem's last Eranos lecture, still pointed to his sustained concern with the *phenomena* of religion.[25] The fundamental entities, or categories, with which Gershom Scholem organized data, in short, were not *archetypes*, but *phenomena*.

It is striking that both Scholem and Corbin claimed that phenomenology was anticipated by the mystics whom they studied. Scholem asserted that the sixteenth-century Kabbalist Cordovero was one: "Cordovero wäre als Phänomenologe."[26] Henry Corbin similarly made such a claim for his theosophists: "Tusi analyzes with the sure hand of the phenomenologist."[27] "Tusi makes a beginning toward this phenomenology, in striking figures."[28] Thus, the idea—explicitly asserted by Scholem and Corbin—is that the scholar studies phenomena *presented in the terms in which phenomena themselves present.* This approach presumes a "religious reality" or, as Gershom Scholem said of Judaism, "a spiritual phenomenon, a living organism."[29] Thus, it may well be that symbols for Gershom Scholem, insofar as they express the "religious reality" of theogonic process, are indeed tautegorical. For Corbin, similarly, something transcending mere physical "life" expressly is made apparent through religious phenomena. These phenomena tautegorically blend into the inchoate world-becoming-God.[30]

The phenomena of religion, accordingly, should be read in themselves as somehow significantly referring to themselves, precisely in order to perceive transcendence through them.[31] Phenomenology therefore, for Corbin, was in tension with historicism: "[We] did not attempt to produce works of pure historical erudition, since, for our part, we have no inclination to confine ourselves within the neutral and impersonal perspectives of historicism. What we have primarily sought to outline is a phenomenology of the Avicennan symbols in their Iranian context."[32] Corbin insisted that such phenomenology penetrated to truths otherwise obscured in historical research. "In every case the revealing light has preceded the revealed light, and phenomenology does no more than uncover later the already accomplished fact."[33] Elsewhere he defined phenomenology as "the recovery of phenomena, i.e. encountering them, where they take place and where they have their places."[34] He was usually careful to distinguish "pure phenomenology" as History of Religion's view of theology.[35] "Pure phenomenology," he explained, was that "analysis which discloses the intention hidden beneath a phenomenon, beneath what is apparent, beneath the *zahir*. So phenomenology is exactly *kashf al-mahjub, kashf al-asrar* (a revealing of the concealed, a revealing of secrets, [SMW])."[36] Perhaps his most succinct formulation of phenomenological method is found in his *History of Islamic Philosophy*. Phenomenological research, he observed,

is based on the rule *sozeïn ta phainomena*, saving the appearances—that is to say, of taking account of the underlying ground of the phenomena, as these phenomena appear to those to whom they appear. The phenomenologist is not interested in material data as such—it is too easy to say of such data that they are "out of date" (our modern scientific data go out of date with the greatest facility after ten years have passed). What the phenomenologist endeavours to discover is the primordial Image—*the Imago mundi à priori*—which is the organ and the form of perception of these phenomena.[37]

Corbin's phenomenology, in part, rested on the Goethean concept of the *Urphänomen*.[38] He described this as "the absolutely primary and irreducible, objective, initial fact (*Urphänomen*) of a world of image-archetypes or image sources whose origin is nonrational and whose incursion into our world is unforseeable, but whose postulate compels recognition."[39] The *Urphänomen*, he insisted, was irreducible. "For no matter how many external circumstances are collated, the sum of them, or their product, will never give the initial religious phenomenon (*Urphänomen*), which is as irreducible as the perception of a sound or a colour."[40] "The experiences of a Shaikh Ahmad, like those of the all the great visionaries, have the characteristics of a basic phenomenon (*Urphänomen*) as irreducible as the perception of sound or color. The phenomenology of religious experience ought neither to deduce it from something else, not to reduce it to something else by illusory causal explanations."[41]

It should be noted, finally, that when Carl Jung came to compose an introduction to Eranos, intended for an American audience in 1939, he had the following to say: "In spite of the great variety of these contributions in form and in subject matter, they are all related to central and transcendent ideas—to the ideology and phenomenology of the way of salvation or redemption."[42]

"DIALECTICAL IMAGINATION" AT ERANOS

The American cultural critic Norman O. Brown, widely read in the 1950s and 1960s, coined the term "dialectical imagination" with explicit reference to Mircea Eliade and Gershom Scholem.[43] The success of the so-called dialectical imagination at Eranos can be gauged by its reception history at that time. Eliade's soon-to-be-celebrated "History of Religions" was predicated on some such dialectic, "the true dialectic of the sacred: by the mere fact of *showing* itself, the sacred *hides itself*."[44] The concept of "dialectics" in fact was long familiar in the work of the historians of religion. Henry Corbin had already addressed "La théologie dialectique et l'histoire" as early as 1934.[45] He was not entirely consistent, however, in his subsequent technical usage of the term "dialectic." But, generally speaking, he counterposed his imaginal gnosis to that of merely academic dialectics. "Passage from our imaginal form to another does not obey any conceptual dialectic."[46]

Gershom Scholem, on the other hand, was more consistent in his dialectics. He stated his position with deceptive plainness. "Mysticism, intent on formulating the paradoxes of religious experience, uses the instrument of dialectics to express its meaning. The kabbalists are by no means the only witnesses to this affinity between mystical and dialectical thinking."[47] In his autobiography, he summarized, in a fundamental statement on dialectics, the relation between Zionism, history, and the very idea of religion:

> . . . the dialectics concealed in this historical consciousness of the Zionists, a consciousness which I shared with all my heart and all my soul: the dialectics of continuity and revolt. But it would not have occurred to any of us to deny the history of our people when we had recognized or rediscovered it as a people. That history was in our bones, whatever we were striving for now. With our return to our own history we, or at least most of us, wanted to change it, be we did not want to deny it. With this *religio*, this "tie to the past," the enterprise was and is hopeless, doomed to failure from the start.[48]

Dialectics, for Scholem, released the historian from postivistic historicism, linking instead the present scholar with prior reality in a direct, if dialectical, connection.

"RELIGIOUS REALITY"

To establish the autonomy of religious phenomena may be the best-known contribution to general thought made by the "dialectical imagination" of the three authors. However, their positioning of religion in the fields of knowledge should, I would suggest, be understood in light of its philosophical background. "Religious reality" was posited to be somehow beyond aesthetics, ethics and logic, inhabiting the domains of neither law, nor art, nor science.[49] But, as has been troubling thought since Kant, if religion resides somehow beyond the good, the beautiful, and the true, what is its distinctive and constitutive "reality"? Eliade and Corbin, in particular, never tired of derogating the historical profession and the social sciences, which, they claimed, "reduced" religion to economics, psychology, society, and the like. One common background for this "antireductionist" attitude was located in the work of Schleiermacher, whose theology strongly influenced Corbin and Jung.[50] The Schleiermacherian *gefühl* (feeling) became, for the Historians of Religions, one of inward "experience." Following Otto and Jung, as well as many esoteric thinkers, Eliade called such experience "numinous." The experience of the "sacred," "numinous," or "holy," in short, was asserted to be the foundational constituent of religion.

Such experience, more particularly, was said to have been the province of the mystic. The mystic, according to Scholem, paradigmatically under-went a deconditioning that brought release from conventional forms (*Ge-stalten*).[51] The mystic thus was a kind of modern *avant la lettre*. But, the medieval mystic, more specifically, adumbrated the modern artist, who likewise approached ultimate reality through symbols.

Scholem's smelting-of-*Gestalten* idea assumed an ideal of radical-re-configuring-after-surfacing-from-a-meltdown; Corbin's *imaginal* was predicated on the ontological unreality of historically objective forms; and Eliade's "fantastic reality" assumed that myth was real and history wasn't. Such presumptions of an archetypal reality more real than ordi-nary reality tended to bleed the ordinary of its interest and its vigor. The mystocentric scholar possessed, however, a surrealistic kind of compensa-tion—"The Certitude of the Never Seen."[52] Theirs was, in other words, an essentially aesthetic approach to religious history, one that celebrated symbolic forms as the central "religious reality."[53]

THE REDISCOVERY OF GNOSIS

> The entire human drama is played out on the
> plane of gnosis and gnostic consciousness. It is a
> drama of knowledge, not a drama of the flesh.
> —*Henry Corbin*

For the analyst Carl Jung, the ultimate dialectic, so to speak, was that of gnosis.[54] Jung insisted that his gnostic approach was psychologically em-pirical, that he was studying a *reality*. He claimed that gnosis, as valid "knowledge," apprehended archetypal reality as such. Henry Corbin, in his tribute "The Time of Eranos," wrapped this toga of higher realism around himself and his cohort; the Eranos men were "gnostic minds."[55] These modern gnostics, it seemed, arrived at their gnosis just as did their ancient gnostic counterparts: *dualistically and anticosmically*.[56] Whether or not such characterizations of gnosis refer to any discernible ancient entity, this label was nonetheless proudly expropriated by Corbin and Eliade. Eliade, near the end of his life, would still identify his own "path" as that of gnosis. Asked whether his path was "gnosis and *jñāna* Yoga" he answered "Perhaps, yes. Gnosis, *jñāna* Yoga."[57]

Scholem, for his part, "rediscovered" gnosis inside Judaism, even if he didn't call himself "gnostic."

> You see, Merkabah mysticism was something specially fitting to the minds
> of Jews for whom there was an inner core for the elect to have religious
> experience of a certain character within the confines of Judaism. They didn't

make a special theology out of it. You can't speak of the "anthropology" of the Hekhaloth texts because there wasn't any. The Merkabah mystics were concerned with the world of the Pleroma which was overwhelming to them. They were concerned with how to get there. This is why I call this Gnosticism.[58]

Corbin, most forcefully of the three, championed a (meta)history of gnosis. He consistently traced ancient dualisms (Manicheanism, Mazdean, Zurvanism) into Islam.[59] Like Scholem, he located a secret doctrine, a gnosis, at the core of his monotheistic object of study. But, in contrast to his Judaist friend, for Corbin this was no dispassionately distanced study. In the last decade of his life, in fact, he called often and openly for a rebirth of gnosis.[60]

> Finally, it should be clearly apparent to everyone why we have associated the concept of gnosis with the look of eyes of fire. Inasmuch as the look of gnosis is a visionary look and not the look of theoretical knowledge, it is wedded to the look of the prophets, spokesmen of the Invisible. To open "the eyes of fire" is to go beyond all false and vain opposition between believing and knowing, between thinking and being, between knowledge and love, between the God of the prophets and the God of the philosphers. The gnostics of Islam, in agreement with the Jewish Kabbalists, have particularly insisted on the idea of a "prophetic philosophy." It is a prophetic philosophy that our world needs.[61]

The philosopher Hans Jonas seems to have provided the primary influence on Scholem's idea of gnosis in the 1930s. Like Jonas, Corbin made an early transition from Heidegger to gnosis, also in the 1930s.[62] But the philosophical position of a modern gnosis remains to be explored, at least in the Anglo-American discussion.[63]

ERGRIFFENHEIT

If a word can be said to have summed up the Eranos experiential stance in the years under study here, it is surely *Ergriffenheit*. *Ergriffenheit*, primal ontic seizure, was a term centrally used both by Heidegger and by Jung in the late 1920s and early 1930s. They applied this image of "being gripped," "being seized," both to the structures of original experience and to the action of an *Ergriefer*, a leader who seizes. Evoked in Heidegger's extraordinary Nietzsche seminars of the 1930s, in Jung's equally extraordinary Nietzsche seminars of the 1930s, as well as in the anthropological idea of *Ergriffenheit* championed in the Leo Frobenius school, *Ergriffenheit* also simultaneously became a founding theorem of the Eranos circle of historians of religion, established in 1933, the year that Weimar died.[64]

Before World War II, Scholem worried about academicism. "Will I, so to speak, suffer a 'professorial death'?"[65] Eranos seemed to assuage this anxiety. After forty years, looking back on his experience at Eranos, Scholem spoke of *Ergriffenheit.*

> Es gibt eine Schwierigkeit, die für alle Eranos-Teilnehmer und wohl auch für viele, wenn nicht alle Redner gilt; nümlich die Schwierigkeit, in einer Spannung zwischen der Distanz zum Gegenstand und der Identifikation mit ihm sprechen su müssen. Für Olga Fröbe war fast entscheidend, das sie Redner suchte, die sich mit ihrem Gegenstand identifizierten. Sie nannte das in ihrer Sprache *"Ergriffenheit."* Sie wollte erfriffene Redner, keine Professoren, obwohl sie alle Professoren hiesßen.[66]

Adorno saw the matter slightly differently. "The rhetorical insistence on being stirred (*Ergriffenheit*) endangered the objective contents of that which matters in particular to someone like Scholem, who is moved (*ergriffen*) through and through."[67]

In any event, like Scholem, Corbin also returned to the notion of *Ergriffenheit* in his own valediction to Eranos. "Parce que ce monde impérissable aura été notre passion, et celle-ci le secret de ce que Madame Fröbe-Kapteyn a si justement encore nommé *Ergriffenheit*—source de cette juvénilité è laquelle faisait allusion Schleiermacher en déclarant: La religion déteste la solitude, et dans sa jeunesse surtout, qui pour tout est l'heure de l'amour, elle se consume en dévorante nostalgie.' "[68]

Finally, it is important to recall that all three of our scholars sought out "the Masters" of traditional mystical sciences. Scholem, the oldest of them, did so when he first emigrated to Jerusalem from Berlin in 1923. The story he told in the opening of his inaugural Eranos essay in (1949), that he met but did not study with these masters, was related in the third person. In a subsequent interview, however, he confirmed that it was he who in fact had rejected instruction by these masters.[69] A few years after Scholem's initial experience, in 1928, Eliade studied with gurus in India, happily submitting to their authority.[70] And in September 1945, leaving Istanbul for Tehran, Corbin eagerly ought out "the traces of the Ishraqiyun." He succeeded in having "serious conversations . . . with certain venerable Shaikhs."[71]

THE PUBLICATION OF THE SECRET

> Only after you have had to keep a secret can you
> learn the true outlines of self.
> —C. G. *Jung*

Instead of reporting their own seizures and ecstasies, the Historians of Religions spoke theoretically about ecstasy and vision, even if they sometimes implied that they knew whereof they spoke. But, in any case, through their scholarly disquisitions on the visions of the past, they transgressed, precisely and routinely, ancient injunctions against such publicity. "We are entering into a period that I would be tempted to call *phanic*. We display in broad daylight texts, ideas, beliefs, rites, etc., which normally should have remained hidden, and access to them reserved only to initiates. . . . 'Transmission through misunderstanding' is characteristic of the present civilization."[72] These observations of Eliade may perhaps be born out, for example, in the proliferation of Sufi teaching, indeed, active patronization by Sufis of publication in the last two centuries.[73] The theorists of esoterism at Eranos, in any event, sought to perpetuate ancient secret teachings by publicly teaching those secrets today. Scholem acknowledged just how historically peculiar this must appear.

> The public character of the main works of the old Kabbalist literature is the most important warranty of its secret. For we do not see anything any more, and when are we addressed? No kabbalist work has been attacked because of its popularizing tendencies, because of the alleged betrayal of the secrets of the Torah as was the book '*Emek Ha-Melech* by Jakob Elchanan Bacharach from Frankfurt on the Main, which was published in 1658. But if one opens this folio today, it becomes evident that our perception of this betrayal of mysteries must have vanished. There is hardly a less understandable book than this "Valley of the Kings." So are we again dealing with that mystical-anarchic policy that protects secrets better by pronouncing them than by keeping silent about them? And which one of all pronounced worlds could be more sunk into its mysterious pronunciability than the world of the Lurianic Kabbalah?[74]

By publicly pronouncing their secrets, mystics succeeded in "keeping" those mysteries. Taking up this mode, the three Historians of Religion wrote "phanically," in Eliade's phrase. They too, as Scholem implied, protected secrets by pronouncing them.

Leo Strauss's essay "Persecution and the Art of Writing" famously suggests one kind of esoteric *écriture*; kabbalah and Sufism are another kind.[75] The former, philosophical esoterism, is a theatrical display of camouflage; the other, mystical esoterism, is a sequestration of positive content. The traditional philosopher's esoterism hides from the hoi polloi; the mystic encrypts the innermost message in strata of conceits. Which kind of esoterism, then, did the History of Religions writers practice? The Historian of Religions, in pronouncing secrets with such authority, intimated a certain knowing beyond research. Their widely selling secrecy bespoke not gnosis as such, however, but another strategy of writing. They each wrote "indirectly" in various genres and formats. But while this "art of writing" treated mysticism historically, it cannot be reduced to a mystical esoterism. Nor is it identical with philosophical esoterism.

Nevertheless, to opt for the other obvious conclusion, to accept them as initiates, that is, to see them as cloaked avatars of privileged understanding, may be to misconstrue their conceits. Beyond whatever instrumental functions it performed, their indirection was convincing because it implied the traditional possibility of direct metaphysical knowledge; they thereby presented themselves as exemplars, if only allusively. That one can today understand such things; that the modern reader can still have access to the godhead; that the history of tradition—however posthistorically attenuated—is yet unbroken: that was the implied promise of History of Religions. Eliade told an interviewer, "I made the decision long ago to maintain a kind of discreet silence as to what I personally believe or don't believe."[76] This "discretion" may suggest, at least to some observers, that Eliade knew more than he was saying. But such an implication was not testable, and so their enticing "understanding" could not in fact be replicated. The substance of the mystical secret could not be conveyed. Still, they implied that the ancient secrets could be interpreted today. Mystical secrets *could be understood*. And the History of Religions was the vehicle for that understanding.

HIDDEN LIFE

> We are interested in history because therein are
> hidden the small experiences of the human race,
> in the same way as there are hidden there the dy-
> namic light of the future.
> —*Gershom Scholem*

How so? What secrets expressly were hidden in the "phanic" monographs of the History of Religions? One possibility is that these friends implied secrets as something like the aura of the History of Religions. The notion of aura, originally an occultist idea, was famously adapted by Walter Benjamin in his celebrated essay, "The Work of Art in the Age of Mechanical Reproduction."[77] Scholem saw an aura at the heart of the Kabbalistic paradox. "This alchemy of the law, its transmutation to the transparent, is one of the deepest paradoxes of the Kabbalah, for what could be principally less transparent than this glimpse, this symbolic aura that now appears."[78] This aura was one of gravity, antiquity, and authenticity.

Gershom Scholem embraced, in his groundbreaking *Major Trends in*

Jewish Mysticism, a "quest for the hidden life of the transcendent element."[79] He reiterated this point decades later: "[T]he Kabbalist had a
fundamental feeling that there is a mystery—a secret—in the world."[80]
For Scholem, anything could be a symbol—"it need only have something of the spiritual 'charge' of the intuitive heritage which lends the
world meaning, gives it character, and reveals its mystery."[81] And this
mystery can reveal itself today: "[The] secret life it holds can break out in
you or in me."[82] Or, as he put it elsewhere, Judaism "is a phenomenon in
which the not-yet-revealed, the hidden, and the anticipated, flowing like
the remnants of the riches of the past, are still present."[83]

Mircea Eliade similarly claimed "to interpret the message hidden by
the reality of the story."[84] But this was no act of demystification, the
unsympathetic attitude of which Eliade never tired of attacking. "One
day we shall be blamed for our 'demystification' by the descendents of
those we once colonized. . . . Such a 'demystifiying' attitude ought to be
arraigned in its turn, on charges of ethnocentrism, of Western 'provincialism,' and so, ultimately, be 'demystified' itself."[85] The ultimately inverse
operation, a complete remystification, seemed to be the project of Corbin. "All the more significant, then, is the reactivating of those archetypal
themes which took place freely, so to speak, under the cover of anonym-
ity."[86] For Eliade, finally, the Historian of Religions negotiated the same
dialectic as ever: "[T]he true dialectic of the sacred: by the mere fact of
showing itself, the sacred *hides itself*."[87]

CONCLUSION: *RELIGIONSWISSENSCHAFT ALS BERUF*

> Dir steckt der Doktor noch im Lieb [The Professor
> still lurks in your anatomy].
> —*Mephistopheles to Faust*

In the following chapters I will try to interpret not only the claims and
the successes but also the difficulties of the esoterism outlined in this
chapter. Even as he acknowledged the dialectical tension between "identification and distance"—the title of his 1978 valedictory address at
Eranos—Scholem rather elided its difficulty (*Schwierigkeit*). And that difficulty is that Scholem—like Corbin, and, indeed, all scholars who retro-
ject theosophy into the core of their respective traditions—appropriated assumptions from the traditions in a way that derives rather too
unproblematically from certain early modern theories of so-called tradition. As I will try to show in the chapters that follow, Schelling, Molitor,
and von Baader, in the nineteenth century, transformed what they called
theosophy—which in turn they received from the sixteenth-century Jakob

Boehme—into "myth as tautegory." This tautegory would be taken up as a "phenomenologically" accurate portrayal of the past by the Historians of Religion. This "tautegorical" interpretation of "tradition" privileged mystical symbolism in the study of religion. Corbin and Eliade demanded acquiescence to the proposition that this esoteric core was the religious stuff of religion, that this was religion as such. In other words, this theosophical assumption, and the mystocentrism they derived from it, led them to certain conclusions about an autonomous reality for religious phenomenon; conclusions that have as much to do, perhaps, with early modern notions of esoterism as they do with contemporary practices of critical inquiry. In any case, however ironic it may now seem retrospectively, it was by this means that they institutionalized, in the academic study of religion, an original esoterism.[88] Near the end of his life, Corbin penned a tribute to Eliade in which he celebrated their common cause at Eranos, "brothers in arms . . . on the same side of an invisible front."[89]

Religion as such. To identify the hierophany, the self-revealing of the sacred, one must experience its *numinosity*. Corbin encountered the aged Rudolf Otto, who coined the term *numinous*, in Marburg in 1930; soon thereafter, in November 1932, Olga Froebe-Kapteyn also made this same pilgrimage. At that latter meeting, Otto proposed and Froebe-Kapteyn accepted the name *Eranos*.[90] Those who proudly associated themselves with this name, who in fact led it during its golden age, included Gershom Scholem, Henry Corbin, and Mircea Eliade. It carries to this day a numinous aura.[91]

Toward the Origins of History of Religions:
Christian Kabbalah as Inspiration and as Initiation

Only the poet has re-integrated
the world that in the rest disintegrates.
—*Rainier Maria Rilke*

THE MYTH OF REINTEGRATION

The word *esoterism*, so often misused, refers to the
unavoidable necessity of expressing the reintegration of the human being in symbols.
—*Henry Corbin*

. . . the aim of every symbol: the reintegration of
man into the All . . .
—*Mircea Eliade*

"In my book *Mitul Reintegrării (The Myth of Reintegration)* I traced the
opposites that are found together in primitive rites, myths, and metaphysics. We shall have to return to these problems later on."[1] Eliade described the background to his writing *Mitul Reintegrării* in an essay
eventually published in English under the title "Mephistopheles and the
Androgyne."[2] In another essay extracted from *The Myth of Reintegration*,
he spoke directly to the concept of "reintegration."

We meet here one of the dominants of the whole spiritual life of "primitives": the desire to be integrated into the all . . . the reintegration of man
into the primordial Cosmos. Moreover, it is not difficult to observe that the
majority of symbolisms which we have mentioned in these notes have no
other function than to *unify*, to *totalize*, to construct a *center*. . . . Everywhere, back of this symbolism, we find a tendency toward unity towards
reintegration. . . . This simultaneity of meanings in the symbol is expressed
better when we take into account of the aim of every symbol: the reintegration of man into the All, [not] the annihilation of life and the Cosmos, but
rather the reintegration into the All.[3]

Eliade used the term extensively throughout his career, applying it to all his principle interests—alchemy, Yoga, Shamanism, and the like.[4] The ultimate source of the concept seems to be *Traité de la réintégration des Êtres créés dans leurs primitives propriétés, vertus et puissance spirituelle divines,* published in 1770 by Martines de Pasqually (1725–1774). Martines de Pasqually is best known today as the mentor of Louis-Claude de Saint-Martin (1743–1803), eponymous founder of the so-called Martinist order.[5] Eliade concisely identified their original program. "I cannot examine here the central thesis of Martines de Pasqually; it suffices to say that for him *the goal of initiation was to reintegrate man* with his lost 'Adamic privileges,' i.e., to recover the primeval condition of 'men-gods created in the image of God."[6] Henry Corbin also employed the key word "reintegration."[7] "The word *esoterism,* so often misused, refers to the unavoidable necessity of expressing the reintegration of the human being in symbols."[8] Corbin and Eliade, in fact, shared some inspiration if not initiatic descent from Martines de Pasqually through Louis-Claude de St.-Martin, the *philosophe inconnu.* Eliade apparently derived his connection largely through René Guénon (1886–1951), whom he read before the war, while Corbin's commitment to an initiatic esotericism emerged late in life. In any case, both were involved with so-called speculative masonry, though by uncertain channels of influence.[9] Although it may seem intuitively unlikely to the casual reader of Gershom Scholem, he too was not untouched by the myth of reintegration. In late 1934, Scholem wrote letters to Walter Benjamin describing his reading of Louis Claude de Saint-Martin.[10] By the end of the decade, he was using the phrase to typify a key Kabbalistic concept. "Salvation means actually nothing but restitution, re-integration of the original whole, or *Tikkun,* to use the Hebrew term."[11] Scholem again translated *reintegration* as *Tikkun* in his 1955 Eranos lecture on reincarnation.[12] Some years later, the full, telltale phrase *the reintegration of all beings* emerged in a crucial passage of a major speech the great Kabbalah scholar delivered at a meeting he hosted of the International Association for the History of Religions. "There is, then, *the reintegration of all beings* into a state of peace and harmony, but, as a matter of fact, this reintegration is much more than restoration. It is not the conservative element of turning back to a projection of the past into the future, that gives it is explosive power; it is rather the utopian hope that redemption will contain much more than any past, including any golden age."[13] Scholem delivered these lines at virtually the same time that he composed the entry on Martines de Pasqually for the pages of the new *Encyclopedia Judaica.* This timing is noteworthy inasmuch as Scholem, in his Jerusalem speech, employed Pasqually's full phrase, *the reintegration of all beings,* which title he cited in the *Encyclopedia Judaica* article.

A late phase of Christian Kabbalah is represented in Martines de Pasqually's *Traité de la réintegration des êtres*, which greatly influenced theosophical currents in France. The author's disciple was the well-known mystic Louis Claude de St. Sartin. Pasqually himself was suspected during his lifetime of being a secret Jew, and modern scholarship has in fact established that he was of Marrano ancestry.[14]

Scholem's use of *tikkun* as *reintegration* suggests the further possibility, which he never states directly, that he may have been drawing on Pasqually's own translation. That is, as Kilcher and others suggest, it may be that Pasqually, versed to some unknown extent in Kabbalah, originally devised the phrase *the reintegration of all beings* as a translation of *tikkun*.[15] This may be significant, for one thing, because it would constitute one more piece of evidence in support of a scholarly consensus agreeing that Pasqually was not only a Jew by origin but was also somewhat learned in Kabbalah. "Christian Kabbalah" was never a consistently Christian tradition but had in fact been in conversation with Jews and Jewish Kabbalists throughout the early modern period.[16] Early influences on Scholem's conception of Kabbalah, it is now generally acknowledged, included Baader, Schelling, and Molitor.[17] Molitor, as Christian Kabbalist, had perhaps the single biggest impact on Scholem's conceptualization of Kabbalah.[18] Moreover, the most widely read scholars of Kabbalah in the generation before Scholem were Adolph Franck and Paul Vulliaud, both of whom, in addition to their studies in Jewish Kabbalah, also wrote significant works on the Martinist tradition.[19] Christian Kabbalists, furthermore, bequeathed not only to Corbin and Eliade but also to Scholem the concept of *theosophy*, a notion at the heart of their History of Religions.[20] Scholem's original conception of Kabbalah, especially his metatheory, was in certain respects more beholden to Schelling, Baader, and Molitor than it was to the Kabbalistic tradition itself. He initially read Kabbalah through the lens of Christian Kabbalah. More precisely, he entered it through the theosophies of Christian Kabbalah. Scholem, then, not only associated with contemporary theosophists of an Christian Kabbalah orientation but was himself originally inspired by these sources.

"TRADITION," CHRISTIAN KABBALAH, AND GERSHOM SCHOLEM

In the first words he uttered in a lecture at Eranos, Scholem seemed intentionally to distance himself from the living tradition of Kabbalah. He began his inaugural lecture at Ascona with "a short but true story."

> In 1924, clad in the modest cloak of modern philology and history, a young
> friend of mine went to Jerusalem, wishing to make contact with the group of

Kabbalists who for the last two hundred years have there been carrying on
the esoteric tradition of the Oriental Jews. Finally he found a Kabbalist, who
said to him: I am willing to teach you Kabbalah. But there is one condition,
and I doubt whether you can meet it. The condition, as some of my readers
may not guess, was that he ask not questions.[21]

This "friend," of course, was Scholem himself. That he was, in this opening
gambit, himself "clad in a modest cloak" and thus not telling a "true"
story may indicate that he was, rather, employing a "higher" sense of
truth, that of myth. Given that this anecdote opened a lecture on "Kabbalah and Myth," this might not seem an unwarranted reading. That he
began with a "story" is in itself significant, particularly considering that
he then continued these introductory remarks by embracing Schelling's
"narrative philosophy" as his very definition of myth. It is also important
to note that in this first lecture at Eranos he began by "announcing" his
rejection of initiation nearly half a century earlier. Scholem's "true story,"
with its characteristically understated complexity, quite effectively expressed his paradoxical relationship with the initiatic tradition of Kabbalah.

Scholem told his first Eranos audience, in short, that he had rejected
direct initiation. He was not, he himself confessed, initiated directly into
the Kabbalistic mysteries.[22] Given the depth of the background Eliade
had in Guénonism and the increasingly heightened esoteric rhetoric of
Corbin, Scholem would hardly seem to fit this picture. This apparent
lack of fit precisely is what makes his esoterism so remarkably illuminated
when it is reread in the light of what we now know about Corbin and
Eliade. "Tradition," in Scholem's usage, is not so far removed from
Eliade's conception as it would seem. It has been argued plausibly that
"Tradition" as used in the Guénonist circles was first employed by Molitor as a translation of "Kabbalah."[23] Scholem's use of the term "Tradition" clearly enough derived from Molitor, while for Eliade the derivation is through Guénon, who in turn seems to derive from a Martinist
trajectory. A common Christian Kabbalah origin of this trajectory is unmistakable. All this may seem unfamiliar, perhaps, to many readers of
such classic essays as Scholem's "Revelation and Tradition as Religious
Categories in Judaism," originally published in the *Eranos-Jahrbuch*
in 1962, or "The Crisis of Tradition in Jewish Messianism," from the
Eranos-Jahrbuch in 1968. The former, in fact, begins with a long quotation from Molitor, and the latter ends with verses of Goethe.

It may reasonably be concluded that the use of the category "tradition" in Scholem, like "traditional society" in Eliade, shares a formative
source in Christian Kabbalistic usage. Scholem insisted that there was in
his day no living, authentic mysticism in the contemporary world.[24]

While it would therefore be patently absurd to consider Scholem an "initiated" or "practicing" Christian kabbalist, it is not at all implausible on the face of it to read his framing conceptions of Kabbalah as having a Christian Kabbalistic inspiration. His lifelong acknowledgments of his debt to Molitor say as much. This was a literary debt, to be sure, if not an initiation by the book.

ELIADE'S "BAPTISM BY INTELLECT"

> On sait que Mircea Eliade insiste sur la nécessité, pour l'homme d'aujourd'hui, de passer par le livre, par la culture, s'il veut s'initier.
> —*Antoine Faivre*

Mircea Eliade began his career in North America, it will be recalled, with the Haskell Lectures at the University of Chicago, published as *Rites and Symbols of Initiation*.[25] But it was only in his journals that he was somewhat more explicit about his initiatory connections. "*NB*: I feel that, in initiatory doctrine and rituals, I have discovered the only possibility of defending myself against the terror of history and collective desires."[26] Eventually, Eliade delivered a lecture, "Initiation et Monde Moderne," before an audience of French Freemasons.[27] This lecture is remarkable in the oeuvre of Eliade, and the form of its publication is rather revealing. The first volume of the French Masonic journal, *Travaux de Villard de Honnecourt*, which his lecture inaugurates, prints his lecture framed by introductions and interviews.[28] There is much that can be inferred here concerning his close association with initiatory practice and practitioners.[29] Eliade's lecture, for example, was followed by an interview in which Eliade was invited to elaborate on his themes. Several interesting features of this lecture and interview present themselves. First, it is a version of a lecture he had given and published on several other occasions.[30] Each version contains elements, whole paragraphs, of the others, but they are otherwise distinct. The *Travaux de Villard de Honnecourt* version seems almost certainly designed for its audience. Specifically, Eliade devoted most of the first section of this lecture to the Jewish and "Judeo-Christian" initiatory traditions, which, he claimed, fed into Gnosticism as well as into the subsequent esoteric traditions of Judaism and Christianity. That these claims were favored in the Masonic forum at which he was the honored lecturer is virtually certain. This reading is confirmed by its conclusion, in which he underscores the initiatory dimension of *reading* ("initiation livresque") in the modern world. "Dans la perspective de ce nouveau modèle d'initiation, la transmission des doctrines ésoteriques n'implique plus une 'chaîne initiatique'; le texte sacré peut être oublié pendant les siècles, il suffit qu'il soit redécouvert par un lecteur compétent pour que son message redevienne intelligible et actuel."[31]

Beyond doubt, then, Eliade intentionally obfuscated—or *camouflaged,* to use his favored term—many of these esoteric relations.[32] One example may suffice here. In a 1979 review-essay devoted to A. K. Coomaraswamy and to Corbin, which he published in his own journal, *History of Religions,* Eliade spoke of Corbin's interest in secret organizations ("what Corbin called the *'chevalrie spirituelle'*").[33] Eliade went on to note that Corbin

> . . . thought that scholars and philosophers who do not share in [the reductionistic] fallacy ought to abandon their eagerly accepted subaltern positions in contemporary academia and rebel against the academic and cultural dictatorship of 'scientism," "historicism," and "sociologism." Accordingly, they should reassemble and constitute, not a new type of "Theosophical Society,' but a new type of university. . . . For this reason, and *with the collaboration of some thirty university professors.* . . . Corbin founded, in 1974, the Centre International de Recherche Spirituelle Comparée [Université de Saint-Jean de Jerusalem]. . . . *Following the model of Eranos,* the lectures were published annually.[34]

What Eliade does not say is that he was one of these "thirty university professors." On 8 July 1975, Eliade recorded the following in his journal.

> In the evening we have dinner at Corbin's. Henry is completely satisfied with the outcome of the lecture series that took place at The University of Saint John of Jerusalem. *Although I am one of the founding members,* it was impossible for me to go to that colloquium, but I share his joy in finally seeing one of his geatest desires take shape: to bring together a group of scholars, theologians, and philosophers belonging to the three traditions dealing with the Bible, to form them into a sort of Hermeticist circle, and to have address an audience, *restricted, of course, but of the elite.*[35]

It lies beyond the purposes at hand to document in detail the many available examples of this sort of intentional inconsistency in Eliade's statements concerning contemporary initiatic groups.[36] Antoine Faivre, another of those chosen thirty founders, addresses Eliade's special approach to initiation explicitly.

> "We are condemned," notes Mircea Eliade, "to learn about the life of the spirit and be awakened to it through books. Erudition is "baptism by Intellect" . . . Mircea Eliade shows how the profane itself reflects the mythic and by integrating a poetics into his scientific project he makes felt the nature

and the exigencies of a quest that can aptly be called traditional. . . . The exegeses of Ananda Coomaraswamy, Mircea Eliade, Henry Corbin, and Seyyed H. Nasr always start with the notion of *philosophia—theosophia—perennis*, and it is to this that their hermeneutics always returns. But not one of them neglects erudition, critical apparatus, or the historical and philosophical tools that constitute a specific aspect of modernity. With them, university scholarship becomes the aid, today indispensable, of Tradition, which they approach both as savants and philosophers.[37]

The relations between Faivre and Eliade were reciprocal. In Eliade's review of Faivre's edition, he concludes that such "contributions admirably illustrate the cultural relevance of unraveling the "secret history" of the post-Enlightenment era."[38] Once one understands Eliade's submerged commitments to this "secret history," certain aspects of his project for the "New Humanism" that was to be the History of Religions become clearer.

To take one last example, Eliade reviewed Scholem's anthology of Eranos lectures, *On the Kabbalah and its Symbolism*. Of all things, Eliade interpreted Kabbalah here in terms of "cosmic Christianity." He concludes with this paragraph, which appears to be a *non sequitur*: "Pico della Mirandola was not only a great scholar, but he was also a good and sincere Christian; surely he knows what he was looking for in learning Hebrew and trying to decipher and master *Magia et Caballa*."[39] A quick review of Eliade's lifetime infatuation with Christian Kabbalah explains this comment. The budding Romanian scholar enthusiastically pored over Christian Kabbalah when he was twenty years old, and later often referred to these studies as the impetus that drove him to his famous sojourn in India. Eliade bolstered this claim in his journals of 1957.[40] In 1964, he similarly wrote of "Renaissance man's longing for a 'primordial revelation' which could include not only Moses and *Cabbala* but also Plato, and first and foremost, the mysterious religions of Egypt and Persia . . . a longing for a universalistic, transhistorical, mythical' religion."[41] In interviews in 1978, the Historian of Religions once again articulated his formative excitement at the idea of Christian Kabbalah. "I was equally excited by the fact that Pico knew Ficino's translations of those texts and that he had learned Hebrew, not just in order to understand the Old Testament better, but, above all, in order to understand the Kabbala."[42] Finally, in the last interview he granted, just months before his death in 1986, Eliade reiterated this view of his past nostalgically. "I wanted to add to the understanding of Western culture, to do what [Giovanni] Pico della Mirandola did in the Renaissance, when he learned Hebrew and studied the Cabala . . . and I thought that one could go even farther down, not stopping at the Cabala and Zarathustra."[43]

RÉNÉ GUÉNON AND MIRCEA ELIADE

> Le but unique et final de l'initiation est la réintegra-
> tion des sous-multiples dans une Unité Divine.
> —*Stanislas de Guaïta*

"Reintegration," then, was a technical term used by Martines de Pasqually and Louis Claude de Saint-Martin, by one of Guénon's Martinist
initiators, Stanislas de Guaïta, and eventually by Guénon himself. That
this "counterrevolution" had some sustained impact on subsequent
French cultural life is by now a historical commonplace.[44]

Eliade understood "reintegration" to refer to the coincidence of opposites, a usage explicitly beholden to René Guénon (1886–1951), founder
of the so-called Traditionalist school.[45] Guénon emerged at the French
fin de siècle in a milieu of Freemasonry, Martinism, Templarism and Illuminism, to establish what came to be known as Traditionalism. Guénon
in his youth became an initiated Martinist. Between 1906 and 1912, he
was associated with the Martinist lodges established by Papus (Dr. Gérard Encausse, 1865–1916).[46] Papus founded the Supreme Council of the
Martinist Order in 1891.[47] One Guénon initiator, Stanislas de Guaïta
(1861–1897), headed the The Kabbalistic Order of the Rose-Croix (Ordre Kabbalistique de la Rose-Croix).[48] A subsequent "revivification" of
"l'Ordre du Temple," undertaken by "plusieurs membres de l'order martiniste," was led by Guénon as "chef" in 1908.[49]

Eliade emerged at a geographic distance from this milieu, and he
downplayed this dimension of his program during his American incarnation. His interest in the occult sciences, however, was lifelong. He had
written an appreciative article on Julius Evola's "The Value of Occultism
in Contemporary Culture" as early as 1927 and published *Occultism,
Witchcraft and Cultural Fashions* in 1976. In the 1930s, as his biographer put it, "it is [Oliver Leroy, Guénon, Evola, and Coomaraswamy],
evidently, that Eliade wishes to associate himself methodologically."[50]
And in a collection titled *Fragmentarium* published in the 1930s, Eliade
praised Guénon for his unequivocal contempt (*mépris*) of the modern
world, proclaiming that *he is a true master (il est un vrai maître)*.

C'est ce que pensent aujourd'hui biendes gens, peut-être les plus intelli-
gents de ce siècle. Parmi lequels nous ne pouvons pas ne pas nommer René
Guénon, en qui, entre autres nombreuses vetus, s'est concentrée une formi-
dable capacité de mépriser, en bloc, le monde moderne. Je ne pense pas qu'il
ait existé quelqu'un d'autre méprisant son époque plus catégoriquement que

ce prodigieux René Guénon. Et jamais on ne sent transparaître, dans son mépris compact, olympien, une trace de colère, un soupçon d'irritation, une ombre de mélancholie. *Il est un vrai maître.*[51]

Mac Linscott Ricketts, biographer of the young Eliade, has shown at length that "works of Coomaraswamy, Mus, Guénon and Evola . . . had a major impact on Eliade's methodology and vocabulary in the late 1930's."[52] Reminiscing on his first meeting with Evola in 1937, Eliade seemed equivocal. "I admired his intelligence and, even more, the density and clarity of his prose. Like René Guénon, Evola presumed a 'primordial tradition,' in the existence of which I could not believe; I was suspicious of its artificial, ahistorical character."[53] A close reading of this passage in its entirety shows, however, that their difference was one of degree and not of kind. On the one hand, Eliade affirmed his Italian friend's Traditionalism. "From a certain point of view-that of an exemplary, ahistorical 'tradition'—he was right." The difference between them, Eliade said, was that he, unlike Evola, was not despairing, but rather continued to make culture even in "a crepuscular age." And in July 1974 Eliade devoted nearly two pages of his journal to reflecting on the death of Evola. Here again, he makes the same point that he did in the *Autobiography*, not that Evola was wrong in any way but simply that they wrote for different audiences. "The books I write are intended for today's audience. Unlike Guénon and his emulators, I believe I have nothing to write that would be intended especially for them."[54] Both these final reports of Eliade on Evola make Eliade's identical point about his relationship to Evola's Traditionalism: "Traditionalists" like Evola and Guénon were not incorrect, but he simply did not want to limit his audience to their "initiated" groups alone. Another report in his journals seems to clarify his attitude to Guénon. In late 1977, Eliade noted succinctly that "Réné Guénon ended up discovering late in life the *real* sources, both Oriental and Western, of esoteric traditions, and above all understood their meaning."[55]

When Eliade publicly grappled with Guénon's *philosophia perennis* in his Freud Lecture of 1974, he appeared to counterpoint a pessimistic "esoterist" to optimistic "occultists," explicitly terming these as "two opposite understandings of the occult tradition."[56] It is necessary to look more closely at this essay, "The Occult and the Modern World," to see why this "opposition" of the "esoteric" and the "occult" was another example of his camouflaging his sources. Eliade derived enjoyment from the humorous setting of this lecture: the twenty-first annual Freud Memorial Lecture, published initially in the *Journal of the Philadelphia Association for Psychoanalysis.*[57] He clarifies his terminology: "[T]his distinction [between 'esoteric' and 'occult'] is of consequence, and it will help us to understand *the parallel roles* of occultism and esotericism in modern times" (emphasis added). The treatment of Guénon is the key here: "in this learned and brilliantly written book"; "[t]he most important and significant contemporary representative of esotericism"; and "more significant than the rationalistic views"; "we hasten to add that [Guénon's] doctrine is *considerably more rigorous and more cogent* than that of the occultists *and hermeticists* of the nineteenth *and twentieth* centuries."[58] Since the 1950s, Evola and Guénon had been the leading theorists of Traditionalism's revolutionary antimodernism.[59] Along with Eliade they strove to distinguish themselves from "mere" occultism: their effort was (in the Guénonian vocabulary) to establish themselves as the true elite, as opposed to the pseudo-elite of the occultists. Guénon, Evola, and Eliade all toyed with Theosophy and magic until the 1920s, and all three eventually settled on Traditionalism as a more exalted elitism, by the 1930s. The result was that the philosophical masterworks of each—Evola's *Revolt Against the Modern World*, Guénon's *Crisis of the Modern World*, and Eliade's *Cosmos and History*—all are antihistoricist works that employ world history, especially the theory of world cycles, to condemn the present moment as the *Kali Yuga*, the lowest conceivable moment in cosmic history. This planetary pessimism amounted to a cosmic catastrophism. Eliade embraced it, with reference to Guénon: "the 'posthistoric era' is unfolding under the sign of pessimism."[60]

Eliade, then, had joined Guénon and Evola in the 1920s and 1930s as Traditionalists who "belong to the same international community of scholars dedicated to the study and interpretation of all aspects of religious realities."[61] Guénon and Evola wrote their classic works on perceived threats to the so-called Traditional World in the 1920s and 1930s, Eliade his in the 1940s. In no place did Eliade disavow the diagnosis of the danger articulated by these Traditionalist comrades outside the academy. The evidence suggests, therefore, that Eliade did not disagree with them on this point. Evidence from within the initiatic world confirms this impression. Certainly, as he said in a letter of 26 September 1949, Guénon saw Eliade as a kind of fellow-traveler.

> Since you speak of Eliade, I have already reviewed several of his works, books and articles. . . . You will note that I treat him rather carefully and that I try above all to refer to that which is good; . . . he is basically very nearly in agreement with traditional ideas, but he does not dare to show it in his writing, since he fears colliding with officially admitted opinions; this produces a rather unfortunate mix . . . we hope, however, that some encouragement will help make him a little less timid.[62]

In his chapter on silence and secrecy in *The Hermetic Tradition*, Eliade's friend and colleague, the Guénonian Julius Evola, identified "symbols of *a spiritual reintegration.*"[63] The Guénonian position is sometimes known as "integralist" and was referred to this way by Evola.[64] "Reintegration," in short, was a technical term in the Guénonian lexicon, as it had been in the earlier Martinist vocabulary. In 1935, Evola identified *reintegration* as the very counter-revolution against modernity catalyzed by his master Guénon:

> . . . an *authentic counter-revolution* [which] begins to dominate and give a direction, in several countries, to wide sectors of the new generations. It would be interesting to determine to what degree and in what form these currents, which are *radically opposed to democracy and socialism* . . . can provide the superior foundation necessary to begin *the arduous task of reintegration in the sense indicated by Guénon*, and thus a work endowed with a metaphysical, transcendent, ethical, and social character.[65]

In light of the counterrevolutionary nucleus to Guénon's "Tradition," the reader should not be surprised to find Eliade employing "reintegration" to describe (and normatively endorse) an ostensibly original politico-cultural program. "[T]the civilising mission of Christianity has been so remarkable. *For, by Christianising the ancient European religious heritage, it not only purified the latter, but took up, into the new spiritual dispensation of mankind, all that deserved to be 'saved* of the old practices, beliefs and hopes of pre-Christian man . . . the Christianisation of the peasant levels of Europe was affected thanks above all to the Images: everywhere they were rediscovered, and had only to be *revalorised, reintegrated and given new names."*[66]

Eliade added elsewhere that "[every] reintegration is a totalization."[67] This totalization, by definition "total," patently does not exclude the political dimension of social existence. "Reintegration" was used by Guénonian Traditionalists to refer, on one level, to the basic processes of return to a primordial condition.[68] In fact, Guénon himself used the term to refer to such a process of return in Kabbalah. He did so, suggestively, in pointing out that the Hebrew word *Kabbalah* means "tradition," and that the "reintegration" envisaged by Pasqually pointed back to the Edenic *Pardes* of the Kabbalah.[69] "Reintegration," for Guénon's Traditionalism, could be used in a Kabbalistic sense, but it could also be used in a political sense.[70] Eliade used it in all these senses.[71]

CORBIN AND THE RESURRECTED TEMPLE

> . . . the initiate, he who has experienced the
> mysteries, is he who knows.
> —*Mircea Eliade*[72]

Of the trio of Historians of Religions, Corbin was the only one whose Christian Kabbalism was explicit, both in his own statements and in those of his fellow travelers. The form it took, in the last decade of his life, was a fairly explicit "speculative Masonry."[73] Corbin's first lecture at Eranos was on initiation.[74] Gilbert Durand, a passionate disciple of Corbin, after Corbin's Eranos career, memorialized Corbin's Masonry and Templarism, with detailed reference to initiation and the Rectified Scottish Rite. He introduced his Masonic hommage this way: "Henry Corbin *parce qu'il était des nôtres à plus d'un titre*, méritait cet hommage ému que Villard de Honnecourt, dont il était membre d'honneur"[75] In this course of this essay, Durand reveals that Corbin experienced his own "time of Pentecost"—presumably some sort of transfiguration—while on pilgrimage in Scotland in July 1978.[76]

The Rectified Scottish Rite looked back to Pasqually for inspiration. His teachings drew on the notion perhaps most central to Christian Kabbalah, the claim that embracing Kabbalah leads back to the "true Judaism." As Christopher McIntosh puts it, "Pasqually believed that the Jewish tradition had been perverted by its orthodox practitioners, but that certain "true Jews" had preserved it in its purity. Clearly, he believed that his order was in some sense helping to restore the true Judaism, by which may have meant the Cabala."[77] Saint-Martin, as initiated disciple of Pasqually, elaborated this mystical philo-Semitism. "Si le Peuple juif a été le dépôt de semblables instructions, s'il a posséde un temple quie semble être le hiéroglyphe universel, si ceux qui y remplissaient les fonctions nous sont annoncés comme dépositaire les lois du culte et opérant même tous les faits dont j'ai demontré que la source était dans l'homme, il est probable que le Peuple juif est en effet le Peuple choisi par la Sagesse Suprême pour servir de signe à la postérité de l'homme."[78]

These passages illuminate the increasingly explicit statements concerning Christian Kabbalah made by Corbin in the exhilarated last years of his life. "Plus encore, il y aurait de nombreux neo-gnostiques d'origine juive et des néo-gnostiques chrétiens, mais ils partageraient ensemble un même point de vue, plus secret que touis les autres sans doute, car ils n'envisageraient rien de moins qu'une sorte *de reconversion du christianisme à ses origines, c'est-à-dire au judaïsme*."[79] Corbin then made it even clearer, within the limits of his "art of writing," what he implied by this necessary reconversion to Judaism: "This is what we have in another place called the paradox of monotheism and it is a constant theme in all *those doctrines in the religions of the book which are in one way or another related to the Kabbalah*."[80] Corbin's reversal of conventional emphasis in this last sentence should be marked: the Abrahamic religions "relate to" Kabbalah, and not the other way round. What these religions share is not a common history, a common ancestor in Abraham, or a shared heritage in ethical teachings. Their unity is to be found in their relation to Kabbalah.

CHRISTIAN KABBALAH AND THE ORIGINS OF THE HISTORY OF RELIGIONS

> . . . how many secret, underground threads I was to discover between my passion for the Italian Renaissance and my vocation as an Orientalist.
> —*Mircea Eliade*

In sum, Christian Kabbalah provided key terms, including "reintegration," "tradition," and "theosophy," and a formative intellectual inspiration for Scholem; Eliade may or may not have been an initiate, but certainly traveled in close proximity with initiates (Evola, Guénon, Corbin, to name a few); and Corbin certainly embraced initiatory traditions fully, if only in the final years of his life. Together they found inspiration in those Western esoteric sciences deriving from Jacob Boehme by way of his spiritual descendents Pasqually, Saint-Martin, Schelling, Molitor, and von Baader. Scholem drew his philosophical inspiration from his early study of these thinkers, while Eliade, at virtually the same time in the 1930s, wrote his dissertation on the origins of this phenomenon during the Florentine Renaissance. Eventually, Corbin's intimate relations with this same tradition surfaced explicitly in the last decade of his distinguished career. Corbin, quite unabashedly, and Eliade, at most obliquely, each portrayed himself to be a spiritual heir—initiate?—of this selfsame "tradition." Scholem most emphatically did not; but, as in so many other sectors of his richly multidimensional mind, here too he remained dialectical (as he would say), openly in conversation (as we might say) with this "tradition." Perhaps here, as important as any I have been able to identify, we find an intellectual context for the History of Religions as they conceived it, a context heretofore unremarked. The History of Religions in their conception operated as a kind of Christian Kabbalah.

It is therefore useful to reflect on the reasons for this convergence of interests. Christian Kabbalah, it may be argued, was a notable, original effort at the outset of modernity to address the emerging question of religious plurality. There was not one revelation, but many, and, conversely, there were not many truths, but one original source of truth (*prisca theologia*). Religious multiplicity, by any definition, was the social reality to which Christian Kabbalah responded. Esotericism, insofar as it posited a transcendent unity to world religions, in this light is linked, historically speaking, to the rise of comparative religion. Both sought solutions to the problem of revelational diversity.

It is in this context that one of the seeming anomalies in any positing of significance to the grouping of Scholem-Eliade-Corbin may be clarified. Scholem, who might seem the least likely of the trio to be fairly characterized in this way, in fact may be the strongest case. That is, his Sabbatian theory was of a piece with a theory of enlightenment. And this theory was, most importantly, predicated first and foremost on the supposed apostasy of its central figure. In other words, the torn condition of the Jew in the modern world was symbolized dramatically in this tragic exemplar. That dual identity was to be both Jewish and, to whatever extent one had absorbed or "assimilated" general culture, non-Jewish *at the same time*.[81] Scholem's career centered on Sabbatai Zevi, a leader of world Jewry who converted to Islam. The Kabbalah scholar never tired of highlighting the significance of this perplexing fact. Christian Kabbalah explicitly attempted some such transreligious religion. The very designation "Christian Kabbalah," after all, implies a revision of traditional boundaries between Judaism and Christianity. Franz von Baader thus could assert that Pasqually was a Jew and Christian *at the same time*.[82] Through Christian Kabbalah, one could be a "true Jew" without being an ethnic Jew or a practicing Jew.

From the perspective of Christian Kabbalah, all people of religion, not just Jews, were in this same modern boat, at least with regard to their root identity in an Abrahamic faith system. Here we approach a convergence with the origins of the History of Religions. A founding father of nineteenth-century comparative religion, Max Müller, famously suggested that "[t]o know one is to know none,"—and he was correct, at least in the following sense. The preponderance of religious people do not need the category *religions*: the local believer alone knows religion in the singular. Conversely, there can be no knowledge of ordinary-life religion-in-the-singular by "religionists"; critical students of religion who theorize about "religion" can only know a composite religion in the plural, *religions*. The Historians of Religions were inclined to paradox, perhaps, because of the nonexistence of *religions* in the real world. In other words, their generalist idea of *religions* may not represent the reality of *religion* as practiced in most places most of the time. In this light, such esoteric roots of "comparative religion" as those of Christian Kabbalah become more significant. The supposition of a common core to religious expression and experience had been pioneered, at least in part, in those esoteric circles.

Whether as inspiration or as initiation, then, Christian Kabbalah cannot be avoided in any rounded understanding of the rise (and decline) of the History of Religions. If there is an "untold story" in the present project, it may be located in the shared Christian Kabbalist sources of Scholem, Corbin, and Eliade.[83] This is a story not yet told in scholarship. Eliade alluded to it in terms of a "secret history" of our era.[84] We need not mystify that history to study it seriously. It is the history of thinking on religion that starts from the fact of being religiously numerous—and goes from there to defend against that fact, inescapably doing so through the very forms of that fact. This *dédoublement*, in which the thinker imaginatively projects into a unifying perfection outside pluralistic social conditions, into a singular theophany accessible as symbols, disrupts an unproblematic relation to everyday belief and practice. It thus seeks, out of this originative rupture, a religion resistent to rupture. Such reintegration is found in the "hidden life" that is the real Tradition, in the theosophical history of *religion after religion*.

CHAPTER 3

Tautegorical Sublime: Gershom Scholem and Henry Corbin in Conversation

GERSHOM Scholem was almost certainly the leading Judaist of this century. Henry Corbin was one of the world's most influential Islamicists during the same years.[1] Each was the leading authority on the esoteric traditions of their respective monotheistic tradition. They were also acquainted for fully fifty years, and friends for over thirty years.[2] After World War II, from 1949 to 1978, they met together almost every August at Eranos meetings. They cited each other in their scholarship and eventually contributed to each other's *Festschriften*. Both were subsidized by the Bollingen Foundation. They even, at times, shared the same translator.[3]

Perhaps most significantly, each approached his respective monotheistic tradition resolutely "in its own terms." By thus emphasizing the autonomy of religion, they established the study of Judaism as a religion and the study of Islam as a religion in ways which otherwise would not have been possible. For the discipline of the History of Religions, it was Scholem and Corbin, more than any other Judaist or Islamicist, who made Judaism and Islam safe for study. Finally, they did so on the basis of certain parallel assumptions about religion. Most significantly, both became world famous by boldly relocating mysticism at the center of their respective nomocentric monotheisms. For these two scholars, mysticism, not law, formed the central feature of Judaism and Islam.

The first documented contact between Scholem and Corbin was Scholem's letter, dated 1937 October 21, in response to Corbin's (still unpublished) invitation to contribute to a new journal. Scholem said, "Je suis persuadé qu'une intime et étroite communauté d'étude peut être profitable pour nous deux."[4] Little could he know, in those darkening years, just how this optimistic sentiment would be fulfilled.

Scholem and Corbin already shared a number of personal connections in the 1930s. These included Fritz Lieb, the Swiss Protestant Socialist follower of Karl Barth and scholar of Pietism, who was simultaneously a close colleague of Corbin and of Scholem's intimate friend Walter Benjamin.[5] Lieb was also strongly affected by Lev Shestov, who likewise influenced Scholem at that time.[6] Another intermediate connection between Scholem and Corbin was Martin Heidegger. Corbin was the first French translator of Heidegger, and visited him in Germany in the 1930s. Scholem, in these same years, was strongly influenced by Heidegger's student Hans Jonas's study of gnosticism. Scholem belonged to a study circle with Jonas soon after the philosopher fled to Palestine.[7]

There is no question that Gershom Scholem and Henry Corbin not only personally revered one another long after that, but that each held the other in deep intellectual respect. In his later years, Scholem paid Corbin warmly admiring tributes both public and private. In 1973, Scholem sent greetings for Corbin's seventieth birthday.

> Voilà maintenant 25 ans que nous nous connaissons, et je suis heureux d'avoir eu la grâce de connaître en vous l'un des quelques savants dont l'érudition soit d'une envergure véritablement spirituelle et toute illuminée par la pénétration des choses elles-mêmes. Vous êtes, cher Corbin, l'un des rares historiens de la religion dont on puisse dire qu'ils savent ce qu'ils savent. Outre tout cela, votre grande distinction et l'humanité que vous avez en tout ce qui est humain m'ont toujours impressionné.[8]

In a letter dated 17 June 1973 Corbin thanked Scholem with equally warm enthusiasm.

> Non seulement vos livres, mais vos conférences à Eranos, notre contact annuel prolongé, m'ont révélé beaucoup, beaucoup de choses. Je vous dois en grande partie le sentiment de notre communauté dans la tradition abrahamique, et la conviction que les racines profondes de cette communauté sont en l'ésotérisme. Vous savez combien j'y insiste chaque fois que j'en ai l'occasion. C'est vous qui vous apportez encore le soffle prophétique, dont la privation a conduit notre monde à l'étouffement et aux horreurs. Soyez remerciés encore, vous et vos amis, de nous transmettre ce message dont nous ne pouvons nous passer.[9]

Five years later, in 1978, Scholem made his admiration of Corbin public. Speaking for the last time to the Eranos circle, he singled out Corbin.

> Wir hörten Redner wie Corbin, der aus einem unerhörten Gefühl des Eindringens, der Fast-Identifikation und gleichwohl der Distanz eines tief wissenschaftlichen Geistes heraus sprach, der nicht als Vertreter einer bestimmten Sache erschien, sondern als Betrachter, als Mensch, der aus der Kontemplation un der distanzierenden Erkenntnis wirkte, die ohne diese Distanz gar nicht möglich wäre.[10]

Given the personal and intellectual connections linking Scholem and Corbin, it seems warranted to probe these associations in some detail. And given the demonstrable commonalities shared between these two Historians of Religions, it is all the more striking that they ended up with

ultimately divergent conceptions of the History of Religions. I shall conclude, appropriately for men who positioned paradox at the core of their
conceptions, with this paradox.

"ROMANTIC RELIGION"

The place to start, perhaps, is with Scholem and Corbin's mutual attraction to certain early German Romantic thinkers.[11] Of these, they were
both deeply and explicitly influenced by the work of Johann Georg Hamann, Friedrich von Schelling, and Franz von Baader.[12] In Paris, in 1939,
Corbin delivered a series of lectures on Hamann shortly before he left for
an unexpectedly prolonged sojourn in Istanbul.[13] In particular, Hamann's
Aesthetica in Nuce (*Aesthetics in a nutshell*) was prized and cited by both
Scholem and Corbin, who translated it into French. It is quite apt, then,
to assert with Muhsin Mahdi that "Corbin was in many ways the last of
the German Romantics."[14]

Scholem was deeply influenced by German Romanticism, but the
depth of that influence remains to be gauged accurately. To some he is a
"figure of romantic anti-capitalism."[15] There is little dispute that Scholem
emerged, in a general sense, out of a kind of neo-Romantic revival that
reached its peak during the Weimar period. The History of Religions,
more generally, was itself, if indirectly, also a product of that moment.[16]
Gershom Scholem, it may be noted, met the spiritual leader of Weimar
Jewry, Leo Baeck, in 1922 and had "many more" encounters with him.[17]
Scholem borrowed the notion of Romantic Religion from Baeck, though
his usage reversed Baeck's emphasis.[18] "Following the termination [*sic*] of
the late Dr. Leo Baeck, we may call [mysticism] the romantic stage of
religion, in contradiction to its classical stage, which saw the formation of
great religious systems and their crystallization in the soil of forms, in
rituals and in institutions."[19] Baeck was responsible for Scholem accepting
the invitation to Eranos, a story now told many times.[20]

It is rather less well understood that, more so than Hamann, the stronger influences on both men were the late esoteric Romantic philosophers
Schelling and Baader. This influence, unlike the early, diffuse, and largely
aesthetic impact of Hamann, fundamentally shaped their understanding
of world history and was sustained as such throughout their respective
careers. The friends Schelling and Baader, in particular, provided the
young friends Corbin and Scholem with a theory of so-called theogonic
process, in which world ages reflect an unfolding inside God. Baader, of
particular significance for Scholem, understood Kabbalah almost uncan-

nily. Baader's synopsis of Boehme, according to Scholem, "reads exactly like a versified paraphrase of *Zohar* I, 17 ff."[21] The system of Romantic esoterism generally was known by them as *theosophy.*[22]

NACHTGESCHICHTE

A kind of ontological uneasiness queasily pervaded the esoteric Romantics' theosophy. Corbin savored the unsettling phrase "the great silent clamor of beings," which he discovered in his favorite sixteenth-century Isfahani philosopher, Mullâ Sadrâ.[23] This "great silent clamor" may be compared instructively to Scholem's parallel invocation of "the tremendous agitation that came into the world with the book of Job."[24] For both theosophic scholars the world itself was anciently out of joint. Their resonating imageries of ontic anguish echo a similarly clanging claim registered by Carl Jung. Jung resoundingly identified an ontological catastrophe at the core of things. "An unusual scandal was blowing up in the realm of metaphysics, with supposedly devastating consequences, and nobody was ready with a saving formula which would rescue the monotheistic conception of God from disaster."[25] The contemporary universe, in this theosophical view, finds itself in a state of unrest because its primordial condition was deranged. For Corbin, this dark vision was derived from Franz von Baader. "[The] great theosophist Franz von Baader . . . well understood that the book of Genesis begins only with the creation of the visible universe, and that this beginning is not an absolute beginning. Evil did not begin with or through man, but independently of him. Franz von Baader speaks of cosmic catastrophes, 'great catastrophes which were brought about before the coming of man.' "[26]

With good reason, Ernst Benz spoke (in an Eranos lecture attended by Corbin) of Baader's "profound interest in the dark side of existence."[27] Such a vision of a fallen universe undoubtedly, though differently, underwrote the gnosticism—ferocious for Corbin, conflicted for Scholem—that supported the central superstructure of their respective theosophies. One of the few contemporaries who perceived this darkness accurately was Theodor Adorno. In his subtly insightful and affectionately critical birthday salute for Scholem's seventieth birthday, Adorno recognized the paradoxical implications of Scholem's use of Baader.

> One of the central aspects of Scholem's work is a representation of the processes of secularizing mysticism, its affinity to enlightenment. His deep insight, which was forever unwilling to give up closest contacts with the facts was unable to blind itself against the logic of such secularization. The mystic

undercurrent of Jewish tradition, which his entire works are devoted to, is due to a concept of divinity as something which Baader called theogonic process, *in itself eminently historical.*[28]

For Adorno, Scholem's theosophy was not merely a species of metahistory. In this same tribute, Adorno went on to characterize Scholem's attraction to the *Nachtgeschichte*, the "nocturnal history," of the Jews. This insight is particularly significant because the metahistory of the theogonic vision, as I have suggested, is inseparable from its intrinsic darkness. This is only partly explained by the fact that Scholem found his alternative, against-the-grain *Nachtgeschichte* in gnostic currents, hidden esoteric streams. And these gnostics themselves, like Baader, espoused a kind of cosmic *Nachtgeschichte*, "a profound interest in the dark side of existence."[29]

TAUTEGORICAL SUBLIME

> "I am that I am" said the God of Abraham. Only some such divine tautology would seem to do justice to us all: the old woman who sees ultimate meaning in her grandchild, the mathematician who sees it in a formula, the tribesman who sees it in a crocodile. The meaning of life is that it should mean. At everyday levels surely meaning is one with nourishment.
> —*James Merrill*[30]

Tautegory, a central hermeneutic principle shared by Corbin and Scholem, also derived from the esoteric Romantics. "Tautegory" apparently was a neologism coined by Friedrich W. J. von Schelling.[31] Schelling, perhaps as much as any thinker, was an early tutelary spirit for Corbin and Scholem. His notion of "tautegory" may have come to Scholem and Corbin by way of the leading Schellingian exponent of their youth, Ernst Cassirer, whom Scholem heard lecture and Corbin met in person. They took from the Schelling-Cassirer theory of symbolism the crucial replacement of allegory with tautegory: the religious symbol is not to be understood in terms of a system of reference outside the symbol, as in allegory, but rather the symbol carries its own meaning, in reference to itself. This self-referential meaning of the symbol was dubbed *tautegorical*.

Scholem's first Eranos essay, "Kabbalah and Myth" (1949), an essay in which he in effect announced the major themes of his synthetic Eranos years, stated unequivocally his Schellingian identification of myth as "narrative philosophy." Corbin likewise embraced this notion at the core of his own system. Corbin dubbed his own project "prophetic philosophy": "A prophetic philosophy is thus a *narrative philosophy* absolved of the dilemma which obsesses those who ask: is it myth or is it history?"[32] The resolution of this false dichotomy for Corbin was Schelling's *tautegory*. Corbin was most explicit on this point in his enormous, and enormously revealing, "*The Imago Templi* in Confrontation with Secular Norms."[33] Near the beginning of this extended 127-page essay, he noted that "the *Imago Templi* is not allegorical but 'tautegorical'; that is to say, it should be understood as concealing the Other whose form it is. It is to be understood in its identity with that Other, and as being itself the thing which it expresses. It will thus be clear that we do not intend to take up the task of the psychologist, still less to subject the *Imago Templi* to the categories of positive historical criticism."[34] Later in this essay, he explains that "the *Imago* is the form in which both the one and other integrally manifest themselves. This privileged imaginal form can also be called *tautegorical*."[35]

One may call this view "the tautegorical sublime." What is sublime in this view is its liberating apathy. Released from a need to deliver religious phenomena to a meaning outside themselves, ancient spiritual phenomena are now let be. The documentary remainder of religious history, the symbolic heritage of the past—angels, *sefirot*, hierophanies—could now successfully resist condescending "explanations" which read them against their original spirit. They are now allowed to be themselves; they are themselves meaning; they mean themselves. These traditional symbols demand to be read in their own terms. This revision of the visionary into a visionary hermeneutics generated a revolutionary rereading of myth as a kind of tautegorical sublime. The key was the rediscovery of what Corbin called "the privileged imaginal form."[36]

"A SHADOW OF THE LAW":
THE SCOURGE OF LEGALISM

> Si l'on a vraiment compris de quoi il s'agit et ce
> qui est en cause, on ne reste pas neutre devant le
> choix entre l'Islam légalitaire et l'Islam spirituel.
> —*Henry Corbin*

The sustained insight to mount and maintain this visionary hermeneutics required a radical selectivity. And, indeed, the object of their inquiry did not include all of monotheism. Law, said conventionally to rest unquestionably at the center of the Judaic and Islamic systems, was excluded on principle from the theosophical purview. Corbin, especially in his last years, felt released to inveigh openly against his old enemy, "legalistic religion."[37] It is instructive to compare two of the more explicitly confessional texts published by Corbin and Scholem. Both address the question of law.

> I believe that Shi'ism is the only religion that has permanantly preserved the relationship of divine guidance between God and humanity forever, and continuously perpetuates the *wilayah*. Judaism ended the prophethood, which is a true relationship between God and the human world, in Moses, and after that did not recognize the prophethood of Christ or Muhammad, and has thus disconnected the relationship; and similarly the Christians have stopped with Christ, and the Sunnite Muslims with Muhammad, and after the completion of prophethood in him they do not recognize the existence of any relationship between the creator and the created. And it is only Shi'ism that, while considering the period of prophethood ending with Muhammad, keeps the *wilayah*, which is that relationship of guidance and completion, forever alive.[38]

One can find Corbin's attacks against legalism interwoven throughout every book he wrote. To take one more example, it is interesting to note the objects of opprobrium in the following polemic. "[The] exoteric, deprived of its theophanic function, degenerates into a covering, a hollow cortex, something like the corpse of what might have been an angelic appearance, if this would be conceivable. Everything, then, becomes institutionalized; dogmas are formulated; *legalistic religion triumphs*."[39]

To these comments the following aphorisms ventured by Scholem may be compared instructively.

> As nature, viewed the Kabbalistic way, is nothing but the shadow of the divine name, so one can also speak of a shadow of the law, which it casts longer and longer on the life of the Jew. But the stone wall of the law becomes gradually transparent in the Kabbalah, a glimpse of the reality encompassed and indicted by it breaks through. This alchemy of the law, its transmutation to the transparent, is one of the deepest paradoxes of the Kabbalah, for what could be principally less transparent than this glimpse, this symbolic aura that now appears?[40]

Kabbalah functions for Scholem's Judaism, in this one respect, as Shi'ism does for Corbin's Islam: these esoteric traditions render the exoteric law "transparent."[41] Scholem did not abhor Jewish law (*Halakha*) in the way that Corbin seemed to loath Islamic law (*Shari'ah*). The Israeli scholar insisted on this point in 1977: "I am among those who respect the *Halakha* (despite some empty and slanderous words that have been said about me), and consider it to be a central problem."[42] Nonetheless, law drops out of the center of the study of monotheism for him as it did for his friend Henry Corbin.[43]

"SCIENCE IS SCHOLEM'S INCOGNITO"

> But let us understand clearly that for yet some
> time we shall be few in number and that we shall
> have to take refuge behind the veil of a certain
> esotericism.
>
> —*Henry Corbin*

Such a view of monotheism without law, perhaps, could not comfortably be espoused openly. Corbin's esoterism, in fact, *was* public, celebrated internationally, even during his lifetime. Scholem's form of esoteric writing, however, remains a matter of controversy. Only rarely did those close to him broach this question. Joseph Weiss, one of Scholem's closest students, was one who did so.[44] Weiss published a tribute to his teacher on the occasion of his fiftieth birthday.

> What is the method of his esoterics? His esoterism is not absolute silence but
> a kind of camouflage. By use of thick volumes of texts and philological re-
> search he publicly reduces the character of the metaphysician to that of the
> scientist. But his metaphysics reveals itself in disguise, camouflaged as sen-
> tences and half sentences among "purely" scientific analyses up to total inde-
> cipherability—or in the shape of an unusual adjective which says nothing to
> the unfamiliar but all to the knowing one. Thus the secret metaphysician
> dresses as an exact scientist. Science is Scholem's incognito.[45]

Until recently, one could only speculate, perhaps, on the privileged access Joseph Weiss had to Scholem. But with the publication of Weiss's letters, we know that he had a remarkably intense, if conflicted, relationship with his master.[46]

"THE ANTI-EXISTENTIALIST IDEA"

By the 1950s, one avowed target of the leading Eranos contributors was something they called "existentialism." Mircea Eliade was inclined, for example, to draw contrasts between "the very difference that distin-guishes the archetypal (traditional) anthropological position from the ex-istentialist (historical) position."[47] Corbin, for his part, had been preoccupied with questions of essence and existence since the early 1930s, publishing a study on "Transcendental et Existential" in 1937.[48] But after the war, and especially with the heating of the Cold War, "existentialism" came to be associated, at least in Eranos circles, with a certain pathology of modernism—historicism, Marxism, existentialism, in the litany of Eliade.[49] Scholem returned to the attack on so-called existentialism throughout his Eranos essays.[50] In his famous polemic against Martin Buber, delivered at Eranos in 1967, Scholem accused the senior scholar of Hasidism of serving at "the front rank" of existentialism; of suffering from a "strong tinge [of existentialism] . . . I would be the last to deny that;" and claimed that Buber read existentialism into the Hasidic texts.[51] The topic of existentialism similarly was central to his late "Reflections on Jewish Theology."[52] Scholem, quite simply, saw his historical work as opposed to existentialism: "It may be that historical criticism does not really amount to much, but we have nothing better. And in an era of pompous and hollow 'existential analysis,' it behoves a scholar in the humanities to make his stand clear."[53] Most powerfully and centrally, Scholem concluded his great essay "Toward an Understanding of the Messianic Idea"—one of the two or three most influential essays in Jewish thought written in this century—with the pronouncement that "the Messianic idea is the real anti-existentialist idea."[54] Years later he quoted the paragraphs in which this sentence was located as "my own personal motto."[55] Around the same time, Corbin emphasized "the radical difference separating Mullâ Sadrâ's metaphysic of *existence* from what has in our day taken the name 'existentialism.'"[56] Existentialism, then, was another common animus characteristic of their thought. Existentialism was seen by both to be one flavor of the tainted fare that is modern thought.[57]

SECULARIZATION, OR, RELIGION AFTER RELIGION

> My secularism is not secular.
> —*Gershom Scholem*

Kabbalah and Sufism, then, served them as esoteric religion alongside the exoteric religion of law. The Historians of Religion themselves analogously seemed somehow religious even as they themselves rejected exoteric modes of belief and practice. To put the point in terms of the paradoxes they preferred, they were antimodernist moderns, whose modernism was defined by its opposition to modernity. Scholem seemed to despise the "secularization process . . . the barbarization of the so-called new culture."[58] Corbin, similarly, approved Chesterton's caricature of modernity as a "world full of Christian ideas gone mad."[59] Even more forcefully, he asserted the following: "In our time the Grand Inquisitor has been secularized; he no longer speaks like a theologian, in the name of a transcendent God and a magisterium whose power extends to the beyond. He speaks like a sociologist and a technocrat, in the name of collective norms, limiting all finality to this world."[60]

Scholem, for his part, did not practice traditional Judaism but always insisted, "My secularism is not secular."[61] Scholem made this point unmistakably, just as he always stressed that he believed in God and was by no means an atheist. That being said, he felt keenly the inherent *religious* promise of secularization.

> When religion undergoes, as it does so often and so visibly in our days [14 July 1968], the process of secularization, that is to say when it is interpreted in apparently irreligious terms, we encounter a characteristic shifting of emphasis: what was formerly taken as a state of redemption, especially in its messianic connotations, by now becomes the condition in which alone true human experience is possible. The unredeemed state is no longer worthy to be called human. The redeemed state is where human experience begins.[62]

THE PARADOXES OF MONOTHEISM

> Perhaps the most important function of religious symbolism—especially important for the role it will play in later philosophical speculations—is its capacity for expressing paradoxical situations or certain patterns of ultimate reality that can be expressed in no other way.
> —*Mircea Eliade*[63]

The foregoing similarities serve as background necessary to grasp their contrasting views on the paradoxes of monotheism itself. Yet, ultimately, Corbin and Scholem, two of the greatest scholars of monotheism, came out almost as opposed as possible when addressing the challenge of secularization. For Scholem, the messianic future contained great promise. Secularization revealed novel religious forces. For Corbin, secularization was the Grand Inquisitor, or Leviathan, or Antichrist. While both espoused a kind of religion after religion, one was relentlessly, even violently anti-modern. The other was in a sense modernist into his marrow.[64]

Consider Scholem's lecture "The Crisis of Tradition in Jewish Messianism," delivered at Eranos in 1968.[65] Here he announced to his readers that Jewish Messianism eventuates in crises that seem to turn Judaism inside out. "This new Judaism has in principle already completed the inner break with the Jewish tradition even where it continues to draw sustenance from it, and it has confirmed that break by symbolic acts and rituals."[66] This seems to summarize Scholem's own position with regard to Judaism. The crisis of tradition is still tradition, both remaining within its spirit and yet leaving its current forms behind. If this relationship to tradition was paradoxical, Scholem did not shy away from this conclusion. In fact, Scholem's own philosophy was so centrally concerned with paradox that he placed an epigraph to this effect on the frontispiece of his masterwork, *Sabbatai Sevi, the Mystical Messiah*. Elsewhere he asserted flatly that "mystics become involved in paradox in every age . . . the very idea of such a history is paradoxical to begin with."[67] He deemed Sabbatai Zevi "the living archetype of the paradox of the holy sinner."[68] At the conclusion of his greatest essay, "Redemption through Sin," he invoked "a faith pregnant with paradoxes."[69] In the end, according to Scholem, "God can appear as not-God." Here is his paradox of monotheism in a nutshell. Gershom Scholem seemed to prefer his religion "the more paradoxical the better."[70]

Already in his early study of Hamann in 1939, Corbin similarly located the paradoxical principle he sought. "Le paradoxe correspond exactement à l'uni-totalité de l'être humain, à la fois comme homme caché et homme exterieur. Simultanéité qui vait conduit le Mage [Hamann] au principe de la *"coincidentia oppositorum."*[71] Over a generation later, Corbin titled a vivid final collection of his essays *Le paradoxe du monothéisme*.[72] His massive lecture at Eranos in 1976, reprinted as the title essay in that collection, deployed Heidegger to explode monotheism in philosophical terms even as he employed Jung to implode monotheism in psychological terms. In thus reconciling these twin incendiary apostles of Nietzsche, Corbin accomplished his paradoxical task of having his Islam and immolating it, too.[73]

The transgressive implications of this position should not be underestimated. Corbin tended to obfuscate these implications even as Scholem made them the core of his research program. In the case of Scholem's great studies of the antinomian Messiah Sabbatai Zevi, the paradox of an antinomian monotheistic messiah rested on a "seemingly inexhaustible" paradox: *redemption through sin*. For Scholem and his colleagues, to be sure, such paradoxes were not examples of ultimate contradiction, or blatant violations of logic. Along with Mircea Eliade, Henry Corbin, Carl Jung, and other Eranos luminaries, Scholem subsumed the apparent contradiction of mere paradox into the higher continuities of *coincidentia oppositorum*, the coincidence of opposites, a doctrine they all employed.[74] For Scholem himself, the rational paradoxically reopens a transcendent access to the transrational, just as historicism returns the historian of mysticism to the untramelled freedom at the end of history. In transtemporal terms, his dialectic ascends, like a ladder undercutting itself at every rung attained, from the pit of history all the way into that blue messianic heaven where laws of logic, historical laws, moral laws, are transvalued and made anew.

A central paradox of their shared tautegorical sublime, in short, was their monotheism beyond exoteric ethics. When the visionary materials of monotheism are read with a second naiveté, as both Scholem and Corbin claimed to do, then those materials no longer merely enjoin a believer to pious ritual action. As symbols instead of commandments, they are to be "experienced" not as commanding ethical voices but rather as transmoral theophanies. This emphasis on the visionary image effaced, in a sense, the voice of ethical authority. Monotheism is thereby transmogrified into gnosis, its ostensible opposite number. The gnosis-soaked symbol is sufficient, it would seem, to conduce its viewer to a new world. Left behind, however, were the legally binding norms of monotheism, norms inextricably characterizing everyday belief and practice. Judaism and Islam, in other words, had passed through the looking glass of theosophy, emerging unrecognizable to most Muslims and Jews.

RELIGION AS SUCH

> I consider religion the center of everything—
> more so than, say, the social sciences.
> —*Gershom Scholem*

Given this theosophical revision of monotheism, all the more striking, then, is the extraordinary success of the History of Religions practiced by Henry Corbin and Gershom Scholem. Ironically, their interpretation of religion is itself religious, even as it is postreligious; its watchword was tautegorical, rejecting all nonreligious explanations of religion. It is itself a paradox—a purportedly "religious" study of monotheism that rejects monotheism's fundamental emphasis on the transcendence of God and the demands of law. And yet they have been perhaps the most productively stimulating teachers for students of monotheism in this century.

The Historian of Religion, epitomized by these scholars, epitomized the study of religion as religion. It is sometimes forgotten that Gershom Scholem was for decades one of the world's only Judaists who studied Judaism *as a religion*.[75] True, he studied its internal developments and was not a "comparativist." But his analysis of Kabbalistic symbols unfolded along lines unmistakably familiar from contemporaneous History of Religions. Most important, his emphasis on "religious realities" was consonant with the parallel approach of his Eranos colleagues Henry

Corbin and Mircea Eliade. In other words, Gershom Scholem *was* a Historian of Religions. The significance of this deceptively simple fact should not be missed.

For example, Scholem asserted *the* basic assumption of his great *Origins of the Kabbalah* to be that "the Kabbalist movement in Judaism cannot be described adequately according to the categories of the history of philosophy; it can only be explained in terms of the history of religions . . . "[76] He was surely reserved in his generalizations concerning religions in the plural, but he certainly was not averse to such assertions. "In all religions, the acceptance of a divine revelation originally referred to the concrete communication of positive, substantive, and expressible content."[77] "The historian of religion in particular has no cause to express moral condemnation of the pseudepigraphist."[78] This simple point, then, may be remembered: Scholem understood himself to be a Historian of Religion, that professional with a particular calling to *understand* religion. Corbin, for his part, stood by the principle of religion's tautegorical irreducibility, the very watchword of the History of Religions. "La tendence de notre époque nous conduit trop souvent à vouloir expliquer un phénomène religieux par les causes non religieuses. On s'est donné beaucoup de mal par expliquer le shî'isme par des circonstances politiques, sociales, géographiques ou autres. Ce faisant, on n'a oublié qu'une chose: si une religion déterminée existe, la première et dernière raison du phénomène, c'est l'existence de ceux qui la professant."[79] Here Corbin annunciated the tautegorical sublime as working principle: *the first and last reason for a religious phenomenon is the existence of those who believe in it.* Corbin's tautegory elsewhere is delivered apodictically: "[T]he true meaning is derived not from conclusions reached through deductions or inference but can be unveiled and transmitted only by 'the one who knows.'"[80] One suspects that Scholem would never say such a thing. So why did he not criticize such gestures when Corbin made them? In fact, he seemed to praise Corbin precisely on this tautegorical point: "You are, dear Corbin, one of those rare historians of religion of whom one can say that they know what they know."[81]

Gershom Scholem, however, insisted that the study of religion must be dialectical: his ardent dialectics encompassed appreciation and critique, identification and distance, philology and theosophy. Corbin's genius, by contrast, placed the emphasis elsewhere; in fact, squarely in the *elsewhere* itself, in the transcendent realms available to visionaries only. Scholem, consistent with his dialectics, could honor that position even if he could not unequivocally espouse it. Corbin, for his part, often cited Scholem to make his own points, even as he implicitly rejected Scholem's insistence on scholarly distance. In the end, Scholem was a historian's historian, while Corbin was the standard-bearer of the esoterist assault on historicism. Scholem remained sympathetic with the esoterist position, even if he kept esoterism in dialectical tension with historicism. He was happily aware that this position may have seemed paradoxical—"the more paradoxical the better."

One can conclude that the cordial detente between Scholem and Corbin in the end, may mislead readers into seeing more in common between them than stands up under historical scrutiny. This is not to diminish the importance of their common ground.[82] One prime difference between them, in the end, was Scholem's commitment to Judaism and Zionism. Corbin, by contrast, was neither Christian nor Muslim. For Corbin, the individual Gnostic, the individual modern esoterist, "the one who knows" is the exclusive exponent of true religion. For Scholem, not the individual but the collective ultimately matters as the object of inquiry. He thus insisted that Kabbalah was the "historical psychology" of Judaism and therein its significance properly was to be located. Scholem's public commitment to the historical struggle of his people and his nation is beyond dispute. Corbin's commitment was more elusive. This difference, I believe, accounts for their divergent readings of secularization. But even here, there are paradoxes within paradoxes: Corbin's passionate commitment to a traditional Iran manifested itself in intimate allegiance to the secularizing Peacock Throne of the Shah.

The conversation between these exemplary modern religious thinkers was thus riddled with paradoxes. While both men were preeminent historians of their chosen monotheistic traditions, they read those traditions resolutely against the grain, even as they asserted the tautegorical primacy of the original symbol. This paradox, when pressed hard enough, yields, I think, the following conclusion. What they championed as the most "traditional" theosophy appears as an expression of a curiously emphatic modernism: antinomian, individualistic, and secular. One may call their paradoxical approach *religion after religion*.

Monotheism presents paradoxes to Henry Corbin and Gershom Scholem. As the very designation suggests, Judaism and Islam are religions of the One God (*mono-theos*), and yet they were claimed best to be apprehended not through the One but through the Many, through manifold symbols. They argued that these symbols, especially Kabbalistic *sefirot* for Scholem and angels for Corbin, refer to themselves "tautegorically." The Historians of Religion also presented monotheism as paradoxical insofar as it is purports to be a religion of revealed Law. For both scholars, the "secret" of monotheism is somehow "beyond" the Law. They differed, however, on the promise that modernity presents to monotheists. Still, they agreed that the traditional symbols and antinomian esoteric traditions of monotheism should remain the spiritual tools for monotheists today. Their distinctive approaches to their respective religions, however paradoxical—or perhaps *because* they were paradoxical—remain in both cases preeminent examples of the "religious study of religion," of a History of Religions that claims to respect the autonomy of traditional religious expressions by refusing to "reduce" religions to economics or psychology. The final paradox, perhaps, is that this approach, which seems on principle to respect traditional monotheistic belief and practice, flies in the face of monotheism's classical theology with its esoterism and flouts monotheists' everyday ethics with its antinomianism.

CHAPTER 4

Coincidentia Oppositorum: An Essay

It is impossible to portray life as a whole except as
a coincidentia oppositorum.
—*Ernst Cassirer*

Verbindet die Extreme, so habt ihr die wahre
Mutte.
(Unite the extremes, then you have the true
meaning.)
—*Friedrich Schlegel*

MIRCEA ELIADE showcased the *coincidentia oppositorum* (coincidence of
opposites) as both the title (*Two and the One*) and alternate title (*Mephistopheles and the Androgyne*) he assigned to one of his most popular essay
collections. This collection was then reprinted under a title taken from
the essay forming its core, "Mephistopheles and the Androgyne *or* the
Mystery of the Whole." Eliade, in fact, claimed the *coincidentia oppositorum* to be so central to his understanding of the sacred and the profane, and evoked it so often, that his conception of it has drawn ample
study. It hardly seems necessary, therefore, to recapitulate his version
here.[1] On the other hand, it is little noted that Henry Corbin and Gershom Scholem also discovered this idea to be a key to their respective
hermeneutics of monotheistic theosophy. This shared theosophy of *coincidentia oppositorum* may fairly be said to have dominated the History of
Religions as they conceived it.

This chapter responds to this imposing conception in light of their
thought in its integral entirety. In what follows I accordingly shall recon-
noiter this notion, first, to elucidate its usage in the History of Religions.
I hope as well, however, to approach a critique of its application in the
History of Religions. In order best to accomplish this task I have sought
orientation for this claim in its larger intellectual context. *Coincidentia
oppositorum,* as it turns out, leads historical inquiry into certain impulses
constitutive of their historical moment.

My intention here, I hasten to emphasize, is not to dispute the "larger"
general significance of this concept. Examples of its import in various
fields of thought are abundant. The anthropologist Claude Lévi-Strauss

asserted that "[thought] always works from the awareness of opposites towards their progressive mediation."[2] Theories of opposition are often adduced in cultural analysis.[3] Such concepts as complementarity are similarly common in some sectors of scientific explanation. The dictum of the physicst Niels Bohr to the effect that a "deep truth" is one whose "opposite also contains deep truth" is well known.[4] Philosophers have even found the reconciliation of opposite already inherent in the Kantian "Enlightenment": "Unity resides in agreement. The resolution of contradiction is the system *in nuce*."[5]

Coincidentia oppositorum often has been interpreted to be a genre of paradox, though, of course, not all paradoxes are *coincidentias*. Particularly among popularizing religious thinkers, it is not uncommon to utilize paradox in the effort to transcend perceived limitations to rational thinking. One thus reads of "new logics," "transcendental logics," "ways of breaking the Law of Identity," and the like. These presumed transrationalities have been construed variously to be mystically synchronic (Joseph Campbell, "A both equals and does not equal B");[6] progressively diachronic (Ernst Bloch, "S is not yet P");[7] and metaphysically precise riddles.[8] But, from the perspective of the present inquiry, such paradoxes are not, in fact, pure *coincidentia oppositorum*. In these cases this notion is not adduced as being the central principle of organization within the divine. It is this insistence that epitomizes the theosophical reading of this idea on the part of the History of Religions.

While, then, *coincidentia oppositorum* obviously is an important idea in the history of thought, and is often utilized in popularizations, its centrality in the postwar History of Religions suggests something beyond its purely philosophical use or popular misuse. In the present context, *coincidentia oppositorum* also possesses historical significance. It was the expression, so to speak, of its cultural moment.

PREDECESSORS: CUSA, HAMANN, JUNG

> I began, Lord, to behold thee in the door of the
> coincidence of opposites, which the angel guard-
> eth that is set over the entrance into Paradise.
> —*Nicolas of Cusa*, The Vision of God

Eliade employed the formulation "*coincidentia oppositorum*" dozens of times throughout his long writing career. Although he vaguely acknowledged that Nicolas of Cusa (1401–1464) deserved credit for this formulation, he usually cited it without reference to the Cusan. One place where he did give this credit is thus worth noting. After noting that he had published a book in Romanian on this subject in 1942, he demurred from

resuming today all the themes dealt with in that work of my youth. I propose to present only a certain number of traditional rites, myths and theories associated with the union of contraries and the mystery of the totality, with what Nicholas of Cusa called the *coincidentia oppositorum*. It is well known that for Nicholas of Cusa the *coincidentia oppositorum* was the least imperfect definition of God . . . .but I do not intend to enlarge on those theological and metaphysical speculations. . . . It is the pre-history of philosophy, the presystematic phase of thought that should, I think, claim our principal attention at the present day.[9]

This chapter, however, precisely concerns "the systematic phase of thought."[10] How appropriate was it to appropriate the Cusan in the way that Eliade did?[11] At this point it suffices, perhaps, to note that Eliade seems to see *coincidentia oppositorum* as the warrant to obviate history. His contribution, according to his own emphasis, lies with the *pre*historical "rites, myths and theories." This, of course, was not the emphasis of Nicolas of Cusa.

There is some history to Eliade's forgetting Cusa's contribution. Johann Georg Hamann wrote both to Herder and to Kant regarding *coincidentia oppositorum*, under the misapprehension that the idea derived from Giordano Bruno; he did not know the Cusan connection.[12] Hamann also adduced *coincidentia oppositorum* in a crucial letter of 27 July 1759, in which he broke from Kant.[13] Hamman's influence on Scholem and Corbin, as I have tried to show in the previous chapter, was both early and sustained.

Perhaps the single figure most responsible for bringing together our three Historians of Religions was Carl G. Jung. Jung never tired of the coincidence of opposites, one of the most frequently applied ideas in his volatile array of theory. He consistently stressed its explosive implications: "When opposites meet there is a whirlwind."[14] *Complexio Oppositorum*, his preferred version of the Latin phrase, played a central role in his work right through to such late books as *Response to Job* and *Memories, Dreams, Reflections*.[15] Mircea Eliade, for one, believed that Jung's usage in those later works carried with it world-historical significance. He therefore contrasted Jung to Hegel, precisely on the basis of *coincidentia oppositorum*.[16]

Coincidentia oppositorum has been invoked on more than one occasion as the very Leitmotif of the Eranos overseen by Jung. For example, Joseph Campbell exclaimed that "even a passing glance at the names of the scholars contributing [to Eranos] will suffice to make Jung's great point, that dividing walls are transparent, and where insight rules beyond differences, all the pairs of opposites come together."[17] Walter Corti, an associate and occasional publicist for Eranos, referred to "le cercle de la *coincidentia oppositorum* des orateurs."[18]

SCHOLEM, ELIADE, CORBIN

> The keynote of [mysticism] is invariably a reconciliation . . . of the opposites of the world, whose contradictoriness and conflict make all our difficulties and troubles.
> —*William James*

The leading participants at Eranos themselves certainly used this idea to describe essential features of their theory of religion. Scholem, as early as his classic pre–World War II lectures, adduced the *coincidentia oppositorum* to explain the Zoharic *sefirot*. "From the contemplation of these Sefiroth he proceeds to the conception of God as the union and the root of all these contradictions."[19] Scholem, many years later, described a Kabbalistic notion, "indistinct unity" [*ahduth shava*] as a *coincidentia oppositorum*.[20] Such judgments were applied in other places in his philological work. "This is the unity of opposites symbolized in the word *shamain* [heaven] = the harmony of the fire of Judgment—*esh*—with the water of compassion—*mayim*. . . . The Tree of Life unites within itself these seeming opposites—fire and water in a harmony of oneness."[21] Scholem thus used the idea to refer to operations inside the divine realm.

Not merely theosophical, not only a characterization of the inner workings of the Kabbalistic godhead, *coincidentia oppositorum* also expressed, for Scholem, his own dialectical mode of thought, as reflected on non-descriptive levels of conception and expression. David Biale has made this point succinctly.

> His account of the development of Kabbalistic messianism into apocalyptic heresy and finally secular enlightenment rests on his theory of the productive conjunction of opposites: myth and monotheism, mysticism and rationalism, apocalyptic messianism and secularism. Where previous historians saw only unresolvable contradictions and negations, Scholem argues that continuities can be established between seeming opposites.[22]

One can find Biale's claim corroborated, I think, in Scholem's justly celebrated revolutionary/conservative thesis. Indeed, here, mysticism itself is defined as a union of opposites. Scholem thus solved a theologico-political dilemma—if not *the* theologico-political dilemma—by having mysticism fuse the opposites.[23] Scholem said something rather similar about the freedom inherent in tradition, that tradition is "the force within which contradictions and tensions are not destructive but rather stimulating and creative."[24]

Already in his early study of Hamann in 1939, Corbin similarly found the paradoxical principle he sought. "Le paradoxe correspond exactement à lúni-totalité de lêtre human, à la fois comme homme caché et homme exterieur. Simultanéité qui avait conduit le Mage au principe de la *'coincidentia oppositorum.'* "[25] But only in his great monographs of the postwar period did Corbin fully embrace *coincidentia oppositorum*. Perhaps most vividly, Corbin implemented this concept to elucidate his theory of the "imaginal" and of "the spiritual body" in *Spiritual Body and Celestial Earth*. For Corbin, both "Spiritual Body" and "Celestial Earth" were to be read as *coincidentia oppositorum*. "Finally, [Hurqalya] is therefore, an *interworld*, limiting and conjoining time and eternity, space and transspace, just as its immaterial matter and its celestial Earth are also sign of its *coincidentia oppositorum*."[26] "Briefly, the mediation that interiorizes the transmutations accomplished in the course of the real operation engenders the *spiritual body*, which is a *coincidentia oppositorum*."[27] Eventually, in his monumental late essay, "The *Imago Templi* in Confrontation with Secular Norms," Henry Corbin identified *coincidentia oppositorum* as nothing less than the key to the kingdom of spiritual regeneration itself. "The Order had but a single aim: the regeneration, the new birth, brought about by the re-establishment of the identity between macrocosm and microcosm. The all-powerfulness of the active Imagination . . . puts into operation an alchemy which comprises a conception of the world, an ethic and an eschatology . . . the philosopher's stone is to be found only through the *coincidentia oppositorum*."[28]

Again, as was the case with Scholem's Kabbalah, the point here is not that Sufism itself did not originally exhibit such a process. Corbin showed this to be the case in the chapter titled "Twofold Dimension of Beings" in *Creative Imagination in the Sufism of Ibn ʿArabi*.[29] In the same volume he cited Abu Said al-Kharraz: "[God] is a *coincidentia oppositorum*."[30] "How do you know God?" "Through the combination of opposites."[31] And Corbin cited "the definition of knowledge by Abu Said al-Kharraz, often quoted by Ibn ʿArabi: I have known God by His bringing together of opposites."[32]

At this point, it seems worthwhile to cite at some length the mature conclusions of Franz Rosenthal regarding *coincidentia oppositorum* in Sufism. No acolyte of Ibn ʿArabi, Rosenthal sums up a major study of the great Andalusian mystic's relation to philosophy with the following restrained comments, of no small relevance to the present discussion.

Even more than other mystics and intellectuals, Ibn 'Arabi showed himself fond of the combination of contraries for the purpose of drawing attention to his ideas. Knowledge is at the same time ignorance, being might be conceived as non-being, right guidance implies both bringing near and keeping away, freedom is slavery. It would seem to be fair to describe him in this manner. The attempt made here to let his own statements speak for themselves and to see him as he might have seen himself lead to his characterization as both broadminded and intolerant, both liberal and conservative, both extremely learned and narrowly focused, both extraordinarily original and totally traditional, both a thinker and beyond thinking—in short, both a philosopher and a mystic.[33]

HISTORY

Only in Europe . . . has the human mind dared to
act in the way that *assumes incompatibles.*
—*Denis de Rougemont*

Denis de Rougemont provided an important personal connection between the members of the trio. His location in their network of intellectuals and in the dissemination of their work reveals something of the interpenetration of their circles. He edited the Barthian journal *Hic et Nunc* with Corbin as early as 1931–33; Eliade published de Rougemont's response to Ernst Jünger's essay on "The Gordian Knot" in the first volume of *Antaios*.[34] And de Rougemont cited Corbin and Eliade in his own work and was supported by the Bollingen Foundation, which also published some of his works.[35] His *Man's Western Quest: The Principles of Civilization* was published by Harper and Row in Ruth Nanda Anshen's World Perspectives series in 1957. Eliade's *Myth and Reality* was published in the same series in 1963.[36]

The epigraph to de Rougemont's *Man's Western Quest: The Principles of Civilization* was taken from Heraclitus: "Whatever are opposites cooperate/ and from the divergent proceeds/the most beautiful harmony."[37] He then devoted an extensive disquisition to *coincidentia oppositorum*, which he called "Thinking by Tensions."[38] His case, however, unlike the rather more gnostic Christianity favored at Ascona, argued for a vigorously explicit Europeanist Protestantism, with the paradox of the incarnation serving as a kind of prototype for advanced civilization. "The dogma of the Man-God was . . . the supreme model of *an unthinkable but true* polarity, which requires, once it is accepted, a profound reform of our intellectual categories."[39] Among these categories, for de Rougemont, were nothing less than history and even the cosmos itself. He thus could track the cultural centrality of *coincidentia oppositorum* from Guelph/ Ghibellines to waves/particles. De Rougemont, a Swiss patriot with connections to Jung and the Bollingen Foundation, felt warranted to speak, finally, of "an age-old drama of opposites."[40] Meanwhile, Jung writes in *Mysterium Conjunctionis*, "Even the names of God reflect this complementary dichotomy."[41]

De Rougemont may be taken here as an example of one kind of thinking, one that may illuminate the use of this concept at Eranos. From a philosophical point of view, however, such sweeping metahistorical gestures were not without their attendant dangers. The most dangerous implication of this tendency, perhaps, is that it collapsed the distinction between historical reality and historical ideal. Steven Schwarzschild once spoke to this point incisively, with reference to German historicism.

> Most importantly, the equation, simply put: "real Germany=metaphysical Christianity," had the obvious advantage that it could claim to be both a descriptive as well as a prescriptive, an empirical as well as a normative, truth. As Hegel put it, "the true now is the actuality of true eternity." In Iggers' less philosophical and theological language, "German historicism assumed that the existing institutions and positive laws themselves represented rationality and morality." In Troeltsch's proclamation "Only history reveals value." *Am deutschen Wesen soll die Welt genesen.* Or to put it aphoristically: these people wanted to have their "ought"-cake and eat the "is"-cake, too.[42]

The result would seem to be a kind of historicism without history. Elements of the transrational inside history anticipate the perfected condition beyond rationality at the end of history. What amounted to a theology of history presumed a perfection hidden inside imperfect historical experience.

POETICS

> It is a poetic liberty to state together two contradictory propositions.
> —*Rabbi Meir of Rothenberg*

Friedrich W. J. von Schelling (1775–1854) was perhaps the key Romantic philosopher of remythologization, which return to myth he characterized as "theosophy." This mystical romanticism elevated poetics to a categorical status. According to Moshe Schwarcz, "[the] chief significance of ['the aesthetic idea' of Schlegel, Schelling, and Hegel] was the demand for a union of opposites."[43] Tzvetan Todorov observed the following analogous point. "As for the symbol, it is characterized by the fusion of two contraries, the great and the particular, or to use Schelling's favorite formula, by the fact that the symbol does not simply signify, but also *is*."[44] Such an emphasis was adopted from the German Romantics by Samuel Coleridge. A. R. Ammons, one of our greatest living poets, had this to say about the poetics which Coleridge thus derived.

> Once every five hundred years of so, a summary statement about poetry comes along that we can't imagine ourselves living without. The greatest statement in our language is Coleridge's in the *Biographia*. It serves my purpose to quote only a fragment from the central statement: that the imagination—and, I think, poetry—"reveals itself in the balance or reconciliation of opposites or discordant qualities." This suggests to me that description, logic, and hypothesis, reaching toward higher and higher levels of generality, come finally to an antithesis logic can't bridge.[45]

Roman Jakobson, from the perspective of linguistics, provided a less poetic but nonetheless relevant explanation of poeticity in his essay "What Is Poetry?"

> Why is all this necessary? Why is it necessary to make a special point of the fact that the sign does not fall together with the object? Because besides the direct awareness of the identity between sign and object (A is A_1), there is a necessity for the direct awareness of the inadequacy of that identity (A is not A_1). The reason this antinomy is essential is that without contradiction there is no mobility of concepts, no mobility of signs, and the relationship between concept and sign becomes automatized. Activity comes to a halt, and the awareness of reality dies out.[46]

Jakobson defined poeticity, those intrinsic contradictions constitutive of poetry as such, by "the mobility of concepts." In signficant contrast to the "freedom" of *coincidentia* in the theories of Jakobson, however, the philosopher of language Umberto Eco warns that the freedom of the literary *coincidentia oppositorum*, left unregulated, can drift off into infinity.[47]

> Hermetic thought states that our language, the more ambiguous and multivalent it is, and the more it uses symbols and metaphors, the more it is particularly appropriate for naming a Oneness in which the coincidence of opposites occurs. But where the coincidence of opposites triumphs, the principle of identity collapses. As a consequence, interpretation is infinite. The attempt to look for a final, unattainable meaning leads to the acceptance of never-ending drift or sliding of meaning.[48]

A shining example of such drift is found in Hans Richter's description of the "new" in Dada:

> At the time we were convinced that we had set foot in a completely unknown territory . . . In fact, however, this idea of the "unity of opposites" has been known under the name of "contingence" for a very long time . . .

The realization that reason and anti-reason, sense and non-sense, design and change, consciousness and unconsciousness belong together as necessary parts of a whole—this was the central message of Dada.[49]

POLITICS

> If one is called upon to renew a state, then one must follow principles which are in constant opposition to each other (des principes constamment opposés).
>
> —*Napoleon*

One may accept or reject the collapse of opposites in poetry. Little might seem to be at stake. But when the poetic creation results in the *myth of the state*, in a spiritual nationalism, then how is it that such a poetic *coincidentia* can be said to found a political solidarity? "Credible impossibility" was Giambattista Vico's "proper material of poetry." Vico argued that it "gives rise to a sense of omnipotence."[50] For Vico, the poet on this poetic basis founds society itself. We are not far from Scholem's aesthetic theory of tradition as the foundational force of creative contradictions.

Robert Sayre and Michel Löwy have found the *coincidentia oppositorum* central, for example, to Romanticism. "But what exactly is Romanticism? An undecipherable enigma . . . because it is a *coincidentia oppositorum*: at the same time (or alternately) revolutionary and counter-revolutionary, cosmoplitan and nationalist, realist and fanciful, restorationist and utopian, democratic and aristocratic, republican and monarchist, red and white, mystical and sensual."[51]

While there is little question of a common background of History of Religions in nineteenth-century German romanticism, it is much less well known that the Historians of Religions, more immediately, shared certain roots in the so-called Conservative Revolution of this century. Armin Mohler, a leading figure in the postwar revival of this movement, has spoken of "Konservative Revolution als coincidentia oppositorum."[52] Pierre Bourdieu, less sympathetically, has also observed this tendency in Heidegger.

> [Heidegger] accomplishes the conservative revolution (*die konservative Revolution*) in philosophy. And this he achieves through a strategy typical of the conservative revolutionaries (and particularly of Jünger): the stategy which consists of jumping into the fire to avoid being burnt, to change everything without changing anything, through one of those *heroic extremes* which, in the drive to situate oneself always in the beyond the beyond, unite and reconcile opposites *verbally*, in paradoxical, and magical, propositions.[53]

Bourdieu goes on to elaborate that

> [the] solution to the antinomy is obtained by pushing it to an extreme: as in mystical thought, tension pushed to its extreme is resolved by a complete reversal of the thesis into the antithesis. It is this same magical logic of the marriage of opposites which leads this extremist fringe of the conservative revolutionaries to think up the concept of Führer, which articulates an extreme case of the paradox it is supposed to resolve, by fusing the cult of the hero with a mass movement.[54]

Theodor Adorno similarly described the terrible efficacy of anti-Semitic propaganda as arising from "the agitator's dream, a union of the horrible and the wonderful, a delirium of annihilation masked as salvation."[55] The merely conservative revolutionary and the full fascist have, at times, effectively used "the same magical logic of the marriage of opposites." This "logic" Saul Friedländer identifies as an ideological core.[56] "There is an identifiable fascist ideology . . . [The fascist revision of Marxism] brought about the coincidence of political and ideological opposites, of themes from the radical right and the radical left, that is the most fundamental feature of fascism."[57]

Friedländer, in his *Reflections of Nazism*, returned to and elaborated these insights. "In this contradictory series, it is not one thing or another that is decisive by itself; it is their coexistence that gives the totality of its significance."[58] He reflected on

> the imponderable elements, the fusion of opposites that I have tried to illuminate. Neither liberalism nor Marxism responds to man's archaic fear of the transgression of some limits of knowledge and power (you shall not eat the fruit . . .), thus hiding what remains the fundamental temptation: the aspiration for total power, which, by definition, is the supreme transgression, the ultimate challenge, the superhuman combat that can be settled only by death.[59]

Fascist thinkers, to be sure, were well aware of the power generated by opposites as they collapsed in on themselves. George Mosse located just this power in National Socialist rhetoric: "Finally, Alfred Rosenberg put it succinctly: death and life are not contraries, but linked to one another. Through the benevolence of God's fate, these contraries are dissolved within eternity. . . . Death is constantly dissolved into a higher synthesis. . . . The concept of the Third Reich repeats such dialectic: 'we must have the strength to live by antithesis.' "[60]

The strength (or slipperiness) of this principle seems almost to be the essence of the political principle itself. One may note that the very names of the social phenomena associated here sound like coincidences of opposites: National Socialism; Conservative Revolution; "Reactionary Mod-

ernism."[61] Today, spiritual descendants of the original "Konservative Revolution" perpetuate this "magical logic." Julius Evola, longtime colleague of Eliade, for example, and a leading neofascist ideologue, used
the *coincidentia oppositorum*.[62] Louis Pauwels, another significant influence on Eliade and one of the most prominent conservative revolutionaries in France in the 1970s and 1980s, coauthored a popular paperback
with the title *Impossible possibilities*.[63]

Today, as between the world wars, this tendency of thought, this se-
duction of thought, persists. Bourdieu helps explain

> the paradigm of all the philosophical strategies of the conservative revolution
> in philosophical matters. These strategies are always grounded in a radical
> overcoming which allows everything to be preserved behind the appearance
> of everything changing, by joining opposites in a two-faced system of thought,
> which is therefore *impossible to circumvent*, since, like Janus, it is capable of
> facing challenges from all directions at once: the systematic extremism of
> essential thought enables it to overcome the most radical theses, whether
> these spring from the left or the right, by moving to a pivotal point where
> right becomes left, and vice versa.[64]

Release/constraint; ascension/binding; antinomian/authoritarian: all
these *coincidentias* have a political life too. That this political life is relevant to the History of Religions is rarely indicated by the Historians
themselves. They generally preferred to locate it as a dynamic inside ancient esoteric texts, if not in the Godhead itself. The inherent theologico-
political problem, however, is left unspoken. One does not neutrally
"describe" the coincidence of good and evil in the past or inside the
divine life without making assumptions about such a coincidence (or lack
thereof) here and now. But such implications were not usually publically
addressed by our Historians of Religions.

ETHICS

The real opposites are ethics and aesthetics.
—*Thomas Mann*

The contemporary *coincidentia oppositorum*, for this reason, may appear
to some to be an apotheosis of evasion. To others it may seem ambivalence as first principle; or, as Denis Hollier has said of Georges Bataille's
thought, equivocation as law.[65] Whether one considers Scholem's paradigm of the "holy sinner" or Mircea Eliade's motto, *Felix culpa*, by definition the *coincidentia oppositorum* of good and evil, however uncomfort-
ably to its beholders, is beyond good and evil.[66] But—and this is the

point now reached in the argument at hand—it is often if not always traded off against an opposition to the reality of evil. This seemingly irrefutable relativization of evil should raise a warning flag for the current study of religion. Inasmuch as *coincidentia oppositorum* reigned supreme in the study of religion as conceived by Scholem, Corbin, and Eliade, it should provoke this concern.

The paradigm case, alas, is that of *coincidentia oppositorum* after the Holocaust, an event that of course touched each of our thinkers. Pairs of opposites, as Hans Jonas lugubriously put it, were obliterated there.[67] Primo Levi, similarly mourned the common fate of "the drowned and the saved"—all such pairs of opposites, he sadly observed, were annihilated in the Nazi death camps.[68] One of the disturbing effects of an overly enthusiastic implementation of *coincidentia oppositorum*, in short, is to erase differences, important differences, differences that matter in some meaningful human sense. If we efface the is/ought distinction, for example, we may also eradicate the need to heal. One may justly worry about an understanding of religions that celebrates the erasure of oppositions at its center. The collapsing of opposites can dissipate the power of ethical imperatives, the foundational demands to cure the world, which demands other theories argue to constitute religion's core. It is, on such an alternative reading, more important for religions to heal than to know the godhead. On this reading, what matters for most religious communities is what really can be done, not what may exist in some platonic stratosphere of the spirit. Sigmund Kracauer identified the boundary concisely: "The *coincidentia oppositorum*, which Cusa in *de vis. Dei*, called the wall of paradise behind which dwells God, does not materialize this side of the screen."[69]

The struggle with, the struggle over, *coincidentia oppositorum* on the part of Historians of Religion defines much of the present project. The point of the foregoing is not that *coincidentia oppositorum* is "wrong" or "bad" but that its tenuous doublesidedness tends to give permission for equivalent ambivalence on the part of students of religion. This is not to deny the significance if not centrality of this idea in the history of the study of religion. Sigmund Freud is remembered for his essay "The Antithetical Sense of Primal Words," which famously attempted to explain the union of opposites in language and religion.[70] He influentially expressed this point as a universal: "Religion is based on 'primary process' where contradictory ideas can simultaneously be maintained."[71] Gary Lease, more recently, similarly sees "religion" itself as the place where irreconcilables are, if not exactly reconciled, at least maintained: "[R]eligion appears to be the location of the struggle over *paradoxes*, i.e., the attempt to *maintain* paradoxes without resolving or dissolving them."[72] *Religion after religion*, the operating theory underlying the History of

Religions, fits such definitions. This stance toward religion is itself religious, even as it is postreligious; it is itself a paradox, perhaps a *coincidentia oppositorum*, and, indeed, may be one of the most productively stimulating for students of religion in this century. Lezak Kolakowski made a fundamental point concerning students of religion, which may help us understand *religion after religion* as *coincidentia oppositorum*. "Thus we notice a strange convergence between the cognitive attitude of a radical mystic and that of a radical skeptic. By virtue of a *coincidentia oppositorum* the mystic and the skeptic turn out to be twin brothers in epistemology."[73] One recalls the paradox pronounced aphoristically by Scholem: "God will appear as non-God."[74] Twin brothers in epistemology, the opposing skeptical and gnostic personae of the Historians of Religion are fused, reconciled, in a *coincidentia oppositorum*. And in this *coincidentia oppositorum* of the skeptic and the gnostic, perhaps only through such a Janus-faced personality, might God appear as non-God.

A NEW LOGIC?

> But, while in theology peacemakers are pronounced blessed and are they who inherit the kingdom of dogma, in philosophy synthesizers are often blasted and castigated as infringers upon the Law of Contradiction.
> —*Harry Austryn Wolfson*

As I have noted, it is not hard to find defenders of *coincidentia oppositorum*, who tend still to posit it as the theological basis for a "new logic." One finds this, for example, in an exposition of Jacob Boehme's theosophy. "When once a *Coincidentia oppositorum* is thus postulated then two basic laws of thought are abnegated; the law of contradiction and the law of the excluded third. A new logic appears. Aristotle had asserted that where there is disparity there can be no love. But Boehme saw deeper."[75]

Since the 1950s, when they began to be widely read, "new logic" was seen to be an achievement of the Historians of Religion. Norman O. Brown, drawing on Scholem and Eliade, pointed to it in his influential *Life Against Death*.[76] Later, in his *Love's Body*, Brown brought this notion to a climax: "To seduce the world to madness. Christ is within the wall of paradise, which is the wall of the law of contradiction; and the destruction of the law of contradiction is the supreme task of higher logic."[77]

Jorge Luis Borges, also arriving at his international readership at the same time, popularized *coincidentia oppositorum* in his *ficciones*, relying, like Eliade, on Nicolas of Cusa.[78] Stanislav Lem, the Polish science fiction writer and critic of distinction, instructively criticized Borges on his use of *coincidentia oppositorum*. "It might be called *unitas oppositorum*, the unity of mutually exclusive opposites. What allegedly must be kept separate for all time (that which is considered irreconcilable) is joined before our very eyes, and without distorting logic."[79] He adds, "Le Bon has already said in his work on humor, we always look disdainfully down upon the mechanic, for a mechanical process always lets the strange and surprising get away . . . The cause of his work's mechanistic sickness is this, I think: from the beginning of his literary career, Borges has suffered from a lack of a free and rich imagination."[80]

The "mechanistic sickness" perceived by Lem in Borges's *coincidentia oppositorum* in turn recalls Rudolf Otto, who was so much an influence on Eliade and Corbin. Otto argued that there was something monstrous in the "scientism" of theosophy. "For the characteristic mark of theosophy is just this: having confounded analogical and figurative ways of expressing feeling with rational concepts, it then systematizes them, and out of them spins, like a monstrous web, a science of God, which is and remains something monstrous."[81]

For Otto, theosophy's monstrosity was its scientization of the divine. Lem, in his criticism of Borges, similarly identified "mechanistic sickness" as a theological problem. "Even this great master of the logically immaculate paradox [Borges] cannot alloy our world's fate with his own work."[82] Scholem, like Lem and unlike Henry Corbin or Mircea Eliade, similarly recognized "the danger of theosophical schematism, or, as S. R. Hirsch put it, magical mechanism."[83]

Some see new logic, then, where others see monstrous mechanism. The promise of *coincidentia oppositorum* would seem to have been the promise of a new, theosophically derived logic—a logic mechanistic for Hirsch, even monstrous for Otto. History of Religions, however dangerously, purported to discover in the most mystical documents of the past the key to this "new logic." This "discovery," as I have tried to illustrate elsewhere in this volume, spoke to the crisis of the times. The past was made to answer the present.

At the risk of psychologism, one may venture the following tentative explanation for the rise of this "new logic." Raised in halcyon childhoods among the *haute bourgeoisie avant la guerre*, the Generation of 1914 understandably resisted the reality that lacerated their adolescence. In one response, the conceptual kind outlined here, they responded by, as it were, expanding dialectically in antipodal directions at once, in a kind of metaphysical compensation for the irreconcilable tensions put upon them. With contradictions resolved in what Freud called "the omnipotence of the wish," they thus found *coincidentia oppositorum* to be an almost ideal rationalization after the fact. These Historians of Religions lived under the consequent pressure of a terrible paradox; that their anti-modernism was inextricable from the modern condition itself. This, perhaps, was their *coincidentia oppositorum* at bottom: that their "transgression as norm" was not so much a release from the modern condition so much as it was a heightened characterization of it.

But the modern facts, the sheer realia, of generational, engendered, confessional, class-correlated, racial, and rational strife—the opposites dominating our actual lives—remained ever so stoutly in position.[84] And there we find them, inside history, as ever. The actual civilizational contradictions, differences of labor and sex and cuisine and nation, have not yet evaporated. The conflict of these oppositions, one might safely say, is our time, is time, if not our condition as such. The timeless oceanic *coincidentia oppositorum*—the *oceanum mysteriosum Dei*, to appropriate the phrase of Saint Jerome—floats out there, through the wall of time; it is not our time, at least not yet. In the mere light of historical day, it seems surely impetuous to dwell on the godhead, as if that "black sun" could ever act as a revealer.[85] The unmanifest, in fact, by definition does not manifest the revealing. The secret in all this is paradoxically unmysterious; what does the revealing, for students and scholars alike, is the angel delegated to direct us, each according to one's own capacity. That angel is reason.[86] And we are enjoined by that angel to remain agnostic concerning the upper regions from whence she was sent. What's up there she knows, but we (mere students of religion) may never know. A mystocentric emphasis on *coincidentia oppositorum* reinforces the *status quo ante* of critical understanding by retrojecting the current flaws of creation back into a unifying godhead. The problem, alas, is that we are limited in our capacity to *know* that godhead.[87] The Mephistophelean implication of *coincidentia oppositorum* is "gnostic" in the etymological sense of "gnosis"—it supposes a "knowing" beyond human knowledge. But without acknowledgment of the limitations of human knowledge we lose the little orientation available to us.[88] For every phantasmic footfall in the imaginal dimension, we divest ourselves of some concomitant confidence, lose further capacity for coordinating ethical and rational direction.

CONCLUSION

His firm stanzas hang like hives in hell
Or what hell was, since now both heaven and hell
Are one, here, O terra infidel.

—*Wallace Stevens*

Coincidentia oppositorum may seem to some to be a bold posture, a mode of operating solo, a defiantly courageous way of flouting the terrifying contradictions of life. It appears not so much a concept as a condition; not so much irrational as the shout released as reason hits its limit, the *cri de coeur* arising when reason breaches its proper domain. At the same time, in its own coincidence of life and afterlife, it appears also as the retrospective point when reason inscrutably eulogizes itself, with philosophical equanimity. *Coincidentia oppositorum*, after all, by definition is *both/and*; it subsumes the best of ideas and the worst of ideas; it "unites" the best and the worst, however, into something literally unimaginable, morally objectionable, and technically unteachable. I am reminded, finally, of the words of a perceptive contemporary. Having attended closely this all too human oddity, he concluded that "we can learn something by examining the absurd, be it only this: that we are again overwhelmed by the transcendent beauty of the principle of contradiction."[89]

Part II

POETICS

CHAPTER 5

On Symbols and Symbolizing

Eranos is, as it were, a gigantic symposium on
Symbolism.
—*R. J. Zwi Werblowsky*

"I HAVE NO SENSE": ON THE
AUTONOMY OF THE SYMBOL

As for the symbol, it is characterized by the fusion
of two contraries, the great and the particular, or
to use Schelling's favorite formula, by the fact that
the symbol does not simply signify, but also is . . .
—*Tzvetan Todorov*

R. J. Zwi Werblowsky, a student and associate both of Scholem and of
Jung, recalled that "Jung once remarked, in one of his most profound
sayings, that a symbol could never be defined but only translated—into
another symbol."[1] Along somewhat the same lines, Joseph Campbell,
one of the leading popularizers of Jung and of Eranos, delivered a lecture
titled "The Symbol without Meaning," at Eranos in 1957.[2] And Scholem
composed a poem on the uncanny painting by Paul Klee, "Angelus
Novus," which included the following strophes.[3]

> Ich bin ein unsymbolisch Ding
> bedeute was ich bin
> du drehst umsonst den Zauberring
> Ich habe keinen Sinn.

> I am an unsymbolic thing.
> My meaning is what I am.
> You turn the magic ring in vain.
> I have no sense.[4]

"The symbol signifies nothing and communicates nothing, but makes
something transparent which is beyond expression," Scholem wrote, with
reference to Kabbalah.[5] Though they "signified nothing," Scholem nonetheless fervently believed in the power of symbols. Nowhere was this

more movingly expressed than in his essay "The Star of David: History of a Symbol."

> Something of the secret of man is poured into symbols; his very being demands concrete expression. The great symbols serve to express the unity of his world. . . . Anything in that world can become a symbol; it need only have something of the spiritual "charge," of the intuitive heritage which lends the world meaning, give it character, and reveals its mystery. . . . Thus the symbol transmits something of the emotional life crystallized within it to the consciousness of those who regard it with the eyes of believers.[6]

In this, I think, Corbin and Eliade would lend assent: the symbol is intrinsically empty yet at the same time is the single most powerful vehicle for spiritual communication. This intrinsic emptiness they usually described as *transparency*. More precisely, the symbol was not quite empty, but rather in itself was solely an access point into the transcendent realm, a higher reality inaccessible, so it was claimed, by any other means.

Behind this idea lay Goethe's "realism of the symbol," which was defined by Nietzsche as a "language of the universal." Another participant at Eranos, Erich Heller, summarized this Romantic symbology. "This realism of the symbol is the common property of all great art. . . . It describes; and in describing it opens our eyes to what really is. And what really is is not a dream or a shadow, nor the meaningless agony of the Will, nor the abstractions of Reason, but the living revelation of the unfathomable."[7] Empty of intrinsic content, universal in origin, and autonomous in its contact with that transcendent origin, this "symbol" derived unmistakably (if not exclusively) from German Romanticism. Jung came eventually to place epistemological priority for God in the psychic substrate of symbols. In his Yale University Terry Lectures of 1937, he said as much. "We might, therefore, conclude that the symbol, spontaneously produced in the dreams of modern people, means the same thing—*the God within*."[8] A short time later, in 1939, he bluntly exclaimed to a seminar that "God is a symbol of symbols!"[9]

HAMANN

> On the gates of this theology I would inscribe the profound words of Johann Georg Hamann, Language is the mother of reason and revelation.
> —*Gershom Scholem*

One such forefather of this inspired linguocentrism was Johann Georg Hamann, "The Magus of the North" (1730–1787).[10] The young Scholem collected Hamann's works, in fact reading Hamann before he read the *Zohar*.[11] Hamann, Scholem noted, anticipated Walter Benjamin's famous dissertation on Baroque allegory.[12] The young historian of Kabbalah wrote to his older friend Benjamin that he, Benjamin, was "the legitimate continuator of the most fruitful and genuine traditions of Hamann and Humboldt."[13] Eventually, Scholem's Eranos lectures carried prominent citations from Hamann. Even late in his career he would revert to Hamann. "This is the fundamental thesis of linguistic mysticism, as it is indicated by Johann Georg Hamann with masterly laconicism; language—mother of reason and revelation, their *alpha* and *omega*."[14] Scholem and Benjamin, however, were hardly alone in rediscovering Hamann. The interwar Hamann reception spread to Paris as well. Henry Corbin delivered lectures on Hamann in Paris between 1936 and 1939.[15]

The 1930s Hamann reception was also significant for the so-called Conservative Revolution, whose best-known names, Jünger and Heidegger, were to be influential on our Historians of Religions.[16] Hamman thus had a marked influence on Ernst Jünger, Eliade's close colleague and coeditor.[17] Jünger's affinity for Hamann led him to quote the Romantic thinker: "Meanwhile, our phantasies, illusions, *fallaciae opticae*, and fallacies stand under God's realm."[18] Hamann was adduced in 1950 by Heidegger, at a time when Heidegger was enjoying a major impact on Jünger and Eliade: "I am still waiting for an apocalyptic angel with a key to this abyss."[19] Such resonant utterances of Hamann were particularly appealing to those who seek to plumb the depths of symbolism.

GOETHE

> Tout l'éphémère ne rien que symbole.
> —*Henry Corbin's version of Goethe, 1957*

> Tout l'éphémère n'est qu'un symbole.
> —*Henry Corbin's version of Goethe, 1969*

Goethe, much more so than his predecessor Hamann, exerted a tenacious influence over Corbin and Eliade, and a significant (though lesser) influence over Scholem. Most especially, all three found his second *Faust* to be a most precious touchstone.

Corbin was a lifelong, ardent Teutonophile.[20] He was also a well-known translator from the German in the 1930s. When he later translated the famous couplet of Goethe, *Alles Vergängliche/Ist nur ein Gleichnis*, he did so with an interesting twist.[21] In fact, the first time he translated he explicitly commented on his own translation: "Que l'interprétation de la Croix par l'Ismaélisme ne nous apparaisse pas comme une dévalorisation de ce réel don nou nous faisons une conception si unilatérale. Loin de là, symbolisme implique valorisation éminente. Tout léphémère ne rien que symbole. Il faut plutôt traduire: *rien de moins qu'un symbole.*"[22] Goethe's famously aphoristic penetration was never lost on Corbin. As an epigraph to a selection from the thirteenth-century Sufi Ibn 'Arabi, Corbin applied a couplet from the last scene of *Faust*, part 2; "Das Unbeschreibliche, Hier istss getan" [Here the indescribable/actually takes place].[23]

Henry Corbin's *Man of Light in Iranian Sufism* devoted its concluding section to Goethe's *Farbenlehre* (Theory of colors). Speaking of him as a "sort of Iranian Goethe," Corbin summarized the teachings of al-Kirmani, a nineteenth-century master of the Shaikhi school.[24] Corbin returned to this comparison, evoking again this flattering comparison with "our eminent Shaikh."[25] In the later context, our eminent French Islamicist asserted that Kirmani "reaches heights foreshadowed by Goethe at the conclusion of the second Faust: an eternally Feminine."[26] The "Prologue of Heaven" from *Faust*, part 2, figured prominently in Corbin's dramatistic exposition of Islamic mysticism.[27]

For Corbin's version of Sufism, spiritual hermeneutics meant the "transformation of everything visible into symbols, the only means of signifying what is to be signified."[28] Corbin shared with Scholem a strong conception of "the symbolical nature of all that exists."[29] Scholem thus would use phrases quite similar to those of Corbin: "What makes *Kabbala* interesting is its power to transmute things into symbols."[30] Scholem's Kabbalists, like Corbin's Sufis, then, are those mystics for whom "everything takes on a symbolic character." "The *sefirot* are '*der Gottheit lebendinges Kleid*,' the living garment of the deity, to quote from Goethe's *Faust*."[31] As has recently been made clear, however, it was not so much directly from Goethe that Scholem "rediscovered" the primacy of the symbolic over the allegorical. A more immediate source seemed to have been Friedrich Gundolf (1880–1931).[32] It was typical of Scholem, in any case, that he was aware of the irony of Goethe's dominance among his contemporaries. "Thus, almost all the most important critical interpretations of Goethe were written by Jews!" he exclaimed.[33] Still, for however many ironies he belittled, he himself remained, in certain crucial cultural respects, a German Jew, as his friend and colleague George L. Mosse has properly observed.[34] And so, just as for his fellow German Jews, Goethe found pride of place (if rather selectively) in Scholem's work. Thus, when ending his classic essay on "Revelation and Tradition as Religious Categories in Judaism," originally delivered at Eranos in 1962, he turned to Goethe to sum up his sense of the "ancient truth" in "genuine tradition."

Das Wahre war schon längst gefunden,
Hat edle Geisterschaft vervunden,
Das alte Wahre, fass es an.

[The truth that long ago was found
Has noble Spirits bound,
The ancient truth, take hold of it.][35]

By citing Goethe in the original German to conclude this lecture, itself delivered and originally published in German, Scholem points to ironies of which, as I have said, he was among the first to be aware. Similarly, when he spoke on "My Way to Kabbalah" on the occasion of receiving the Literary Prize of the Bavarian Academy of Arts in 1974, Scholem cited Goethe's *Faust* to describe his own Hebrew studies![36] And in his letter to Aniela Jaffé explaining why he accepted the original invitation to Eranos, Scholem cited the example that "even Goethe" had flaws, in order to explain why he accepted the analogously large flaws of Freud and Jung.[37]

Eliade, like Corbin, possessed a passion for Germany and things German in the 1920s and 1930s. At that time Goethe became one of his personal touchstones of greatness. "[Voltaire] encouraged my dreams of a univeral spirit. . . . [but w]hen I discovered other universal authors, especially Papini, and later Goethe and Leonardo da Vinci, I ceased to read him."[38] At the end of his career he still placed Goethe in the cultural pantheon. "We must take seriously these oeuvres—in the same way we take seriously the Old Testament, the Greek tragedies, or Dante, Shakespeare, and Goethe."[39] And Eliade compared himself to Goethe on many other occasions.[40] He made clear, for example, that the "sorrows of young Goethe" were, to use a favorite Eliadism, "paradigmatic" of initiation: he cites *Dichtung und Wahrheit* as evidence that Goethe underwent a shamanic ordeal of transformation.[41] Even at the end of his life, he noted, "I resemble, or want to resemble, Hasdeu, Cantemir, and Goethe."[42]

Clearly, then, Eliade understood his role in history to be a very great one, modeled directly on that of "the universal Goethe." Thus he wrote of "a grand destiny" to speak for the entire "young generation" and "my destiny" to be both "authentic Bucharestian" and "universal man."[43] This was even more clearly stated much later in life: "As Gide has rightly observed, Goethe was highly conscious of a mission to lead a life that would be exemplary for the rest of humanity. In all that he did he was trying to *create an example*. . . . As Paul Valéry wrote in 1932: He represents for us, gentlemen of the human race, one of our best attempts *to render ourselves like gods*."[44] In 1959, Eliade stated flatly, "As always, I see Goethe's destiny as my own."[45]

What was that Goethean destiny? In 1973, he noted that "Goethe improves with each new reading. I reread in a single sitting *Dichtung und Wahrheit*."[46] Just after this reading, Eliade reflected on *Gespräche mit Goethe*, in which Goethe speculates on God destroying and recreating the cosmos.[47] This remythologizing *Naturphilosophie* seems to be the key to his devotion to Goethe. Eliade thus attributed to Goethe his own most fundamental metaphysical assumptions: that the cosmos operates on the principle of Nature, whose Mystery consists of a rhythm of death and rebirth. The alchemist "cooperates with Nature," acts alongside God, in this work.[48]

The "Faustian" and even "demonic" propensities of the perfected man, a theme dear to the demiurgic Goethe, thus were understood to be practically unlimited. Goethe spoke of an "empirical demonology."[49] Eliade wrote "empirical" studies of demonology from his "Notes on Demonology" (1939) through his *Occultism, Witchcraft and Cultural Fashions*.[50] Eliade's Faustianism, then, merged with a similarly Goethean "diabolism" and stayed situated progammatically and permanently at the core of his metaphysics: "It isn't by chance that Goethe searched throughout his life for the true place of Mephistopheles, the perspective in which the Demon who denied life could show himself paradoxically as its most valuable and tireless partner."[51] In November 1968, Eliade again reverted to Goethe, confiding to his journal that, whenever he felt "tired, sick, depressed (and how not, since I don't yet know what sickness I'm suffering from?)," he would read Eckermann's *Gespräche mit Goethe*. "And I find that, later, I am calmed, comforted. The mystery of this *total* attraction for Goethe still fascinates me. A thought or a page of his, any work in connection with him, projects me into a sthenic, luminous, familiar universe. I feel like shouting: That is my world, that is the reason that I was created, etc."[52] Eventually, he read *Dichtung und Wahrheit* yet again near the end of his life and was "surprised by the exasperating egocentrism of my dear Goethe."[53]

For Goethe, the symbol was a "living, instantaneous (*lebendig-augenblickliche*) revelation of the inscrutable."[54] The Goethean symbol as revelation itself was then shared by Corbin, Scholem, and Eliade. Corbin used both of Eliade's perennial terms for revelation, "hierophany" and "theophany." He explicitly cited Eliade on this usage.[55] Corbin's own definitive treatment was published in part 2 of *Creative Imagination in the Sufism of Ibn 'Arabi*, especially in "The Creation as Theophany" and "Theophanic Imagination and the Creativity of the Heart." For Corbin, scripture and earth, revelation and creation, were themselves theophanies. Eliade's symbol similarly was a kind of stargate, an access point opening out into the infinite; the locus of revelation, available wherever symbols are apprehended. For the Historians of Religions, the theophanic power of the symbol was—as Goethe had already shown them with genius—unsurpassable.

CASSIRER AND THE "PHILOSOPHY OF SYMBOLIC FORMS"

In one of his final books, *Essay on Man*, Ernst Cassirer summarized the human being as *animal symbolicum*.[56] Eliade employed a parallel Latinism. "Man being *homo symbolicus*, and all his activities implying symbolism, every religious fact has necessarily a symbolic character."[57] For the present discussion, perhaps the key significance of Cassirer's work lies with its rethinking of the "philosophy of mythology" of the late Schelling.[58] The Historians of Religion followed Cassirer in his appreciation of Schelling's late philosophy, borrowing from him, for example, the concept of *tautegory*.[59] On the other hand, they rejected what they felt were both the "bourgeois" and the neo-Kantian elements of his work.

In general, they seemed to prefer more venerable (and less contemporary) authorities. Current theories of symbolism, of which Cassirer's was the best known, interested them only slightly. In addition to Schelling and Hamann, Goethe was certainly preferable to more recent authorities on the symbol. Corbin, however, did meet Ernst Cassirer, "qu'il élargit ma voie ver ce que je cherchais et pressentais obscurément, et qui evait plus tard toute ma philosophie du *mundus imaginalis* dont je dois le nom à nos Platoniciens de Perse."[60] Corbin also employed Cassirer's phrase "the philosophy of symbolic forms."[61] Scholem eschewed Cassirer. By contrast, he explained that he and his friend Benjamin looked for more extreme inspiration than that provided by Cassirer, whose university lectures did not appeal to them. "We were proponents of radical demands."[62] Eliade seems to have cited Cassirer only once, to exemplify a vague "vogue for symbolism."[63] All three knew the work of Ernst Cassirer on symbolism, then, and acknowledged its importance—even as they distanced themselves from it.

"SYMBOL" VS. "ALLEGORY"

> It is beginning to be realized that the rediscovery of symbolism is perhaps the most important discovery of our age.
>
> —*Mircea Eliade*[64]

Eliezer Schweid and Susan Handelman have shown that for Gershom Scholem, the Goethean distinction between symbol and allegory "has the status of a methodological principle."[65] It is not clear whether Scholem or Benjamin had the idea first. According to David Biale, Benjamin originally took the idea from Goethe.[66] Jeffrey Mehlman notes that "the disjunction introduced through allegory into the structure of the symbol is perhaps the central intuition of [Benjamin's] thesis on *The Origin of German Tragic Drama*. Where man is drawn toward the symbol, allegory emerges from the depths of being to intercept the intention, and to triumph over it."[67] Benjamin, it seems, retrieved allegory, rejecting the romantic symbology of Scholem.[68] In the end, they differed, even if they agreed on the general significance of the problem.

As I have noted, Jung said something similar, that the symbol can only be translated into another symbol.[69] Eliade noted simply that the symbol "cannot always be translated into concepts."[70] Paul Ricoeur developed this point in his *Symbolism of Evil*, a book explicitly indebted to Eliade.[71]

> Symbol and allegory, then, are not on the same footing: symbols proceed hermeneutics; allegories are already hermeneutic. This is so because the symbol presents its meaning transparently in an entirely different way than by translation. . . . It presents its meaning in the opaque transparency of an enigma and not by translation. Hence, I oppose the *donation of meaning in trans-parency* in symbols to the *interpretation by trans-lation* of allegories.[72]

While Scholem and Eliade stood on the same side of the allegory/symbol contrast, it was Henry Corbin who devoted his ample philosophical energies to articulating its necessity. In his definitive defense of the *mundus imaginalis*, he made this point as powerfully as anywhere in his corpus:

> [T]he current attitude is to oppose the real to the imaginary as though to the unreal, the utopian, as it is to confuse symbol with allegory, to confuse the exegesis of the spiritual sense with an allegorical interpretation. Now, every allegorical interpretation is harmless; the allegory is a sheathing, or, rather, a disguising, of something that is already known or knowable otherwise, while the appearance of an Image having the quality of a symbol is a primary phenomenon (*Urphänomen*), unconditional and irreducible, the appearance of something that cannot manifest itself otherwise to the world where we are.[73]

He reiterated this symbological credo, defined by its ardent opposition to allegory, throughout his work, so much so that he may be said to have created an esoteric philosophy of symbolic forms unparalleled in this century. Given the comparative neglect into which it appears to have fallen, it is perhaps worthwhile to cite several of his reflections at some length.

The symbol is not an artificially constructed *sign*; it flowers in the soul spontaneously to announce something that cannot be expressed otherwise; it is the *unique* expression of the thing symbolized as of a reality that thus becomes transparent to the soul, but which in itself transcends all expression. Allegory is a more or less artificial figuration of generalities or abstractions that are perfectly cognizable or expressible in other ways. . . . The exegete should beware lest he thus close to himself the road of the symbol, which leads out of this world.[74]

To the straightforward exoteric reader what appears to be the true sense is the literal reading. What one proposes to him as the spiritual sense appears to him as the metaphoric sense, as an "allegory" which he confuses with "symbol." For the esoteric it is the opposite: the so-called literal sense is only a metaphor (*majâz*). The true sense (*haqîqat*) is the event which this metaphor conceals.[75]

The difference between "symbol" and what nowadays is commonly called "allegory" is simple to grasp. An allegory remains on the same level of evidence and perception, whereas a symbol guarantees the correspondence between two universes belonging to different ontological levels: it is the means, and the only one, of penetrating into the invisible, into the world of mystery, into the esoteric dimension.[76]

Allegory is rational, remains signifying on identical planes of consciousness, whereas

the symbol announces a plane of consciousness distinct from that of rational evidence; it is the "cipher" of a mystery, the only means of saying something that cannot be apprehended in any other way; a symbol is never "explained" once and for all, but must be deciphered over and over again, just as a musical score is never deciphered once and for all, but calls for ever new execution.[77]

Corbin, of the three Historians of Religion, developed the most complete and sophisticated esoteric theory of symbolism.

TRANSPARENCE OF THE SYMBOL

There each man
Through long cloud-cloistered-porches, walked alone,
Noble within perfecting solitude,
Like a solitude of the sun, in which the mind
Acquired transparence and beheld itself
And beheld the source from which transparence came . . .

—*Wallace Stevens*

For Scholem, "the symbol 'signifies' nothing and communicates nothing but makes something transparent which is beyond expression."[78] His trope of transparency, like other features of the theory of symbol in the History of Religions, derived from German romantic aesthetics. Inspired by these contemporaneous romantics, Samuel Taylor Coleridge, to take one example, exalted the symbol's "translucence of the special in the individual . . . above all by the translucence of the eternal through and in the temporal."[79] Jonathan Z. Smith has properly noted the popularity of this perspective on symbolism in the History of Religions. "The symbol, while possessing no ontological status of its own, has quite consistently been held to be transparent to the realm of being, of ultimate value."[80]

In some of the most eloquent passages in his work, Scholem summarized his symbology of transparence with succinct penetration. Commenting on the thirteenth-century mystic Abraham Abulafia, he observed the transformative potential of a true understanding of symbol. "All that which occupies the natural soul of man must either be made to disappear or must be transformed in such a way as to render it transparent for the inner spiritual reality, whose contours will then become perceptible through the customary shell of natural things."[81]

> All creation, from the world of the highest angel to the lowest realms of physical matter, refers symbolically to the law which operates within it—the law which governs the world of the Sephiroth. In everything something is reflected—one might just as well say—from the realms which lie in the center of it. Everything is transparent and in this state of transparency everything takes on a symbolic character. This means that every thing, beyond its own meaning, has something more, something which is part of that which shines into it or, as if in some devious way, that which has left its mark behind in it, forever.[82]

Elsewhere he elaborated this perspective.

> In the mystical symbol a reality which in itself has, for us, no form or shape becomes transparent and, as it were, visible, through the medium of another reality which clothes its content with the visible and expressible meaning, as for example the cross for the Christian. The thing which becomes a symbol retains its original form and its original content. It does not become, so to speak, an empty shell into which another content is poured; in itself, through its own existence, it makes another reality transparent which cannot appear in any other form. . . . The symbol "signifies" nothing and communicates nothing, but makes something transparent which is beyond expression. . . . Of such symbols the world of Kabbalism is full, nay the whole world is to the Kabbalist such a *corpus symbolicum*. Out of the reality of creation, without the latters being denied or annihilated, the inexpressible mystery of the God-

head becomes visible. In particular the religious acts commanded by the Torah, the Mitzvot, are to the Kabbalist symbols in which a deeper and hidden sphere of reality becomes transparent.[83]

And even in his most personal "ahistorical" reflections on Kabbalah, Scholem returned to the metaphor of symbolic transparence. "But in the Kabbalah, the stony wall of the law gradually becomes transparent; a shimmer of the reality surrounded and circumscribed by it breaks through."[84] As David Biale aptly interprets this passage: "[T]he Kabbalists transmuted the law into transparency by rendering it symbolic."[85]

These passages make it abundantly clear that the mystical transparence of the symbol was a cornerstone of Gershom Scholem's symbolical understanding of religion. It was no less central in the work of Henry Corbin.

> Symbol is the only possible expression of that which is symbolized, that is to say of the thing signified *with which* it symbolizes. It can never be deciphered once for all. Symbolic perception effects a transmutation of the immediate data (the sensible and literal data), and renders them transparent. In the absence of the transparency brought about in this manner, it is impossible to pass from one level to another.[86]

Several of his works provide extensive discussions of symbolic transparence.[87] Corbin raised it, as all things, to a matter of celestial principle.

> No misunderstanding is possible, however. We are faced with the same imperative as that which is posed to the esoteric hermeneutics of Shi'ism in general: the simultaneity of the spiritual sense and the literal sense, of the exoteric (*zahir*) and the esoteric (*batin*). The situation is, in fact: either this simultaneity is not noticed by the profane, in which case the natural sense forms a protetive wall against any violation of the sanctuary; or else it is known to the spiritual adept, but in this knowledge itself a transmutation of the natural sense occurs, the covering becomes transparent, diaphanous.[88]

Following a technique also practiced by Eliade, these disquisitions on the symbol tended to overlap and interpenetrate, in a recursive, intentionally rhythmic repetition. Corbin's most sustained treatment, perhaps, is found in *Creative Imagination in the Sufism of Ibn 'Arabi.*

> [The active Imagination can] become increasingly transparent, for its sole purpose is to enable the mystic to gain knowledge of being as it is, that is to say, the knowledge that delivers, because it is the gnosis of salvation. This occurs when the gnostic understands that the plemulti [*sic*] successive forms, their movements and actions, appear to be separate from the One only whenthey are veiled by a veil without transparency. Once transparency is achieved, he knows what they are and why they are.[89]

Eliade also favored the metaphor of symbolic transparency. "Above all, the world exists, it is there, and it has a structure; it is not a chaos but a cosmos, hence it presents itself as creation, as work of the gods. This divine work always preserves its quality of transparency, that is, it spontaneously reveals the many aspects of the sacred."[90] Eliade saw this transcendence-by-transparence accessible everywhere. "Every cosmic fragment is transparent; its own mode of existence shows a particular structure of being, and hence of the sacred."[91]

Transparence became, as it were, the color of Eranos itself. The popularizer of Eranos, Joseph Campbell, defined myth as "a metaphor transparent to transcendence."[92] Corbin, in his tribute to Eranos titled "De l'Iran à Eranos," called up its "instants privilégiés où tout s'élucide en une transparence simultanée d'effroi et d'allégresse."[93] Or, even more directly, Carl Jung announced that the "difference between most people and myself is that for me the dividing walls are transparent."[94] And so Corbin's adoption of the Jungian Active Imagination turned out also to emphasize transparence.[95]

> The active Imagination thus induced will . . . function directly as a faculty and organ just as *real* as—if not more real than—the sense organs. . . . The organ is not a sensory faculty but an *archetype-Image* . . . and the property of this Image will be precisely that of effecting the transmutation of sensory data. . . . to restore them as symbols to be deciphered . . . it changes the physical datum impressed upon the senses in a pure mirror, a spiritual transparency.[96]

ALL AT ONCE OR NOT AT ALL

> Even today, the aim of 'reactionary' thought is not to defend the contention that Adam spoke to God in Hebrew, but rather to defend the status of language itself as the vehicle of revelation. This can only be maintained so long as it is also admitted that language can directly express, without the mediation of any sort of social contract or adaptations due to material necessity, the relation between human beings and the sacred.
> —*Umberto Eco*

Transparency, like tautegory, suggests a sublime condition of resistance-less spirit through which perception passes like light itself. Such purity was the ideal condition espoused, however indirectly, at Eranos. It was an intellectual condition beyond intellection; an aesthetic insight after art; a religious attainment after religion. How was it to be reproduced? Both Scholem and Jung used the same expression for such symbolic perception. The symbol, they said, was understood *all at once or not at all.*[97] What may be less than obvious is that Eliade's repeated concern with "totality" is not unrelated to Scholem's repeated considerations of the idea of "Gestalt." Maurice Hayoun, the French translator of Scholem's *The Mystical Shape of the Godhead,* interestingly noted that Scholem used variants on the word "form" (*Gestalt*) no less than 165 times in this book, even using 19 variations of it on a single page.[98] Corbin also employed the German *Gestalt. Gestalt* is, in fact, used by Corbin more or less interchangably with "archetype": "This figure, the *Gestalt,* has completely retained its identity, even though the elements of the context have changed . . . it may happen that her name is no longer pronounced, that a Figure with an entirely different name appears in an entirely different context, and that nevertheless we can still identify the same features, the same *Gestalt.*"[99]

For Eliade, the parallel conception was that of "totality"—as in "the mystery of totality."[100] The totality, the *Gestalt,* of the symbol, image, or myth, could only adequately be apprehended all at once or not at all. And the one best suited, uniquely suited in fact, to understand the totality that is the symbol was the Historian of Religions. This assertion suggests the interesting situation of an implicit polemic against the priority of the very traditions that the Historians studied. That is, the Historian of Religions operates autonomously of these traditions—he does not pretend to be either a spokesman or an official believer—because symbols are autonomous. Eliade's theory of symbolism, resting as it does on these presuppositions, has been studied extensively for the last thirty years.[101] It has long been recognized that his theory of religion is centrally symbological. Large claims rest at its center. These claims can be summarized syllogistically. *If* "the symbol reveals certain aspects of reality—the deepest aspects—which defy any other means of knowledge"[102] *and if* "the historian of religions is in a better position than anyone else to promote the knowledge of symbols,"[103] *then* the following conclusion seems logically inescapable: *The Historian of Religions is in a better position than anyone to reveal the deepest aspects of reality. This privilege is made possible only through the symbol.*

CONCLUSION: TAKING SYMBOLS SERIOUSLY

> But the attempts to discover the hidden life beneath the external shapes of reality and to make

visible that abyss in which the symbolic nature of
all that exists reveals itself: this attempt is as important for us today as it was for those ancient
mystics.

—*Gershom Scholem*[104]

The Historians of Religions *took religion seriously* and, more particularly,
took symbols seriously. They took symbols to be revelatory, and they accepted their message in the terms prescribed by traditions. Or did they?
In fact, by dehistoricizing symbols into phenomenology, Corbin and
Eliade divested symbols of their original embeddedness in some historical
solidarity. Such decontextualizing selections of symbols, however, did not
merely remove them from their setting in life. At the same time, it removed them from lived traditions and recast them as a newly accessible
route to the absolute; it relocated them from their organic settings into a
synthetic esoteric tradition. By *choosing* their symbols, their own eclectic
"tradition," they thereby pieced together original artifacts from the raw
materials of history. The focus on symbols allowed these modernist authors to *choose* their religious objects—choice being eminently modern.
They chose, as they suggested, to pass through the "transparent" symbol
into some transcendent referent. *Through the wall of time*—that is,
through the separating wall between historical life in our society and the
symbolic galaxy of the godhead—the Historians of Religions lept. But
where they landed was not in any actual historical communities of the
past. Rather, they arrived at an "ideal" transparence, outside societies of
the past or the present.[105]

It is not insignificant to recall that Eliade, Corbin, and Scholem each
rejected critique of ideology in favor of retrieval of tradition as early as
the 1920s.[106] Traditional systems of symbols were to replace the dread
actuality of a perceived collapse of European civilization. What constituted the real difference between their advances in the History of Religions,
and what went before? And the answer: symbols were *both more and less*
real for them. In their comprehensive recapitulations of symbols, individual symbols became relativized, systematized, and each one's organic integrity ultimately *reduced* into the context of the totality. But this theosophic reordering of them, of course, still asserted each symbol to be a
capstone on the archway into the infinite.

The choice of the *total symbolic system* constituted a central difference
between these three thinkers. For Scholem, the Jewish mystic, the true
Kabbalist—in fact, any mystic, in his conception—operated out of the
profoundest depths of his singular tradition.[107] For Eliade and Corbin, in
sharp contrast, the holism of the symbol omnidirectionally opened the
most eclectic reconnections *between* total systems. Ultimately, Scholem

rejected mastery in this sense—the master as omniscient browser—while Eliade and Corbin epitomized it. But the brunt of all their symbologies, nonetheless, rested on *the transposability of symbols. In the transposability of symbols was the continuity of tradition*. That one symbol can be transposed across time—the rediscoverers of myth seized this insight as somehow primary, the very *via regia* leading into a present "religious reality." Here was the implied promise of generational continuity. The past was not lost. The approach privileging symbolism, moreover, thus was claimed to be an extension of traditional modes of approaching reality. In other words, a "religious study" of religion, epitomized especially by Eliade and Corbin, fundamentally asserted a claim about the very survival of "real" religion, through the exclusive route of traditional symbols. Symbols promised to open out transparently to the absolute. And only the contemporary "hermeneut," according to the esoterism of Eliade and Corbin, could orient otherwise lost moderns on this royal road of traditional symbols. In this way, the young aspiring sages of the Generation of 1914 in this way, found themselves, after World War II, to be authoritative gatekeepers of the *via regia*.

If they had not believed that the symbols that they celebrated symbolized something real, they would not have been "Historians of Religions" in the Eranos conception of that calling. Herein, as much as anything, their distinctive vocation (*Beruf*) can be perceived. The History of Religions is the preeminent authority on religious symbols; it was on this claim that the discipline's autonomy depended. The assumption behind this claim should now be clear. *The autonomy of religion rested on the autonomy of the symbol.*

CHAPTER 6

Aesthetic Solutions

Ascona's legacy was new uses of the imagination.
—*Martin Green*

"NEW USES OF THE IMAGINATION": THE HISTORIAN
OF RELIGIONS AS MODERN ARTIST

Is not the position of the spiritual hermeneut . . .
similar to that of the artist?
—*Henry Corbin*

As writers, the Historians of Religions presented readers with a model impossible to copy. That is, while their creations were "about" religion, neither their writings nor the forms of religion they described were, in any direct sense, replicable by the reader. This irreproducibility, I suggest, echoes their very modernity as writers. The History of Religions, in form and in content, positioned itself to be unparalleled, unique, autonomous, a species of one—just as did modern art and the modern artist. This parallel is particularly significant because it was on this basis that the foundational claim for the autonomy of religion could be grounded. Analogous to the autonomy of a "religious reality" that they so importantly championed, the History of Religions itself was to be autonomous. Substantially resonant with this conception, I suggest, was the individualism of the modern artist and the uniqueness of the modern artwork. An appropriate angle of analysis to be pursued, then, is that of *History of Religions as modernist art form.*[1]

Put otherwise, the Historians of Religions transposed social analysis back into aesthetics, into what Schelling, followed by Scholem and Corbin, called "narrative philosophy." Schelling's "narrative philosophy," it would seem, was his kind of answer. As I shall argue in the next chapter, the formative years of Scholem's intellectual development were marked by the shift, especially popular with young Jewish intellectuals in the Weimar Republic, from Kant to Schelling. The "new mythology" thus struck like a revelation: a theory of global coherence had arrived, and just in time. Tillich's popular *Kairos*, a conception shared by Freud, Scholem, and others, reverberated with this sense of new being.[2] Now the world made sense again—but not sense in the life-world, not social sense. If anything, the Schellingian turn *raised the stakes but changed the rules*. But if the human universe was now enveloped in "theogonic process," it was hardly cleansed of social contradictions. Indeed, the kairotic demand for the immediacy of myth reached a peak in daimonic intensity under the Third Reich. One result, then, was a heightening of drama at the expense of peace. Individual and collective strife—the Daimonic itself—was claimed in these years to be a free-floating principle of the age. In fact, this dramatistic self-consciousness reflected a generalized aestheticization. Whether left or right, aestheticization of politics, of society, of life world, was a distinctive feature of the turn to myth in interwar thought.[3]

Such an analogy with modern art is not as unlikely as it may seem at first blush. Scholem, Corbin, and Eliade each enjoyed close proximity to various avant-garde artists. Each was, for a time anyway, close to activists in the dada and surrealism movements.[4] A few examples make this point. The Romanian emigré poets, for example, were one social group that overlapped with the Historians of Religions. The famous dadaist Tristan Tzara, né Samy Rosenstock, was a Romanian Jew who associated, on the one hand, with Eliade's mentor, the Italian dadaist Julius Evola, and on the other with the Paul Celan, the great Jewish poet deeply influenced by Scholem.[5] Another example was the Jewish-Romanian surrealist poet and existentialist philosopher Benjamin Fondane. Fondane, the best-known student of the Russian existentialist philosopher Lev Shestov, dined with Eliade in 1943 and perished in Auschwitz in 1944.[6] Shestov was deeply appreciated by Scholem, who introduced his lecture in Palestine, and by Eliade, who consoled himself by reading Shestov when his first wife died.[7] Fondane was also a friend of Eliade's longtime intimate friend, Emil Cioran, who eulogized the late Jewish poet in print.[8] Shestov in turn had another dedicated follower in the 1930s, the Swiss religious socialist Fritz Lieb. Lieb, during those years, was a close friend both of Walter Benjamin and of Henry Corbin.[9] Such examples of a social interlinking can be amplified.

An adequate inquiry into their History of Religions would necessarily transcend the trio's relations with and attitudes toward contemporary artists.[10] Robert Alter has studied Scholem as a modern, something still little done for Corbin and Eliade.[11] Eliade, of course, was a fiction writer of some note. They each, more generally, developed their own aesthetics. Henry Corbin translated Hamann's *Aesthetica in Nuce*. With its subtitle, "A Rhapsody in Cabbalistic Prose," this work also had an impact on Scholem.

The esoteric theorists, then, associated themselves both with modern art and modernist men of letters. As modernist writers themselves, they successfully located audiences for their peculiarly dramatistic accounts of religion. For all his apparent infatuation with this drama, Scholem alone could allow for scientific falsifiability.[12] As such, he alone of the trio spoke to and for working historians, in a way the others, as sworn enemies of historicism, could not. The others spoke instead to "the reader," *l'homme honnête*, the bookbuyer reflective enough to be drawn to their new accounting of ancient themes.

GENIO LOCI IGNOTO: THE UNFATHOMABLE ORIGINS OF ERANOS

The origins of Eranos, if not precisely discoverable, are amenable to historical inquiry. Before the Eranos meetings were inaugurated in 1933, Ascona had been identified with radical, occultist, and countercultural avant-gardes. This story has now been detailed in Martin Green's *Mountain of Truth: The Counterculture Begins in Ascona, 1900–1920*.[13] Such was the notoreity of Ascona's Monte Verita, the Mountain of Truth, as a center for experimental lifestyles and new forms of art and spirituality, that colorful characters were drawn there from across Europe and the United States. The most notorious visitor, perhaps, was the astonishing Otto Gross, lampooned by Max Brod as Dr. Askonas.[14] Franz Kafka, a most potent influence on Scholem and Brod, was also affected by the Asconan ideal[15]

The study of Yoga, too, was significant in the origins of Eranos. Four of the contributors to the new, international journal *Yoga*, published by Helmut Palmier in 1931, soon became participants at Eranos.[16] Jakob W. Hauer, a contributer to this journal, was one of the first participants of Eranos. He was also, as archival research now reveals, a correspondent of Eliade in the late 1920s and early 1930s.[17] And Jung participated with Hauer in a long seminar during these same years.[18]

The occultist context of Jung's early career, up to and including the origins of Eranos has now been clarified by Richard Noll.[19] The first years of the annual colloquium also retained Ascona's bohemian atmosphere, nicely conjured by Jung's student, Jolande Jacobi. "Stille Gemüter, echte Gelehrte, Mystiker, Snobs, Schwärmer, Menschheitsverbesserer, Propheten, Adabeis and viele anonyme Besinnliche und Wissenschungrige füllten den Saal bis auf den letzten Platz."[20] But the important difference from the earlier Asconan scene was that at Eranos almost all lecturers were academics of some sort. The sociology of the European academy *entre deux guerres* would no doubt shed light on the radical mandarinism of these participants. True to its avant-garde origins, perhaps, this was a mandarinism whose disposition was to diminish the significance of the very academy in which it otherwise thrived.

Of the origins of Eranos it seems inescapable to note one other irony.

Rudolf Ritsema and Gilbert Durand, leaders of Eranos especially in the period after that under study here, have proudly spoken of the "specific propitiousness of the hour of its birth."[21] That year was 1933. They seem to have meant that this year was "propitious" because it responded, however indirectly, to a generalized European crisis. This response was a kind of flight from the contemporary world into eternities, now newly accessible, once known only to visionaries.[22] The origins of Eranos were tellingly located at Ascona among an aestheticizing subculture of world-rejecting avant-garde. The turn East, the turn inward, and the turn to myth were each vectors on this one immense trajectory from the urban century to primordial immediacy. Now, at the origins of things as such, authentic relations with the gods would be rectified. One could again experience religion not through economy or psychology or as society—but *as religion.*

"REPRESENTATIVE THEATER"

Myth expresses in action and drama what metaphysics and theology define dialectically.
—*Mircea Eliade*

The problem for this return to a direct experience of religion was one of representation. How best were past symbolic realities to be represented in the present? If there was a single work of literature that one could point to as the most deeply felt shared inspiration of all three scholars, it may be Goethe's play *Faust*. Drama, more generally, seems to have been an aesthetic form preferred by the Historians of Religions. Eliade was himself a playwright.[23] Scholem enjoyed a certain well-honed and often noted dramatic aspect to his personality. " 'I [Scholem] call myself a metaphysical clown . . . a clown hides himself in theater.' I [Cynthia Ozick] ask whether Walter Benjamin ever hid himself that way. 'Benjamin never played theater.' How much of Professor Scholem is theater? Scholem: 'Ask Mrs. Scholem.' Mrs. Scholem: 'One hundred percent.' "[24]

Corbin's beloved visionary hero, Emmanuel Swedenborg, saw the created cosmos and the uncreated worlds altogether as one "representative theater."

Briefly, everything in the natural world, in general as well as in the most infinitesimal detail, including the constellations, atmospheres, the entirety and the components of the animal, vegetable, and mineral kingdomsall this is nothing more than a sort of "*representative theater*" of the spiritual world, where we can see things in their beauty if we know how to see them in the state of their Heaven.[25]

Corbin, especially at the end of his career, concentrated on, as one title put it, "The Dramatic Element Common to the Gnostic Cosmogonies of the Religions of the Book."[26] In fact, the concept of drama was central to Corbin's larger conception of gnosis. He said so succinctly with regard to Avicenna's "recitals." "By substituting a dramaturgy for cosmology, the recitals guarantee the genuineness of this universe; it is veritably the place of a personally lived adventure. . . . To speak of the Angels of which we are a part, or of their combat as of a combat they wage for a part of themselves, is to refer to a fundamental aspect of the dramaturgy shared by all gnostics, by all who are *strangers* to this world."[27]

Eliade developed an analogous dramaturgy, but for the History of Religions today. In the penultimate paragraph of the epilogue of *Shamanism*, Eliade generalizes the results of his extensive study. "[Every] genuinely shamanic séance ends as a *spectacle* unequaled in the world of daily experience . . . [it reveals] the fabulous world of the gods and magicians, the world in which *everything seems possible* . . . where 'the laws of nature' are abolished, and a certain superhuman 'freedom' is exemplified and made dazzlingly *present*."[28]

This abstraction is only partly helpful in working toward Eliade's self-understanding of his own performance. A passage from his essay "Ropes and Puppets," however, explicitly addressed "the 'dramatic' function of the rope-trick (and similar exploits)."[29]

> The magician is, by definition, a stage-producer. . . . During the magician's trick the spectators are passive; *they contemplate*. This is an occasion for imagining how things may be done without "working", simply by "magic", by the mysterious power of thought and will . . . by the force of their words or thought. To be brief, a whole moral is pointed: that spiritual science is all-powerful. . . . All these thoughts are raised by the contemplation of the "spectacle".[30]

Here one recalls Eliade's conception of the magical "power of thought and will." One will remember that he associates this power preeminently with the Guénonian archetype of the "universal king," this time in the form of the "terrible god," Varuna: "[H]e can do everything because he rules over the cosmos, and he punishes all who break his laws by 'binding' them (with illness or *impotence*) because he is the guardian of universal order."[31] As the archetype for magicians as well, "power is his by right because of his very nature; this power enables him to act through magic, through 'the power of the mind,' through 'knowledge.'"[32] Now Eliade has emphasized that the power of *spectacle*, for the shaman and the magician, operates by such "power of thought and will." Not surprisingly, therefore, he links Varuna, magic, and shamanism: "Suffice to say here that some aspects of the magic (of Varuna's 'bonds') are shamanic."[33]

Eliade's *spectacle*, then, is the mise-en-scène of this archetype, the ritual of this myth.[34] The magician and the shaman perform as "stage-pro-ducers," enacting their identification with Varuna: "*[E]very sorcerer, too, is imitating the terrible sovereign and his divine prototype.*"[35] "[A]ny wizard whatever pretends, at the height of his ritual, to be the Universal Sover-eign."[36] The actors copy the divine original "to the extent that they are charged with *power.*"[37] And in an interview granted late in life he stressed that the shaman was an actor and that shamanism constituted one of the sources of theater.[38] Strikingly, he also claimed the inverse, that the actor is a kind of shaman, undergoing a series of reincarnations: "I am certain that the actor possesses a human experience different in quality from our own."[39]

And what, then, of Eliade's ultimate Varunic exemplar, the perfect form of power, which the shaman makes dazzlingly present, and before which the sorcerer's audience is passive?

> . . . thought itself can be a considerable source of energy . . . the celestial god sees everything and therefore knows everything, and this knowledge . . . is in itself a force (which is found) also in the highly-evolved religions: intel-ligence, ominiscience and wisdom are not only attributes of the heavenly divinity, they are *powers*, and man is obliged to reckon with them. . . . Var-una is indeed a powerful god, a Great Magician, and men tremble before him.[40]

In short: the magician and the shaman act par excellence in a *spectacle*, during which performance they imitate the terrible sovereign, "the fearful magician who 'binds' men from a distance and paralyses them."[41] "But let me point out at once that this notion of universal sovereignty, exer-cised purely by spiritual and magical means, owes its development and its definition of outline largely to the notion of the sky's transcendence. It was some such notion, developing at all sorts of different levels, that made the full picture of "magic sovereignty" possible. . . . [Varuna] is supremely the sovereign god."[42] This Varunic omniscience of the "univer-sal king" homologously is recapitulated by the "planetization" under-taken by the universal scholar, the Historian of Religions.[43] And this global reach was achieved by means of *performance*. The performative dimension of Eliade's conception of the History of Religions remains to be understood.

The "theory of the spectacle," a dramatistic theory of the Eliade's per-formance as a Historian of Religions, is fictionally expressed in his 1978 novella, *Nineteen Roses*.[44] The reader of History of Religions here is ex-plicitly and repeatedly assimilated to the viewer of the spectacle: "*Anyone, any spectator, any reader, can have a similar revelation* . . . [spectacles] illustrate and convey a method of absolute freedom, provided you know, when *reading* them or watching them *performed*, the corresponding code."[45] According to the protagonist, Thanase, no limits are set on the transformative potential of this *Gesamtkunstwerk*: "But through the dramatic spectacle . . . the decipherment of the symbolic, therefore religious, meanings of events can become an instrument of illumination—more precisely, of salvation—of the masses . . . the dramatic spectacle could become, very soon, a new eschatology or soteriology, a technique of salvation."[46]

Of necessity, it follows that Eliade's reader, like his audience, is passive. The Historian of Religions, the "stage-producer," " 'binds' men from a distance and paralyses them."[47] Only rarely, it would seem, have readers of Eliade recognized that that was what he was doing. Richard Gombrich, one such rare reader, recognized that Eliade's "scholarly" speech-act recapitulated the "performance" that he purports to describe. "By quoting passages . . . out of sequence, mostly under other names, Eliade has peformed a variant of the rope trick: plucking the dismembered pieces of the text out of the air, he has 'before the spectators' wondering eyes' reconstituted them into something rich but strange."[48]

Eliade's late fictionalized confession, in *Nineteen Roses*, acknowledged that, in some real sense, he did understand himself to be such a "magician." I know of nothing in Eliade's "ensemble" to contradict this reading of his "Varunic" pretensions. Eliade, at mid-career, served as a professional propagandist for several consecutive Romanian regimes, at a level high enough to earn personal audiences with dictators, and so understood the convertibility of the power of style into the style of power. But he was more than an official rhetor: he was himself a creator of a Wagnerian *Gesamtkunstwerk*, a vast and even total myth. For Eliade, these vocations were continuous. Before and during World War II, he had labored professionally to create an "Aesthetic State"—after the war, he retooled The Work into an aestheticized, metapolitical total discipline.[49] Such a project he outlined during the war. In 1943, the then propagandist Eliade reprinted an essay from 1937. In it he called, rather portentously, for a *Völkisch* theater for the masses. "There are certain themes in our folk literature that are extraordinarily rich, from the dramatic point of view. . . . By means of modern techniques of stage management, the sensation of dreaming, of the supernatural, of the fantastic could easily be realized. And in this collective sensation the words would be more impressive and associations would penetrate more deeply."[50]

Eliade, after the war, assimilated the reader of his new History of Religions to the audience of the traditional sorcerer and the archaic shaman. "The historian and phenomenologist of religions does not confront those myths and rituals as external objects, like an inscription to be deciphered, an institution to be analyzed. In order to understand that world from within, he must live it. He is like an actor assuming his roles, embodying them."[51] Eliade's Historian of Religions himself somehow recapitulated the paradigmatic experience of the traditional believer; only thus could he *see* the real forms, and therefore only in this way could then *show* them to the reader. The demonstration from the deeps *performed* primordial symbols; *represented* them to the student.

MASTERS OF WORLD MAKING

> Everything created
> Is worth being liquidated.
> —*Johann Goethe's Mephisto (cited by Carl Jung,* Response to Job*)*

Masters of symbolic manifestations play with appearances. The symbol leads, like scenes in a scenario, inward to the unseen. In Eliade's esoteric dramaturgy, the dramaturge is assimilated to the demiurge; both are masters of world making. That is, as he explicitly said, they approximate the masters of world making. To begin, they both require a cosmos as tabula rasa. The unknowable, the unseen, the formless, thus was—to use a word favored by Eliade—*homologous* with their originary dissolution of the All.

> I could write an entire book on this . . . Our ideal [as modernists] would be to demolish everything down to ruins and fragments in order to be able to return to full, unlimited formlessness . . . [but the critics can't appreciate] a coherent, poetic language [that would reestablish formal criteria, "re-form"]. . . . That would be to move back into an organized, meaningful world, that is, precisely a world that they claim is not possible today. A traditional novel like *Forêt interdit* seems to them an anachronism.[52]

For Eliade, the pretense that his "traditional novel" should re-form the world was not too much to assume. His archetypal understanding of the sacred revealed to him the demiurgic role of the sacred artist in "cultural renewal."[53] As such, he was to *organize* the world after its reversion to Chaos. Eliade, the aesthetic demiurge of a self-styled *littérature fantastique*, fantasized world destruction, world rebirth. "Cosmic cataclysm" was a favorite theme. This language, explicit and nebulous at once, ostensibly referred both to a macrocosmic "reversion to chaos" and to a micro-cosmic "violent rebirth."[54] This persistent *Weltuntergang* fantasy was it-self predicated on a vision of the "true" ontological unreality of the world, which the Indologist associated with the Hindu doctrine of *maya*.[55] The profane, according to Eliade, are stuck in the idolatrous "state of igno-rance and illusion" which *believes in* the ontological reality of History. History, like society, and like the cosmos itself, in *fact* has no ontological reality in itself. This de-reification of the world, one suspects, pleased its readers with a titillating *coup de bouleversement*. In his guise as exterminating demiurge, the artist Eliade had to imagine the collapse of worlds, unreal anyway, so that he could keep re-creating them.

> The magical structure of play and fantasy is obvious. In its leap it creates a new space with a centrifugal motion, in the center of which stands, as it were, the demiurge, the creative force of a new cosmos. From it, from this actualization of primordiality, everything begins. This leap outside indicates the beginning of a new world. It matters little that *this world will find its own new laws* quickly, laws over which new others will be unable to pass. It *remains a magical, demiurgical creation*, just as a work of art is a creation even if, when completed, it falls under the domination of physical, social, economic, or artistic laws.[56]

Eliade composed this passage in 1932 and republished it in 1981. Its antinomianism and grandiosity aside, Eliade's keynote on "play and fantasy" should not be taken to mean *mere* play and *mere* fantasy. For he meant to create imaginary universes (*univers imaginaire*), fully formed mythological entities. These include, for example, the Dacians, his forebears, whose racial imprint the Iron Guard Legionaries also chauvinistically bore.[57] In other words, the seriousness of his theory, and the implications of its practice, must not be missed. He never intended this demiurgism to be taken as a "merely" symbolic, fantastic or imaginary transformation. He insisted, rather, that the first act of the demiurge was *transvaluative*:

> . . . the joy that a *human being* has created, has imitated God's work, has been saved from a destined sterility, has breached those walls of impotence and finitude. On the one hand there is the formula I am created by God, which inevitably arouses the consciousness of nothingness, of religous fear, of the taste of dust and ashes. On the other hand there is the statement "A human being, like myself, has created, like God, which brings the joy that a fellow creature has imitated creation, has become a demiurge, a force in the creating."[58]

"Destined to sterility," Eliade's demiurge overcomes destiny, thus becoming "like God."

UTOPIAN POETICS

> The discovery of the tremendous poetic potential
> within Kabbalah, in its own unique language no
> less than in its poetry proper . . . has come down

> to us with great richness . . . but the tools have
> not yet been created for understanding the lyric
> plane within the language of the Kabbalists and
> the Hasidim. . . . My own secret longing to do so
> has not been fulfilled and remains unsatisfied.
> —*Gershom Scholem*

Poems by Corbin and Scholem survive.[59] They are not juvenilia, but written at a mature age. Neither Corbin nor Scholem could claim, as did Jung, that he "perpetrated a poem" ("Seven Sermons on the Dead") only as "a sin of my youth."[60] Theirs are didactic verses, so to speak. Scholem's poem has received critical attention; Corbin's none at all that I know of. Forty-eight years old, new to the Eranos circle, having published his first Eranos lecture in 1949, Corbin wrote a private poem, "À Olga Fröbe Kapteyn," in September 1951. It begins this way.

> A l'horizon d'un Derviche
> Pérégrinant sur les hauts plateaux de Perse:
> Des espaces illimités et nus, matière tellurique primordiale,
> Ocre silencieux, s'exaltant aux flamgoiements des aurores,
> Aux fugitives extases des crépuscules.[61]

There is little poetry in Eliade, though Georges Dumézil, perhaps exercising the poetic license of a devoted friend, did once refer to him as "poète."[62]

These amateur poets purveyed a professional theory of symbols as salvational.[63] The poetic solution to the crisis of the modern world variously espoused by Corbin, Eliade, and Scholem may have been a justifiable response to what Scholem's friend Jürgen Habermas, following Weber, called "the rationalization of the lifeworld."[64] But is their aesthetic esoterism any kind of sufficient answer to the disenchantment of the world in fact? What seemed to be a universal panacea turned out to have at most local efficacy. Even if one grants them the presumed panhuman need for the symbol, the social centrality of the symbolist as leader remains to be demonstrated. In other words, if the hero-type of History of Religions is a kind of revolutionary poet, then we know little more than we came in with: that the specialist in symbols proclaims a radical solution that no known social reality has proven practicable. The History of Religions solution, such as it was, floated in an Ascona above the century's terrible fray—as well we already know.

"The Time of Eranos" is not timeliness, but rather a utopian time. The History of Religions response to what Weber called *Entzauberung* didn't "work" because, by its own definition, it should not *work*. It was not designed to be a workable socio-religious program but rather an aesthetic critique; one that, in a sense, did not "reflect" society and thus is not "constructed," but rather operated as an imaginal gods'-eye view from redemption, the view from utopia. It did not start from the concrete given of the modern city or the modern body but rather from the heavenly city and the transfigured body. One may now reject this view as platonism or archetypalism, but such criticism will fall short. It cannot strike the source of this dialectical view because it must, on its own definition, misconceive the relation of worlds. The putative otherworldliness of a symbol-centered History of Religions is neither constructed by worldliness nor ignorant of worldly ways. Rather, it is a double worldliness—it is equivocal, dialectical, inside and outside history, and thus thickly ambivalent. History of Religions is a view from above the neutralized antinomies or complexes that give society dynamism but go nowhere. Utopia, the artwork ideal of the History of Religions, is outside such society in the end, gazing at it from redemption. But insofar as it eventuates in the next world, it remains very much a critique of this world. This critique bears analogies to Scholem's definition of religious power. Scholem expressed this rather directly when he wrote of the "inextricable combination of impulses which were social and beyond the social were what actually integrated them, and it is this which makes the historical impact of the religions."[65]

The dialectical view toward tradition, indeed toward the religious world as a whole, is what constitutes the Whole. The "reality" of religion, in other words, was presumed to reside in its "totality."[66] Their kind of *Gesamtkunstwerk*, then, was not so much a total work of art so much as it was a work of art *about totality*.[67] The "real" *is* the "whole," in this conception. This unrealizable vision elevated a vision no one could actually see. The Historian of Religions made a promise but invited no one directly to fulfill it. The modern master strove rather for another autonomy, perhaps not of *Ars Gratia Artis* but of the self-containment of the "religious reality," *Religion Gratia Religionis*. The ancient vision was "realized" in paperback allusions. Rather like gazing at "Modern Art," the consuming of such History of Religions accordingly required a certain aesthetic aptitude in order for it to succeed as a consumer experience. The paperback, like the museum, made that experience accessible to anyone who could afford its minimal charge. It is this accessibility that perhaps most exemplified the *coincidentia oppositorum* between their modernism and their traditionalism, between the exoteric and the esoteric. Anyone who could afford to buy the book, so to speak, could have a look at the ancient secrets. But the only one who really *saw* was the master of forms, the creator of the Work. For Eliade, the author was active and the audience passive. No accident, perhaps, that they were patronized by one of the century's greatest art collectors, Paul Mellon.

The new universal accessibility of previous "secret doctrine," thanks to his Bollingen Foundation, had, in short, its analogues in the larger marketplace of symbols.[68]

It is apt, by way of conclusion, to switch metaphors to another art form. Symphonically, the Eranos participants insisted on the grand musicality of religion itself as apprehensible solely through symbols; and so the Eranos phenomenologist might conduct all symbols in a score known to him because he, the conductor, conceives the music of revelation as such. "Its meaning, finally: that of a sym-phony whose performance would each time be repeated in fuller and deeper sonorities—that of a microcosm, which the world cannot be expected to resemble but whose example, one may hope, will spread throughout the world."[69] Corbin more explicitly insisted that the musicality of the esoteric was of its essence.

> The unsayable which the mystic seeks to say is a story that shatters what we call history and which we must indeed call *metahistory*, because it takes place at the origin of origins, anterior to all those events recorded—or recordable—in our chronicles. The mystic epic is that of the exile, who, having come into a strange world, is on the road of homecoming to his own country. What that epic seeks to tell is dreams of a prehistory, the prehistory of the soul, of its preexistence to this world, dreams which seem to us a forever forbidden frontier. That is why, in an epic like the *Mathnawí* we can scarcely speak of a succession of episodes, for all these are emblematic, symbolic. All dialectical discourse is precluded. The global consciousness of that past, and of the future to which it invites us beyond the limit of chronology, can only attain *musically* its absolute character.[70]

Such an operatically conceived poetics of revelation resounded stunningly, to be sure.[71] But what remains after the "recitation," the "performance," must be our criticism, critics that we must be. Even in our critique, however, we may still perform this poetics, if only in a different key.

A Rustling in the Woods: The Turn to Myth in Weimar Jewish Thought

Die Zukunft wird die Wirklichkeit der Geschichte.
—Hermann Cohen

THE MOST influential and brilliant students of Hermann Cohen (1842–1918), the neo-Kantian Jewish philosopher of Marburg, largely rejected one of his fundamental views on Judaism. Opposing his characterization of Judaism as the religion definitively opposed to myth—Judaism as virtually identical with a demythologized Enlightenment rationality—these post-Cohenian thinkers turned to a view of myth as a creative and living force. At least three Cohen students, Franz Rosenzweig, Ernst Bloch, and Ernst Cassirer, wrote revolutionary works that innovatively reassessed the relations between myth, the History of Religions, and Judaism. These figures were joined by a much larger cohort in an enthusiastic and influential turn to myth, a cross-section of the younger German Jewish intelligentsia, which included Gershom Scholem, Martin Buber, Alexander Altmann, Aby Warburg, Hans Jonas, and others.

In this chapter I will assess the post-Cohenian turn to myth. I will begin with the year 1923 and its significance. Then I will consider the profound and seriously underestimated impact of the late philosophy of Schelling, with reference to three students of Cohen (Rosenzweig, Bloch, and Cassirer) who were explicitly influenced by the late Schelling in their new approach to myth. I will next explore the theory of the "*daimonic*" ("the rustling in the woods"). Finally, I will consider some results for the History of Religions, especially for Scholem's epochal rejection of the Cohenian view of Judaism as anti-myth. In each case I will suggest that the turn to myth impelled a return to history in Weimar Jewish thought.

1923

The world is collapsing
Behind a thin wall.
Blood-red are the crossbars of windows
As shades of night fall.

—F. Sramek, "Spring 1923"

"We are convinced that today a *kairos*, an epochal moment in history, is visible," proclaimed Paul Tillich in 1922.[1] The first line of Albert Schweitzer's *The Decay and Restoration of Civilization*, published in 1923, was: "We are living today under the sign of the collapse of civilization."[2] Sramek's momentous Czech poem, titled "Spring 1923," began, "The world is collapsing and crumbling/Behind a thin wall." And in the same year, T. S. Eliot, in England, wrote a review of James Joyce titled "*Ulysses*, Order and Myth." Redolent with worry over "the panorama of futility and anarchy which is contemporary history," Eliot concluded with a clarion call: "Instead of narrative method, we may now use the mythical method. It is, I seriously believe, a step toward making the modern world possible for art."[3] If Virginia Woolf was correct that human nature changed in or about December 1910, then one may be permitted to suggest that human nature—at least in its European high-cultural form—celebrated its bat mitzvah in 1923.

This new time was a *quickening*. In Germany, indications were that the old life was dying, and dying fast: by July 1923, $1 equaled 353,412 marks, but by December 1923, $1 equaled 4.2 trillion marks.[4] Time itself seemed almost to swerve, if not curve fully back on itself; one could not go forward; history had ruptured. At just this time, a debate ensued concerning the very character of temporality. On 6 April 1922, Henri Bergson encountered Albert Einstein in Paris, at which confrontation he "attempted to defend the cause of the multiplicity of coexisting 'lived' times against Einstein. Einstein's reply was absolute: he categorically rejected "philosopher's time."[5] Other new theories of time, such as Ernst Bloch's eventually influential "nonsimultaneity of simultaneities," blossomed among radical political philosophers.[6] Gustav Landauer (1870–1919), a pacifist, anarchist, unaffiliated socialist, and man of letters, was fortunate to have his work *Die Revolution* published posthumously by Martin Buber in 1923.[7] In this work Landauer identified "a qualitative differentiation of time."[8] Along with Landauer, the art historian Wilhelm Pinder (b. 1878), who was developing a theory of "the noncontemporaneity of contemporaries," influenced the generational sociology of Karl Mannheim.[9] Mannheim then fully articulated (in Michael Löwy's words) a "new perception of temporality at variance with evolutionism and the philosophy of progress."[10]

It is inside this sense of "new time," breaking forth in 1923, that the turn to myth must first be framed. This philosophical breakthrough affected other areas of culture, starting with the arts. Thus, the Jewish littératur Rudolf Kayser became the editor of the taste-making and pace-setting magazine *Die Neue Rundschau* in 1923—when he also published a work of metaphysical anarchism, *Die Zeit ohne Mythos*.[11] Jews in Frankfurt in 1923 included the young Elias Canetti, a future Nobel Prize–winner for literature, who there immersed himself in the study of Gilgamesh. He was later to recall, "In this way, I experienced the effect of a myth."[12] In Frankfurt alone, Jewish institutes such as the Freies Jüdisches Lehrhaus, the Institut für Sozialforschung, and Aby Warburg's Institute, as well as non-Jewish institutions such as Leo Frobenius's Forschungsinsitüt für Kulturmorphologie were blazing trails backwards into the mythic dimensions of history.[13] Aby Warburg, in 1923, delivered a public lecture on the Pueblo serpent rituals he had witnessed some years before. Extolling snake handling, he concluded that "myths and symbols, in attempting to establish spiritual bonds between man and the outside world, create space for devotion and scope for reason which are destroyed by the instantaneous electrical contact—unless a disciplined humanity re-introduce the impediment of conscience."[14] Warburg's successor was thus accurate in her assessment that "Warburg believed in the power of reason; he was an *Aufklärer* precisely because he knew the heritage of demonic antiquity so well."[15] It was at Warburg's library, not incidentally, that Cassirer was inspired to undertake his monumental *Philosophy of Symbolic Forms*. The turn to myth was a return to history.

Symbolic forms, whether in the thought of Cassirer or Warburg, were not limited to art history, or to the history of myth, but held the key to history itself. Indeed, a reconceptualization of the philosophy of history emerged from this ferment of temporality. A particularly striking result of this new historical reflection was the widely used image of *history turned backward*. For example, George Lichtheim, distinguished historian of Marxism, and translator of Scholem's *Major Trends in Jewish Mysticism*, observed that, in his 1923 classic of Western Marxism, *History and Class Consciousness*, "[the George Lukács of 1923] was in fact returning from Marx to Hegel."[16] The former student of Heidegger, Karl Löwith, eventually wrote his classic treatment of the philosophy of history, *Meaning in History*, chronologically backward, beginning with Jakob Burckhardt and ending with the Hebrew Bible.[17] One might say, in fact, that the watchword of the age was the epigraph Walter Benjamin placed over his ruminations on *Jetztzeit*, and which he attributed to Karl Kraus: "Origin is the Goal."[18] With almost equal epigrammatic force, Cassirer would cite Friedrich Schlegel to the effect that the historian comprises "*einen ruckwarts gekehrten Propheten*, a retrospective prophet. There is also a prophecy of the past, a revelation of its hidden life."[19] This same passage was also glossed by Walter Benjamin.[20] And just as Cassirer could cite Schlegel, so Bloch quoted Hamann: "The field of history has thus always appeared to me like that wide field full of bones, and lo! they were very dry. Nobody except a prophet can prophesy upon these bones that sinews and flesh will grow on them and skin will cover them."[21]

History turned backward on or about 1923, and it turned back to myth. The turn to myth in Weimar Jewish thought is explicable, in the first instance, against the "nonsimultaneity of simultaneities" of 1923. Four students and young associates of Cohen, Franz Rosenzweig, Ernst Bloch, Ortega y Gasset, and Ernst Cassirer, published importantly innovative works in that *annus mirabilis*, in each of which the turn to myth was discernible.[22] But unlike proto-Nazi myth infatuation, their myth studies pointedly were not regressive. By the sharpest of contrasts to fascist primitivism, the Jewish turn to myth was made up of historical flights out of time, pathways into deepened history, reentrances into historical meaning: *myth as history reborn*. In 1923, Gerhard Scholem remained in Germany only until Yom Kippur, after which he immediately made *aliyah* and changed his name to Gershom.

FROM COHEN TO SCHELLING

The ultimate Jewish Kantian of his time, Hermann Cohen, catalyzed a heroic age of remythologization, marked by its reversion from Kant to Schelling.[23] In the brief interim between Hermann Cohen's death at war's end and the momentous year of 1923, young German thinkers turned to myth, especially through study of Friedrich Schelling's "philosophy of mythology."[24] Cohen's conventional view of Judaism as an enemy of myth was not the only such view then being championed.[25] The new science of sociology, especially that of the neo-Kantian founding sociologist of religion, Max Weber (1864–1920), agreed with Jewish thought that demythologization was set in the Bible itself. Weber strove to demonstrate that the rationality of Biblical Judaism was embodied in the social structures of ancient Israel. This latent rationalization then was made consciously manifest by the rabbis of late antiquity, and finally institutionalized by the major Jewish philosophers of the Middle Ages. Weberian sociology of religion thus largely accepted this Jewish self-understanding of the world-historical significance of "ethical monotheism."[26] So too, significantly, did Cohen's "admired colleague," Julius Wellhausen, the dean of the new Biblical Criticism.[27] On the established Jewish thinking, on the Critical Biblicist reading, and on the new sociological understanding, then, Judaism resisted myth from the outset and therefore deserved to be seen as the historic pioneer in the disenchantment of the world.[28]

Against the backdrop of this emerging concensus, the sudden popularity of the "reorientation of European Social thought" among young Jewish intellectuals stands out all the more starkly.[29] So great was the attraction of Jews to the new social thought that by 1924 Friedrich Gundolf could disparage German sociology as "a Jewish sect."[30] But this flight to social theory, further dramatically impelled by defeat in the Great

War, interrupted a fantasy. The Jewish dream of a smooth assimilation to Germanness, becoming fully German, suddenly was disrupted. No longer could Jews sententiously claim, as Cohen did during the war, that "as for our own spiritual life, we have already experienced an intimate religious partnership in the accord that exists *between Jewish messianism and German humanism.*"[31] After the Great War, young Jews could no longer unproblematically sustain such optimism. The immediate postwar shattering of Kantian humanism and positivism coincided, ironically, with the ultimate humanistic achievements of Weber and Cohen: the *Religionssoziologie* of Max Weber was published posthumously in 1922; the *Jüdische Schriften* of Herman Cohen were published posthumously in 1924.[32] At the same time, the precipitous decline of Kant even received offical notice. In 1924 the minister of education for the Weimar Republic, the scholar of Islam Carl Heinrich Becker, observed that Kant held little appeal in these postwar years, whether for the young or the old.[33] What did hold appeal, for old and young, was social theory, Marxist or otherwise. And it was this social reflection which, somewhat paradoxically, provided the impetus for a new embrace of myth.[34]

Ernst Bloch, who had completed his dissertation under Hermann Cohen in 1909, is a representative figure of the almost instant transition from Kant to Schelling.[35] Between 1912 and 1914, Bloch "hung out" with Lukács and other geniuses at the Heidelberg salon of Max Weber. Meanwhile, as the European war was breaking out, the dignified Jewish messianism of Cohen was erupting in this philosophical enfant terrible. Frau Marianne Weber saw him in action: "[A] new Jewish philosopher had just come—a young man with an enormous crest of black hair and a self-confidence equally excessive, who obviously took himself to be the forerunner of a new Messiah and insisted that everyone would recognize him as such."[36] By 1918, less than a decade after finishing his thesis with Cohen, Bloch published *Geist der Utopie*, in which he now held that Myth (*Mythos*) revealed "a becoming of God, a disclosure of the God who is now living and sleeping in man alone, an internal monologue within the creature, a self-disclosure of God before himself, in which, however, the transcendent of God is brought to life."[37] Here we are galaxies away from Cohen's professorial moralism, not to speak of his circumspect, Kantian monotheism. Now the leading motifs of Schelling's *Philosophy of Mythology* were reannunciated. Philosophy is identified with theogony, the becoming of the godhead, which in turn is viewed as world process itself: God unfolds inside history, history inside us.[38] It is not for nothing that Habermas famously dubbed Bloch "The Marxist Schelling."[39]

Bloch was not the only young Jewish social philosopher following Cohen who turned to Schelling during the Great War. The literal rediscoverer of Schelling's lost fragment for a "New Mythology" was Franz

Rosenzweig, who in 1914 identified the manuscript of "the Oldest System-Program for German Idealism" as being authored by Schelling.[40] In the very month that Cohen died (April 1918), Rosenzweig wrote to his mother that "before everything else" he saw Schelling as "his patron saint."[41] In the same letter, he saw himself as "destined" to have discovered the *Systemprogramm*.[42] This was just months before he was to begin the *Star of Redemption*, where he proclaimed that "The Jew alone . . . possesses the unity of myth which the nations lost through the influx of Christianity. . . . The Jew's myth, leading him into his people, brings him face to face with God who is also the God of all the nations."[43] Rosenzweig's "New Thinking," like the emerging "New Being" of Paul Tillich, drew deeply on Schelling's original "New Mythology."[44]

Almost simultaneously, between 1916 and 1918, Gershom Scholem and Walter Benjamin engaged in a ferocious discussion of myth. Benjamin, according to Scholem, "accepted myth alone as 'the world' . . . myth was everything."[45] Precisely at this time, they studied Hermann Cohen together but were disappointed with him.[46] They preferred German Romantic philosophers, up to and including Nietzsche. Of this effervescent post-Cohenian moment he shared with Benjamin, Scholem pointedly observed, "I suppose it was in those days that we especially influenced each other."[47] Much can be said, it is clear, about the multiple cross-fertilizations occurring at that instant. Benjamin, for example, soon thereafter cited both Ernst Bloch and Franz Rosenzweig in his "Theologico-Political Fragment" of 1921–1922.[48]

The most complete and influential exposition of the turn to Schelling was explicated by another Cohen student, Ernst Cassirer, as is well known.[49] What is somewhat less well known, perhaps, is that, at roughly the same time, Heidegger called Schelling's *Of Human Freedom* (1809) "one of the profoundest works written in Germany and thus of occidental philosophy."[50] Heidegger, in general terms, resembled Rosenzweig in underscoring the momentous dimensions of the civilizational shift (*Kehre*) being undergone. And Rosenzweig, like Heidegger, utilized the term *Ershutterung, Shattering*, to describe the crackup of philosophical totality.[51] The future Nazi author of *Being and Time* acknowledged, in fact, that the turn to myth in Weimar thought could be articulated by Jewish philosophers. Heidegger thus accepted "the merit of [Ernst] Cassirer's work insofar as it is the first attempt since Schelling to place myth as a systematic problem within the range of philosophy."[52] It is interesting to recall that a mortally ill Rosenzweig commented on this exchange between Heidegger and Cassirer at his life's end. He made two striking points that are relevant here. First, he noted that the "old Cohen" in fact did lead to the "new thinking." Second, he observed that this new thinking was represented by Heidegger and not Cassirer.[53]

These were not the only crosscurrents feeding the interest in Schelling and the turn to myth. Theorists of religion who also were receptive readers of Schelling at this time included Otto, Jaspers, Tillich, and Barth. The Schelling Revival, in short, caught up philosophers and historians of religion, Jew and non-Jew alike.[54] The turn to myth in Weimar Jewish thought, then, was at the forefront of a turn to myth in European—or at least German—thought at large. The Schellingian detour thus signified a post-Kantian, post-Marxian, post-Weberian, but still dialectical return to history. This may explain its promise to Jewish thinkers (with the unanswered exception of Rosenzweig)—for it promised return to a now deepened history, by an ironic leap backward over Enlightenment Reason, into the archaic depths available inwardly for historical reflection.[55]

"A RUSTLING IN THE WOODS": DAIMONIC ERUPTION

A great poet must be, a profound metaphysician.
He may not have it in logical coherence, in his
brain and tongue . . . but he must have the ear of
wild Arab listening in the silent desert, the eye of
a North American Indian tracing the footsteps of
an Enemy upon the leaves that strew the forest.
—*Samuel Taylor Coleridge*

In the wake of the Great War, trans-European *Krisis* was shattering the solidity of Kantian optimism. One immediate result was a reinvigoration of thinking on human origins. The perception of the "collapse of civilization" impelled students of religion, with their cohorts, to return to "The Beginning," the "Primordium." Lévy-Bruhl in France and Otto in Germany, widely read at this time, analyzed Adam as social actor, interpreting primordial mentality or the original encounter with the numinous in terms of the psychology of a percipient individual.[56] In such intimations of a perfectly creative instant, of a eruptive, initial forming of religious language, one hears echoes from nineteenth-century German philosophy. A formative influence on this view of origins, along with Schelling, no doubt was Nietzsche, who celebrated the "eruptive character" (*Ausbruchcharakter*) of Dionysian release.[57] So too did it become a feature for interwar students of religion as otherwise disparate as Jung, Otto, and van der Leeuw, who each utilized some notion of primal form-creation as the basis in their theories of religion, and who each did so explicitly under the sign of Nietzsche.[58]

For some of the new thinkers, the Original Human was a pristine genius. First Speech, accordingly, paradigmatically was *poetic*. Since the Enlightenment, since Hobbes and Rousseau, and since the first explorers' reports from Africa and the New World, the First Man had been seen as a savage, however Noble. Now the First Man was also a Poet of divine language, of the originary moment when speech first pierced the evanescent noises in the primeval glade.[59] This romantic fiction of the primal individual obviously echoed that of the modern individual, preeminently the poetic genius "finding himself." Schelling provided a typical romantic model:

> In all of us there swells a secret marvelous power of freeing ourselves from the changes of time, of withdrawing to our secret selves away from external things, and of so discovering to ourselves the eternal in us in the form of unchangeability. *This presentation of ourselves to ourselves is the most truly personal experience, upon which depends everything that we know of the suprasensual world. This presentation shows us for the first time what real existence is, while all else only appears to be.* It differs from every presentation of the sense in its perfect freedom, while all other presentations are bound, being overweighted by the burden of the object.[60]

Around 1920, another student of Hermann Cohen, Boris Pasternak, described poetic inspiration this way: "[No] real book has a first page: like the rustling in the woods, it is born Heaven know where, grows and rolls on, waking hidden thickets in its path, and suddenly at the darkest, overwhelming, panic-stricken moment it speaks out from all the tree-tops at once, having reached its goal."[61] Few Jewish thinkers at this time went as far as Pasternak did, preferring not to cross the line from an aestheticized philosophy of history to poetry as such. Bloch and Benjamin befriended the dadaist Hugo Ball in Zurich—author of *Flucht aus der Zeit* (Flight out of Time)—but they could not follow his 1923 defection from dada into "the aesthetic conception of the world" (from which position he gravitated toward Carl Schmitt).[62] For most Jewish post-Cohenians, in other words, the daimonic moment of inspiration was less a figure for poetic insight than an emblem of the meaningfulness of time, of seizing the time, of the momentous first creation of something historically new.[63] For Bloch, such moments were the forward motor of history itself:

> The kindling place of inspiration lies in the *meeting* of a specific genius . . . with the propensity of a time to provide the specific content which has become ripe for expression, forming and execution. Not only the subjective, but the objective conditions for the expression of a [Newness] must therefore be ready, must be ripe, so that this [Newness] can break through out of mere incubation and suddenly gain insight into itself.[64]

Rosenzweig, for his part, spoke of a "new thinking" that "knows it cannot have cognition independent of time . . . one must await the given time; one cannot skip a single moment (*Augenblick*)."[65] Paul Tillich, who published two doctoral dissertations on Schelling, delineated the "ripe moment," *Kairos*. Similar themes are found in Ernst Bloch and Walter Benjamin, both of whom applied the image of *Jetztzeit*, of *Now-Time*.[66] Scholem claimed that mystical symbolism is "perceived intuitively in a mystical *now*.[67] Nor could Cassirer escape his (Schellingian) sense that events of the spirit unfold at "the right time" and must be understood, therefore, as expressions of that time. He followed Usener in observing a critical transition from *Augensblickgötter,* "Momentary deities" to daimonic potencies, and then to the first gods.[68]

> The division of the realm of the "holy" from that of the "profane" is the prerequisite for any *definite* divinities whatsoever. The Self feels steeped, as it were, in a mythico-religious atmosphere, which ever enfolds it, and in which it now lives and moves; it takes a spark, a touch, to create the god or daemon out of this charged atmosphere. The outlines of such daemonic beings may be ever so vague—yet they indicate the first step in a new direction.[69]

Compare Rosenzweig: "Thus the self is born in man on a definite day. Which day is this? It is the day on which the personality, the individual, dies the death of entering the genus. This very moment lets the self be born. The self is a *daimon*."[70]

From such a stark beginning, then, bold sketches of world history intuitively could be derived. For Cassirer and Rosenzweig, this originary moment not only let history be born, but let the self be born as well. In fact, historical periodizations (world ages) and generational metaphors (life ages), flourished among the general interest in organic metaphors.[71] The First Age, for Schelling, had consisted of a force "demonic and heteronomous."[72] The late Schelling spoke tellingly of the "other" who breaks forth out of the "dark depths of nature" out of the "will of the deep."[73] Benjamin, as a young man, "distinguished between two historical ages, of the spectral and the demonic, that proceded revelation . . . [and] the real content of myth was the enormous revolution that polemicized against the spectral and brought its age to an end."[74] The first age of religion according to Scholem, was a world "full of gods whom man encounters at every step."[75] Cassirer, for his part, minutely imagined this primordial religious experience to be a "whispering or rustling in the woods, a shadow darting over the ground, a light flickering on the water: all these are demonic . . . but only very gradually does this pandemonium divide into separate and clearly distinguishable figures (or forms, *Gestalten*)."[76]

The products of such eruptions out of an initial formlessness were understood to be Forms (*Gestalten*). In 1923, Tillich, for example, spoke of the demonic as "an eruption of the irrational ground of any realization of form."[77] Three years later Tillich again asserted, in his famous essay on the Demonic, "the tension between form-creation and form-destruction upon which rests the demonic."[78] Bloch, as noted previously likewise spoke of the "propensity of a time to provide the specific content which has become ripe for . . . *forming*." And forms were first words, symbolic forms: more than poetry, they were prophecy, *divine speech*. For Rosenzweig, "Revelation is always present, and if it occurred in the past, then it was in that past which is the beginning of the history of mankind: it is the revelation granted to Adam."[79] This daimonic theory, then, constituted a vision of the First Human—but not Hobbes's brutish First Man. Rather, this was Adam as Prophet.

These confluent retrovisions—philosophical, psychological, sociological, aesthetic, and especially historical—thus transformed fleeting *daimonic* suddenness (*Plötzlichkeit*) into a theory of *revelatory eruption*.[80] It is hard not to recall here the letter Scholem wrote in 1926 in honor of Rosenzweig's fortieth birthday. Sent from Jerusalem, it begins, "This country is a volcano! It houses language!" He continues, "Those who . . . mustered the daimonic courage (den damonischen Mut) to revitalize a language . . . walked and still walk above this abyss."[81] Eventually, such imagery was consolidated into a full-blown historical psychology, as Scholem came to characterize his consistently daimonic approach. But these myth revisionists also understood that with form-creation, form-destruction came dialetically. And, indeed, the primal eruption of daimonic forces soon evoked darker expression in Heidegger's extraordinary Nietzsche seminars of the 1930s, in Jung's equally extraordinary Nietzsche seminars of the 1930s, and in the anthropological notion of *Ergriffenheit*, primal ontic seizure, championed in the Leo Frobenius school, also based in Frankfurt. *Ergriffenheit*, primal ontic seizure, was a term centrally used both by Heidegger and by Jung in the late 1920s and early 1930s. They applied this image of "being gripped," "being seized," both to the structures of original experience and to the action of an *Ergriefer*, a leader who seizes. Jung's notorious "Wotan" essay of 1936 evoked the contemporaneous German *Ergriffenheit* with familiar imagery—a "rustling in the primeval forest of the Unconscious."[82] *Ergriffenheit* became a founding theorem of Jung's Eranos circle of Historians of Religion.[83]

Understandably, then, theorists of the Frankfurt School increasingly resisted this "new mythology." On their dissident view, the *daimonic* primal scene of *Urreligion* was dangerously regressive.[84] Eventually, Adorno and Horkheimer spoke of *Mana* as "tautology of terror" and "objectified dread."[85] In fact, Adorno came to find a terrifying epistemological error at the heart of this fantasy: "The picture of a temporal or extra-temporal original state of happy identity between subject and object is romantic, however—a wishful projection at times, but today no more than a lie. The undifferentiated state before the subject's formation was the dread of the blind web of nature, of myth; it was in protest against it that the great religions had their truth content."[86]

The quest for an *Urreligion* marked Comparative Religion and Religionsgeschichte in this period, but it was coming under increasingly sharp critique, and not only from Marxists.[87] Of course, even for plodding academics, Durkheim's *Elementary Forms of the Religious Life* and Cassirer's *Philosophy of Symbolic Forms* had already dismantled if not demolished the once towering theories known as "Naturism" and "Animism," associated with Tylor and Frazer. *Mana* now was outmoded. Both for the avant-garde and for the professoriate, a more *true-to-life* theory of religious origins and development was demanded. Biologistic and especially organismic metaphors—*palingenesis, pseudo-morphosis, symbiosis,* and ultimately *Life (Leben)* itself—consequently came into vogue.[88] What mattered now was less Weber's worldviews than the vitality of life itself, a view known as *vitalism*. While not a vitalist as such, Franz Rosenzweig announced at the beginning of his *Star of Redemption* that the "conception of the world (*Weltanschauung*) now has for its counterpart the conception of Life (*Lebensanschauung*)"—and he concluded the *Star of Redemption* with the climactic words, "INTO LIFE" (*uns Leben*). Count Paul Yorck von Wartenberg, whose influential letters to Wilhelm Dilthey were published in 1923—and prominently cited both by Heidegger in *Being and Time* and by Gershom Scholem as the epigraph to his masterwork, *Sabbatai Sevi*—asserted that philosophy "is not science but life, and fundamentally has been life even where it wanted to be science."[89]

All the churning currents of the Weimar *Krisis*—Romanticism, *Lebensphilosophie*, Nietzscheanism, critique of reification, "romantic anticapitalism," vitalism, and apocalypticism—poured into the torrential turn to myth. Perhaps the single strongest stream, at least for Scholem, was Schelling's philosophy of mythology. In this thinking, the daimonic moment unified deep past with projected future, for only out of this instant emanated authentic symbols, which alone linked myth with utopia. The immediate linkage was the living present itself, the "now," the "ripe time." Through this lived immediacy, the daimonic made origins imaginable again. And the reimaginers, during the Weimar years, experienced this revelatory eruption as inciting a new age. By conjuring Adam, they invoked utopia now. Myth thus organically coordinated past, present and future; the artificial splits in time were united in a living being: and so historical life revived.

CONCLUSION

Judaism in the History of Religions
according to Gershom Scholem

Without this *religio*, this "tie to the past," [Zionism]
was and is hopeless, doomed to failure from the start.
—*Gershom Scholem*[90]

Jewish thinkers wrestled the daimon of history without losing social consciousness. Starting in the early Weimar years, Gershom Scholem, Martin Buber, Walter Benjamin, Alexander Altmann, Aby Warburg, Hans Jonas, Hans Liebeschutz, Paul Kraus, Leo Strauss, Hans Levy, Henry Pachter, Martin Plessner, Shlomo Goitein, Hannah Arendt, Theodor Adorno, and Max Horkheimer engaged the problem of religion in society largely through historical and philosophical analysis. That is, these scholars turned to the most "irrational" components of their civilization, preeeminently myth, and they historicized them. In various ways, they set out, as Schelling had proclaimed, "to discover reason in this seeming unreason."[91]

This bold turn from Cohen is also inextricably linked to the dire fate of the Weimar Republic. Those Jewish thinkers who experienced or adopted myth as master concept in the early Weimar years mostly abandoned it after the National Socialist appeal to myth was actualized and the Nazi myth became reality.[92] Not all did so, however. In this regard, Scholem, emigrant in Palestine, presented a characteristically paradoxical contrast to his comrades, Cassirer, Bloch, Horkheimer, and Adorno, who composed their masterworks in American exile. They no longer championed myth, but warned instead, of the dangers of the dialectic of enlightenment and the looming myth of the state. Scholem, the Zionist, meanwhile continued to champion myth. This is the vision set forth in *Major Trends in Jewish Mysticism*, delivered as lectures in New York in 1938, which we now are finally prepared to reread. To this daimonic vision—in which destruction allows construction—he remained true even in his great Eranos lectures, delivered after the war, in Europe, in German.

Scholem's sustained leap, which we can now see was hardly unprecedented in its derivation, was to become, we also know, unparalleled in its impact. For he (perhaps alone) used the category of myth to relocate Judaism permanently in the History of Religions. Nonetheless, the establishment Jewish self-presentation, it must be remembered, remained opposed to this "new thinking." Jewish leadership, intellectual and political, Zionist and non-Zionist, generally continued to portray Judaism as the religion of reason and therefore as the original and final enemy of myth. Scholem's consistent Schellingian scenario of three world ages of religion, culminating in mysticism as the revival of myth, seemingly was designed to smash the clay feet of this shaky consensus.

However, the real greatness of Scholem's accomplishment, in the end, was not purely iconoclastic but rather was to have it both ways.[93] On the one hand, he could resurrect myth as the generative principle of religion. On the other hand, he rejected regression to the archaic, recognizing that the only viable vantage point for the dialectician is ever at the front of the social process. Therefore, he had to work "inside history," even to act, in a sense, as its furthermost incitement onward. In an almost unknown testimony, Adorno strikes the right note. Reminiscing over thirty years of friendship, Adorno observed, "If I am not totally mistaken, Scholem became a historian of Kabbala . . . because he understood its contents to be in essence historical and therefore believed that its discussion had to be a historical one. This kind of historical truth can only be seized at the furthest distance from its origins, that is exactly in complete secularization."[94]

George Steiner's recent offhand observation that Scholem was "a master of disenchantment" similarly may not be wide of the mark.[95] My specific concern has been to place this "disenchanted" History of Religions—Scholem's theory of Judaism—into its intellectual context. It was, finally, a *successfully* post-Schellingian theory of myth. Like Cassirer's *Philosophy of Symbolic Forms*, Scholem's *Major Trends* retrofitted myth to the history of monotheism. In both cases, the *Urgeschichte des Bedeutens*, "the original history of meaning" (in Benjamin's pregnant phrase), initiated cycles of creation and destruction and thus subsumed the intitially disruptive daimonic into a continuing historical dialectic. This continuing vision meant, for one thing, that Scholem (and Cassirer) could then utilize this theory of history as the basis for an applied, practical scholarship. Such academic domestication was possible neither for the revolutionary theories of the Frankfurt School nor for the revelational theology of Franz Rosenzweig.[96] Still, in all these disparate cases, with all their constitutive differences registared, the turn to myth opened a dialectical vision of history as symbolic process. Rosenzweig stressed that revelation "brings an absolute symbolical order into history."[97] Scholem followed Schelling in describing his own symbolic shaping of history as a "narrative philosophy."[98] Beginning at the eruptive moment of the revelation to Adam, these narrative philosophies allowed Judaism to be understood in symbolic terms common to all religions. It too had a myth. It too could pass through cycles of devastation and regeneration; and it too could be reborn. Scholem's world ages—lifted from Schelling's *Weltalter*—then, mark the *Weltgeschichlicher Moment*, the world-historical moment, when Judaism reentered the History the Religions, if not history as such.

Part III

POLITICS

CHAPTER 8

Collective *Renovatio*

The hope and dream of these moments of total
crisis are to obtain a definitive and total *renovatio*,
a renewal capable of transmuting life.
—*Mircea Eliade*

ERANOS IN THE COLD WAR PERIOD

Madame Fröbe-Kapteyn, qui a été l'organe par le-
quel fut adressé à chacun de nous l'appel le con-
viant à l'imprévisible rencontre, l'a écrit très justement: Eranos n'était possible qu'en un temps de
détresse comme le nôtre.
—*Henry Corbin*

In 1949, the first year of the Cold War and the year that Corbin and
Scholem first spoke at Eranos, Eliade published *Cosmos and History*, with
its heartfelt chapter on "The Terror of History."[1] It seems almost trite to
observe, at century's end, that the History of Religions was born in a time
of crisis. Still, at the risk of this banality, it is perhaps worthwhile to recall
that that birth did *not* take place during the height of wartime crises,
from 1914 to 1945. Rather, it occurred during its anxiously quiescent
aftermath, at the beginning of the long stretch of peace conventionally
called the Cold War. The 1950s were famously and understandably "an
age of anxiety" (in W. H. Auden's phrase), what Eranos founder Froebe-
Kapteyn called "un temps de détresse comme le nôtre."[2] "In such a time
of distress as our own" the Historians of Religions came to Eranos to
address, directly and indirectly, the crisis of the times.

This chapter discusses the idea of *renovatio* as it unfolded in the Eranos
years of Scholem, Corbin, and Eliade, from 1949 to 1978. Given that
this period was immediately preceded by multiple upheavals of emigra-
tion, exile, defeat, genocide, war, revolution, and, eventually, national
regeneration, it is hardly surprising that the theme of collective *renovatio*
preoccupied them. Of the three Historians of Religion, Scholem had perhaps suffered the greatest personal trauma, having lost a brother in the
concentration camps, and having just witnessed the War for Indepen-

dence of the State of Israel. Still, Scholem's "terrible crisis in Jewish history" was seen by him to be at the same time a moment of unparalleled opportunity.[3] For all three, as I want to show, all hope was not lost.

"THE COSMIC CRYPT": CRISIS
EXPRESSED IN TERMS OF MYTH

> The first stage of our regeneration is our recall from the land of oblivion or kingdom of death and darkness, for this is indispensable for our entrance into the path of life.
> —*Louis-Claude de Saint-Martin*

As a shared point of traumatized departure, they each perceived the worldly situation to be dark indeed. For Corbin, echoing an image from Heidegger, even the heavens darkened.[4] "For the darkening of the world, the flight of the gods, the destruction of the earth, the transformation of man into a mass, the hatred and suspicion of everything free and creative, have assumed such proportions throughout the earth that such childish categories as pessimism and optimism have long since become absurd."[5] These words originally were retained in the republication of Heidegger's *Introduction to Metaphysics* after the war. Corbin himself, speaking of gnosis, seemed to echo this tenebrous imagery of "a darkening from heaven to heaven, a zone of deepening shadow in the face of which we can divine that the situation of man in this cosmos will not be resolved by philosophical descriptions alone."[6] In the same discussion, Corbin went on to characterize gnosis in seemingly Heideggerian terms, as a worldview built on " a 'drama,' *a fall of being*, long before the appearance of earthly man. He shares in this drama because he is of the same celestial race as the original dramatis personae."[7]

In such a "gnostic" view, our world is a pit, a mistake, a foul abortion. Given the planetary desperation to which we all have fallen, the only way left is up and out. Renewal is all. It has been disputed that gnosis bears, by definition, anticosmic tendencies of its essence.[8] But for Corbin, at least, such was indeed an essential characteristic of gnosis. "The Cosmic Crypt," for example, is the title of a memorable chapter in his *Avicenna and the Visionary Recital.*[9] Here he submits gnosis to "phenomenological analysis." His conclusion is that gnosis shares everywhere the "same dominant: 'estrangement,' the feeling of not belonging here, of being an 'allogene' [stranger]."[10] The world, the body, the heavens surrounding both, are tombs for the striving soul, the soul seeking the only way out, the release known to these authors as *gnosis.*

"SCHOLEM AND THE IDENTITY OF PERSONAL AND NATIONAL REGENERATION"

> In such moments of total crisis, only one hope
> seems to offer any issue—the hope of beginning
> life over again. This means, in short, that the man
> undergoing such a crisis dreams of new, regener-
> ated life, fully realized and significant.
> —*Mircea Eliade*

Mircea Eliade was, at a remarkably precocious age in the early 1930s, "the leader of his generation," the philosopher Nae Ionescu's next-in-line.[11] Julius Evola's *Revolt Against The Modern World* was published in 1934; and he hoped to become the spiritual leader of fascism.[12] Something of this sort seemed, at least until 1933, to have been what Jürgen Habermas called Heidegger's "bizarre plan."[13] As for Heidegger's translator, Henry Corbin, he concluded "The Time of Eranos" with a phrase whose aspirations are not less grandiose, calling for a spiritual rebirth "whose example, one may hope, will spread throughout the world."[14] And Scholem, for a brief time in adolescence, even toyed with the idea of his own messiah-hood![15] Each of these thinkers, then, at least for a time, played with the linkage between his unique form of thought and a grand hope for collective renewal.

In the cases of Henry Corbin, Gershom Scholem, and Mircea Eliade, the idea of collective rebirth was more than a youthful infatuation.[16] The national idea was generative. It is necessary to understand these ideas as various expressions of "spiritual nationalism"—Scholem's Zionism; Eliade's active and eventually official support for a succession of Romanian regimes; and Corbin's Iranian romantic nationalism—to understand its relation to their theory of monotheism. All were European emigrants who lived outside Europe for most of their careers; all had access to or were intimate with heads of state; and all wrote influentially on the question of religion and nationalism. They thus were importantly engaged in the nationalistic struggles of Iran, Romania, and Israel. In an encyclopedia article on "Jewish Mysticism and Kabbalah" published in 1946, Scholem made his view clear. He began his discussion of the "general characteristics" with the following assertion: "In its development, the movement of Jewish mysticism was characterized by an ever-growing tendency to become a social and national factor."[17]

These spiritual nationalisms emerged not only internally from their respective spiritual traditions but perhaps primarily borrowed from contemporary French and German traditions. Of the two, the German influence was stronger. George Mosse's well-known essay "Gershom Scholem as a German Jew" clarifies Scholem's specific debt to German culture.

The esoteric, the interest in mysticism, could best grow on German soil, where both were closely connected to the revival of nationalism during the last decades of the nineteenth century. Had Scholem been born or worked in England or France, for example, such approaches to Judaism would not have lain so readily at hand. The identity of personal and national regeneration which Scholem assumed—and which was not only common to modern nationalism but one of its principle characteristics—must be mentioned as well.[18]

The deaths of Hermann Cohen and Max Weber at the beginning of the 1920s and of Rosenzweig and Kafka at that decade's end signaled the transition toward the countermodernism of Scholem's mature thought. Scholem seemed uninterested only in Weber. In this as in so many other senses, Scholem presented a rather pure paradox, for his own theory may be seen as a kind of Weberian sociology without society. His muted rejection of Weber, was, in a sense, more telling than his louder dismissals of Marx and Freud, Jung and Cassirer.[19] In fact, in certain respects he was a typically conflicted post-Kantian of his time, requiring yet denying society's claim on meaning.

The aesthetic "new mythology" associated with Schelling, with its sometimes frenzied flight from the restrained Weberian *Weltanschauung*, made its claim on the young Scholem. Sometime in the early 1920s at the latest, he already understood that his own Zionist worldview would be grounded in a fervent, revisionary historiography. In this scenario, the heroes of Jewish history would be gnostics, anarchists, nihilists. Despite Scholem's marked palingenetic propensity—as if always fullborn, to appear without predecessors, to overcome, as Harold Bloom would have it, the anxiety of influence—a number of writers in fact already had portrayed Sabbetai Zevi as the prototypical revolutionary before Scholem wrote "Redemption through Sin." In each case, moreover, this was done from an aestheticizing perspective. Georg Lukács, Ernst Bloch, Rudolf Kayser, and Martin Buber each had lionized the false messiah as a forerunner of the modernist avant-garde long before Scholem composed his definitive work.[20] It therefore seems significant that, when Scholem composed "Redemption through Sin" in 1936, he cited none of these aesthetic leftist thinkers as the forerunners of his thinking. Instead, he noted the Zionist revisionism undertaken in Hebrew by Shai Ish Hurwitz and in Yiddish by Zalman Rubashov (Shazar).[21]

Arnaldo Momigliano, who studied in Germany in the 1920s, once remarked that we will not understand the formative philosophical influences on Scholem unless we can distinguish between Catholic and Protestant trajectories of German Romantic philosophy.[22] Scholem, Momigliano noted, was fully formed in the crucible of *Catholic* philosophy. Indeed, the most important influences on Scholem from German philosophy were Catholic mystical philosophers, Hamann, Molitor, von Baader, and Schelling, each of whom enjoyed something of a mini-revival in the 1920s.[23] But the 1920s themselves present yet another historical context for Scholem's ramified relations with German philosophy. Scholem was quite careful later in life to dissociate himself from the German philosophers of Jewish descent who were highly popular during his formative years. Thus he derided Simmel and Scheler, dismissed Cassirer, and ignored Husserl. Despite his protestations, it can be shown that Scholem's theory of symbolism is in certain respects close to that of Cassirer, just as he sometimes called himself a phenomenologist, as had Scheler and Husserl.[24] Scholem, in short, consistently downplayed the German influences on his thought, whether of German nationalism, of contemporary German-Jewish writers on Sabbatai Zevi, of German Catholic thought, or of contemporary phenomenology. As Mosse observed, however, the convergence of "the esoteric, the interest in mysticism" along with the identification "of personal and national regeneration" typified the German intellectual milieux in which he was nurtured. Scholem may have rejected these influences, but not without indebtedness.

ELIADE AND THE "NEW MAN"

> The new man or the renewed nation presupposes a great spiritual renewal, a great spiritual revolution of the whole people, a revolution that is opposed to the Spiritual direction of our day and an explicit offensive against this direction.
> —*Corneliu Zelea Codreanu*

> The Legion [Iron Guard] member is a new man, who has discovered his own will, his own destiny. Discipline and obedience have given him a new dignity, and unlimited confidence in himself, the Chief [Codreanu], and the greater destiny of the nation.
> —*Mircea Eliade*

Eliade espoused a different but perhaps equally vehement version of "spiritual nationalism." In his autobiography, Eliade evoked the spiritual revolution of the Legion of the Archangel Michael in its own terms, without the slightest criticism: "[For Codreanu] the Legionary movement did not constitute a political phenomenon but was, in its essence, ethical and religious. He repeated time and again that he was not interested in the acquisition of power but in the creation of a 'new man.'"[25] Eliade in this passage did not provide the historically necessary context of this theme. As George Mosse put it, "a fascist revolution must recognize 'the primacy of the spiritual.' Not control over the means of production was important, but the 'new man' about whom all fascists talked."[26]

Atrocities were undertaken by the Legionary "New Man." Codreanu himself had exhorted the "New Man" to undertake such actions, in order thereby to create Himself by eliminating the Old Man, "totally cleansed of today's vices and defects. In place of the corrupt specimen, who now dominates our political life, a new man of integrity and strong character must rise."[27] I cite here " 'The New Man" in Alexander Ronnett's *Romanian Nationalism: The Legionary Movement.* In the same passage, the "corrupt specimen" is identified as "the Jews."[28] This book was published in 1974, at a time when Ronnett was serving as Eliade's personal physician and dentist. Himself a flamboyantly unrepentant Legionary, Ronnett recently "insisted" to an inquiring journalist that "his patient was once a prominent Guardist."[29]

Nor was this a theme restricted to his Guardist phase in the 1930s. Immediately after World War II, Eliade again evoked the "New Man." This proclaimed renovation of humanity retained the overtones of the prewar *Übermensch*: "[F]or what is involved is creating a new man and creating him on a superhuman plane, a man-god, such as the imagination of historical man has never dreamt it possible to create."[30] Similarly, also in the late 1940s, he attributed this ideal not only to the next stage of evolution but also to its earliest stages. "[The] orgy transports man to an agricultural state. By abolishing norm, limit, and individuality . . . man hopes, by identifying himself with formless, pre-cosmic existence, to return to himself restored and regenerated, in a word, '*a new man.*'"[31]

Eliade's "new man," then, was one key theme linking his prewar agitations with his postwar corpus of writing. The rebirth of "Man," as such, meant a collective *renovatio* sufficiently triumphant as properly to be called revolutionary. It should not be forgotten, finally, that Louis-Claude de Saint-Martin, the eponymous "founder" of Martinism to whom Eliade was indebted, wrote a book titled *Le Nouvel Homme.*[32] Speaking of the movement inspired by Saint-Martin, Eliade stressed that "most of these groups and secret societies were animated by a profound hope in an imminent *renovatio.*"[33] One wonders how this assertion is to be read in light of the sentence that concluded Eliade's 1960 lecture. "And it is in this responsibility [for the renewal of the world] that one must look for the origins of all forms of politics, both "classical" and "millenarist."[34]

"SUMMONS TO A PALINGENESIS":
CORBIN'S ARYANISM AND THE REBIRTH OF HISTORY

[Shi'ite thought] today has the character of a
summons to a palingenesis.
—Henry Corbin

Henry Corbin concluded his *History of Islamic Philosophy* with these
words: "But the lessons to be learned from our Islamic metaphysicians is
that they never imagined that their esotericism—that is to say, their interiority—was possible without a new inner birth. A *tradition* lives and
transmits life only if it is a perpetual *rebirth*."[35] Although he spoke of "the
perpetuity and the palingeneses of the world of the Gnosis" he seemed
not to restrict his concept of rebirth within these bounds.[36] Corbin discussed all the aforementioned emphases within the nominal forum of the
History of Religions, or, more technically, as a self-described phenomenologist of religion. That is to say, like Gershom Scholem, Mircea Eliade,
and others with whom he was closely associated, with whom he met at
Eranos for a quarter-century, and with whom he published and whose
work quoted each other, he articulated his program hermeneutically,
through the reading of traditional texts. Moreover, like these fellow phenomenologists of religion, he articulated a certain *spiritual nationalism.*
In Corbin's case, this choice of texts were not only Islamic, and not only
esoteric, but specifically esoteric texts associated with Iran—in fact, with
what he characterized as the primordial Aryan heritage of Persia. Since
this point is controversial, if not somewhat delicate, I shall spend rather
more time on it.

Corbin's Iran was, to use his neologism, *imaginal.* The way he put it,
his Iran was not the geographically located nation-state but the idea of
Persia—the archetype, or, perhaps, as one title had it, the *soul* of Iran.[37]
As he put it in his 1951 lecture "Iranian Studies and Philosophy," "[I]f
we always use 'Iran,' we risk an implicit suggestion that this is somehow
identified with the borders and characteristics of a political entity—
whereas the philosopher must look to a different realm of being."[38] I
would call this feature of his thought *Aryanism* for several reasons. This
spiritual nationalism had a complex background. For those familiar with
the history of Islam, he hearkened back, for example, to the *Shu'ubiyya,*
the Persian national resistance to the Arabocentrism of early Islam.[39]
Closer to his own day, he also drew on the once popular *Religionsgesch-
ichtlicheschule,* remarkable for its persistent search for a Iranian gnostic
prototype, the so-called Anthropos, ostensibly inspiring the pre-Christian
gnostic Son of Man figure behind the divinized Jesus.[40] Another dimen-

sion of his Persianism was Indo-European theory, which posited cultural continuities, including Persian, between Europe and India.[41] Most important, the effort of the Pahlavi regime, explicitly an "Aryan" throne, to establish continuities with the glories of ancient Persia fundamentally underpinned Corbin's distinctively Persianizing approach to Islam. Corbin enjoyed close relations with the regime from his arrival in 1945 until his death and its death in 1978. I will develop this point below.

It is not inaccurate to say, in fact, that the whole of his idiosyncratic historiography operated under *the sign of the Aryan*. Corbin's debut publication after he emerged from his wartime retreat was a monograph titled *Les motifs zoroastriens dans la philosophie de Sohrawardi*, dated February 1946.[42] Here he posited a transhistorical trajectory reaching from the ancient Persian prophet Zoroaster through the gnostic prophet Mani, spanning the medieval philosophers Suhrawardi and Mulla Sadra, and eventuating in the Peacock Throne of Reza Shah Pahlavi, under whose exalted auspices he himself operated. In 1951, he published "Iran, Homeland of Philosophers and Poets," which reiterated this metahistorical vision in even starker terms. Here he begins with "Zarathustra, the prophet of the Aryans," evokes "the last great sovereign of Iran, Reza Shah Pahlavi," speaks of a north-south axis on which the "great drama of the Aryan nation" operates, and closes with an invocation of Hegel, Schelling, Boehme, Wagner's Tristan, and the Nordic visionary Swedenborg.[43] In June 1978, just four months before his death, he reaffirmed and made explicit the Germany-Iran twinning that runs throughout his lifework. On that occasion he confessed again that both Germany and Persia were "homeland[s] of philosophers and poets" and that his encounters with each had a complementary relation with the other.[44] Thus could he rather coyly claim elsewhere that "the experiences of the Iranian Spirituals evoke in each of us comparisons with certain spiritual facts from other sources."[45]

The work that most fully sets forth Corbin's Aryanism is also one that has received almost no attention in scholarly literature. In 1961 he published the original French version of *The Man of Light in Iranian Sufism*. Here Corbin did nothing less than assimilate the themes of a visionary Germany with those of a spiritual Persia into a singular Aryan *Weltanschauung*, a worldview of the "other" world. Subsequently translated and reprinted on a number of occasions, this work opens with the proclamation that "contrasts between Eastern and Western man, between Nordic and Southern man, regulate our ideological and characterological classifications."[46] He then provides a disquisition on "Symbols of the North."[47] Toward the end of this book, he notes that the fourteenth-century Semnani faced "the very same [metaphysical] situation as did Nietzsche: "[T]he mortal danger described by Semnani . . . is the every same situation with which the West came face to face when Nietzsche cried out: 'God is dead.'"[48]

Nor is this (self-consciously) cryptic book the only one that continued to ply these Prusso-Persian themes. They are reiterated in his *Spiritual Body and Celestial Earth*, translated for the Princeton Bollingen series and recently reissued in paperback. Here, he espouses his typical eschatology, holding that the Zarathustran Savior and the Coming Imam comprise a single archetype, that of "spiritual knights" waiting to "return for the final battle."[49] It recurs in his extreme praise of Carl Jung, when he predicts that the ultimate savior would come "from the race of Zarathustra."[50] Indeed, Corbin called Jung's *Response to Job* a latter-day Zervanism, in a review that Jung praised as the only one of "hundreds of review" that truly understood him.[51]

In all this, Corbin applied an unreconstructed Aryan triumphalism.[52] Put another way, his Persia was Zarathustran, not so much a Middle Eastern nation-state as a post-Nietzschean response to the Death of God.[53] A few months before his death, he confessed in a letter that he felt certain culture spheres were closest to the "imaginal world": "I believe that this imaginal world is the locus of the rebirth of the Gods, those of Greek theogony, as well as of Celtic theogony, which with those of the Greeks and the Iranians, *are the closest to our consciousness.*"[54]

MARTIN HEIDEGGER

Martin Heidegger represents one important but heretofore unstudied link between the Historians of Religions. Corbin was the first French translator of Heidegger, with whom he met more than once in Germany in the 1930s.[55] In 1968 he downplayed the formative impact of Heidegger on his Orientalism.

> Il en résulta une pénétration dans le monde germanique qui, semble-t-il, a jeté le trouble dans ma biographie apparente, et je voudrais saisir l'occasion de rectifiere ici. Parce que je fus le premier traducteur français de Heidegger, on a écrit quelque part que, déçu par la philosophie <existentielle>, j'avais cherché refuge dans la mystique de l'Islam. C'est là fantaisie pure. Mes premières publications en mystique islamique (1933, 1935) sont bien antérieures à ma traduction de Heidegger (1938). Il y a des explications plus simples aux pélerinages et pérégrinations d'un philosophe.[56]

> This resulted in my establishing deep links with the world of Germanic scholarship. Since that seems to have been the occasion for some confusion regarding my own biography, I would like to take this opportunity to set things straight. Because I was the first French translator of Heidegger, some-

one wrote that, disappointed by Existentialist philosophy, I subsequently sought refuge in Islamic mysticism. This is sheer fantasy. My first publications in Islamic mysticism date from 1933 and 1935, well before my translation of Heidegger in 1938. No, there are simpler explanations for the various wanderings and pilgrimages of a philosopher.[57]

This disavowal of 1968 was contradicted by Corbin himself in his later autobiographical interview.[58] Finally, it is worth noting that Corbin concluded lectures of 1951 and 1966 by invoking Heidegger.[59]

Scholem was well aware of Heidegger's charismatic influence during the 1920s.[60] Until 1933, Heidegger held considerable influence over a generation of young Jewish thinkers. They included not only his talented students (and Scholem acquaintances) Hannah Arendt, Herbert Marcuse, Hans Jonas, and Karl Löwith, none of whom wrote what could be called "Jewish philosophy," but also such Jewish theologians as Alexander Altmann, Emmanuel Lévinas, Franz Rosenzweig, Joseph Soloveitchik, and Leo Strauss.[61] It lies beyond the scope of the present discussion to demonstrate that Scholem also was influenced by Heidegger. For the moment, I can note only indirect influence. As circumstantial evidence I would cite the impact of Jonas's Heideggerian study of gnosticism on "Redemption through Sin," as well as the fact that Scholem was in correspondence with Henry Corbin when Corbin was undertaking his translations of Heidegger into French during the mid-1930s.[62] Scholem's theory of gnosis explicitly was influenced by the work of Jonas, whose celebrated assessment, "Gnosticism, Nihilism and Existentialism," was markedly Heideggerian. While Scholem cited this essay with approbation in his classic essay "Redemption through Sin," one should not conclude that this was a mere passing interest of his middle years.[63] In fact, he returned to it with the same emphasis thirty-five years later, in one of his last major lectures at Eranos, "Nihilism as a Religious Phenomenon."[64] And, perhaps most strikingly, Scholem's masterwork, *Sabbatai Sevi*, bears on its frontispiece an epigraph from a letter of Count Yorck, a statement precisely analyzed at the culmination of the celebrated treatment of "historicality" in Heidegger's *Being and Time*.[65] Finally, it is interesting to note that Scholem served on the board of editors of the Harper and Row Religious Perspectives series, along with Mircea Eliade. In 1968, while both served on the board, this series published Heidegger's *What Is Called Thinking?* [66]

> One would love to know someday the itinerary which brought the first translator of Heidegger to the study of Ismaili gnosis and the philosophy of Ishraq . . . it is clear that [Corbin] did not sacrifice his first vocation of philosopher . . . the works of Corbin will one day take their rank among the most brilliant *ta'wil* produced by European Orientalism.

Eliade composed these encomia in a 1955 review of Corbin's *Avicenne et le Récit visionnaire*.[67] The same may be said, after all, of Eliade himself: one would love to know by what itinerary the youthful Romanian reader of Heidegger became the masterly Orientalist and comparativist. Turning to the youthful Mircea Eliade, it may be noted that, although he appropriated Goethe's Faustian ambitions, these proved inadequate for the Romanian writer to articulate a philosophy for the "New Generation."[68] It was among contemporary German thinkers that he found a more vitally effective language for his incipient philosophy. The work of Martin Heidegger thus became fundamental for Eliade's thought, though this influence is not apparent until his postwar works. Ivan Strenski, one of the few critics of Eliade to draw out the links between Heidgger and Eliade, notes the following features shared by Heidegger and Eliade: love of the Italian Futurists; emphasis on "earth," or "telluric piety"; the revolutionary will opposed to the bourgeoisie; an existentialist ontology; celebration of "the new generation"; and a stress on archetypal repetition.[69] He also accurately observes that in the 1930s Eliade's "master" Ionescu taught the "Decisionists" Jünger and Heidegger, both of whom became so important in the life of Eliade.[70] Finally, Strenski recognizes that Eliade played a role in relation to Gerardus van der Leeuw that Heidegger did in relation to Husserl: both revolutionized a previous "phenomenology" almost beyond recognition.[71]

One could go further than Strenski.[72] I would emphasize that Eliade's reading of Heidegger is at the root of his "ontologism," his sustained emphasis on the cosmic centrality of "Being-in-the-world." Most fundamentally, the consistent and essential concern with "historicity" and "being" throughout his corpus further belies the impression of a late or superficial reading. Eliade's "ontologism"—only vaguely reminiscent of the formulations of *Sein und Zeit*, but redolent with the gestures of the postwar Heidegger—is central to his thinking, repeated in various forms throughout the corpus: "[T]he *sacred* is eqivalent to a *power*, and in the last analysis, to *reality*. The sacred is saturated with *being*."[73] "The myth defines itself by its own mode of being."[74]

Eliade came to his appreciation of Heidegger early in his career. Following the lead of his master, Nae Ionescu, Eliade taught and studied Heidegger in his Criterion Group, as early as 1933—that is, after the 1933 *Rektorsrede*.[75] "We needed to discuss Heidegger and Jaspers," he explained at the end of his life.[76] In his *Oceanography*,[77] he cited Heidegger as one of "the few able to penetrate the structure of Rumanian thought."[78] While his earliest postwar statement on Heidegger seemed rather equivocal, in fact, Heidegger remained close to his own spiritual life.[79] When Eliade's first wife died in November 1944, he read only the Bible, Kierkegaard, Shestov, Dilthey, and . . . Heidegger.[80] Eliade, meanwhile, had established close contact with intimates of Heidegger, like Ernst Jünger. In 1953, the Heideggerian psychoanalyst Medard Boss, close to Heidegger personally, related to Eliade a journey he had made with Heidegger to Italy.[81]

Throughout the 1950s, then, the Heideggerian influence on Eliade grew. Eventually, he authored a work suffused with Heideggerian themes, *Myths, Dreams and Mysteries*. In his original French version of 1957, he concluded with a remarkable reference to Heidegger. "Many centuries before Heidegger, Indian thought had identified, in temporality, the 'fated' dimension of all existence. . . . When the yogi or the Buddhist said that everything was suffering, that all was transitory . . . the meaning was that of *Sein und Zeit*, namely, that the temporality of all human existence necessarily engenders anxiety and pain."[82] When he published the English version of this work in 1959, he remarked in the foreword that Heidegger's "latest researches" were developing in the direction of being "capable of regenerating philosophical investigation."[83] By 1963, Eliade was praising Heidegger as a matter of fact: "Admirable response from Heidegger to Carnap's attacks" that "being" is not to be understood "logically"—though this, he observes pointedly, is something a "neopositivist or Marxist" wouldn't understand.[84] In 1971, he provided the preface for *Symposion Heidegger*, a Romanian émigré publication that bore a letter from Heidegger immediately following Eliade's prefatory note.[85] Eliade, then, was unmistakable and unshakable in his conviction that Heidegger's fundamental ontology was *the* philosophy of our time: "It is scarcely fifty years since the problems of Time and History came to occupy the centre of Western philosophical thought."[86] His last explicit statement on Heidegger was also the most lavishly laudatory, to say the least. At the aforementioned public lecture at the annual meeting of the American Academy of Religion, on the subject of "Mythologies of Death," Eliade concluded by referring to the work of Heidegger as "the most profound and seminal," "decisive," "fundamental," "grandiose," and "acute."[87] Even in a subsequent interview he referred to Heidegger's "mature and profound thought processes."[88]

Collective *renovatio* follows the radical rejections that typified Heideggerian planetary *Kampf*. Heidegger's erstwhile student Karl Löwith characterized Heidegger's stance of absolute rejection as follows. "What remains guiding in everything that Heidegger thinks and says is a motto from Kierkegaard: 'The time of distinctions [*Distinktionen*] is past.' The distinctions which Heidegger leaves behind are the traditional distinctions [*Unterscheidungen*] of the philosophical disciplines, e.g., physics, ethics, and logic."[89] Hugo Ott, another of Heidegger's most distinguished students, emphasized that Heidegger rejected not only the distinctions of Western philosophy but also those of ethical monotheism. "Heidegger declared the God of the Jews and the Christians to be finally dead; and, often enough, he proclaimed anew this philosophical abolition of a personal God, of a Creator-God, of a Savior-God. In so doing, he emphatically denied, of course, the need for an ethic based on the Decalogue."[90] Heidegger thus set a momentous, even epochal, example, one that, so to speak, transcended both Athens and Jerusalem. This "planetary" enormity loomed large over religious thinkers at mid-century, the Historians of Religions not least of all.[91]

Heidegger's influence on the History of Religions, however, may seem mostly muted, though Eliade was the most explicit about it. But Heidegger's example, as a thinker who shattered both European civilizational norms and staid monotheistic conventions, remained an unsurpassable horizon for each of our trio of historians. Scholem, of course, was never the fervent Heideggerian that Corbin and Eliade had been. But even the Zionist who abandoned Heidegger's Germany could not entirely move beyond that horizon: many of his Jewish intellectual peers, including Adorno, Rosenzweig, Jonas, Arendt, Altmann, Strauss, and Löwith, responded (in one way or the other) to Heidegger.[92] In terms of the larger organization of forms of knowledge, then, it may be concluded that so-called Continental Philosophy was, in this period, overwhelmingly dominated by Heidegger just as so-called History of Religions was dominated by Eliade, Corbin, and Scholem. The relations between these two discourses remains to be traced in detail.

NEW LAW IN THE MESSIANIC AGE

> And he knew deep in his heart that he was the chosen one, the one to seek and to find his people's soul. And the Dreamer—his name already marked him as the Awaited One: Scholem, the perfect one, prepared himself for his task and began to forge the weapons of knowledge.
> —*Gershom Scholem, 22 May 1915*

The coming identification of God and man, announced portentously by Jung, seems not quite a messiah, but also not quite an Antichrist. Jung understood his announcement to be, in some sense, the manifesto for a new age of humanity. In the sense I have explored, it was, perhaps, best understood as the prophecy of *gnosis as the next epoch*; as the coming convergence of history into psychology, psychology into history, psychology into religion, and religion into psychology in a reunification of the individual with the collective.[93] As collective *renovatio*, this soteriology spoke to the end of history.

Gershom Scholem spoke to this point in a plenary address before a meeting of the International Association of the History of Religions.

> When religion undergoes, as it does so often and so visibly in our days [14 July 1968], the process of secularization, that is to say when it is interpreted in apparently irreligious terms, we encounter a characteristic shifting of emphasis: what was formerly taken as a state of redemption, especially in its messianic connotations, by now becomes the condition in which alone true human experience is possible. The unredeemed state is no longer worthy to be called human. The redeemed state is where human experience begins.[94]

This raises the question of what is meant by "the redeemed state." Corbin called this doctrine of the immanence of perfection "realized eschatology."[95]

This realized eschatology, it seems, emerged from the eschatological imagination. To see this age tottering into its conclusion, driving toward some greater perfection, suggests that realized eschatology, at least in the forms it took in this present purview, underwrote nothing less than modernity itself. "Realized eschatology" is a sign of overcoming the opposites ruling the present, oppressive epoch. And androgyny, the unification of sexual opposites, stands, then, for release from existing constraints. These constraints, to be sure, were not only sexual, but legal and moral, political and ethical, as well.[96]

In fact, one might say, with a certain descriptive accuracy, that modernity itself operated for our Historians of Religion as a kind of false messiah. This world age, that is, not only promises on principle but seemingly delivers in practice a manumission from the bondage of the old law. This secularization is descriptively the case, just as is its objective failure to replace that old law with one recognizable again *as law*. Nonetheless, the present secular modernity, for our Historians of Religions, is peered at through the god's-eye-view of a presumed perfection, from paradise now.

WELTALTER: TRANSGRESSION AS NORM

> Chaque époque rêve la suivante.
> —*Theodor Adorno*

Joseph Campbell's *Hero with a Thousand Faces* popularized, as perhaps did no other book, the Eranos worldview.[97] No book may have done more to bridge the elite Eranos discourse with a budding "New Age" religion, which "spiritually" was to bloom fully some years later. *Hero with a Thousand Faces* identified one big myth, the so-called monomyth. But if there was a mythic story at the center of the *collective*, as opposed to Campbell's *personal* myth propagated at Ascona, it may have been the historical myth of "world cycles." The old world, the modern world cycle, is "a'dying"—and therefore new norms, new postethical norms, now hold true. Today, in short, Halakha, Shari'a, and Ecclesia are no longer operative, at least as regulative ideas in religious history. Their appeal to the theory of world ages made law evaporate. One consequence of this collective monomyth, this epochal self-understanding, was its disintegrating effect on norms of "this world." Thus, historic, legal, and sexual constraints are, in principle, no longer binding on the gnostic now released on his or her own recognizance, as it were.

Each of the historians of religions wrote extensively on the theory of *Weltalter*, or world ages.[98] Scholem wrote perhaps half his vast corpus on the phenomenon of Sabbatian messianism. He also ended his *Origins of Kabbalah* with an extended discussion of an otherwise obscure treatise (*Sefer Temuna*) on world ages.[99] Eliade wrote throughout his career on the Hindu theory of world ages, which seemed to underpin his implied belief that we are presently living in an age imminently due for dissolution (Kali Yuga).[100] And Corbin, at least as much as his colleagues, made this idea central to his Orientalist studies. Putting it in Shi'ite terms, for example, he saw the present age as leading to "the cycle of spiritual initiation in the 'Friends of God succeeding the cycle of legislation prophecy.'"[101]

Corbin and Eliade, not incidentally, themselves wrote repeatedly on the great antinomian revolutionary, Sabbetai Zevi. When they came to address Judaism, they applied Scholem's version of Jewish history almost verbatim. In fact, both wrote essays and even whole chapters in which they described Judaism as such in Sabbatian terms. This Judaism was, in their description, a monotheism almost wholly without law. Judaism, for these Historians of Religion, was identical with Scholem's version of Sabbatianism.[102] That they could so resolutely and unflinchingly coronate such an antinomianism as an authoritative "description" of the most ancient ethical monotheism was possible in part because they operated in a larger intellectual milieu in which it was, at least for a time, routinely revolutionary to assert transgression as norm. Georges Bataille, another philosopher interlinking the three antinomian scholars of monotheism, exemplifies this milieu. It was, incidentally, thanks to Bataille that crucial masterpieces of Walter Benjamin survived the war years. Bataille had met Scholem's friend Benjamin at sessions of the Parisian Collège de Sociologie (1937–1939). Bataille later also helped Eliade get established in Paris, just after the war.[103] Leaders of the Collège, which convened to address "sacred sociology," included Roger Caillois—who later edited the journal *Diogenes,* which published Scholem and Eliade, and whose work *Man and the Sacred* was a formative influence on Eliade—and Denis de Rougemont—who edited the journal *Hic et Nunc* with Corbin, and who cited him for decades, eventually authoring a laudatory article on Corbin in Corbin's *Festschrift.*

THE NEW AGE

> Hermeneutics as science of the individual stands
> in opposition to historical dialectics as alienation
> of the person.
> —*Henry Corbin*

A manifesto like Henry Corbin's "The Time of Eranos" rather unmistakably announces the religious equivalent, for dislocated emigré intellectuals, of Cold War anticommunism. Theirs was a spritualized, internationalist version as opposed to the local, chauvanist varieties grounded in nationalisms. Henry Corbin's Lutheran hermeneutics of the 1930s seemed to inform this postwar stance. *Here I stand*: the post-Lutheran Henry Corbin retained the individual's heroic faith and opposed him to an oppressive collective. After the War, Corbin articulated his post-Christian theology explicitly in terms of the collective *renovatio* offered by Shi'ism. "L'Islam shî'ite pose par excellence à la théologie chrétienne la problème théologique de l'histoire des religions post-chrétiennes. Il est possible que cette question implique une grande aventuree, rien de moins qu'une métamorphose, voire une *totale rénovation spirituelle* pour un bon nombre."[104]

It is not an accident that a certain sort of post-Christianity, so-called New Age Religion, emerged during the Cold War. Religious intellectuals like the Historians of Religions spearheaded a notion of religion that seemed to transcend denominational boundaries even as it presumed some kind of transcendent unity to world religions. The geopolitical antagonism of the Cold War, seemingly so constitutive of the age, stimulated at the same time what seemed like a planetary ecumenicism. This Eranos kind of public gnosis, popularized by Jung, Campbell, and Eliade, could espouse its identity, *seriatum*, with alchemy, shamanism, yoga, Templarism. Such a secularized esoterism, of course, is now familiar in its subsequent popularized forms as (tellingly) New Age Religion.[105] Their characteristically promiscuous application of correspondences, often claimed as a Hermetic principle, underwrote a riot of analogies. Unifying these globalizing linkages, the Principle of Totality was seen to be the "final" point. The ultimate version of the Principle was the Universal Man; the culmination of symbols into one big archetype, what Campbell's *Hero with a Thousand Faces* called "the monomyth," or what Jung called "The New Incarnation," the god-man to come in the Next Age: "the identity of God and man."[106] Eliade put it (unblinkingly) as follows. "Suffice it to recall that the freeing of Nature from the laws of Time went hand in hand with the deliverance of the alchemist himself. In Western alchemy, much later, the redemption of Nature, as demonstrated by Jung, completed the redemption of man by Christ."[107] The New Age is the age of this collective redemption.

Eliade took note of the nascent New Age in his Freud Lecture of 1974, "The Occult and the Modern World."[108] Here the theme of collective *renovatio* came to the fore. According to the historiography espoused in this lecture, the literary lineage running from Goethe's *Wilhelm Meister* to Balzac's *Séraphita* was characterized by "a hope in a personal or collective *renovatio*—a mystical restoration of man's original dignity and powers; in sum, the literary creations reflected and prolonged the conceptions of seventeenth- and eighteenth-century theosophists and their sources."[109] This purported mini-renaissance of theosophy, Eliade continued, was followed by the "illuminating contributions" of contemporary scholars, of whom he specifies Scholem and Corbin. Under the rubric "The Hope for *Renovatio*," Eliade then portrayed the counterculture of 1974 as "a rejection of Christian tradition in the name of a supposedly broader and more efficient method for achieving an individual and, by the same stroke, a collective *renovatio*."[110] As for René Guénon, with whose case Eliade concluded, "there is no hope for a cosmic or a social *renovatio*. A new cycle will begin only after the total destruction of the present one."[111] Eliade, in his concluding remarks, did not choose between these two alternatives— between the optimistic and the pessimistic accounts of coming *renovatio*— but the clue to his preference for Guénonian catastrophism is alluded to in the final pages of this lecture. This preference is clearly supported by other sources.[112] For Eliade, in short, collective *renovatio* will come after a total annihilation of this stage of history.

APOCALYPSE YESTERDAY

Eliade's alchemical "completion" of the "redemption of man by Christ" is illuminated by reference to Henry Corbin's notion of "realized eschatology" and with Scholem's concept of "the redeemed state." This "redemption" implied, in short, a theory of religion after the law, life in the aftertime, a theory whose opposition to secularization succeeded because it is almost perfectly adapted to it; a perfectly theorized secularity.

This idea also coincided with the trope of "freedom" so prominent in the Cold War. *Antaios* was subtitled "a *Journal for the Free World.*" So too Scholem could embrace a "radical new freedom" and Eliade could write a tome titled *Yoga: Immortality and Freedom.*[113] The apocalypse has happened. Apocalypse yesterday. The new age is our age, and the old gods are an old story for us—the new story is the new myth, one that explains our freedom to us. The apocalypse becomes the modern itself: *Eranos is afterward as such.*

Such a stance was hardly unproblematic. For one thing, it seemed to fly in the face of Corbin and Eliade's otherwise insistent rejection of modernity. Collective *renovatio* seemed necessary, from the outset, because the perceived terror of the times demanded it. There is, however, no rational means by which one can demonstrate that "modernity" as such is worse than "traditional life." Any such assertion cannot be a rational proposition. The mythic character of this form of world rejection becomes apparent in the totality of its claims. It is a sacred narrative, a totality, a worldview. One thing that distinguishes *religion after religion* from other totalizing antimodernisms is its "traditionalist" posture. Ironically, then, it espoused a past that never was in opposition to a present that never is. Perhaps these great scholars selected the solution of a *coincidentia oppositorum*—this world age is the best of times *and* the worst of times, as it were—because they needed a both/and answer; because they wanted to have their "freedom" cake and yet wanted to have it "traditionally" too. Their deaths, in a world-historical irony, clustered around 1989, the postapocalyptic end of the Cold War, which brought in its wake if not "collective *renovatio*," if not "reintegration," at least the return of religion.

CHAPTER 9

The Idea of Incognito:
Authority and Its Occultation
According to Henry Corbin

HENRY CORBIN produced scholarship prolifically for nearly fifty years. But his voluminous corpus is that rarity, one whose breadth easily is matched by its depth. My intention in this chapter, therefore, cannnot be to provide a comprehensive review of this vast and subtle body of work. Rather, I want tentatively to explicate one aspect of his vision, the idea of *hidden authority*. I want to suggest that the theory of discipleship espoused by Corbin, especially when understood in light of its historical and political contexts, is one we embrace at our own intellectual peril.

Before I begin my exposition proper, I should note that Corbin never pretended to speak otherwise than normatively. As I shall show, he openly, often angrily, reviled historicist analysis and social-critical inquiry in the name of his self-designated "prophetic philosophy." And he never pretended to be a historian, at least in any sense recognizable to working historians in North America. I underscore this point because I intend to engage Corbin's normative views, and not his historical method, monography, or conclusions.[1]

THE CAREER

Before I can come to these substantive concerns, I should briefly review his remarkable career. While it can and has has been divided according to various other criteria, I will conveniently describe it as transpiring in three phases, that of Paris in the 1920s and 1930s, Istanbul from 1939 to 1946, and Tehran/Paris from 1946 to his death in October 1978, just weeks before the return of the Ayatollah Khomeini. It is this last phase, of course, which is of primary concern here.

Corbin completed his Catholic education in 1923, at the age of twenty. During the 1920s, he studied medieval philosophy with Gilson, and Sanskrit with Louis Renou, before turning to Arabic and Persian. In retrospect, he now appears to belong fully to the generation of young European Catholic intellectuals who radicalized their lapse from the Church.[2]

These young intellectuals turned away from Europe and the Church to existentialism, paganism, Islam. To the end of his life, Corbin excoriated the Church as what was in effect a Great Satan.[3] Islam seemed to have served as his means of escaping the Church—for example when he claimed that the "phenomenon of the Church doesn't exist in Islam" (*Le phénomène Eglise n'existant pas en Islam*).[4] Similarly, as he put it in 1959, "Shi'ite Islam poses par excellence the theological problem of post-Christian history of religions to Christian theology."[5]

His academic mentor was the leading French Islamicist of his day, Louis Massignon (1883–1962)—himself a pious lay cleric in the Roman Church. In the first years of the 1930s, Massignon handed him the works of Shihab al-Din Suhrawardi with the comment, "*I think there is something in this book for you.*"[6] By 1933 Corbin was already publishing studies on and translations of Suhrawardi.[7] Meanwhile, he was energetically involved in intellectual and cultural circles, especially those surrounding Karl Barth and Martin Heidegger. In 1938, Corbin became the first French translator of Heidegger, even as his Heideggerianism soon took the unique form of a Lutheran Orientalist gnosticism.[8] Corbin also translated Hendrik de Man's *The Idea of Socialism* with Alexandre Kojève, himself soon to be famed in the halls of the Sorbonne for his lectures on Hegel and the end of history.[9] Down the hall, Corbin ended his Parisian 1930s with a series of memorable lectures on the "Magus of the North," the early German romantic thinker Johann Georg Hamann.[10]

In 1939, Corbin left for Istanbul on an ostensibly three-month-long mission that lasted six years. The prolific writer published nothing in this period. "In the course of those years . . . I learned the inestimable virtues of Silence, which initiates call 'the discipline of the arcane' (*Ketman* in Persian). One of the virtues of this Silence was to be put in solitary company alone with my invisible Shaykh, Shihaboddin Yahya Sohravardi, who died a martyr in 1191, at the age of 36, the very age that I was at that time."[11] Corbin's autobiographical fragments, as well as his biographers, claim that these war years in Istanbul were devoted to the solitary study of and translation of Suhrawardi manuscripts.[12] The associates in Istanbul whom he later identified included Germans and Romanians.[13] Nor did the Vichy Government dismiss him from his post. There is no evidence, however, that he was a supporter of the Vichy government. But he did quote with approbation the Vichy supporter and fascist ideologue Maurice Bardèche in his 1965 Eranos lecture, specifically in the context of defining the characteristic attitude espoused at Eranos.[14] As a repeated visitor to Germany in the 1930s, as a close colleague of leading fascist sympathizers throughout Europe, as a lifelong Teutonophile, and as a sworn enemy of liberal democracy and secular humanism, it would not be inconceivable that Corbin supported Vichy. In any event, this possibility suggests various readings of his statement that "[i]n the course of those [Istanbul] years . . . I learned the inestimable virtues of Silence, which initiates call 'the discipline of the arcane.' "[15]

Corbin broke this public silence in 1946, launching an academic publishing career that blossomed immediately and flourished unabated until his death in 1978, when he was one of Europe's best-known scholars of Islam. In these thirty-two years he divided his time between Paris and Tehran. He enjoyed the protection and support of the Shah of Iran; succeeded Louis Massignon as *directeur d'études* at the École pratique des hautes études at the Sorbonne; lectured almost annually at the Eranos meetings in Switzerland; and was subsidized and published in this country by the prestigious Bollingen Foundation.

OVERVIEW OF THE THEORY

The work produced by Corbin from 1946 to 1978 is daunting in scope, complexity and subtlety. Without pretense of completeness, therefore, I will now highlight five interpenetrated and overlapping leitmotifs of his work in this period: *esoterism*; *antimodernism*; *angelology*; *the theory of the imaginal*; and the *idea of the incognito*.[16] I might just note that the Tehran phase with which I am primarily concerned began when Corbin was forty-two years old. The mature program he annunciated in 1946, then, never changed, but only deepened and developed along lines fully in place at that time. For that reason I feel justified in generalizing about the work as a whole. Finally, for my purposes, I will concentrate on the last of the five, and review the first four rapidly.

First, his scholarship comprised an *esoterism*. Corbin variously described his approach as esoteric, gnostic, or theosophical; he rejected such labels as myth, magic, and mysticism. His mature theory, rather, situated itself, on the one hand, in the Western occult sciences, alchemy and hermeticism, and, on the other hand, in the lineage of medieval philosophical esoterism. If I were to characterize developments within his esoterism, I would say that in the first part of the Tehran phase Corbin emphasized the individual and philosophical dimension; in its second phase, the last fifteen or so years of his life, he concentrated on the collective and occultist nature of the esoteric imperative.[17]

Antimodernism is a second feature of this thought, closely related to the first. Corbin consistently and uniformly excoriated the characteristic developments of intellectual modernity, especially historicism, sociology, and secularization. As he put it near the end of his life, "The norm of our world can assume all manner of names: sociology, dialectical or non-dialectical materialism, positivism, historicism, psychoanalysis, and so forth."[18] Elsewhere in the same essay he exclaims, "Sociologists and phi-losophers of history . . . are the docile followers of Pharaoh."[19] Four months before his death he inaugurated the Université Saint Jean de Jerusalem. In this fiery opening address he contrasted so-called Occiden-tal science and Oriental gnosis, posing the pointed question, "Will there really be a renewal of gnosis, bearing witness to the fact that gnosis can-not remain indefinitely absent and that its banishment was a catastro-phe?"[20] For Henry Corbin, modernity *is* catastrophe. In his last major statement he "sets the same catastrophe at the center of world history: the destruction of the Temple, of the same Temple."[21] Just eight months before his death he restated this emphasis in his favorite (Heideggerian) fashion: "To confuse Being with being is the metaphysical catastrophe."[22] This confusion typifies the central philosophical disaster at the dark heart of contemporary intellectual life.

A third distinctive element of Corbin's thought was its *angelology*. Here, more than anywhere else, I believe, Corbin's brilliant insights and far-reaching vision produced a valuable result. Inasmuch as this makes up the substance of his theology, it is outside my scope here. I simply note that he saw this angel-centered theosophy to be diametrically opposed to the historical study of religion: "[A]ngelology and sociology must remain forever foreign to one another."[23]

Following on his angelology, Corbin concomitantly elaborated what might be called a unified field theory of religious experience. This theory rested on his conception of the *imaginal*.[24] He posited a suprasensible and submundane dimension of experience that he called the *mundus imaginalis* (*al-ʿalam al-mithal* in Arabic), a "*third world* halfway between the world of sensible perception and the world of intelligibility."[25] With an admixture of ardor and erudition perhaps unparalleled in contempo-rary scholarship, Corbin argued for the ontological reality of the objects of visionary experience. In careful contrast to the merely *imaginative* projections of the human psyche, he coined the celebrated term *imaginal* to refer to this reality.[26] This emphasis on the reality of the imagination's objects has made Corbin a favorite of theorist of poetics for decades, culminating in his preeminent influence on James Hillman's post-Jungian archetypal psychology, predicated as it is on a "poetic basis of mind."[27]

THE IMAM PARZIFAL: THE IDEA OF THE INCOGNITO, AND "*LA NOTION DE GUIDE*"

I come now to my main concern, Corbin's theory of hidden authority. *The idea of incognito* dominated the discourse of Henry Corbin and re-mained at the center of his "notion of the guide."[28] One need not be distracted by the charlatan example of Madame Blavatsky, who channeled the Mahatmas from Tibet, to find serious occultist claims of hidden mastery that influenced Corbin. Though such examples can be found in the recent history of Western Occultism, of which literature he was a dazzling master, Corbin located his primary models closer to his Iranian home. I am not the first to observe that Corbin's Islamicist mentor, Louis Massignon, enjoyed such an intense and sustained relationship with the tenth-century martyr al-Hallaj as to have seemed virtually possessed by that millennium-old Sufi master.[29] Corbin's uncanny relationship with another medieval mystical Muslim martyr, Suhrawardi, bears more than a passing resemblance to Massignon's with al-Hallaj. Still, Corbin never personalized this phenomenon, never encouraged some literalistic overemphasis on time travel, astral body, or mere reincarnation. Instead, he argued for the "spiritual" centrality of guidance beyond geography and temporality. He grounded this defense, perhaps most importantly, in Shi'i imamology, especially in the Occultation, *ghayba*, of the last Imam.

Even here, in his treatment of Shi'ite imamology, the central institution of the imamate and its eschatology, Corbin still sustained a markedly Aryan emphasis. The Iranian case recapitulated for him the chivalric Parzifal of the Grail legend.[30] The Grail Castle, located in "The Cosmic North," is the spiritual center, the goal of the true chivalric Quest.[31] The operatic Corbin, who characterized Jung's *Response to Job* as an "oratorio," could declaim that "one cannot . . . speak of the Temple of the Grail without opening one's inner vision and hearing the musical dramas of Richard Wagner."[32] Similarly, in conflating German and Persian "angels" (the Teutonic Valkyrie and the Persian Fravarti), he asserted that

> the theme of comparative research consociating Fravartis and Walkyries, would reveal all its potentialities *only on condition of searching, even of calling, for its reflowering in the course of time.* We recall here a conversation with the late Gerhard (*sic*) van der Leeuw, who himself, as a good phenomenologist, could do justice to Richard Wagner on this point.[33] As he pointed out, and as we wholly agreed, though Wagner treated the ancient Sagas in a very personal manner, he at least had a penetrating and subtle comprehension of the ancient Germanic beliefs.[34]

Zarathustra, Parzival, and the Hidden Imam, then, are secret Aryan rulers in the darkness, higher entities who guide us in our blindness toward the light. These hidden beings he traced to pre-Islamic Mazdaism.

> To live long years of meditation in Iran, encountering beings whose spiritual and religious individuality is among the most rebellious with regards to orthodoxy . . . to live among these naked mountain summits, iridescent against the heavens, which seem to virtually retain, and summon, the very dreams

and visions for which they have so long formed the background . . . perhaps, after all, there is some continuity of celestial presences which imposes itself here, presences which once transfigured this land through the holiest Light of Mazdaism, the Xvarnah.[35]

This Light was passed to the Imans. Corbin asserted many times, with various permutations that "[the imamate] is a spiritual kingship above the visible world that operates incognito, something like the role of the dynasty of the Grail."[36] The Hidden Imam, like the eternal Parzifal, is a world master in occultation, a Pole, one who upholds the world in his invisibility, "since it is through them that the effusion of divine grace still arrives in this world; and if it should ever happen that an epoch were deprived of them, the world would perish in an irreversible catastrophe."[37]

Corbin expanded this theory of the Pole who upholds the world to encompass a general phenomomenology of the visionary, one that universally posited an imaginal reality of hidden, distant, or ancient masters. Such paradigms of hidden authority as Zarathustra, the Hidden Imam, or Parzifal—there are many more in the Corbinian oeuvre—ultimately were subsumed, however, into Corbin's metapolitical agenda. As I have tried to show, he anticipated, called for, even demanded, the reconstitution of a hidden order, a chivalric order, one obviously presuming political action, though of an entirely cryptic kind.[38] This call to collective action naturally assumed that the hidden masters, the secret knights, exert not only authority but some specifiable kind of direction.

"SPIRITUAL MEANING CAN BE REVOLUTIONARY": VISIONARY KINGSHIP IN THE GEOPOLITICS OF THE COLD WAR

The question of direction, therefore, should next be pursued. What human guides led Corbin, and in what direction? I turn now to Corbin's most powerful postwar patrons, the Shah of Iran and Paul Mellon.

The crescendo of Corbin's intimate relation with the Shah's Pahlavi regime, perhaps, was the spectacular 1971 activities commemorating the two thousand five hundredth anniversary of the "founding of the Persian Empire" by the Emperor Cyrus. Included in these events, sponsored by the throne and directed by a small committee that included Corbin, were elaborate publications, including the *Acta Iranica* and the massive *Commemoration Cyrus*.[39] In 1974, the Shahbanou, Farah Diba, the Empress of Iran, created the Imperial Iranian Academy of Philosophy. Its flagship journal, *Sophia Perennis*, edited by Corbin's disciple Seyyed Hossein

Nasr, carried a programmatic essay by Corbin as its lead article.[40] The Imperial Iranian Academy of Philosophy also published his major editing projects and sponsored one of his last books.[41]

Beyond such sponsorship, Corbin's closeness to the throne can be seen more directly in his influence on the self-understanding of the Shah and his wife. The Imperial couple, Francophone and Franophile by cultural background and inclination, drew indirectly on Corbin's construction of Iranian spirituality in various published statements.[42] Particularly striking are the official interviews with the Shah published in 1977.[43] In a chapter titled "The Divine Spark," the Emperor of Emperors, His Imperial Majesty Shahanshah Aryamehr claimed mystical visions and lifelong divine guidance, invoked the twelfth Imam, denounced modernity and Marxism, and counterpointed the material and spiritual realms—all themes favored by Corbin. The Shah claimed, pointedly, that "the spiritual [world] seeks to maintain good traditions of the mind, the spirit, the morals, the religion and the ethos and civilisation of the Aryans."[44] Moreover, Corbin was an intimate of the Pahlavi high functionary Feyridoun Hoveyda, who published a virtually hagiographic article on him, in French, shortly after the disasters of 1978.[45] A year before Corbin died and Khomeini returned, Nasr had already written an equally hagiographic overview on Corbin, followed with his bibliography, in an issue of *Sophia Perennis* dedicated to the venerable French sage. The disciple could be quite explicit about the master's influence on "the Prime Minister, Amir Abbas Hoveyda, who has known Corbin since his own student days in Paris and who is an avid reader of Corbin's works."[46] Nasr, even closer to the throne, as a young man in 1972 had been made president of Aryamehr Institute of Technology.[47] Such examples can be multiplied.[48]

The Pahlavi impact on Corbin was of course direct and fundamental, and it did not go unacknowledged. His masterwork, the four-volume *En Islam iranien*, bears the inscription (as I translate it from the French): "This work is published with support accorded on the occasion of the 2500th anniversary of the Iranian Empire by The National Iranian Society of Petroleum, the Iranian Ministry of Culture and Arts, and The National Iranian Commisssion for UNESCO/the Center for the Study and Presentation of Iranian Culture."[49] Similarly, in the last paragraph of his monumental *History of Islamic Philosophy*, he announced "an event of major importance for the intellectual life of Iran: the multiplication of Iranian universities with the encouragement of the reigning sovereign, Muhammad Rida Shah Pahlavi."[50]

In addition to the support of the Iranian regime, it is also important to note Bollingen support for Corbin. The Bollingen Foundation was founded and funded by the oil magnate Paul Mellon, which also served as patron of the Eranos meetings, for which it provided subsidization. Mellon's Gulf Oil controlled vast interests in Iran.[51] Corbin's self-described "spiritual" Iran served the Shah's "imperial" Iran, a Cold War ally who stabilized extraction of petroleum for a billionaire American, who in turn, from his profits, subsidized that "spiritual" self-image.

I am aware that some may protest that this line of inquiry is irrelevant to our understanding of Corbin. But how is it inappropriate to speak of petroleum geopolitics in reference to a man who entered the intimate circles of the prime minister of an major oil exporter; whose major work was funded by its oil cartel; and who was the recipient of lavish patronage from the personal foundation of the "oil baron" who supported that state and controlled as much 40 percent of that cartel? Certainly, in the case of the historical study in hand, such patronage is a legitimate object of inquiry.[52]

THE ART OF WRITING AND
THE THEORY OF SECRET AUTHORITY

How then are we to assess the patron Mellon's impact on Corbin? One prewar insight into this postwar question presents itself.[53] Their connection came through Carl G. Jung. On 24 June 1936, in a seminar on Nietzsche's Zarathustra, Jung spoke on the topic of spiritual directors. The ancient Essenes were gnostics, he claimed, who initiated John the Baptist, and through him, Jesus of Nazareth. And how did Jung explain this initiation? He used the term *Ergriffenheit*.[54] Evoking "a catastrophic wind that breaks into social existence" (*Brausewind*), he described it as

> the simile for the peculiar collective movement by which people are seized, *ergriffen*. . . . That is the manifestation of the spirit in its most original form. So a savior is one who seizes, the *Ergreifer* who catches people like objects and whirls them into a form which lasts as long as the whirlwind lasts, and then the thing collapses and something new must come. That is the great wind described in the Pentecostal miracle.[55]

Jung's notion of *Ergiffenheit*, being seized by a cyclonic archetype, was taken up by the founder of the Eranos group, Olga Froebe-Kapteyn, who used it to epitomize the daimonic imperative of her group, founded in the fateful year 1933. When Corbin wrote a retrospective on the group, and later when Gershom Scholem wrote his own reflections on Eranos, they returned nostalgically to the term *Ergriffenheit*.[56]

This usage is further clarified when one reads the subsequent passage in Jung's 1936 Zarathustra lecture. This brings us back to the topic of this chapter. Jung went on to observe that "[These ancient gnostics] were sort of *directeurs de conscience* for rich people at courts, and we have evidence that they were called in in cases of particularly ticklish dreams."[57] Here Jung suggests that the spiritual director, a dream analyst for rich folks, is the *Ergriefer*, one who seizes. And who is seized? *One* who was swept up in these claims was in attendance that day in 1936. She was a rich American woman, perhaps the richest American woman. She was Mary Conover Mellon (1904–1946), a patient and devotee of Jung.[58] It was through her devotion, and later in her memory, that her husband Paul Mellon established the Bollingen Foundation, which subsequently funded Jung, Corbin, and Eliade on and off until each enjoyed the stabilization of his fame.[59]

Another figure who not incidentally connected Jung with Mellon was the founding director of the CIA, Allen Dulles. Dulles, who spent much time with Jung during World War II while he was station chief of the OSS in Zurich, later personally exculpated both Jung and Olga Froebe-Kapteyn from accusations of having been Nazi sympathizers.[60] Mellon served in intelligence during the war, while Dulles was instrumental in securing needed foreign oil reserves for the Cold War, oil reserves that were of course also beneficial to Mellon's Gulf Oil. Kermit Roosevelt, the CIA operative responsible for fomenting the 1953 Iranian coup in support of the Shah, was later made a vice-president of Mellon's Gulf Oil Corporation.[61]

What did Corbin learn from Jung? It should be remembered that Jung was sometimes designated the "Spiritus Rector" of Eranos, though he apparently never referred to himself this way.[62] Jung thus modeled a certain type of mastership, that of a master who denied he was a master, a master openly in hiding, a gnostic spiritual director. As such, he provided a living example to the younger scholar.

HIDDEN IDEOLOGY: HISTORY OF RELIGIONS AS "PROPHETIC PHILOSOPHY"

But of course Corbin was not a psychologist. What *was* Henry Corbin? I do not mean what was his religion, though it is itself not obvious that Corbin was either a Christian or a Muslim. I want to frame my conclusion instead as an answer to the vexing question not of his religious identity but of his professional identity.

One might well conclude with the obvious perception that Henry Corbin was what he seemed to be, an academic Islamicist. But his object of inquiry was "Islam" only in his imaginal sense. That is, by "Islam" he did not mean the Islam of Muhammad, the Qur'an, or the *shar'iah*, and certainly not that of Ayatollah Khomeini. One searches in vain in his many books, in fact, for any sustained discussion of Muhammad, the Qur'an, or religious law, not to speak of Islamic society in any form whatsoever. Instead, Corbin found in Islam the gnosticism he needed to transcend "the catastrophe of the Church," the "legalism" and "literalism" he demonized as "Ahriman." And it was furthermore in the Shi'ite notion of the Hidden Imam that Corbin discovered this needed gnosis.[63]

What then was he, if not an Islamicist? Corbin, as I have tried to show, also was neither of the other things usually said of him: he was neither a historian of religions nor an academic philosopher. At various points he makes this explicit.[64] In fact, what he practiced was nothing less than prophetic philosophy. As he put it in his major statement on "The Situation of Esoterism": "All this calls for a prophetic philosophy going hand in hand with an esoterism."[65]

I can therefore legitimately conclude that Corbin understood himself to be a prophet, in his special sense of that term. That is, he claimed that the hidden master alone initiates the disciple, for "contemplative prophetism" recognizes no "dogmatic magistery or Council."[66] "The calling of a *nabi* [prophet] is the most personal of callings; it is never a function conferred (and still less exercised) by a collectivity or a magistery."[67] He was, in short, a self-designated prophet, one more explicitly so with every passing year.

CONCLUSION: DISCIPLESHIP AND THE AMPHIBIAN PROFESSOR

I have answered the question of Corbin's identity—he was not a professor so much as a prophet. Rather, more accurately, he was an amphibian professor, publicly holding a professorship at the Sorbonne while conducting a private war on reason. Corbin was an apostle to the classroom.[68] And indeed, he was a prophet who sought disciples among our students and received plenty of them. His successful appeal was an escape from open rational inquiry in favor of a more exciting, surreptitious quest. We must acknowledge that this appeal is dangerous once we admit, however unappealingly, that the emperor is naked: *that the esoteric art of writing is, in plain language, also a form of lying.* The esoteric writer feels obliged to dissemble, covering half-truths in something exotic like camouflage, or heavenly deception, or higher truth, or the idea of the incognito. But our work as historians of religion is pointless if it is not honest: we cannot have a functioning history of religions that operates incognito. I stand firm with Max Weber: "[I]n the lecture-rooms of the university no other virtue holds but plain intellectual integrity."[69]

Henry Corbin, I think, might not have been displeased to be charac-

terized as a *dangerous* man.[70] When he called for a "total spiritual renovation" ("totale rénovation spirituelle") he was calling for a final eschatological battle against the powers of darkness.[71] That is, he enjoined
nothing less than "combat for the Soul of the World."[72] He inveighed
against the Church and Hegel as sources of totalitarian darkness, in a
titanic Twilight of the Gods that would crush any adequacy of mere rational conversation.

Given, then, his apocalyptic insistence, we therefore are entitled (if not
obliged) to scrutinize his rhetoric of secret leadership carefully. What I
have found in the foregoing preliminary review of the evidence is that he
announced a leadership even as he deflected attention from it. Corbin's
"idea of the incognito" was that the gnostic elite need proceed esoterically, under the cloak of secrecy. My concern, to speak plainly, is that
such hidden authority demanded by Corbin was in fact but another spiri-
tualized version of an all too familiar assault on democracy and science.
Corbin's program, that is, fits with his cohort of European religious intellectuals in the Generation of 1914: a radical traditionalism, a revolutionary conservatism, a reactionary aggression that was profoundly, instructively, equivocal about—when it was not identical with— fascism.[73]

A final word on Corbin's "combat for the Angel," what one might call
the fight for the signifier. What he espoused was an authoritarian hermeneutic in which all is symbol, but nothing explicitly is symbolized.
Thus, open access, critical dialogue, community, are eliminated in favor
of a pseudomeritocracy of Masters of the Whole. They alone mediate the
Whole, for they alone are spiritually qualified hermeneuts of the symbol.
And how did this hermeneutic operate? In Corbin's occult science, the
principle of analogy reigned supreme; images meaningfully, almost magi-
cally, correspond to each another in an infinite play of signifiers. These
radically eclectic connections are not obvious on the surface of things but
must be revealed from the depths by the visionary leader. This
procedure is typical of what is called Traditionalism. The Traditionalist
school specializes in syncretism, in which the transcendent unity of world
religions proliferates endlessly analogous symbols, whose inner logic can
only be shown by a master.[74] As Umberto Eco has pointed out, this kind
of so-called Traditionalist syncretism is also a fundamental of fascist
thinking.[75] While I would not claim that Corbin was fascist, I am saying
that he cannot be understood historically unless he is seen in the light of
such contemporaneous themes in fascist thought.

Given what we now know about the life and work of Henry Corbin,
this assertion is not only fair but necessary. Though he rejected the notion of himself as historian, we historians are entitled (if not obliged) to
assess him in historical terms. These terms, I insist, must be apposite to
his occult politics and his syncretistic traditionalism. And since, on the

basis of this occultist syncretism, *he* declared war on *us*, and since his war on us more than circumstantially resembles related wars on modernity, we would in fact be obtuse not to register the worldly thrust of this otherworldly bellicosity. After all, those who adulate Corbin, and they are many, usually ignore his blatant aggression. But this pugnacity—what he called "the combat for the Angel"—is in his own terms inseparable from his scholarly production. I am addressing, in short, the central paradox of Henry Corbin's career: he declared war on the West but was warmly welcomed as a great Western Sage. So he should be. But perhaps this paradox, vivid and legitimate as it is, ought to force us to rethink the meaning, at least in his case, of the incognito assumed by such a "prophetic philosopher."

The concern of the present work is to recover the legacy of the History of Religions for the next generation of critical students of religion. Rather, my effort has been, at least, to reflect on the origins of that legacy in its era. One conclusion that emerges from reflecting at length on Corbin's "idea of incognito" is that it is only recoverable if it is historicized; if it is understood illuminated in the light of its times. If not, if it is taken literally, then Corbin—the nemesis of all literalisms—is betrayed. But he need not worry in his grave. His incognito was shouted to the rooftops, after all, and therefore, as a proudly proclaimed paradox, *cannot* be taken literally. This is not to say that I seek to unmask him and fail. It is to suggest, however, that the new History of Religions can only be self-respecting if it accepts its intellectual obligations to unmasking, when indicated, while simultaneously respecting the self behind the mask. We will be obliged to point out disguises when they conceal the truth; but we will also be obligated, equally, in perdurable deference, to honor, as indicated, the veils that may protect another truth.

Part IV

HISTORY

CHAPTER 10

Mystic Historicities

This awesome giant, our history . . . this great
creation, filled with explosive power, compounded
of vitality, wickedness and perfection . . .
—*Gershom Scholem*

COUNTER-HISTORY

Counter-history is ultimately more true than history.
—*Henry Corbin*

A stumbling block often encountered by new readers of Mircea Eliade is
the discovery that the History of Religions oddly is defined by its
opposition to history. Gershom Scholem's version of History of Religions
seemed to obviate this dilemma, inasmuch as he championed historical
research and the historical method. Henry Corbin used a variety of terms,
such as "imaginal" and "prophetic," to characterize his stridently antihistoricist Islamic studies. But all three shared a developed interest in
metahistory. Both Scholem and Corbin thus spoke of "historiosophy."
They also spoke of their own work in terms of a kind of "counter-history."[1] Corbin used the term himself, and Biale has effectively applied it
to describe Scholem's theory.[2]

Corbin seemed, of the three, to have developed, on a philosophical
basis, the foundations for a full-blown metahistory. "The epochs of the
spiritual world are totally different from the epochs of the exterior world
of geology or of sociopolitical history. The epochs of the spiritual world
make up a history *sui generis*, which is in its very essence *imaginal* history."[3] Elsewhere Corbin spoke of "metahistory" and "hierohistory."
Metahistory, he asserted, "bestows meaning on history, because it makes
it into a hierohistory. In the absence of metahistory—that is to say, in the
absence of anteriority 'in Heaven'—and in the absence of an eschatology,
to speak of a 'sense of history' is absurd."[4] Corbin adopted the related
conception of "historiosophy" from von Baader and Schelling. "By contrast, that which certain Western philosophers, like Baader, and Schelling,
have called *Historiosophy* would not be able to do without a metaphysics,

for if one ignores or excludes the hidden, esoteric sense of things, the living phenomena of this world are reduced to those of a cadaver."[5] Elsewhere he struck a Heideggerian note, invoking the notion of "being thrown into history," in order to underscore his preference for Historiosophy.

> Take note! When a man lets himself be thrown into history he can go through all the philosophies of history he likes, he can legislate in the name of a historical causality which ignores all metaphysic, he can behave like a complete agnostic. This is no longer possible when history is interiorised, integrated into man's consciousness. . . . Only that which theosophists like Franz von Baader or Schelling have so rightly named "historiosophy" can now be pursued.[6]

In the light of such claims for a counterhistory, it is surprising and instructive to recall that each produced major histories, including Scholem's *Sabbatai Sevi, the Mystical Messah*, Corbin's *History of Islamic Philosophy*, and Eliade's three-volume *A History of Religious Ideas*.[7] It may seem strange that these avowed exponents of counterhistory wrote such histories at all. And, to be sure, each articulated a distinctive explanation for his usually dialectical relationship with historical research. Corbin seems to have been the one unconflicted esoterist among them. But even he recognized that "such an esoterism . . . will have to attune itself to the 'historical trend.'"[8] Elsewhere, he explained the underpinning idea operative in such assumptions, to wit that "under the appearance of historical contingencies, the secret law that gives rhythm to spiritual history imposed itself."[9]

Thus, their notion of counterhistory implied a study into some secret inside historical time. By means of their presentation of their historical materials, beyond sheer philological expertise, the Eranos scholars appealed to their readership on the strength of a metahistorical hint—*that they know more than they are historically saying*. Rather than leave their readers with a merely humanistic understanding (*Verstehen*), they intimated *real* knowledge, immediacy, insight into the transhistorical depths of religious phenomena. However, by the lights of their own phenomenology, they studied religious history from an insurmountable distance. That is, the phenomenologists'-eye-view was said by its proponents to "perceive" structures that are abstractions, ideal types that do not exist as such. This argument makes up the brunt of the classic treatment of phenomenology of religion, Van der Leeuw's *Religion in Essence and Manifestation*.[10] In "bracketing" the life world out of phenomenological enframement, the religious "realities" left on view are those of an ideal type, a *univers imaginaire*. Thus, Henry Corbin, Gershom Scholem, and Mircea Eliade each argued mightily that a *metahistorical reality* is involved. Henry Corbin claimed that the *imaginal* is actual; Mircea Eliade equated "sacred" with "reality"; and Gershom Scholem asserted that a "religious reality" transcends social life.[11] In other words, each posited a distinctive form of "reality" that was at once symbolic and "really real."

THROUGH THE WALL OF TIME

> And perhaps it wasn't so much the key that was missing, but courage: courage to venture out into an abyss, which one day could end up in us our-selves, courage also to penetrate through the sym-bolic plain and through the wall of history.
> —*Gershom Scholem*

This "religious reality" was characterized by its transcendence of time. Eliade thus included a chapter in his collection *Myth and Reality*, which bears the title "Time Can be Overcome."[12] Behind this idea lurked the inspiration of Réné Guénon, whose assertions on this score typically were apodictic. "He who cannot escape from the standpoint of temporal suc-cession so as to see all things in their simultaneity is incapable of the least conception of the metaphysical order."[13] One who did imply his own escape from "the standpoint of temporal succession" was Eliade's coedi-tor of *Antaios*, Ernst Jünger.[14] Shortly after beginning the *Antaios* proj-ect, Jünger published a book called *Against the Wall of Time* (*An die Zeitmauer*).[15] Eliade's position blended his influences from Jung and Guénon, among others. It was definitively articulated in the fateful sum-mer of 1968, when he was still coediting *Antaios* with Jünger: "The structure of the sacred in the human consciousness is built on the struc-ture of synchronicity, as opposed to the diachronic structure of radical historicism."[16]

Throughout his sprawling corpus, Eliade returned to the concept of the abolition of time as the key to access to the sacred. His most explicit discussion, perhaps, is to be found in his 1952 Eranos lecture "Indian Symbolisms of Time and Eternity."[17] Here he states this proposition pow-erfully.

The total present, the eternal present of the mystics, is stasis or non-dura-tion. . . . He whose thought is stable and for whom time no longer flows, lives in an eternal present. . . . The 'favorable moment' of enlightenment may be compared with the flash that communicates a revelation, or with the mystical ecstasy which is prolonged, paradoxically, beyond time. . . . All this proves, I think, that there is no break in continuity between the man of the archaic societies and the mysticisms attaching to the great historical religions: both are striving with the same strength, though by different means, against *memory* and Time.[18]

This theory is elaborated in *Yoga*, which, in its final paragraph, concludes that the ideal of Yoga "is to live in an 'eternal present,' outside of time."[19]

Henry Corbin, for his part, proposed a distinctively esoteric theory of time, "discontinuous, qualitative, pure, psychic time."[20] The absolute discontinuity of time means, for the Prophetic Philosopher (as Corbin styled himself), that things do not cause others things to happen.[21]

> The fundamental idea is this: visible, apparent, outward states, in short, phenomena, can never be the causes of other phenomena. The agent is the invisible, the immaterial. Compassion acts and determines, it causes things to be and to become like itself, because it is a spiritual state, *and its mode of action has nothing to do with what we call physical causality*, rather, as its very name indicates, its mode of action is *sympatheia*.[22]

The encounter with theophany, with transfigured reality, utterly alters the sense of time itself, leading to ". . . the idea of tradition whose line is vertical, longitudinal (from Heaven to Earth), a tradition whose moments are independent of the causality of a continuous physical time."[23] There are, for Corbin, two kinds of time: lived psychic time and abstract psychic time, one successive and one simultaneous.[24] "The only 'historical causality' is the relations of will between acting subjects."[25] History is composed of "connections without cause."[26]

> If the chronological succession does not suffice to give us knowledge of a causal historical filiation between these recurrences, at least we see arising between them the continuity of a "hierophanic time," which corresponds not to the external history of the sects and schools connected with the Gnosis, but to the cyclical presence of their "archetype," to their common participation in the same cosmic dramaturgy.[27]

For this concept of "hierophanic time," Corbin cited Eliade's *Patterns in Comparative Religion*, the original French version of which had appeared not long before.[28] Elsewhere, Corbin drew on Eliade to establish the metahistorical basis for his hermeneutics in what, borrowing from E. Souriau, he called "the founding will":

> What really confers meaning is the historically new fact, the founding will which brought possibilities into flower, into being-in-the-present then and there. . . . As personal act, this 'philosophical founding' is an irreproachable witness to the significance *in action* of a motif, and leads the possibility of the past back into the present. It is essentially a *hermeneutic*—by *under-*

standing it, the interpreter implicitly takes on responsibility for what he understands. This is also what Mircea Eliade refers to as a 'valuation of hierophanies.'[29]

Scholem, of the three, was far and away the least explicit in his concern for the abolition of time. Perhaps his most important published comments are to be found in his 1962 Eranos lecture, "Revelation and Tradition as Religious Categories in Judaism."[30] He sets the tone with a lengthy, evocative citation from J. F. Molitor, which begins, "Scripture crystallizes incessantly flowing time and sets forth the evanescent word as a perpetual present with firm and lasting features."[31] Scholem underscores the eternal character of Torah, according to the Rabbis, who "make absolute the concept of tradition in which the meaning of revelation unfolds in the course of historical time—but only because everything that can come to be known has already been deposited in a timeless stratum."[32] The "course of historical time," the timelessness of its source notwithstanding, is the bearer of revelation. With this emphasis in mind it may be possible, perhaps, to identify Scholem's response to Eliade's notion of the abolition of time. I suggest that this response may be found in "On Sin and Punishment. Some Remarks concerning Biblical and Rabbinical Ethics," the contribution made by the Kabbalah scholar to Eliade's Festschrift, *Myths and Symbols*. "According to the Kabbalists, the infinite can operate unbroken and without conflicts only in the infinite itself. It is the nature of the decision to create which makes such a conflict-free action impossible; it must call forth an entanglement and disharmony in everything finite. But with this, I fear, we are already far away from the original point of departure of our Biblical consideration."[33]

CREATIO EX NIHILO AS ERROR

Corbin was trained and practiced as a philosopher, by contrast to the historians Scholem and Eliade.[34] But "more" than a "mere" academic philosopher of religion, Corbin explicitly identified himself as a "prophetic philosopher," to use his own designation. One of his primary tasks, then, was to set forth nothing less than a "prophetic philosophy," a historiosophy, a visionary history of this and all the other worlds, rhythmically recurring through the *Weltalter*, the Ages of the World.

Eternal recurrence, with its myth of worlds following cyclically on earlier worlds, thus directly displaced the monotheistic doctrine of *creatio ex nihilo*, creation out of nothing in a moment in time.[35] *Creatio ex nihilo*, for Corbin, becomes the world as imagination.

We might even go so far as to ask whether there is not a necessary correlation between this idea of a *creatio ex nihilo* and the degradation of the ontologically creative Imagination and whether, in consequence, the degeneration of the Imagination into a fantasy productive only of the imaginary and the unreal is not the hallmark of our laicized world for which the foundations were laid by the preceding religious world, which precisely was dominated by this characteristic idea of the creation.[36]

Corbin let there be no mistakes on this score: "Creation is not *ex nihilo* but a theophany. As such, it is Imagination."[37] Real creation takes place inside the divine, in a "*histoire intradivine*, non pas une Histoire du sensordinaire de ce mot, mais une Histoire intemporelle, éternellement achevée et éternellement commençante, donc simultanément et éternellement tout entière (*simul tota*) sous tous les formes et à toutes les ètapes de son autogénération comme Dieu personnel."[38]

Scholem had already alluded to the transformation of this *creatio ex nihilo* from the rabbinic to the Kabbalistic conception, in *Major Trends in Jewish Mysticism*, to the effect that "creation out of nothing thus becomes the symbol of emanation."[39] He began his 1956 Eranos lecture, "The Creation out of Nothing and the Self-Contraction of God," with a citation of Eliade on the general absence of a concept of *creatio ex nihilo* in the History of Religions at large.[40] Scholem thus remarked, rather pointedly, on the distinctiveness of this Jewish concept. Scholem's citation of Eliade relied on the latter's celebrated and widely cited emphasis on myths of creation as rituals of repetition.[41]

Creatio ex nihilo, a fundamental conception in the history of monotheistic thought, thus was marginalized by the three Historians of Religions. Each did so by means of a selectivity, a choice to look consistently elsewhere in their respective subjects. The resulting emphasis was that of a kind of gnostic preference for a certain alternative mythic scenario. Instead of a personal God willing Creation out of nothing at a moment in time, Corbin and Eliade preferred instead the recurring, cyclic process of birth and rebirth inside the divine life—theogonic process, in their favored phrase from Schelling. While there is little reason to doubt that this was indeed an enduring preference in the esoteric traditions, it is not nearly so obvious that these esoterisms were central to the monotheisms as such. In other words, the centrality of esoterism stressed by the Historians of Religions may have shunted aside the claims these monotheisms normatively made about themselves. In so nudging God from His role as Creator within these traditions, they could shove into His place Nature, or Life, or the Cosmos. For this move they drew from *Naturphilosophie*. And to this extent, Scholem parted company with Eliade and Corbin.

"PERFECT NATURE" AND NATURPHILOSOPHIE

Das Judentum ist die Historie selber.
—*Gershom Scholem*

The secret law governing history is a law of nature—but not empirical nature, and therefore not natural law. Rather, historical reality is conditioned by the laws identified in the philosophical tradition known as *Naturphilosophie*.[42] This view was popularized by Corbin as "The Hermetic Idea of Perfect Nature."[43] Corbin's scintillating exposition of this idea so impressed Scholem that he cited it, as illumination of Kabbalistic symbolism, in two of his Eranos essays. Most strikingly, he concluded his Eranos debut, "Kabbalah and Myth," with this citation, explicitly citing Corbin.

> But if symbols spring from a reality that is pregnant with feeling and illumined by the colorless light of intuition, and if, as has been said, all *fulfilled* time is mythical, then surely we may say this: what greater opportunity has the Jewish people ever had than in the horror of defeat, in the struggle and victory of these last years, in its utopian withdrawal into its own history, to fulfil its encounter with its own genius, its true and "perfect nature"?[44]

Elsewhere, Scholem explained that this "seeing of one's own self is thus turned from a prophetic into a messianic experience."[45] This eschatology also recurs, perhaps tellingly, in Scholem's contribution to Corbin's *Festschrift*.[46] Scholem's use of "perfect nature," to be sure, was explicitly beholden to Corbin.[47] Again, in his essay "Walter Benjamin and His Angel," he borrowed from Corbin to illuminate the personal philosophy of his dear friend Benjamin.[48]

History itself assumes mystical properties when, on its encounter with "perfect nature," its true personality as Anthropos is revealed. Nature itself, the entirety of the cosmos, by means of the illuminated imagination, can be seen, that is, as a Great Man, Macanthropos.[49] The Historians of Religions wrote extensively on this theme. Personification of Nature is the essential teaching of *Naturphilosophie*, from which intellectual tradition they variously descended.[50] Eliade was the one writer of the three who explicitly placed this notion at the center of his thought. His widely used textbook, *The Sacred and the Profane: The Nature of Religion*, includes as its central chapter "The Sacredness of Nature and Cosmic Religion."[51] "Cosmic Religion" was Eliade's shorthand for his theory of sacred nature, of which he was exceedingly proud. Thus, for example, on 1 June 1960, he noted in his journal, "I think I can count myself among the rare Europeans who have succeeded in revaluing nature, by discovering the dialectic of hierophanies and the structure of cosmic religiosity."[52]

Nature, when "perfected," reveals transcendence and freedom transparently through it. For Eliade, alchemy "implicitly pursues the 'perfecting' of nature—that is, in the last analysis, its absolution and freedom."[53] In one of his final public lectures, he again stressed the point that "the tendency of nature is toward perfection."[54] Ending (as he began) on an eschatological note, Eliade carried this tendency into the present, suggesting the existence of a contemporary *Naturphilosophie* holding that "everything in the universe possesses consciousness."[55]

Here again Scholem balked. In the name of Jewish theology he rejected *Naturphilosophie*. "Any living Judaism, no matter what its concept of God, will have to oppose pure naturalism with a definite no."[56] To be sure, some pantheistic Jewish thinkers of the Middle Ages went so far as to assert that "reality itself as a whole is the mystical shape of the deity," imagined at times as a celestial Man, a Universal Anthropos.[57] But "Jewish faith in God the Creator will maintain its place, beyond all images and myths, when it is a matter of choosing an alternative: the world as Creation and the world as something that creates itself by chance."[58]

On this point, Scholem's personal commitment forced him to part company, decisively, from Corbin and Eliade. By his personal commitment I mean not to Judaism but rather to the theologico-political project of Zionism. It cannot be emphasized strongly enough that this crucial factor led Scholem to reject a soteriology of nature. In plain terms, Scholem alone of the three committed himself to identifying with and living publicly in a religious community, a corporate religion with a political profile. This commitment he took seriously enough to face squarely the real question: "*Whether, when, and in what form religion will be an effective force in society.*"[59] Corbin and Eliade chose esoterism, which by definition begs this question, avoiding a public accounting of its demands.

In the end, Scholem did not break off his fruitful conversation with them, but he did see their *Naturphilosophie*, it would seem, as a smuggled sort of secularization. "It smuggles an absolute value into a world which could never have formed it out of its own resources, a value pointing surreptitiously to a teleology of Creation which is, after all, disavowed from a purely naturalistic rationalistic view of the world."[60] Theirs was a *trans*rationalistic naturalism, but one that, nonetheless, aspired to the perfecting of nature as the consummation of history. Their alternative science, predicated on this view, was nothing less than a gnosis, a project of Redemption. Corbin insisted without the least equivocation that this project proceeds not as a public activity in building a new society, but rather secretly, "in the night of symbols."

If a certain science of our times views Nature [as a corpse], it may be said that it is this transgression which all esoterisms have subsequently tried to redeem, and that is their significance for a spiritual history invisible to historians of external events . . . no esoterism, until the coming of the Iman, can be anything more than a *witness*, recognized by a small number, ridiculed by all the others, and not progressing except in the night of symbols.[61]

Speaking not of this esoterism but of "pure," that is, rationalistic secularization, Scholem answered his own question concerning "whether, when, and in what form religion will be an effective force in society." He did so not with a prophecy but with a prescription. "I consider a dialogue with such secularization about its validity, legitimacy, and limitations as fruitful and decisive."[62] *Mutatis mutandis*, the same may be said of his conversation with Corbin and Eliade.

REALIZED ESCHATOLOGY

When one encountered one's "perfect nature," a new condition, entirely renovated, replaced the tired life of the old world. Scholem expressed this total renewal in terms of traditional Jewish messianism. "[W]hat was formerly taken as a state of redemption, especially in its messianic connotations, by now becomes the condition in which alone true human experience is possible. The unredeemed state is no longer worthy to be called human. The redeemed state is where human experience begins."[63] Corbin defined the *corpus mysticum*—in a phrase ironically anticipating current jargon—as "virtual paradise."[64] The favored and repeated anecdote Corbin used to exemplify this point came from his meeting with D. T. Suzuki. This story is worth reproducing at length.

I should like to mention a conversation, which strikes me as memorable, with D. T. Suzuki, the master of Zen Buddhism (Casa Gabriella, Ascona, August 18, 1954, in the presence of Mrs. Fröbe-Kapteyn and Mircea Eliade). We asked him what his first encounter with Occidental spirituality had been and learned that some fifty years before Suzuki had translated four of Swedenborg's works into Japanese; this had been his first contact with the West. Later on in the conversation we asked him what homologies in structure he found between Mahayana Buddhism and the cosmology of Swedenborg in respect of the symbolism and correspondences of the world. . . . Of course we expected not a theoretical answer, but a sign attesting in a concrete person of an experience common to Buddhism and Swedenborgian spirituality. And I can still see Suzuki suddenly brandishing a spoon and saying with a smile: "This spoon *now* exists in paradise . . ." "We are *now* in Heaven," he explained.[65]

At the end of his life, Corbin came to call this present condition of perfection "realized eschatology." In his most revealing and confessional essay, published four years before his death, Corbin extrapolated from the evidence of the Dead Sea Scrolls community to posit a universal condition of perfected time.

> The time of the prophets and of prophetic visions was not *within* the time of History. The Copernican reversal of the question was made necessary by the existential phenomenology of the *Imago Templi* that we are attempting to elucidate. Faced with a Church which had become a historical power and a society in the time of this world, the longing for the Temple is a longing for . . . a present which is not the limit of past and future in historical time, but the *nunc* of an eternal Presence. This "realized eschatology" was the restoration of Paradise, the restoration of the human condition to its celestial status.[66]

"The existential phenomenology of the *Imago Templi*" is eternal Presence—accessible in this instant, the now. Just as, in the mystic historicity, the sequence of moments in the past are made concurrent in the heart of the gnostic, so too is the future now present, eternally. The Eschaton is realized. Now's the time.

EPOCHE AS MESSIANIC TIME

> All prophets—there is no exception—have prophesied only for the messianic time (*epoche*). As for future time, what eye has seen it except you, Lord, who will act for him who is faithful to you and keeps waiting.
> —*Maurice Blanchot*

The phenomenological *epoche* pioneered by Husserl was transformed in the phenomenology of religion practiced at Eranos.[67] The first, intervening transformation of *epoche* came at the hands of Husserl's student, Heidegger. Also much influenced by Heidegger, and soon substantially to influence Eliade, Gerardus van der Leeuw then made *epoche* central to "the phenomenology of religion" and in this role stood as a presiding presence in the first meetings at Eranos.[68] By contrast, Corbin was fervently committed to the absolute truth prophetically and theophanically revealed by "phenomena." And that truth, at the end of his life, was revealed to be the mystical reality of a Temple Order. "The phenomenologist's task is now to discover a *counter-history* 'more true than history' in the evidence *a parte post* of the Templar tradition—evidence that confirms the secret survival of the Order of the Temple until its resurgence."[69]

The Historians of Religions, in the final, postwar phase of their theoretical development, recapitulated a minimessianic moment. Phenomenological "bracketing" (*epoche*) paralleled a (putatively temporary) release from norms, which release they asserted to typify the final time. The phenomenologist in this sense appeared as a living precursor of a future condition, of that "redeemed" condition in which characteristically human sympathies are suspended. The phenomenologist thus operated in a kind of paradisal space made possible by a "perfect nature" presumptively available now.

"MY OWN PERSONAL CREDO"

> There are those for whom the past is over. There
> are those for whom the past is still to come.
> —*Henry Corbin*

Scholem, it would appear, lived not merely in his prized paradoxes, but in Zeno's paradox especially. Infinitely deferred but always drawing closer, the messianic era will never quite arrive. Scholem, who began his college studies in mathematics, discovered that the concept of the asymptotic best described this perpetually progressive nonarrival. "The discursive thinking of the Kabbalists is a kind of asymptotic process."[70] Even within the Kabbalistic system, he argued that the *sefirot* "approach the substance of the *Ein-Sof* asymptotically . . ."[71] Yet more strikingly, at the conclusion of one of his most personal essays, he applied this same metaphor to his dear friend Walter Benjamin. Benjamin's last writings suggested that the Messiah can enter at any second. This, according to Scholem, summed up "the Judaism . . . Walter Benjamin approached asymptotically throughout his life, without ever attaining it."[72] Here again, as was the case with *coincidentia oppositorum*, one finds the descriptive and biographical conflated.

On the other hand, perfection is possible *now*. Eliade famously evoked the "terror of history" even as he called up the very real possibility of "transcending the human condition" *now*.[73] The power of such concepts as "virtual paradise" and "realized eschatology" and "perfect nature" and "the redeemed state" is that they bear in their very character a presumption of perfection *now*. Their reader thus is led, however implicitly, to see that no one is excluded from such potential. Even if one is not perfect now, this perennial possibility of perfection, in such reading, becomes a "religious reality" *now*.

Scholem, in what he called his "personal credo," summed up this felt sense of the inadequacy of anything less than redemption. But the irony of the ages, according to his conception, was that precisely this messianic expectation cast the length of history into an asymptotically extended shadow. He felt an acute, even poignant, sense that the price of messianism, in the meantime, is that "there is nothing concrete which can be accomplished by the unredeemed."[74] Here may be the annunciation of the condition Lutz Niethammer has called *Posthistoire*.[75] In the Messianic era the "forbidden is permitted," just as certain holy men were said to be "beyond law," even in this posthistorical era. Thus, the ultimate *coincidentia oppositorum* for history presents an apocalypse now, realized eschatology, the end of history inside history.

For the Historians of Religion, history was less and more than it appeared in the eyes of literalistic historicists. It was less because, especially for Eliade, this Idealism demanded that the only really real is the sacred.[76] "Whatever the historical context in which he is placed, *homo religiosus* believes that there is an absolute reality, *the sacred*, which transcends this world but manifests itself in this world, thereby sanctifying it and making it real."[77] But history was more, too. It was more than merely passing phenomena because history, in miniature, could symbolize the vastest events of the cosmos. This representation was perceptible, however, only to the "ones who know." As Scholem put it, "The history of the world unfolds according to an inner law that is the hidden law of the divine nature itself. *Every gnosis transforms history into a symbol of cosmic processes*."[78] Corbin quite similarly speaks of "that history which for Shiʻites, theosophists and Ismailis is nothing but the metaphor of The True Reality."[79] For Eliade, the transformation of history into symbol took various forms. Perhaps his most emphatic example concerned the world-historically unique contribution of what he called "Judaeo-Christianity." "[The] great originality of Judaeo-Christianity was the transfiguration of History of theophany. . . . From the standpoint of the history of religions, Judaeo-Christianity presents us with the supreme hierophany: *the transfiguration of the historical event into hierophany*."[80]

All these mystic historicities reversed the normal expectations one brings into the reading of concrete events. For those few capable of an extraordinary apprehension of symbols, the concreteness of event is rendered transparent, as a stunning reversal occurs: history itself becomes a symbol, the world itself a theophany, the created universe a glyph to be deciphered. In a sense the glove is tugged inside out as the cosmos becomes myth and myth in turn turns into a cosmos unto itself. In this reversed world, appearance and reality trade places in a strange and perhaps dangerous dance. "In short, if we are to achieve a phenomenology which is integrally true, we must see things and perceive each other as we would if we were 'decorporized,' at least momentarily, so that the appearance would actually be the *apparition* of what *is* in reality, with nothing external to misrepresent what is inward."[81] Scholem, for one, recognized the dangers of such an exquisite dissolution. "Utterly free, fettered by no law or authority, this 'Life' never ceases to produce forms and to destroy what it has produced. It is the anarchic promiscuity of all living things. In this bubbling cauldron, this continuum of destruction, the mystic plunges."[82] To be thus taken apart and put back together backward—the very mystery of rebirth, for Eliade—was not merely dangerous, but the ultimate, exemplary danger.[83] "By crossing, in ecstasy, the 'dangerous' bridge that connects the two worlds and that only the dead can attempt, the shaman proves that he is spirit, is no longer a human being . . . the mystical experience of the 'primitives' is a return to origins, a reversion to the mystical age of the lost paradise."[84] The counterhistory employed by the Historians of Religions, at the risk of this *daimonic*, risked all—and won, at least insofar as they passed symbolically through some such transformation in their telling of this particular tale, this story of the mystic's history according to the History of Religions.

CHAPTER 11

The Chiliastic Practice of Islamic Studies According to Henry Corbin

> I am still waiting for an apocalyptic angel with a key to this abyss.
> —*J. G. Hamann, cited by Martin Heidegger*

ONE must study the totality of Corbin's published work to understand that this great Islamicist was something other than an Islamicist.[1] He wrote what he came to call "prophetic philosophy," a kind of esoteric science complemented by the acceptable apparatus of footnotes.[2] Influences on this elaborate conception, however, have not yet been traced in full, though many of them are by now well known. Corbin's esoterism blended medieval philosophy, occultism, History of Religions, Lutheran theology, Shi'ite ideology, into a brilliantly polished, absolutely authentic, and utterly irreproducible mixture. It is my conviction that he may have been the most sophisticated and learned esoterist of the century.[3] While there have been some serious works written on his thought in France, no sustained work has yet been done in English.[4]

CORBIN ALS APOCALYPTIKER

Corbin's apocalypticism was at least as much beholden to Schleiermacher and Barth, Otto and Heidegger, Jung and Swedenborg, as it was to the giants of Shiite and Sufi thought. He translated Heidegger and Barth before he translated Suhrawardi. He did not begin his extended annual visits to Iran until he was forty-two years old. The taproots of his system, it seems, are to be found in his youthful transition from fin-de-siècle French Catholicism to an idiosyncratic, Weimar-era, radicalized German Lutheranism. The next major transition in his life, into that of an ardent Iranophile, put the flesh on bones already firmly structured by the end of the 1930s. By that time, he was a cosmopolitan Parisian in his late thirties writing, translating, and lecturing on Barth, Kierkegaard, Hamann, and Heidegger.

The operating system, so to speak, around which he built his arcane and erudite theosophy, then, primarily was German in provenance. To a certain extent he made this origination clear in his own autobiographical statements.[5] Its implications remain to be plumbed, however. One, it seems to me, is that Nietzsche is a more significant figure for understanding Corbin's theory of Islam than Muhammad is. Consider the gnostic revolutionary spin Corbin put on his Nietzschean proclamation that "God is Dead" in his 1954 Eranos lecture: "Here it is not our task to apprehend in terms of pure phenomenology the consequences, *a parte Dei*, of homoousia and incarnation. God has ceased to be the Eternal in heaven. . . . But consciousness would fully 'realize' the event that had taken place, and Nietzsche would cry out: 'god is dead, he has died of pity for men.'"[6] In a subsequent lecture, he would again speak of the Death of God as a fait accompli. "This position and function [as supreme Principle and Cause] have been attributed to [the personal God] by every politico-religious *magisterium* so that this God to whom it attributes supreme power may in His turn guarantee the delegation of this power to it. In the end the day comes when this God of the non-gnostic monotheistic religions is declared to be dead."[7] One wonders what the vast proponderance of Muslims possibly make of this.

A key to this most un-Islamic reading of Islam may perhaps be found in its indebtedness to such early influences as Martin Heidegger. Karl Löwith's evocation of Heidegger as teacher—he was Löwith's teacher—bear informative parallels to Corbin in nearly every respect.

> Raised as a Jesuit, he became a Protestant out of indignation, a Scholastic dogmatist through schooling, and an existentiell pragmatist from experience, a theologian on the basis of tradition and an atheist as a researcher; in the guise of a historian of his tradition, he was really a renagade against it. Existentiell like Kierkegaard while possessing the will-to-system of a Hegel, as dialectical in method as he was single-minded in content, making apodictic claims out of the spirit of negation, silent in respose to others but uncommonly curious, radical regarding what is ultimate and inclined toward compromise in everything penultimate—this was the mixed effect that the man exerted on his pupils, who nonetheless remained captivated by him because he far exceeded all other university professors in intensity of philosophical willing.[8]

DECISIONIST *POSTHISTOIRE*

In the supercharged atmosphere of the 1930s, Corbin brought Heidegger's "end of metaphysics" into conversation with Barth's "theology of crisis" to forge a post-Christian apocalyptic theology. In 1933, Corbin published "La théologie dialectique et l'histoire."[9] Barth's deeply influential *Commentary on Romans* finds its impact here, in Corbin's translation: "Le jugement de Dieu est la fin de l'Histoire, et non le commencement d'une seconde histoire."[10] In the mid-1930s, Corbin was close to Alexandre Kojève, cotranslating a book with him at the time when the Russian emigré philosopher was conceiving his influential theory of the end of history. Closely related to this theme of *Posthistoire* was the decisionism that provided an impetus; one that could thrust posthistorical man out of dreaded modernity and into another, mythic world. Corbin was already sounding the sonorous tones of decisionism in the 1930s.[11] In his introduction to Manichean hymns published in 1937, for example, he spoke self-reflexively as he described the gnostic position: "La cosmologie n'est vraie que dans la ré-invention de la foi, dans l'expérience individuelle authentique. C'est pourquoi la sotériologie, le salut, l'histoire finale du monde, n'est pas un chapitre succédant à sa constitution, à sa création primordiale. La création *est en même temps* l'eschatologie . . . c'est par cette *décision* primitive que le monde *est* une histoire."[12]

In 1935, Denis de Rougemont cofounded with Corbin the theological journal *Hic et Nunc*—"petite revue de pensée religieuse qui se réclamait de Kierkegaard et de sa double descendance—'existentiell' et nietzschéenne par Heidegger, 'dialectique' et calviniste par Karl Barth."[13] Sketching Corbin's position at that time, de Rougemont quotes Corbin to the effect that "par 'existence' nous ne pouvions entendre que *décision concrète* . . . dans l'instant, *hic et nunc*."[14] Mircea Eliade, it is interesting to note, reiterated such a theme in the "Conclusion" to *Patterns in Comparative Religion*. "Resistance is most clearly expressed when man is faced with a *total demand* from the sacred, when he is called upon to make *the supreme decision*."[15]

THÉOLOGIE CHRÉTIENNE DES RELIGIONS: SHI'ISM AS PROTESTANT ESCHATOLOGY

When one considers the vast Corbin oeuvre in its fullness, it becomes apparent that he was not *ultimately* interested in Islam. He plainly was not interested in Islam in the terms recognizable to most Muslims or even to most Islamicists. Of the 445 pages of his *History of Islamic Philosophy*, some 14 are devoted to the Qur'an, 20 to the Sunni Kalam, and another 20 pages to "Sunni Thought." Less than one-eighth of the whole, then, is devoted to what, statistically, makes up the bulk of Islamic religious thought. A work of awesome learning, which purports to redress imbalances, *History of Islamic Philosophy* seems to overcompensate rather severely. These proportions are, if anything, even more extreme in their disparity if one considers Corbin's work as a whole.

His defense, to the extent that he might have offered one, is that Shi'ism makes urgent, total demands. Conventional rationality, which may apportion the facts quite differently, is simply irrelevant to the case. For this case, according to Corbin, is that Shi'ism is par excellence an eschatology: "[T]he metaphysics of Mullâ Sadrâ seems to me to correspond strictly to the Shi'ite urgency, which maintains man in a state of tension and striving, because his perspective is essentially eschatological, and is oriented towards the *Parousia* of the 'Awaited-for Imam'."[16]

It is telling, however, that he homologized this Shi'ite eschatology, in turn, with a certain Western esoteric eschatology. "[L]a métaphysique du shi'isme est essentiellement, comme celle de Berdiaev, une métaphysique eschatologique. L'une et l'autre se conjoignent pour nous convaincre que ce n'est pas en tentant de rivaliser avec les idéologies socio-politiques issues de la sécularisation du christianisme, que le christianisme parviendra à concevoir et à formuler une *'théologie chrétienne des religions.'*"[17]

In short, Corbin's theory of Shi'ism was identical with his "Christian theology of religions." This was a post-denominational, freelance theology, one which poured itself inside Shi'ite sources with a genius for sympathetic representation. Corbin's Christology, in fact, became indistinguishable from Shi'ite and Sufi Christology. At the end of his life, as he wrote more explicitly, if not feverishly, on what he called *Harmonia Abrahamica* (Abrahamic Harmony), it became "clear" to his readers that that indistinguishability was the point all along.[18] This seems epitomized by his citation of a couplet from the Persian poet Hafiz, "which I would gladly take as my personal motto": "Let the inspiration of the Holy Spirit but breathe once more—Others in their turn will do what Christ has done."[19] He left no doubt, then, that he was practicing a "comparative philosophy" that presumed a visionary philosophy transcending conventional denominational limitations.[20] The visionary achieved a transcending unity of Abrahamic faiths. And, in the end, this achievement carried with it explicitly eschatological significance. "L'approfondissement comparatif nous permettrait se saisir ce qu'ont en commun les 'religions du Livre,' dans leur attente d'une pentecôte encore à venir."[21]

"THE THEOLOGY OF THE HISTORY OF RELIGIONS": THE TIME OF ERANOS AND THE ENDS OF HISTORY

Corbin may have been, along with Adolf Portmann, the distinguished Swiss biologist, the most enthusiastic booster of Eranos in its "golden age," roughly from 1950 to 1975. In "The Time of Eranos," an essay he published several times, Corbin articulated perhaps the most emphatic and moving manifesto of the *Eranos-Tagungen* (as they were called by participants). The end of history would seem muted here. But this essay, perhaps his most important treatment of an esoteric theory of time, delves deeply into the problem of duration.[22]

The real end of history for Corbin was found in resymbolization, the process by which individuals departed from the crowd and became truly themselves. In the world of symbols there is neither before nor after. This blessed simultaneity, comprehensible only to those who learn to interpret signs, means that the believer must be a kind of hermeneut. "It is 'interpreting' the *signs*, explaining not material facts but ways of being, that reveals beings. Hermeneutics as science of the individual stands in opposition to historical dialectics as alienation of the individual."[23] Aside from being the vibrant expression of a committed cold warrior, on the offensive against "historical dialectics," Corbin reveals here the philosophical basis for his assault on historicism.[24]

> Past and future thus become *signs*, because a sign is perceived precisely *in the present*. The past must be "put in the present" to be perceived as "showing a sign." . . . In short, the whole contrast lies here. With *signs*, with hierophanies and theophanies, there is no making history. Or rather, the subject that is at once the *organ* and the place of history is the concrete psychological individuality. The only "historical causality" is the relations of will between acting subjects.[25]

But it was in his Eranos lecture of 1965 that Corbin presented perhaps his most explicit statement of what may be called Eranos eschatology.

> We can speak of the configurative action of the Spirit, of form as a task to be accomplished by the Spirit (which is our theme in *Eranos*), with full meaning only if we are in possession of a space into which we can project the totality of this form. *Such a space was known to the science of religions and to traditional theologies as the eschatological dimension*, in which the spring of the arch is achieved—a spring which will never be ours so long as we remain on this side of our "scientific" proof.[26]

It is interesting to note that Corbin, more than once, credited Eliade with supplying his understanding of "the theology of the History of Religions." At the Eranos lectures, some of Eliade's technical vocabulary, especially "cyclical history" and "theophany," began to be employed by Corbin. In *Creative Imagination in the Sufism of Ibn ʿArabi*, the section on "Theophany" finds Eliade cited four times.[27] And in his massive late Eranos lecture (well over 100 pages, and bearing 294 footnotes), "*The Imago Templi* in Confrontation with Secular Norms," Eliade's sacred/

profane dichotomy is positioned noticably near to what Corbin called "the key to my hermeneutics."

> Profane history sees mankind as mankind has created itself; History is the creation that man regards as his own, and of which he is the result. Sacred history or hierohistory reascends to events that are prior to the world, prior to the destruction of Temple, because it is by this Temple that I was created, and its *Imago* exists within me. This is the key to my hermeneutics, the sacred norm which determines the ascent from world to world.[28]

The intrinsically conflictual character of this quest should not be minimized. The "sacred norm" is intelligible only by means of identifying "profane history" so that one can be liberated from its bondage, in order then to ascend "from world to world." This is possible, in turn, only to the extent that one can name the Adversary, the Ruler of This World. For Corbin, one of his several names was *Ahriman*.

AHRIMANIA

Ahriman is best known as the final Persian version of the diabolical half of ancient Zoroastrian dualist myth. Aristotle already reported on this Magian Deity in his *De Philosophia*. This quasi-demonic Adversary was transposed eventually into gnostic versions. Like Leviathan, he was also identified with Satan by the Church Fathers.[29] Found also in Greek and Latin versions, as well as in Mithraism (as *Deus Arimanius*), in Manichaeism, and even in some versions of Islamic cosmology, this demon's late Zoroastrian incarnation as "Ahriman" has attracted much ideological attention in twentieth century cultural criticism. Carl Jung, Joseph Campbell, Denis de Rougemont, Mircea Eliade, and Henry Corbin employed the myth of Ahriman-as-planetary-antagonist in ways that tended to blur into a kind of philosophical anti-Judaism.

Gnostic anti-Judaism is implicit in the identification of Ahriman with Jehovah. The dominant figure of Eranos, its presiding presence, *Spiritus Rector*, and primary permission giver, Carl Jung himself, identified both Leviathan and Ahriman with Jehovah in *Response to Job*, a book rightly attacked by Martin Buber for its gnostic anti-Judaism. Perhaps the most perfectly gnostic document of the century, *Response to Job* became Jung's single most important text for mounting a post-Holocaust assault on the God of the Jewish people.[30] Other examples from the Eranos and Bollingen group could be added. Joseph Campbell, in his widely read *Masks of God*, likewise identified Ahriman, or Angra-Mainyu, with Jehovah.[31] And Eliade's Romanian volume, *The Myth of Reintegration*, bore a chapter on Ahriman and Ohrmazd.[32]

We find a related mythic slur purveyed by yet others in their intimate circle. Here the idea is not that the Jewish God is Ahriman, but that the Jews were responsible for creating Satan out of Ahriman. One widely read member of this circle was the Swiss man of letters Denis de Rougemont. De Rougemont was one of the first beneficiaries of the Jungian Bollingen Foundation—in fact, he was the recipient of personal patronage from Jung's patient, Mary Mellon, the founder of Bollingen.[33] Ahriman comes up in de Rougemont's treatise on evil, *The Devil's Share*, which was written on the estate of Mary Mellon. In this wartime volume, he baldly proclaimed that "The Devil is a Jewish invention . . . as the Panzer division is German . . . it was the Rabbis who contrived to make use of the legend of Ormuzd and Ahrimane."[34]

Corbin's was perhaps the most complex and significant Eranos treatment of Ahriman as planetary antagonist—and the one that is also least obviously a case of what Scholem called "metaphysical antisemitism." De Rougemont was a very close friend and theological ally of Corbin in the 1930s and continued to use Corbin's work in his own essays throughout his life.[35] As I noted in the preceding chapters, a virulent anti-modernism had featured centrally in Corbin's thought since the 1930s, when he elaborated a "crisis theology," alongside de Rougemont.

Corbin launched his postwar academic career as a Persianist. The ancient Persian god Ahriman, in the following decades, became for him a prime symbol of the all-too-loathsome modern world. In one of his first and most widely read Eranos essays, Corbin hammered away at Ahriman, which he termed the *principle of active nihilitude*.[36] "For Ahriman is the legitimate prince of this world; moreover, although he is a Power of Darkness, this Darkness is an aspect of the supreme godhead itself. Iblis-Ahriman is never invested with a legitimate sovereignty, he is the Adversary pure and simple."[37] He elucidated this negative world principle emphatically at the end of his life: "The norm of our world can assume all manner of names: sociology, dialectical or non-dialectical materialism, positivism, historicism, psychoanalysis, and so forth."[38] For Henry Corbin, modernity, so described, was an Ahrimanic catastrophe. He "sets the same catastrophe at the center of world history."[39] It is the time of the catastrophe which succeeded the day when Adam . . . surrendered the secret and the vision of Paradise to the rage and mockery of Iblis-Ahriman."[40] In fact, technology utterly has ravaged the world:

What we call the Western venture is the application of the intelligence to the scientific investigation of a nature that has been desacralised, which must be violated in order to find out its laws and to subject its forces to the human will. It has brought us to where we are now. . . . A work of nothingness and of death which must be looked in the face if it is to be denounced, in the way in which the Sages of ancient Persia, who were the first if not the only ones to do so, looked into the eyes of the atrocious Ahriman.[41]

Finally, at his life's end he reiterated that the human condition as such is a "promethean tragedy, but it is also an ohrmazdian tragedy (the invasion of Ahriman)."[42]

I must be perfectly explicit here. There is no evidence that Henry Corbin was anti-Semitic. That being said, Corbin did revile Ahriman, the planetary antagonist, in terms that the reader could associate with rabbinic Judaism. That is, the enemy, the catastrophe, for Corbin was *legalism*.[43] Corbin remains famous for his gnostically dualistic division of Islam into mysticism and legalism, Sufism and the "église," the Church, of Islam. Legalism, of course, is a routine trope of anti-Semitic rhetoric.[44] And so it is fair to say that Corbin's cosmic exaggeration of a primordial split between letter and spirit, between legalism and esoterism, is at once paradigmatically gnostic and implicitly anti-Jewish. Gnosticism, it is worth remembering in this connection, was once called by Gershom Scholem "the greatest case of metaphysical antisemitism."[45] Thus, while Corbin meant no known offense to Jews, he also never repudiated the implications of his imagery, which thrived in circles around him throughout his long life.[46]

Corbin, I would add, wrote an ecstatically laudatory review of Jung's *Response to Job*, which is today included in the current French translation of that booklet. Jung in return praised Corbin's essay as the only review of dozens published that really understood him.[47] In retrospect this is not surprising, since Corbin and Jung proudly (if esoterically) proclaimed themselves to be gnostics. They agreed, in effect, on the fundamental (if esoteric) principle that the High God of the Hebrew Bible was in fact a monstrous demiurge, one of whose many names is Ahriman.

CONCLUSION: CORBIN AND THE END OF RELIGION

> Heretics of all religions, unite!
> —*Henry Corbin*

Henry Corbin died on 7 October 1978. On 7 August of that year, he wrote some of his last words. As was common in the works he wrote in the 1970s, this penultimate text, "Le combat pour l'âme du monde ou urgence de la sophiologie," did not concern Islam as such. And then, weeks later, Khomeini returned from Paris. Corbin's genius spelled the end of a certain Islamology, and that may not have been such a bad thing. Still, it would be dangerous to confuse his theory with a reliable rendering of Islamic eschatology. As he himself insisted, he did not study eschatology: as he might have put it, he *was* eschatology.[48] Corbin declared eschatological war on history, on "legalism," even on the "non-gnostic monotheistic God." This fact translates into a disturbing irony. Henry Corbin, to put it bluntly, declared himself the enemy of Islamic history, of *shar'iah*, even of the Allah of the overwhelming majority of Muslims.

In the end, Corbin made himself, if not an immortal scholar per se, surely a great religious visionary; indeed, one of the most inspired esoteric writers of the century. Yet the character of his religion remains, perhaps *must* remain, inaccessible to the student of his teachings. He called himself, at times, a "philosopher of the West."[49] Roger Arnaldez asked and answered his own question: "A-t-il été lui-même un 'initié'? La question est indiscrète et il suffit de savoir qu'il appartient à cette famille d'esprits fortement portés vers l'ésoterisme et le gnosticisme."[50] However indiscreet, it must, for the sake of the truth, be asked. Like his hero Goethe, Corbin would have been happy, I believe, to have each part of his corpus read as "fragments of a great confession." The historian of the History of Religions is justified, I believe, in reading Corbin's essays—written each in so intimately, ardently, insistently personal a style—likewise as such confessions.[51]

One of my concerns here, then, is to understand Corbin's hermeneutics of Islam as itself a kind of millenarianism. It constituted, in short, a *religion after religion*. Reading his visionary essays one is again reminded of Löwith's penetrating observations on his erstwhile teacher, Martin Heidegger.

> But the basis that serves as the background for everything said by Heidegger, and that permits many to take notice and listen attentively, is something unsaid: *the religious motive*, which has surely detached itself from Christian faith, but which precisely on account of its dogmatically unattached indeterminacy appeals all the more to those who are no longer faithful Christians but who nonetheless would like to be religious.[52]

Corbin claimed, much as did Eliade, that he was championing a foreign tradition in and of itself, and that he likewise was the most vigorous opponent of all those explaining it in terms not its own.

> La tendance de notre époque nous conduit trop souvent à vouloir expliquer un phénomène religieux par des causes non religieuses. On s'est donné beaucoup de mal pour expliquer le shî'isme par des circonstances politiques, so-

ciales, géographiques ou autres. Ce faisant, on n'a oublié qu'une chose: si une religion déterminée existe la première et dernière raison du phénomène, c'est l'existence de ceux qui la professent.[53]

Still, without question, most Muslims know nothing of Martinism, Swedenborg, Templars, or Franz von Baader.[54] Corbin's identification of Muslim "spirtualité" with these European esoterisms, while he at the same time routinely derided the ancient, legitimate, legal tradition and the everyday practices of living Islam as "légalisme," forces the historian of Islamic studies into a uncomfortable bind. Henry Corbin's legacy, by consequence, seems destined to be almost tragically mixed.

Perhaps the deepest irony to emerge from the present investigation, to state it directly, is that Corbin the Islamicist did not represent Islamic tradition. The Iranian Revolution was an implicit repudiation of his idiosyncratic version of Iranian tradition, in the name of an authentic indigenous religiosity. The ironies of his indisputable commitment to native Iranian cultural development, therefore, are nearly too painful to contemplate today. In the spring of 1957, he was able to broadcast these stirring words into Iran, counseling radio listeners on the development of their intellectual institutions.

L'Université de Téhéran est en train de réorganiser tout l'enseignement de la philosophie. Il est urgent en effet que, parallèlement aux rénovations matérielles, se produise une renaissance philosophique; urgent que se forme une génération de jeunes philosophes iraniens, faute de laquelle le pays serait en péril de perdre conscience de son destin. . . . Si les méthodes que la philosphie occidentale met en oeuvre de nos jours pour comprendre "au présent" la signification de son passé, peuvent aider nos amis iraniens à retrouver dans leur philosophie traditionnelle le sens de l'homme en quête de la connaissance de soi-même, alors ils n'est pas douteux que si Mîr Dâmâd mérita, il ya trois siècles, d'êtres appelé le "Troisième Maître," nous verrons surgir quelque jour celui qui méritera d'être appelé le "Quatrième Maître."[55]

Little could he know that that "Quatrième Maître," Fourth Master, for millions of Iranians, would be the Ayatollah Khomeini.[56]

There can be, I think, no gainsaying Corbin's love of Iran and of Iranians. But his unmitigated rejection of the body and of society, of social differences and historical change, of routine ritual and the diversity of religious expression—these were limitations on his historical consciousness which resulted in devastating consequences. One can say, as many do, that he was a poetic exemplar of a sort, and I tend to agree with these voices. At the same time, historical research and its unreliquishable values, most especially the inescapable demand of evidentiary adequation, simply falls aside when the poetic quotient flies off the scale into the outer limits of gnosis. Henry Corbin was a genius, and students of Islam will not stop studying his many works. But he himself, with quite conscious intent, apocalyptically imploded the study of Islam into his very person, in an ultimately incommunicable kind of millenial interiority, after which we pick up the pieces and keep on seeking the truth.

The pieces are the pieces of religion. Corbin proclaimed "Heretics of the world unite!" not only as an obvious play on a communist slogan. The unity he enjoined was postdenominational. This new religion was one he hoped would come after the Ahrimanic reign of legalistic religions. He looked to Eliade and Scholem, he looked to Eranos more generally, for bridges to this future. Religion after religion, then, would be the unity of gnostics everywhere. There is no evidence and no reason to believe that Scholem heeded this call. Eliade was more amenable. Muslims, nearly all the Muslims of the world, reject such abjurations. It remains for the next generation of Historians of Religions to decide for themselves. Corbin's religion after religion, neither a Christianity nor an Islam, calls to heretics, to gnostics. A new History of Religions may decide that a critical study of religions cannot found itself on this militant rejection of the self-understanding of millions of ordinary believers.

CHAPTER 12

Psychoanalysis in Reverse

Depth psychology has taught us that the symbol
delivers its message and fulfills its functions even
when its meaning escapes awareness.
—*Mircea Eliade*

GIVEN the long-term participation by the Historians of Religion in the
meetings inspired by Carl Jung, it seems virtually unavoidable that any
study of their theories of religion must carefully assess their respective
positions in relation to psychology. This, however, is a particularly vex-
atious area of research, inasmuch as each explicitly opposed the reduction
of religious realities to psychological forces. On the other hand, each
scholar, at the same time, was accustomed to employing psychological
categories—of which archetypes are only the best known—to interpret
religious materials.[1]

PSYCHOANALYSIS IN REVERSE

For Eliade, preeminently, the promise of his new History of Religions was
to reverse the direction of history, to follow the signals of myth back to
original consciousness. Eliade's History of Religions in this sense constitutes a *psychoanalysis in reverse*, to adapt a concept developed by Leo
Lowenthal and Theodor Adorno.[2] This analogy is not reductionistically
imposed on Eliade, for he himself precisely positioned his History of Religions directly in opposition to psychoanalysis: "But there can be no question of confusing their frames of reference, nor their scales of values, nor,
above all, their methods."[3] Eliade was always explicit on this score. Referring to a psychological study of "primitives," for example, Eliade proposed "to reverse the terms of comparison."[4] More generally, he noted
that, as opposed to all forms of social and psychological critique, his new
school demanded "demystification in reverse."[5]

> Marxism and depth psychology have illustrated the efficacy of the so-called
> demystification when one wants to discover the true—or the original—sig-
> nificance of a behavior, an action, or a cultural creation. In our case, we have
> to attempt a demystification in reverse; that is to say, we have to "demystify"

the apparently profane worlds and languages of literature, plastic arts, and cinema in order to disclose their "sacred" elements, although it is, of course, an ignored, camouflaged, or degraded "sacred."[6]

The "creative hermeneutics" of symbolism, he asserted, "does not mean rationalism, rather the reverse."[7] He reiterated this idea in his journal. "Therefore it is necessary to apply a demythologization in reverse."[8] He claimed that one of the differences between him and his friend, the Italian fascist man of letters Julius Evola, was that he wanted to include "on a new Noah's Ark . . . also the poetic, historical, and philosophical understanding of *The Divine Comedy*. The limiting of the hermeneutics of European spiritual creations exclusively to their 'esoteric meanings' repeats, *in reverse*, the reductionism of a materialistic type illustrated so successfully by Marx or Freud."[9] The Romanian emígré moreover posited an ideal personality type, that of the hero capable of violent rebirth, whose struggle is seen as a recovery of lost sexuality: "But the *tantrika* strives to *repeat this process the reverse way*."[10] That is, this hero-type strives to redynamize an "impotent" Supreme Being.[11] Finally, he went so far as to characterize his History of Religions, the system predicated on this personality type, as "metapsychoanalysis."[12]

Eliade's intention, plainly, was to turn back the clock on Freud's advances. In a discussion of "Symbolism and Psychoanalysis" dating from 1952, Eliade described Freud's sexuality theory as a "fixation" on the "concrete."[13] These were opening shots in Eliade's postwar war on Freudian theory.[14] The overdetermined language Eliade wielded in this assault left little to the imagination. Typically, this juggernaut of rhetoric was cast in terms of that which is assailed, the Freudian Imagination itself: "The brutal language of Freud and his orthodox disciples . . . translate[s] an image into a concrete terminology by restricting it to any one of its frames of reference [which] is to do worse than mutilate it—it is to annihilate, to annul it as an instrument of cognition."[15] He went on to characterize it further as "psychic disequilibrium," "partial," "incomplete," "false," an "aberration," and "frankly, faulty."[16] He continued the diatribe with the accusation that psychoanalysis deals with "manifestations of a psyche in crisis, if not in a state of pathological regression."[17] Near the end of his career, he lampooned Freud with the apocryphal remarks of "an anonymous British psychoanalyst": "We are born mad; then we acquire morality and become stupid and unhappy; then we die."[18] Therefore, he felt himself entitled to contrast healthy Yogic psychology with "the ignorance of the scientists."[19]

Eliade, beyond any doubt, was opposed to psychoanalysis both programmatically and passionately. For History of Religions to be established, two "difficulites have to be overcome," historicism and psychoanalysis.[20] That these two are linked, however, is also certain: "Psychoanalysis . . . introduces historical and individual time into therapeutics."[21] Freudian theory, like Marxist historicism, according to Eliade, was to be identified as a Jewish sin.[22] One source of his enmity was his repulsion at what he explicitly associated with Jewish exclusivism: "Psychoanalysis satisfied the thirst for the absolute, characteristic of the Judaic genius, the belief that there is a *single* royal road to the Spirit, and it betrays the specifically Hebraic revulsion toward pluralism, polytheism and idolatry."[23] Eliade likened the psychoanalytic concern with sexuality and life history to a "fixation" on the "concrete," an accusation that parallels the accusation of "literalism," of the preference of the "letter" over the "spirit." The championing of "History of Religions" over a Jewish-identified "psychoanalysis," then, was historically depicted by Eliade in terms to parallel the triumph of Christianity over "history." In both cases, it will be noted that this polemical dichotomy is not the only animus toward Jews that stimulated Eliade's reading of "history." It was, as well, historical analysis itself that he claimed to have been successively epitomized in the Hebrew prophets, in Marx, and in Freud.

Eliade's anti-Freudianism was reiterated throughout his postwar writings, but, in fact, his writings in Romanian before the war were at least equally condemnatory of "materialism, Freudianism, Marxism." For example, in his *Fragmentarium*, published in Bucharest in 1939 and more recently in French translation, he spoke of these social sciences reaching "subhuman levels" resulting in "sterility of spirit."[24] In "The God Who Binds," the first major scholarly paper he published after the war, he even suggested that the historicized "decadence" or "degeneration" of symbolism was almost inhuman, "for it is very commonly the case that pathological variants of religious complexes also have a superficially simian appearance."[25] His antipathy was directed toward a "degenerate" Freudian theory, which was identified as being Jewish, and which was precisely positioned as the diametric opposite to the History of Religions. The Chicago Historian of Religions remarked, as I have noted, on "the characteristic of the Jewish genius, the belief that there is a *single* royal road to the spirit."[26] To this singularity he contrasted his own royal road: "[W]e do not doubt that the 'creative hermeneutics' will finally be recognized as the royal road of the History of Religions."[27] The polemical motifs of Marx and Freud usually came in pairs, almost invariably set in paired opposition to his own royal road. In a typical instance, Eliade begins his vast *Patterns in Comparative Religion* by straightforwardly claiming that "to grasp the essence [of symbolism] by psychoanalysis . . . is false."[28] Shortly thereafter he reasserted that Freud was wrong, linking him this time with Marx.[29] The scathing polemics that open *Images and Symbols* restate these points even more vehemently. Such pungent remarks are found throughout the journals as well. Even in a late collection of essays, he startlingly accused Freud of a recapitulation of killing of God. "Probably, [Freud] thought that he found proofs of the killing of God the Father among his Viennese patients. But this 'discovery' was tantamount to saying that *some modern men were beginning to feel the consequences of their 'deicide'*."[30]

Given the foregoing, he well understood the "Freud Memorial Lecture" of 1974 to be one of the most ironic invitations he ever received.

> Why the devil did I accept a year ago this invitation to the Philadelphia Society of Psychoanalysis? I was undoubtedly enticed by the very fact of having been invited, I who for thirty or forty years have continued to denounce Freud's theories concerning religion. For two things, one, I told myself: either they've read nothing I've written, or in the opposite case, they want me to present my own theories, which means they've stopped stiffening on dogmatic and intransigent positions and are opening up, in principle, to criticism of the Freudian dogma.[31]

Still, he returned to Sigmund Freud, even if only to reverse his meaning. Thus it may be noted that he acknowledged two Freudian ideas to have influenced the History of Religions: the bliss of origins and return to origins through memory.[32]

HENRY CORBIN AND CARL JUNG

Corbin appropriated Jung as much as Eliade rejected Freud. Of the three scholars under discussion here, only Corbin was ever anything like an "orthodox'" Jungian. Both Scholem and Eliade, for example, used the term "archetype" while denying that they used it in a Jungian sense.[33] But Corbin extensively employed the technical vocabulary of Jung's Analytical Psychology, including such terms as *individuation, archetype, mandala, quaternity, shadow, active imagination, Self, synchronicity, coincidentia oppositorum*, and *animus/anima*.[34] In a rather pure form, at least in the 1950s, he folded Shi'ism into the Jung cult, proclaiming in Jungian idioms that "to know one's self, one's soul, one's anima, and therewith all the universe of the soul, is to know one's Imam."[35] His world of visionary forms was a veritable *Mundus archetypus*.[36]

Corbin, however, seems not to have come into contact with Jungian thought until his Eranos years. If it is possible to locate a moment when Corbin's Jungianism was consolidated, it seems to have been his review of *Response to Job*. His own testimony to this fact is eloquent: "[C]'est 'en Eranos' que le pèlerin venu de l'Iran devait rencontrer celui qui par sa 'Réponse à Job' lui fit comprendre la réponse qu'il rapportait en lui-même de l'Iran. Le chemin vers l'éternelle Sophia. Que C. G. Jung en soit remercié."[37]

It must be emphasized, nonetheless, that Jungian terminology was but one of many vocabularies employed by the eclectic Corbin. And Jungianism, on close inspection, seems only to have risen to the fore in the work he produced primarily in the 1950s and 1960s, with a progressive deemphasis by the 1970s. *Avicenna and the Visionary Recital*, originally published in 1954, is by far his most Jungian work. *Spiritual Body and Celestial Earth* and *Creative Imagination in the Sufism of Ibn ʿArabi* contain a considerable number of Jungian notions as well. On the other hand, he found it necessary to exclude Jungian terminology rather rigorously from his *History of Islamic Philosophy*.[38] And the works from the 1970s generally emphasized occultist and esoterist traditions to the comparative exclusion of Jung.[39] To a certain extent, then, Jungian ideology served a transitional purpose for Corbin. It seems not to have been primary in the way that either theology or theosophy was for his thought. And, in fact, a few months before his death, in his only autobiographical statement, Corbin insisted, as did Eliade and Scholem, that he too was not a Jungian. "Moi-même je fus ami avec Jung. Je ne fus jamais un 'jungien'."[40]

It may be added that his influence on post-Jungian psychological thought, through the agency of James Hillman, is without question the most pronounced such influence of the three.[41] Still, Corbin was a richly syncretistic philosopher whose work is variously beholden to Luther and Schleiermacher, Hamann and Goethe, Heidegger and Barth, not to speak of its almost bafflingly manifold esoteric sources. Only his early Eranos lectures, especially those delivered in the 1950s, while Jung was still alive, positioned the Jungian idiom at the forefront of his presentation.

SCHOLEM AND DEPTH PSYCHOLOGY

> How can one speak of a history of the private
> realm or of those things that are between man
> and his Creator?! Yet, nevertheless, there certainly
> is! The entire history of religions is built upon the
> development of those impulses
> —*Gershom Scholem*

Gershom Scholem certainly held no public brief for psychoanalysis.[42] His disavowal is well known: "In treating the history and world of the *kabbalah*, using the conceptual terminology of psychoanalysis—either the Freudian or the Jungian version—did not seem fruitful to me."[43] According to Joseph Dan, Scholem used to say of Freud, "I have read dozens of better mythological concepts of the soul than his."[44] He nonetheless held Freud in high esteem, referring to him as a "first-rate mind" in the same breath as he so characterized Kafka and Benjamin.[45] Elsewhere, he went so far as to call him a genius.[46]

That being noted, Scholem, especially in the 1930s, did favor vocabulary familiar from Freudian thought. For example, he seemed to have espoused an "Id" concept, implied in such formulations as "anarchy in every human soul"; "libidinal forces"; "the more primitive region of the soul in which long-slumbering forces are capable of sudden resurrection"; "the darker aspects of Kabbalistic ritual, reflecting man's fears and other emotional states"; "instincts of anarchy and lawlessness that lie deeply buried in every human soul."[47] His deeply felt intuition of the dark side, so to speak, in fact underpinned his very analysis of Sabbatianism in "Redemption through Sin," arguably his most important essay. "Herein lay the psychological basis of that spirit of revolt . . . the whole Sabbatian psychology in a nutshell."[48] He also used the notions of the uncanny and of latency.[49] It may be remembered as well that, in the one of the landmark moments in the early history of so-called psychohistory, he diagnosed Sabbatai Zevi to be a manic-depressive.[50]

There is no question, more generally, that he assumed some depth psychology, at least as far as he was accustomed to employing the dyad conscious/unconscious. For example, in his justly influential characterization of mystical experience as simultaneously conservative and revolutionary, he asks the following question:

> Is it correct to distinquish these two attitudes toward authority as conscious and unconscious? Are we justified in saying that the religious authority is a conscious power in the mind of the mystic, while his conflict with it is rooted in the unconscious layers of his experience? Undoubtedly there have been mystics in whom the dividing line between conscious and unconscious coincided with the dividing line between their conservative and revolutionary tendencies.[51]

He wrote these lines when he was more than fifty years old, and republished them when he was over sixty. They were not, then, a relic of his youth that he jettisoned in maturity.[52] Perhaps most interestingly, in this regard, he went so far as draw notice, on several occasions, to what he believed was a Hasidic predecessor of the concept of the unconscious.[53] In fact, he concluded his lecture on the Tzaddik by citing the Maggid of Mezhirech, to the effect that "[t]he Tzaddikim make God, if one may phrase it thus, their unconscious."[54] He also praised the work of his friend, the Jungian analyst Siegmund Hurwitz, who was working along these lines.[55] Jung, in these same years, was arguing that the "unconscious" was first discovered by the ancient gnostics.[56]

According McGuire's official history of the Bollingen Foundation—a privileged and generally reliable source of information—"During Jung's lifetime, [Jung and Scholem] enjoyed a warm intellectual friendship."[57] In fact, even before he met Jung, Scholem did employ the concept, or at least the term, of "archetype," as when he deemed Sabbatai Zevi "the living archetype of the paradox of the holy sinner."[58] After meeting Jung, he continued to use the concept, speaking of "archetypes of all creation" and "the archetypes of all being."[59] As late as 1969, he was speaking at Eranos of rabbis as "archetypal representatives of the ideal *Talmid Hakham* [rabbinic scholar]."[60] Elliot Wolfson thus has called Scholem's approach one of "contextual archetypalism."[61] Joseph Dan would, then, seem to be mistaken in his blanket assertion that Scholem's "views clashed diametrically with the Jungian approach."[62] David Biale is closer to the mark when he more accurately observes that "Jung's dialectic between the conscious and the unconscious, repeated on the social level as myth, resembles Scholem's dialectic between rationalism and irrationalism in Jewish history."[63] Scholem himself seemed to feel not that Jung's ideas were all wrong but that such psychologizing needed to be philologically grounded, as he wrote to Morton Smith in 1950.[64]

Finally, it must be stated that Scholem understood both Freud and Jung to be great men. He explicitly addressed this point. In the often cited letter in which he explained why, despite Jung's apparent collaborationism—on the basis of Jung's famous "I slipped up" confession—the Jerusalem scholar decided to attend Jung's Eranos. In that letter, now published for the first time in its full form, it turns out that Scholem added an additional statement, which he explicitly requested Aniela Jaffé not to publish, even as he gave permission to cite the body of the letter.

Neither was it my task to idealize the image of C. G. Jung in this sketch, nor to reduce it. However, it was important to remove the image from "the parties' hate and favour." It is, most of the time, hard for man to keep his position and retain his own dignity when next to the great. This leads to indiscriminate glorification on the one hand and to similarly indiscriminate exaggeration of actual existing faults on the other. Not even the image of Goethe, which had been held unimpeachable, was—as the latest literary history proves—immune to this. The images of Freud and Jung did escape this fate just a little.

It is harder to bear the fate of one's own greatness than to accept and bear the greatness of someone else. Greatness has an effect like an intrusion of the transcendental and is a task of life that borders on the extreme. Therefore the personality has the strongest impact in which greatness unites with humaneness, the singular with the collective, the spiritual light with wandering in the dark.[65] From the suffering of this tension, understanding, comprehension, or love towards the world awakens in great artists or scientists, in great men.[66]

MOSES AND MONOTHEISM

Three disparate works dating from the period of the Third Reich form an intellectual frame for Scholem's groundbreaking essay "Redemption through Sin": Jonas's *Gnosis in spätantiker Geist* of 1934, Freud's *Moses and Monotheism* of 1937, and Horkheimer and Adorno's *Dialectic of Enlightenment* of 1944.[67] Of this family of texts, Jonas's work on Gnosis had the first, deepest, and most lasting impact on Scholem. Jonas belonged to an intimate study circle (designated "Pilegesh"/"Concubine") with Scholem in Palestine in the mid-1930s.[68] And Jonas's formulation of the role of Gnosis in religious history, centrally emphasized in "Redemption through Sin," continued to be cited by Scholem until the end of this life.

However, *Moses and Monotheism*, written at precisely the same time as "Redemption through Sin," bears interesting, unremarked parallels to Scholem's landmark essay. In both cases a hero of Jewish history is portrayed, with seeming perversity, to be a paradigmatic lawbreaker. This revision is, paradoxically, held to deepen the greatness of the hero for his people. In both cases a radically new critical analysis demystifies a Jewish protagonist in the very face of Nazi assault. Freud dethrones a prophet king, and Scholem, so to speak, glorifies a scoundrel. In both cases, this paradoxical strategy was explicitly undertaken by Jewish writers during the Third Reich as a paradoxical kind of national self-defense.

The third member of this contemporaneous group is Max Horkheimer and Theodor Adorno's *Dialectic of Enlightenment*.[69] In this work, as with those by Jonas and Scholem, the irrational by-products of cultural development, especially myth, are seen as evolving in a dialectic of creation and destruction. Rationality is no unequivocal apogee of progress. Rather, Reason and its subversive other, myth, operate in a civilizational synergy. These works also engaged anti-Semitism explicitly. Scholem told his friend Hans Jonas that Gnosticism was "the greatest case of metaphysical anti-Semitism," a line repeated by Corbin.[70] Freud's *Moses and Monotheism* espoused the psychological theory that Christianity, having murdered its Jewish "father," is necessarily anti-Semitic.[71] And *Dialectic of Enlightenment* included a ferociously reproachful chapter titled "Elements of Anti-Semitism: Limits of Enlightenment."

Of these works of genius, however, Scholem's was the only one written from an explicitly Jewish perspective, was the only one to deal with Judaism as such (as opposed to anti-Semitism), was the only one to zero in on the core metaphysical paradox at work, and thus went far further than any of the others in rendering its strange service to the rebirth of the Jewish people. Scholem, a romantic visionary of sorts, felt passionately that this rebirth could not be founded on historical positivism, bourgeois moralism, or Kantian humanism. If it was to respond adequately to the negativist, amoral, and inhuman reality of its day, Zionism needed to deepen and expand its sense of historical self. This meant being daring enough to think heretofore unthinkables.

Freud, Adorno, Horkheimer, and Jonas were serious thinkers compelled to reflect on the perversity of history. Scholem, similarly, was a historian driven philosophically to engage a monumentally perverse moment in Jewish history. It is truistic—and therefore painfully inadequate—to observe that the driving necessity, from either side, was that of catastrophe. It is inadequate if for no other reason than that it begs the essential question. This question obsessed Scholem, and he returned to it with all his might after the catastrophe, after the Shoah. In any case, not surprisingly, each of these works offers the reader a theory of catastrophe. The audacity of these works—the characteristic tonality of each is at once austere and hysterical, magisterial and overwrought—is meaningfully captured in their respectively preposterous hypotheses. Audacity withstood catastrophe by means of a preposterous moral inversion of historical reasoning.[72]

One need not go so far as Harold Bloom, who sees in Scholem one of the three greatest Jewish minds of the century, along with Freud and Kafka.[73] But one could argue that the paradoxical morality espoused by Scholem bears important parallels to the function of neurosis for Freud. The creative potential, if not the sheer psychological bravura, of these revisionary inversions of conventional history should not be underestimated.

"EXPERIENCE"

> Every religious experience after revelation is
> a mediated one.
> —*Gershom Scholem*

Eliade's Jungian position, adopted only in the 1950s, established a landmark in the progressive psychologization of the idea of religion. The mutual influences on Jung and Eliade, including such figures as Kierkegaard and Otto, had extended the inwardness of Protestant "faith" to a pure condition of interiority. Schleiermacher, in this connection, had a particularly significant impact on Carl Jung. This sense of the numinously meaningful inner life could, then, especially at the hands of Jung, seize on the "totality" of the "psyche" as being no longer God, but rather what remained as a ghostly imprint of His aftermath—"the God-image."

Corbin in turn approved Schleiermacher's claim that "there is a mode of knowledge which is intuitive, divinatory, combining the action of imagination and feeling, and which as such is the mode, essentially, of religious knowledge."[74] Legitimate religious "knowledge" meant for Corbin only the strongest possible epistemology, that of "gnosis."[75] Gnostic knowing alone, then, yielded for the scholar of the religious past a properly profound knowledge of its truest inner life. This "inner truth" was to be grasped as a whole. "For all this makes up an organic whole, of which the philosopher's thought is the seed and his experience the substance."[76]

Gershom Scholem long sought something rather similar in his study of the historical past, even as he was always wary of it. At a critical junction in his precocious youth, he asked Walter Benjamin whether Judaism "is still alive as a heritage or an experience, even as something constantly evolving, or did it exist only as an object of cognition."[77] As David Biale has pointed out, as early as 1917 the young Scholem opposed "experience" as such. "In place of 'experience' Scholem advocated education by example."[78] The nineteenth-century sciences, he complained, "demanded for themselves the right of the mysteries of creation and the wretched experience of the 'disenchanted' world, which they called *Erfahrung* (experience) set itself up as eternal."[79] In his "Unhistorical Aphorisms" he dryly submitted the aphorism, "Experience (*Erlebnis*) can only know Nothingness (*Nichts*)."[80] In his rigorous critique of "Martin Buber's Conception of Judaism," he excoriated the vocabulary of dialogue articulated in Buber's philosophy. "They continue to terminate in a hypostatization of the old concept of *Erlebnis* onto the ontological realm."[81]

What was at stake in Scholem's thought, nonetheless, was the nature of "true human experience." "What was formerly taken as a state of redemption, especially in its messianic connotations, by now becomes the condition in which alone *true human experience* is possible. The unredeemed state is no longer worthy to be called human. The redeemed state is where human experience begins."[82]

Eventually, Scholem came to represent one side of an extensive controversy concerning ostensible "experiences" in Merkabah mysticism.[83] Scholem elsewhere cited Immanuel Kant against those who denied the significance of religious experience. "I am not orthodox, but it is evident to me that without the restoration of such a 'fruitful bathos of experience' (*fruchtbaren bathos der Erfahrung*), which arises out of the reflection and transformation of human words in the medium of the divine, nothing of your project can be realized."[84]

Corbin, for his part, wrote a letter to the editor—the only letter to the editor I know him to have written—of *Revue de métaphysique et de morale*, which was published in 1963. He attacked the Guénonian position that Ibn 'Arabi's visions were "essentiellment impersonnel et non individual." Corbin argued that Ibn 'Arabi's *Futuhat* "est essentiellement fondé sur les expériences visionnaires, ses intuitions et ses songes les plus personnels."[85] Eliade also wrote regularly on religious experience. One of his best-known essays was titled "Experiences of the Mystic Light."[86] But, in fact, Eliade, dependent for this point on René Guénon, found the significance of the sacred not in experience per se but rather almost exclusively in the impersonal.[87] Corbin and Eliade still seemed somewhat—though only somewhat—to take the psychology of religious experience as such more seriously than did Scholem. That being said, it will be noticed by any honest reader that our Historians of Religions were unconcerned with the "psychology of religious experience" taken in psychological terms alone. This they collectively derogated as mere "psychologism."

INDIVIDUUM EST INEFFABILE

> The idea of an individual who is himself his
> species is the idea of the Angel.
> —*Henry Corbin*

In 1740, Goethe wrote to Johann Kasper Lavater (1741–1801), "Have I not already written to you, '*Individuum est ineffabile*,' from which I derive a whole world?"[88] In 1947, Leo Baeck, who had been the spiritual leader of German Jewry in its darkest years and was then an aged Holocaust survivor, employed this phrase as the title of his lecture at Eranos.[89] Corbin, for his part, eventually reiterated this Goethean theme as a Leitmotif of Eranos itself. "There is no explaining the initial fact of which we are speaking, for it is individual and singular, and the individual can be neither deduced nor explained; *individuum est ineffabile* . . . the individual as the first and only concrete reality. . . . Hermeneutics as science of the individual stands in opposition to historical dialectics as alienation of the person."[90]

For Corbin's Jungian-inflected view of the individual, the self is transformed to Self, the mere little man to Cosmic Anthropos, by means of "*exemplification*, which constitutes the individual person and raises him to the dimension of an archetypal Person."[91] Corbin's pointed contrast between *individual* and *collective* runs throughout his postwar thought. Hans Schmid-Guisan, an old friend of Jung, wrote a now forgotten allegory of the conflict between two opposed forms of life, which he termed

Collectivopolis and *Individua*.[92] Corbin discovered Schmid-Guisan's now largely forgotten book, *Comme le jour et la nuit*, with its introduction by Jung.[93] The Islamicist then used it as a pretext to contrast "individualism" (not quite identical with Jung's "individuation") with "collectivization." "The vertical dimension is individuation and sacralization; the other is collectivization and secularization."[94]

Catalan author Eugenio d'Ors was praised both by Eliade and by Corbin for his *bon mot* that the angel is its own species.[95] "This secret [of the angel] is also the secret of the 'power of the keys', the keys of the personal, spiritual Temple"[96] For Corbin, the *potestas clavium*, the "power of the keys," was the insight that undergirds his angelology: that the individual, through encounters with his Angel, transcends mere selfhood to become a kind of Universal Man.

"ENORMOUS TELLURIAN FORCES"

Another means of accessing universals was from below. Our authors each wrote of certain "telluric" forces. The 1953 Eranos meeting was devoted to the theme "Mensch und Erde," "Man and Earth." Eliade spoke on "La Terre-Mère et les hiérogamies cosmiques," Corbin lectured on "Terre Céleste et corps de résurrection d'après quelques traditions iraniennes," and Scholem devoted his talk to "Die Vorstellung vom Golem in ihren tellurischen und magischen Beziehungen." Although the title of Scholem's address included the adjective "tellurischen," this modifier was dropped from the English translation. But it remained, in the body of the text, in Scholem's reflections on the Golem. "Here then we have a truly tellurian creature, which, though animated by magic, remains within the realm of elemental forces. . . . So also in the kabbalistic development of the golem, the tellurian and magical elements converge in a way that is specifically defined . . . [so that] the golem once again becomes the repository of enormous tellurian forces which can, on occasion, erupt."[97]

Ivan Strenski, one of the few critics of Eliade to draw out the links between Heidegger and Eliade, observed their shared emphasis on "earth" or "telluric piety."[98] The *völkisch* dimension of Eliade's work drew on a perhaps uncynical respect for peasant piety, for quasi-pagan "cosmic christianity," for folklore and folklife as metaphors for cosmic origins.[99]

Corbin's paean to the Angel of the Earth, and thus to all things telluric, was his *Spiritual Body and Celestial Earth*, delivered at Eranos and published by Bollingen. He opens this movingly poetic piece of scholarship with the assertion that "the telluric glory is the liturgical creation, the hierurgy of that Earth angel whose features are perceived as a glorified human image."[100] What he does not tell the reader is that he once perpetrated a poem upon precisely this theme. Titled "Théologie au bord du lac," it came to him at Lake Siljan, in Sweden, on 24 August 1932: "Terre, Ange, Femme, tout cela en une seule chose, que j'adore et qui est dans cette forêt."[101] Two decades later, Corbin penned a private poem, "À Olga Fröbe Kapteyn," in September 1951. It begins this way:

A l'horizon d'un Derviche
Pérégrinant sur les hauts plateaux de Perse:
Des espaces illimités et nus, matière tellurique primordiale . . .[102]

In other words, Corbin at his most private and intimate, resorted to the "telluric" as a foundational conception. "Terre, Ange, Femme"—Earth, Angel, Woman—was such a conception.

"THE REAWAKENING OF OLD MENTAL STRUCTURES"

Die Vorzeit hat sich weider aufgetan
[Antiquity is revealed once again].
—*F. W. Von Schelling*

The telluric force erupts from the depths but only into the few individuals capable of such experiences. For these special few, this force could volcanically reconfigure their very worldview through a transvaluation of all value. They were the exceptions who saw through this world age to a new world reborn. The "exception," on the collective level, thus implied a new cycle of history releasing the dead hand of the past. On the individual level, however, the exception to the rules of conventional society was epitomized in the gnostic person. This impact of hierophany on historical reality provided Historians of Religion Corbin and Eliade with a raison d'être for their phenomenology of vision, a kind of visionary exceptionalism that could be taken seriously even while remaining respectably inside the academy. These "phenomenologists of religion"—under a Nietzschean influence diffused through a Jungian prism—thus glorified a heroism of private insight.[103] They claimed to find "structures of consciousness" and "modes of being" and "hierophanies" and "religious realities" and "archetypes" *out there in history but also in here available to the needy reader.*

The fit between apparent description and magisterial prescription belonged to the researcher, the exceptional scholar with firsthand insights into these things. As Eliezer Schweid said of Scholem, "God Himself is hidden, and the mystic breaks through to the hidden realms. This involves great daring and danger; upon reflection, one will realize that the very daring and danger which are present along the entire way themselves embody the experience of breakthrough to hidden depths. It is thus that Scholem characterizes mysticism."[104]

The Historians of Religion claimed not to be this mystic per se, but rather one who has recapitulated the breakthrough *intellectually*. One is reminded of the Historian of Religions as performer, telling secrets that are, paradoxically, protected precisely by means of their publication.[105] The gnostic modern, whether the Eranos scholar or his reader, thus was implied to recapitulate such mystic breakthroughs of old. Eliade with Scholem is rather more honest than Corbin on this point. Scholem addressed this idea provocatively in the famous parable that forms the conclusion of *Major Trends in Jewish Mysticism*. The scholar of religion who tells the story of the believer is the latest placeholder for that authentic believer of the past. The last in the line of tradition, the scholar of tradition, still belongs to a golden chain, unbroken yet, linked to an ultimately hierophanic past.[106] What still remains at the end of the chain is the insight of the scholar, which still is communicated, in turn, to the last reader.[107]

In all this—the telluric, the daimonic, the eruption from the depths—certain assumptions about experience inevitably were at work. The Ancient Discovery of the Unconscious was recapitulated by modern gnostics. Scholem found it in Kabbalah.[108] Most important, in this regard, was Scholem's pioneering article in which he claimed to have discovered the unconscious in the concept "Kadmut ha-Sekhel" of the Hasidim.[109] Jung, similarly, found the unconscious in ancient gnosis. "My enthusiasm arose . . . they were the first thinkers to concern themselves . . . with the contents of the collective unconscious."[110] And Eliade invoked an analogous notion, but in reverse; a hieropompic descent into the depths, on the analogy of a kind of sacred spelunking.

> When Jung revealed the existence of the collective unconscious, the exploration of these immemorial treasures—the myths, symbols and images of archaic humanity—began to approximate its techniques to those of oceanographers and speleologists.[111] Just as deep sea diving and cave exploration revealed elementary organisms that had long ago disappeared from the earth's surface, so analysis discovered a deep psychic life hitherto inaccessible to study.[112]

"HISTORICAL PSYCHOLOGY," "PSYCHOCOSMOLOGY," AND "ANTHROPOCOSMIC DESTINY"

> I was planning then, in May of 1940, to write a book, *Anthropocosmos* . . . but I wrote almost nothing.
>
> —*Mircea Eliade*

Although they were mature scholars before World War II, the respective systems of Scholem, Corbin, and Eliade were considerably broadened and refined after the war. As is well known, Eranos provided each an annual opportunity to present thematic lectures to an international audience. This new context allowed them to reflect synthetically on their specialized studies in an expanded, indeed, self-consciously global, forum. Their entry into Eranos also allowed them, as well, to speak of "religious realities" in planetary perspective. Finally, Eranos provided an opportunity to exploit the fruits of their philological labors to address, if indirectly, contemporary conflicts.

One psychological assumption they shared, which perhaps most exemplifies their emerging synthesis, was that which Scholem termed "historical psychology."[113] Scholem found this phenomenon in Sabbatian teaching, in which, he claimed, "the metaphysical and psychological elements are closely intertwined; or, to be more exact, they are one."[114] Later, at Eranos, he spoke of the "peculiar unity of [history and psychology] which constitutes the decisive step taken by Kabbalistic theosophy."[115] In fact, he introduced his first English-translation "Eranos" volume in just such terms, in an essay previously published in an issue of the Swiss magazine *Du* dedicated to Eranos.[116]

Of the works that perhaps more than any others propelled Corbin and Scholem out of the level of great specialists into the ranks of international sagehood, two books stand out. Both were translated by Ralph Manheim, perhaps the preeminent translator from German in his day. Manheim translated some sixty-seven Eranos lectures, edited in six volumes for the Bollingen series by Joseph Campbell, published between 1954 and 1968. The works he translated by Corbin and Scholem, however, were the first of their synthetic Eranos lectures to reach the English-reading public. Corbin's *Creative Imagination in the Sufism of Ibn ʿArabi,* largely made up of Eranos lectures published in the *Jahrbücher* in 1955 and 1956, was published in the Bollingen series in 1969. Scholem's *On the Kabbalah and Its Symbolism,* which collected Eranos lectures delivered between 1949 and 1957, was published in Manheim's English translation in 1965. This publishing history is apposite to understanding certain statements made in these two books, which take on a somewhat different cast when read in the light of each other. In this light, certain apparent parallels are of interest.

The creature-Creator typifies the *coincidentia oppositorum.* From the first this *coincidentia* is present to Creation, because Creation is not *ex nihilo* but a theophany. As such, it is Imagination. The Creative Imagination is theophanic Imagination, and the Creator is one with the imagining Creature because each Creative Imagination is a theophany, a recurrence of the Creation. *Psychology is indistinguishable from cosmology; the theophanic imagination joins them into a psycho-cosmology.*[117]

While Scholem's emphasis is different, it is interesting to note that he concluded *On the Kabbalah and Its Symbolism* by begging off from just such claims. "The golem has been interpreted as a symbol of the soul or of the Jewish people, and both theories can give rise, no doubt, to meaningful reflections. But the historian's task ends where the psychologist's begins."[118]

Just as Scholem nonetheless spoke of "historical psychology," so Corbin similarly spoke of "psycho-cosmology."[119] Eliade preferred a closely analogous concept, "anthropocosmic destiny." "It is not a matter of making objective or scientific observations but of arriving at an appraisal of the world around us in terms of life, and in terms of anthropocosmic destiny, embracing sexuality, fecundity, death and rebirth."[120] Closely related formulations of Eliade's included "cosmo-physiological mysticism"[121] and "anthropo-cosmos."[122] Psychoanalysis of the individual, finally, has been reversed into that of the cosmos. Eliade already proclaimed this process, the world process of symbolization, in the final paragraph of his first masterwork, *Patterns in Comparative Religion*. "[Symbols] identify, assimilate, and unify diverse levels and realities that are to all appearances incompatible. Further still: magico-religious experience makes it possible for man himself to be transformed into a symbol. And only in so far as man himself becomes a symbol, are all systems *and all anthropo-cosmic experiences possible.*[123]

CONCLUSION: THE SUPREMACY
OF THE HISTORY OF RELIGIONS

The psychologists, C. G. Jung among others of the first rank, have shown us how much the dramas of the modern world proceed from a profound disequilibrium of the psyche, individual as well as collective, brought about largely by a progressive sterilisation of the imagination. . . . [However, the] historian of religions is in a better position than anyone else to promote the knowledge of symbols. . . . It is in the history of religions that we meet with the "archetypes," of which only approximate variants are dealt with by psychologists and literary critics.[124]

—*Mircea Eliade*

Ultimately all three scholars claimed unequivocal superiority for the "religious" study of religion over the "psychological" study of religion. Jung seemed to Corbin and Eliade generally not to conflict with such a remythologization; Scholem opted for a quietly peaceful coexistence with

Jung, electing not to engage in his otherwise customary polemics. Eliade, for his part, lionized Jung to the end of his life. He warmed to the subject in a 1978 interview.

> I have a great admiration for Jung, both for the thinker and for the kind of man he was. I met him in August 1950, at the Eranos Conference in Ascona. After half an hour's conversation I felt I was listening to a Chinese Sage or an east European peasant, still rooted in earth mother yet close to Heaven at the same time. I was enthralled by the wonderful simplicity of his presence, by the spontaneity, the erudition, and the humor of his conversation . . . at each meeting I was deeply impressed by the fullness, and what I must call the "wisdom," of his life.[125]

In the end, the Historians of Religion did not reverse psychoanalysis. Rather, they retained operative assumptions that they shared with the depth psychologies of Freud and Jung. Most especially, they posited a kind of unconscious, the eruptive depths that provide contact, by means of symbols, with universal truths. This realm of "religious reality" accessible through its "depths" was never, on their reading, to be identified directly with the psyche. But their notion of religion, at bottom, privileged the experience of symbols above other forms of cognition or perception. They balked at calling this *individual* psychology, each preferring to see in this symbolization the royal road for the individual's transformation, or reintegration, into an "historical psychology." Such was the "anthropocosmic destiny" steering their visionary course. Psyche reverses into cosmos. Still, especially in the case of Eliade and Corbin, the denial that this psyche was psychological seems designed to enable them to have their Jungian cake and eat it too.[126]

Part V

ETHICS

CHAPTER 13

Uses of the Androgyne in the History of Religions

MÉPHISTOPHÉLÈS ET L'ANDROGYNE

The most striking (and the most uncharacteristic) title of the many books published by Mircea Eliade was *Méphistophélès et l'androgyne*.[1] This title had a long history.[2] It was the title of the longest essay in the collection; this article in turn had been his lecture at the Eranos meeting in Ascona, Switzerland, in 1958. Before that, this same material had originally constituted his studies in the late 1930s; they were published during the war, in Romanian, as *The Myth of Reintegration*.[3] The essay itself, in its final English version, alludes to this protracted history in its opening lines. "About twenty years ago [1938], happening to reread the 'Prologue in Heaven' of Goethe's *Faust*, and having just reread Balzac's *Séraphita*, I seemed to see a kind of parallel between the two works which I could not define."[4] Henry Corbin, in full awareness of Eliade's work (and vice versa), likewise investigated the relation between *Faust* and *Séraphita*. Corbin, like Eliade, similarly opened an Eranos lecture with a discussion of *Séraphita*, in 1965.[5] Elsewhere, like Eliade, Corbin also returned to this theme.[6] And Gershom Scholem, to pursue the parallel, showed that such esoteric teachings on the androgyne found their way into the private fantasies of his friend, the philosopher Walter Benjamin.

To untangle the threads of this common interest—indeed, at first, simply to discern the theme itself—I must explicate the connections between various seemingly unrelated texts. These threads include the short story *Séraphita* by Balzac, the novel *Baphomet* by Pierre Klossowski, and a short fantasy by Walter Benjamin. These three works, each in its own way unclassifiable, play on esoteric traditions in such a way as to blur the line between fiction and nonfiction, between spiritual confession and "mere" literature; between allusion to initiatic secrets and excoriation of bourgeois forms of monotheism. After considering these implications, I will conclude with reflections on the influence of these themes on the Mephistophelean theory of religion refined by the Historians of Religion under study here.

SÉRAPHITA

Séraphita, the mystical novel by Honoré de Balzac, was a prized preoccupation of Eliade, one to which he lovingly returned in many forums. In

1947, for example, he described an intense interest in Balzac, devoting a study (which apparently was lost) to him, even planning a book just on *Séraphita*.[7] He kept these larger themes in mind throughout the years. In his 1974 essay, "The Occult and the Modern World," Eliade claimed that in *Séraphita*, "occult themes and ideology reflected a hope in a personal or collective *renovatio*—a mystical restoration of man's original dignity and powers; in sum, the literary creations reflected and prolonged the conceptions of seventeenth- and eighteenth-century theosophists and of their sources."[8]

But it was the title essay of *Méphistophélès et l'androgyne* in which he laid out his theosophical interest in *Séraphita* fully and (with all due esoteric reserve) explicitly. This essay brought together most of the major themes of Eliade at mid-career, and did so, moreover, in a manner in which he was especially accomplished. That is, he spoke of exceedingly well known European cultural figures, in this case Goethe and Balzac, but in such a way that an almost shockingly foreign light was shed on their accomplishments. More specifically, he pulled the historical rug out from under them in a tour de force of erudition designed to relocate their modern fiction in the context of prehistoric myth. And so he concluded:

> Goethe and Balzac both believed in the unity of European literature, and considered their own works as belonging to that literature. They would have been even prouder than they were if they had realized that this European literature goes back beyond Greece and the Mediterranean, beyond the ancient Near East and Asia; that the myths called to new life in *Faust* and *Séraphita* come to us from a great distance in space and time; that they come to us from prehistory.[9]

It is no accident, I think, that both in this essay and in his 1974 "The Occult and the Modern World," Eliade spoke of *Faust* and *Séraphita* in the same breath, as it were.[10] In fact, the title of the essay announces that intention, which then explicitly frames the essay at its beginning and at its end.

Eliade introduced his commentary on *Séraphita* by calling this "the most attractive of Balzac's fantastic novels." This was the case, said Eliade, not because of "the Swedenborgian theories with which it is imbued but because Balzac here succeeded in presenting with unparalleled force a fundamental theme of archaic anthropology: the androgyne as perfect man."[11] This notion of the androgyne as perfect man was repeated almost verbatim by Eliade at the very end of his life, in his entry on "Androgyne" for the *Encyclopedia of Religion*, which he (nominally) edited.[12] In other words, Eliade, on the face of it, and throughout his long career, celebrated an ideal type, the male androgyne.[13] Séraphita, in

Eliade's presentation, is just such a creature: throughout his discussions, Eliade refers to Séraphita as "he." Eliade insisted that Séraphita is not an angel but rather "a perfect man, that is to say a 'complete being.'"[14]

Séraphita occupied pride of place for Eliade because, as the original Romanian title of his study of androgyny suggests, he was primarily concerned with what he called "the myth of reintegration." "Reintegration" was a technical term taken from the occult science of alchemy and from the occult societies of Illuminism.[15] In *Yoga*, for example, he spoke of "the reintegration of the primordial androgyne, the conjunction, in one's own being, of male and female—in a word, the reconquest of the completeness that precedes all creation."[16] Elsewhere he could promote a drive "to accelerate the reintegration of the precosmogonic stage, that is, the 'end of the world,' and on the other hand, to approach God through a progressive 'spermatization.'"[17]

Henry Corbin's comments on *Séraphita* came first in his 1965 Eranos lecture, "The Configuration of the Temple of the *Ka'bah* as the Secret of the Spiritual Life." He opened this long talk with a contrast between two interpretations of Balzac he had read in the preceding year.[18] In a second reading of *Séraphita*, Corbin used "Seraphitus-Séraphita" to epitomize the angel's androgyny.[19] After evoking Balzac's reading of Swedenborg, Corbin explicated the significance of these newly discovered angels on Balzac's imagination.

> Thus was born the idea for a book which would become the mystical master-piece of Balzac, the idea of *Seraphitus-Séraphita*, a single angel, but a double being, masculine and feminine, taking birth in the union of the lover and the beloved; liberating in each other "the angelic creature imprisoned in the physical body," this angel *is* the doubleness of their love. Out of this came the book bearing the definitive title of *Séraphita*, in which a hommage to Swedenborg and his doctrines vibrates in long resonances.
>
> [Ainsi naquit l'idée du livre qui devait être le chef-d'oeuvere mystique de Balzac, l'idée de *Seraphitus-Séraphita*, un même ange, mais un être double, masculin et féminin, prenant naissance dans l'union de l'amant et l'aimée; libérant dans chacun des deux "la créature angélique emprisonée dans son être charnel," cet ange *est* la dualitude de leur amour. D'est le livre qui en définitive porta le titre de "Séraphita," et dans lequel un hommage à Swedenborg et à ses doctrines vibre en longues resonances.][20]

While *Séraphita* is not exactly an obscure work, it may not be obvious to uninitiated readers why it was that Balzac's supposed Swedenborgianism, on the joint reading of Corbin and Eliade, was seized on as being unusually significant.[21] Elsewhere, Corbin clarified this point, in his exposition of the Swedenborgian androgyne. In fact, this was to be one of the most succinct summations of the esoteric theory of androgyny. "The feminine in the human being, or man's internal feminine, is, therefore, man's self, his *proprium*, but a self that is transparent to the Principle that vivifies it, for as celestial man is constituted on the morning of the seventh day, he is *Homo*, masculine and feminine (*mas femineus*, said the alchemist), that is . . . his spiritual constitution was androgynous."[22]

The joint associations made by Eliade and Corbin with the secret societies of Illuminism and Martinism may not be irrelevant to understanding such interest in the androgyne.[23] In an unpublished work on the androgyne, the Russian filmmaker Sergei Eisenstein identified psychological and historical dimensions of the androgyne, but with an important difference. According to a study by V. V. Ivanow, Eisenstein found in Balzac and Swedenborg "a combination of two seemingly opposite 'primeval' themes (archetypes)—*Übermenschlichkeit* and the indivisibility and non-differentiation manifested in Balzac's 'proclivity for depicting secret societies.'"[24] It would seem, similarly, that *Séraphita's* popularity with Corbin and Eliade may be related to esoteric teachings to which they somehow were privy.

AGESILAUS SANTANDER

I turn now to Gershom Scholem. In a truly remarkable essay, "Walter Benjamin and his Angel," Gershom Scholem told the fascinating story of a painting once owned by his friend Walter Benjamin. More precisely, this essay told of at least three angels of Walter Benjamin: the angel depicted in the Paul Klee painting *Angelus Novus*, which was owned by Benjamin; the androgyne Agesilaus Santander described in a revealing eponymous fantasy Benjamin wrote in 1933; and the famous angel of history evoked in his influential "Theses on the Philosophy of History." For the purposes at hand, it is "Agesilaus Santander" which is of immediate concern, though, as I hope to show, the other angels are hardly irrelevant.

First, of course, there is the descriptive fact that, "Agesilaus Santander," would appear to be an *androgynous angel*. Benjamin's cryptic fantasy projects this angel, called Agesilaus Santander, as his inner self. "For in taking advantage of the circumstance that I came into the world under the sign of Saturn—the star of the slowest revolution, the planet of detours and delays—he sent his feminine form after the masculine one reproduced in the picture by way of the longest, most fatal detour, even though both happened to be—only they did not know each other—most intimately adjacent to each other."[25] This creature, Benjamin confesses, bears his own, secret name. As Scholem explains, "Agesilaus Santander is . . . an anagram of *The Angel Satan* (*Der Angelus Satanas*) . . . who is identical with the fallen, rebellious Lucifer."[26] In other words, unlike the androgyne-as-perfect-man with which Eliade identified, or the androgyne-as-angel with which Corbin identified, Benjamin's inner androgyne seems something much closer to a demon; or, at least, a *daimon*. In Benjamin's "fantasia," moreover, the themes of the androgyne and of secrecy intertwined. Perhaps even more important for the purposes at hand, we also find in the "Angel Satan" a coincidence of ethical opposites which mirrors its gender-bending androgyny.

Benjamin, then, embraced another kind of androgyne, in an instructively odd contrast to that of Eliade and Corbin. Benjamin's was no esoteric teaching about superhuman perfection. His alter ego, "Angel Satan," was a satanic sort of bisexual being, less his ideal of perfection than the projected reconciliation of his own inner divisions. This, at least, was Scholem's reading. "In the phantasmagoria of his imagination, the picture of the *Angelus Novus* becomes for Benjamin a picture of his angel as the occult reality of his self."[27] Such hints by Scholem lead the reader laterally from this essay on Benjamin to his primary, contemporaneous studies undertaken as Kabbalah researcher. This is certainly the case with the just mentioned explanation concerning the "occult reality of [Benjamin's] self." The context may help to understand the significance of Scholem's explanation. It comes in a discussion of a fourth angel in Benjamin's work, one conjured in Benjamin's essay on Karl Kraus.

Scholem describes this Krausian angel with the technical term "perfect nature," which he explains as "the expression of the old masters of hermetics."[28] The careful reader of Scholem, the paragon of careful writing, would notice here that the Jerusalem scholar had employed the hermetic notion of "perfect nature" at least twice elsewhere, in lectures on Kabbalah.[29] In both cases, Scholem employed this technical term to define a condition of fulfillment, of collective fulfillment, of utopian redemption. For now, I will merely mark this point, but I shall return to it in due order. For the moment, I would emphasize that Scholem's classic essay, "Walter Benjamin and His Angel," itself serves to link Scholem's autobiographical writings with his Kabbalah studies.

BAPHOMET

> Mais si le Diable, au contraire, si l'Autre était le
> Même? Et si la Tentation n'était pas un des épi-
> sodes du grand antagonisme, mais la mince insin-
> uation du Double?
> —*Michel Foucault, on Pierre Klossowski's*
> Baphomet

Other modern texts celebrating androgyny, I want to suggest, may be usefully adduced to aid in our understanding its uses in "the History of

Religions." This is only in part because the Historians of Religion belonged to some of the same circles as did these fiction writers. Lines of thematic influence are also discernible. I turn now to works of modern fiction that star a divine androgyne called *Baphomet*.[30]

Pierre Klossowski, philosopher, novelist, and painter, brother of the celebrated artist Balthus and uncle of alchemical writer and filmmaker Stansislaus (Stash) de Rola Klossowski, was active in the Collège de Sociologie, where his circles overlapped those of Corbin. Not only was he personally acquainted with both Corbin and Eliade, but he also publicly praised the work of both of them.[31] He was also a friend of Walter Benjamin and a translator of one of his most important essays. In fact, the work of Eliade and Corbin seems to have had at least some important bearing, if not demonstrably direct influence, on his exceedingly strange novel *The Baphomet*.[32]

Novels featuring Baphomet seem to position themselves in a self-dramatizing half-light, teaching esoteric truths secretly in the open, as it were. Perhaps the most significant of these was *The Angel in the Western Window*, the last novel by the fantastic novelist Gustav Meyrink (admired by Borges and Jung, among others).[33] Scholem, as a young man, met Meyrink; on their very first encounter, Eliade asked Scholem about him.[34] Interestingly enough, one finds Corbin citing a volume dedicated to Meyrink little more than a year before the former's death.[35]

Baphomet ranks among the darkest of devilish imaginings, and the most popular of satanic scenarios.[36] This hyperdemonic icon stimulated such destructive satanists as Aleister Crowley (1875–1946), who dubbed himself Baphomet.[37] Here again, perhaps, it is useful to recall Eisenstein's insight to the effect that the androgyne and the mythology of secret societies share a certain semiotic indivisibility or at least a fictional connection to one another. One may perhaps go further, though, and risk asking the obvious question. Does the androgyne emperor—*or is it empress?*—wear any clothes? This question, to which I now turn, is the problem of nihilism.

FAUST

Philemonis sacrum, Fausti poenitentia
(Philemon's sanctuary, Faust's atonement)
—*Inscription on the entrance to Jung's*
Bollingen tower

It should be remembered that, as I noted at the outset, Eliade repeatedly cited *Séraphita* in the same breath as Goethe's *Faust*. "About twenty years ago [1938], happening to reread the 'Prologue in Heaven' of

Goethe's *Faust*, and having just reread Balzac's *Séraphita*, I seemed to see a kind of parallel between the two works which I could not define."[38] The authors I am discussing each in his own way loved Goethe, and perhaps Goethe's *Faust* most of all.

In particular, they took the culminating passage of the second *Faust*, the chorus of the "Mothers" or the "Eternal Feminine," to be the closest thing to genuine revelation anywhere in modern literature. Corbin evoked Faust's Eternal Feminine as the deified goddess Sophia so central to his modern version of gnosis, just as it was also central for Jung.[39] Corbin, through an intepretation of Iranian Shiʻism, evoked this Sophia in movingly ecstatic tones.

> We can say of her through whom earthly existence is transfigured into the dawn of a supercelestial earth, that she is *the* THEOPHANY. The theme rises and expands to such magnitude that our Iranian Shaikh . . . reaches heights foreshadowed by Goethe at the conclusion of the second Faust: an Eternally Feminine, preceding even terrrestial woman because predceding the differentiation of male and female in the terrestial world. . . . Indeed, we have to take feminine as meaning, in the first place, the totality of the beings of the universe of the Possible![40]

Corbin, like Eliade, then, found in the History of Religions a kind of revelation of the androgyne epitomized in Goethe's Faust. Here again his personal philosophy was inseparable from his writing as a Historian of Religion.

I suggested that Scholem's essay, "Walter Benjamin and his Angel," similarly revealed a thread connecting his scholarship and his personal philosophy. This connection was not nihilism—though the philosopher Franz Rosenzweig, who was acquainted with Scholem, did accuse him of being a nihilist—but a kind of deal with or wager on nihilism characterized as a pact with the devil. The point I am making is that Scholem (citing the Islamicist Helmutt Ritter, a German colleague of Corbin in wartime Istanbul) identified Agesilaus Santander's "perfect nature" as the astral body, the personal daimon, of the *Zohar*, and then in turn with "Dr. Faust's Devil, who made a pact with him and thereafter initiates him into the secrets of black art."[41] In short, Scholem, in making these associations, implicitly identified Benjamin's Agesilaus Santander with Goethe's Mephistopheles by way of Corbin's "perfect nature." His personal essay on Benjamin's angel, then, reveals to the close reader, if not a theology of the History of Religions, at least certain linked assumptions that allow the attentive reader to detect themes beneath the surface of the exposition.

NIHIL CONTRA DEUM, NISIS DEUS IPSE

No one can stand against a god unless he is a god
himself.
                              —*Johann Wolfgang von Goethe*

Elsewhere, it seems, Goethe expressed yet deeper implications of his
Mephistophelan *theology*, or perhaps more precisely of this return to
myth. Hans Blumenberg's monumental study *Work on Myth* provides the
background for that myth, which Blumenberg sees as the myth of Prometheus. Prometheus, Corbin tells us, was also the archetype for the
Man of Light, the gnostic Lucifer, literally the Light-Bringer.[42] Blumenberg devotes a chapter to understanding the context of another Goethe
saying. "On July 3, 1810, Goethe delivered this afterdinner observation:
'*Nihil contra Deum, nisis Deus ipse*. A magnificent dictum, with endless
applications. God always confronts himself; God in man again confronts
himself in man.'"[43] As Blumenberg observes, this implied nothing less
than the theosophy of Jacob Boehme, which posits tensions interior to
the godhead, forces actively in celestial opposition; an "intradivine dissension."[44]

Similarly, Corbin, with parallel Prometheanism derived from his beloved Goethe, claimed that "the gnostic is forced, as it were, to reaffirm
God against God."[45] The passage in which this claim is expressed is worth
noting in more detail. In this essay, "The Dramatic Element Common to
the Gnostic Cosmogonies of the Religions of the Book," Corbin delivered a manifesto for gnostics to the gathering of gnostics at the Université de Saint Jean de Jerusalem, which he had founded a few years earlier.[46]
Here the aged Islamicist gnostic not merely embraced but demanded the
rebirth, within Judaism, as its true essence: Sabbatianism. Relying exclusively here on Scholem's researches, Corbin posited an androgynous first
Emanation.

> [*Shekhina*] in its bi-unity, reveals itself, and saves . . . and it is this that has
> been forgotten as a result of later confusion and demoralisation. However, if
> the Jewish people are guilty of this forgetfulness, the same is true where the
> other religions of the Book are concerned. . . . Faced with this danger, the
> gnostic is forced to reaffirm, as it were, God against God, forced to free the
> personal God from the status and function of the supreme Principle and
> Cause, for these do not belong to him.[47]

Corbin had long held the position that conventional forms of monotheistic religions were degenerate and thus deserving of the gnostic onslaught
against them. Jung, another gnostic, similarly spoke of this intradivine

dissension beginning with the book of Job, "Job who expected help from God against God."[48] At the end of his life the Swiss therapist wrote one last time of "God supporting us against God, as Job long ago understood."[49]

Before leaving Goethe it may be remembered that he claimed, in yet another celebrated dictum, to be a pantheist in science, a polytheist in poetry, and a monotheist in ethics.[50] What is apt in the present context is that the androgyne in the second *Faust* is polytheist; is not man, angel, or demon, but nothing less than *another god*. Blumenberg rightly concluded that Goethe's "extraordinary saying" was not Christian but rather gnostic, dualist, positing a demiurgic alternate divinity; an esoteric idea descending from the theosophy of Jakob Boehme.[51] Boehme, especially through his followers von Baader and Swedenborg, was equally an influence on Balzac, Corbin, and Eliade.

THE HISTORICAL PSYCHOLOGY OF THE ANDROGYNE

To recapitulate: the androgyne was a popular trope for totality among the Historians of Religion under discussion here.[52] More specifically, the androgyne was identified as perfect man by Eliade; as Angel by Corbin; as demon by Scholem (in his interpretation of Benjamin); and as the godhead by their common predecessor Goethe. What totalities could be left for the androgyne to represent? At least one more serious possibility remains to be explored.

When Scholem came to discuss the feminine dimension of the divine, he emphasized that *Shekina* symbolized both a sector of the godhead as well as a personification of the Jewish people. It therefore, he insisted, operated as a dialectical unity of history and psychology.[53] The androgyne-as-historical-psychology, in fact, may be the most comprehensive totality of all. Corbin called this totality a "psycho-cosmology."[54]

In fact, the androgyne, especially for Eliade, Jung, and Corbin, never concerned individual psychology, but always collective psychology. The reunification or reintegration of opposites that it represented were meant to be ontogenetic, historiosophic, macrocosmic. Their ultimate androgyne thus was the Perfect Man; Adam Kadmon; the Angel of Humanity; the Holy Spirit; *Homo maximus*; the Macanthropus; the macrocosmic anthropos.[55] This macanthropos, the angelic projection of humanity as such, seems implicit also in Benjamin's "Angel of History." The individual psyche was literally, from this esoteric perspective on cosmic personification, *im*material, no matter whatsoever. Only the whole mattered. The androgyne, in short, was the ideal sign for an eschatological totality.[56]

Finding a name for this totality, of course, is at once obvious and almost impossible. That is, on the one hand, this esoterism is familiar as a variant on contemporary esoteric teachings, doctrines with a profound influence on Corbin, Eliade, and their joint mentor, Carl Jung. Both Corbin and Eliade, moreover, seem to have enjoyed initiatic warrants for their esoterism.[57] This general fact was explicitly evident even on the surface of their writing, a secret held in public, a kind of hiding in the open. On the other hand, the identification of their "inner" teachings and, more recalcitrantly, of their initiators—if they had them—may never be known. They were, at the least, secret groups of some sort, probably Martinist; hence the accuracy of Eisenstein's observation concerning a "proclivity for depicting secret societies."[58]

It is not uncommon for secret societies to position themselves as being released from the moral interdictions that govern conventional social life.[59] Eisenstein spoke to this point. "This unity of the superman and the collective, which is presented mystically and abstractly in *Séraphita*, is depicted concretely and through actual situations in . . . the superman Trompe-le-Mort . . . the omnipotent leader of the criminals."[60] The androgyne as criminal, or at least as symbol of antinomianism, emerges from the foregoing pattern of usages.

The theory of religion implied by these uses of the androgyne, then, presumed an eschatological totality with certain social consequences. A kind of theology of higher crime, analogous perhaps to Sade's "Society of the Friends of Crime," this theory evoked fantasies of release from the natural order—*Gender*—in order to elicit if not accelerate even more potent fantasies of release from the constitutional order—*Law*. Our authors, to be sure, understood such revolutionary potential in these theories. The revolution to come is the ultimate unification of the "superman and the collective," as Eisenstein put it. Scholem's reflections on this point were really quite unequivocal: such a revolutionary superman could well end up being Jacob Frank, "in all his actions a truly corrupt and degenerate individual. Indeed, it might be plausibly argued that in order completely to exhaust its seemingly endless potential for the contradictory and the unexpected the Sabbatian movement was in need of just such a strongman."[61]

CONCLUSION: "TO INTEGRATE THE EVIL ONE"

> Herbert Spencer tells us that the perfect man's conduct will appear perfect only when the environment is perfect.
>
> —*William James*

While one could no doubt read the materials under discussion here in terms of the hydraulic involutions of sexuality, I have chosen not to do so. In this choice I agree with Sergei Eisenstein, who similarly said, with reference to his own discussion of androgyny, that "the abovementioned observations on bisexuality have no relation whatsoever to sexuality in the narrow sense of the word. We are interested in the problem of 're-moving' the biologically sexual interpretation of the concept of opposites in this concept, that is, in the image of an imagined superman unifying opposite poles."[62] In making this point, I am not following Jung, who pretentiously asserted that Freud was stuck in the biological basement of the psyche, while he, Jung, worked in its spiritual attic. Rather, I follow Martin Buber against Jung: "[T]he bridal unification of opposites" always also means a positive transvaluation of evil and negative transvaluation of good.[63] Jung's "wholeness," Buber saw clearly, meant "the integration of evil."[64] And so, when Alan Watts compiled a quasi-Jungian anthology on "myths of polarity," he could proclaim that to "secure this growth of consciousness we must recover the lost or hidden dimensions of our nature; we must, as Jung would say, 'integrate the Evil One.'"[65]

Eliade, for his part, insisted on totality as the ideal for the Historian of Religions. "But Hegel dealt with no more than two or three centuries, whereas the historian of religions is obliged to study and understand the history of the mind in its totality, from Paleolithic man onward."[66] He also insisted that he himself be judged not merely as such a Historian of Religions, but explicitly—to return to my point of departure—like none other than Balzac and Goethe. "In the same way, if I dare to compare myself just for one instant with those giants, it is only the totality of my writings that can reveal the meaning."[67] And that meaning was quite clearly expressed. "Androgyny is an archaic and universal formula for the expression of wholeness, the co-existence of the contraries, or *coincidentia oppositorum*."[68] Reflecting on "balance between two antagonistic forces of good and evil," Eliade commented that that "reminds me of Goethe and especially of C. G. Jung, for whom the ideal of man is not *perfection*, but *totality*."[69]

While Jung insisted that perfection was the problem, and even went so far as to accuse Yahweh and the Jews of a pernicious perfectionism, it is hardly the case that his preferred alternative, wholeness, is necessarily preferable.[70] Jung's and Eliade's "whole man," at the end of history, stands on a pile of corpses, as Benjamin envisioned the scene: "[O]ne single catastrophe that keeps piling up wreckage on wreckage" and throwing it at the feet of the angel.[71] Eliade, Corbin, Benjamin, and Klossowski understood this collapsing of ethical opposites, which led them back to Faust. The esoteric motif of androgyny led repeatedly back, that is, to an identification with the Mephistophelean "other." This regression, perhaps, in the rather bleak light of retrospection, may not be surprising. It leads back to the hubristic condition we tend now to call *Faustian*.

Or, perhaps, *Zarathustran*. Jung spent much of the 1930s teaching a vastly extended seminar on Nietzsche's Zarathustra: his "whole man," ultimately championed in his postwar *Response to Job*, may inadequately but not irresponsibly be identified as a self-appointed successor of the Nietzschean *Übermensch*.[72] For Jung, and then for his associates Corbin and Eliade, esoteric traditions successfully obfuscated the constitutional status of this Brave New Superman. Or perhaps such remystification was the social program all along.[73]

In any case, mediated in all its various intensities and colorations, some such androgyne was central to the Historians of Religion, Corbin, Eliade, and Scholem. It reposed near the core of their preoccupation with gnosis. Henry Corbin, in his retrospective essay, "The Time of Eranos," called the Eranos men "gnostic minds."[74] How the gnosticizing theory of androgyny influenced their studies of religion, however, is a topic for another discussion.[75]

Defeating Evil from Within: Comparative Perspectives on "Redemption through Sin"

> Here precisely is the paradox, the permanant challenge of this Shi'ite Gnosis: to experience the religion of Resurrection, the religion of the Imam, is to penetrate the hidden sense of the positive religion and at the same time to surpass it. And yet the positive religion must be retained, precisely in order to constrain men to exceed it, to call the resurrection of the adepts.
> —*Henry Corbin*

THE GREATEST scholarship requires the closest study. Gershom Scholem's classic essay "Redemption through Sin" remains one of the most influential essays written not only in Jewish Studies but in the History of Religions more generally.[1] It was a tour de force, serving at once as programmatic seed, historiographic manifesto, research agenda, and transvaluational breakthrough. Even after many translations and republications, this essay remains positioned in Scholem's corpus as a vital synthesis of his innovative creativity. But the paradoxical morality articulated by Scholem in "Redemption through Sin" only appears to be utterly novel. In fact, it emerges more and more clearly that his genius, as manifested in this essay, may properly be understood as rooted in its own era.

"Redemption through Sin," published in 1937, can be illuminated when read in the light of contemporaneous currents in European intellectual life. I will concentrate here on "Redemption through Sin" in three intellectual contexts, leaving aside the familiar terrain of Jewish and German influences on Scholem. The contexts I examine are Paris of the 1930s, the burgeoning field of History of Religions, and the Eranos meetings. My precise focus will be Scholem's still-shocking assertion, made in "Redemption through Sin," that evil can be defeated from within.

SCHOLEM AS HISTORIAN OF RELIGIONS

> Evil must be fought with evil. We are thus gradu-
> ally led to a position which as the history of reli-

gion shows, occurs with a kind of tragic necessity
in every great crisis of the religious mind. I am
referring to the fatal yet at the same time deeply
fascinating doctrine of the holiness of sin.
                    —*Gershom Scholem*

The consensus approach to Scholem's multifaceted career has perhaps
been epitomized by his erstwhile student Nathan Rotenstreich, who
characterized Scholem as "a unique synthesis of a bibliographer, editor of
texts, historian, historian of religions, and metaphysician."[2] My point is
not to quarrel with this characterization but to explore the one element
in it that has rarely been discussed: Scholem as Historian of Religions. An
immediate product of the period between the wars, the History of Religions was epitomized in the older generation by Gerardus van der Leeuw
and Rudolf Otto and among the Young Turks by scholars like Henry
Corbin and Mircea Eliade. This History of Religions was identifiable by
its Nietzschean intensity and by monographs bristling with extreme formulations, grandiose projects, and pyrotechnic displays of erudition.

Scholem considered himself such a Historian of Religion, using this
self-designation in "Redemption through Sin," *Major Trends in Jewish
Mysticism*, and throughout the Eranos lectures.[3] Eranos essays such as
"Religious Authority and Mysticism" (1957) and the late "Nihilism as a
Religious Phenomenon" (1974) were framed not as Jewish Studies but
explicitly as studies in the general History of Religions.[4] At the end of his
life he still stressed, in the final version of *Origins of Kabbalah*, that Kabbalah "can only be explained in terms of history of religions."[5]

To understand Scholem's conception of the History of Religions, it is
necessary to start with his attitude to the organization of knowledge
more generally. In his early career, he was ambivalent, to say the least,
concerning the new social sciences, sanguine if not unmoved by the apparent advances achieved by Durkheim, Freud, and Weber. Thus in his
great 1930 essay on Rosenzweig he proclaimed, "The nineteenth century
sciences demanded for themselves the right of the mysteries of creation—
and the wretched experience of the 'disenchanted world', which they
called *Erfahrung* (experience), set itself up as eternal."[6] In Paris during
1927, Walter Benjamin was the first to whom he posed the question
burning in him at that time: Was Judaism "still alive as a heritage or an
experience, even as something constantly evolving, or did it exist only as
an object of cognition?"[7] In other words, Scholem's stated desire for an
integrated science—transcending on the one hand the wretched experience of the disenchanted world and on the other the study of Judaism as
merely an object of cognition—spurred his quest for a total, organic theory of religion.

Insofar as no existing theory of religion fit this bill, Scholem gravitated to the emerging History of Religions as a sympathetic intellectual vehicle. Scholem, of course, eventually entered into the Eranos circle of Historians of Religion, with their embrace of a celebrated phenomenology of religious symbols.[8] It suffices to note here, as I have detailed in chapter 5, "On Symbols and Symbolizing," that Scholem's History of Religions, like theirs, was essentially and explicitly a symbology. As I have shown, Scholem wrote that for Kabbalists, "Judaism was more than anything else a *corpus symbolicum* . . ."[9] In Scholem's first Eranos collection, *On the Kabbalah and its Symbolism*, he wrote, "[Kabbalah reponded to philosophy] in favor of a living God, who, like all living forces, speaks in symbols."[10] He defined a symbol as the "means of expressing an experience that is in itself expressionless."[11]

"A RADICAL CONCEPT OF FREEDOM"

Since Bakunin, Europe has lacked a radical concept of freedom. The Surrealists have one.
　　　　　　—*Walter Benjamin*

The "experience which is itself expressionless" was conceived by Scholem to be nothing less than the very motor force of religious breakthroughs. As he put it resoundingly in the last sentence of "Religious Authority and Mysticism," "It is mystical experience which conceives and gives birth to authority."[12] Mystical experience, according to this theory, is initially if not essentially formless. The smelting and dissolution of religious forms, the intentional descent into formlessness, constitute the very means by which the mystic can effectively reconfigure doctrines, institutions, whole systems of myth. Scholem consistently called this creative condition of formlessness "inner freedom."

He played, moreover, with two interesting variations on this rather romantic idea of polymorphous inner vision. First, he strongly emphasized its impact on society, that is, that it "gives birth to authority." In "Redemption through Sin," more particularly, he stressed that the appearance of the mystical messiah caused "this inner sense of freedom" to be experienced by thousands of Jews.[13] But, in addition to the collective exportation of "inner freedom," Scholem also stressed—and here is where he sounds rather like the other Historians of Religion—that this same "inner freedom" is required for the Historian of Religions himself to understand mysticism.[14] It is in this context that he announced in "Redemption through Sin," in relation to understanding the "powerful constructive impulses . . . [at work] beneath the surface of lawlessness,

antinomianism and catastrophic negation. . . . Jewish historians until
now have not had the inner freedom to attempt the task."[15] Scholem
apparently felt that he had that inner freedom.

Decades later he confessed, "It was not until my fortieth year that I
found the courage to speak out about topics which, at least for me, had
held a strong attraction and fascination." Scholem turned forty in 1937:
the immediate articulations of this "attraction and fascination" were, of
course, "Redemption through Sin," written shortly before his fortieth
birthday, and *Major Trends in Jewish Mysticism*, written just after it.[16] The
"topics . . . that held a strong attraction and fascination" were those of
radical antinomianism. In *Major Trends* he speaks of the "deeply fascinating doctrine of the holiness of sin," while in *On The Kabbalah and its
Symbolism* he confesses that "[o]ne cannot but help be fascinated by the
unbelievable freedom . . . from which their own world seemed to construct itself."[17] As he noted in *Walter Benjamin: The Story of a Friendship*,
"[I]t was the question I grappled with, under varying emphases, for
years."[18]

Marking these themes of symbology and formlessness, inner freedom
and antinomianism, we are prepared to enter Paris of the 1930s.

"A SORT OF MORAL CONSPIRACY": SADE, FRANK, AND THE FRENCH REVOLUTION

> The transgression does not deny the taboo but
> transcends and completes it.
> —*Georges Bataille*

The Berlin-born Jerusalemite historian of Kabbalah might seem to have
had slight associations with the City of Lights. In fact, the Paris directly
apposite to Scholem's antinomianism was a cauldron of European cultural ferment between the wars. Walter Benjamin, Pierre Klossowski,
Georges Bataille, Roger Caillois, Denis de Rougemont, and Henry Corbin are some of the thinkers whose Paris of the 1930s frames "Redemption through Sin" in a properly comparative context. It was in the precursor of this Paris in 1927 that Scholem revealed his breakthrough, "a
very surprising discovery—that is, a messianic antinomianism that had
developed within Judaism in strictly Jewish concepts."[19]

I want to suggest that in the context of this radical Parisian scene,
Scholem's "Redemption through Sin" appears familiarly bold, and not
some sui generis outrage. For that Paris scene was one of regular transgressions, a time for normal enormities. Even before World War I, the
poet Guillaume Apollinaire had announced that the Marquis de Sade was

"the freest spirit who ever lived."[20] Starting in the 1930s, French philosophers Simone de Beauvoir, Maurice Blanchot, Jean Paulhan, Pierre Klossowski, and Georges Bataille celebrated the sovereign transgressor, the Marquis de Sade, as a model of perfect freedom. It was precisely at the same time, and with precisely this liberatory idiom, that Scholem treated Sade's contemporary, Jacob Frank, in "Redemption through Sin."

The Parisian artist and philosopher Pierre Klossowski, for example, linked de Sade to the Revolution in his 1939 lecture, "The Marquis de Sade and the French Revolution." This talk was delivered to the Parisian College of Sociology sporadically attended by his friend Walter Benjamin.[21] Klossowski was subsequently to enjoy a strong relationship with the work of Henry Corbin and Mircea Eliade.[22] In "Redemption through Sin," Scholem likewise links Frank directly to the French Revolution—he even published a book at his life's end with the title *Du Frankisme au Jacobinisme*.[23] In short, Scholem linked the libertine Frank to the eventual Revolution, just as Klossowski linked the libertine de Sade to the Revolution. Furthermore, as we will see, both did so explicitly in terms of a gnostic politics.[24]

Here is Klossowski's summary of the Sadian imperative: "The evil must, therefore, erupt once and for all; the bad seed has to flourish so the mind can tear it out and consume it. In a word, evil must be made to prevail once and for all in the world so that it will destroy itself and so Sade's mind can find peace."[25] Klossowski stresses here that "the evil must erupt once and for all." Analogously, for Scholem, the Sabbatian movement needed the repellent Frank: "[I]n all his actions a truly corrupt and degenerate individual. Indeed, it might be plausibly argued that in order completely to exhaust its seemingly endless potential for the contradictory and the unexpected the Sabbatian movement was in need of just such a strongman."[26]

Just as Satan is said to be the most gripping character depicted in John Milton's *Paradise Lost*, so too is Jacob Frank the truly vivid antihero of "Redemption through Sin," if not of Scholem's entire corpus.[27] Outrageous, lascivious, and cruel, but also fascinating and influential, Scholem's Frank furthermore follows the path of Klossowski's Sade, and stirs the French Revolution.[28] In "Redemption through Sin," Scholem starkly frames the teleological trajectory of Sabbatianism in terms of the Revolution, that is, that it was specifically the French Revolution which made Frank's revolt historically significant.[29] "Seemingly, the [French] Revolution had come to corroborate the fact that the nihilist outlook had been correct all along: now the pillars of the world were indeed being shaken, and all the old ways seemed about to be overturned."[30]

In fact, the shaking of the foundations continued apace. After the Revolution came the Utopian theorist of nineteenth-century Paris, Charles

Fourier. In Paris of the 1930s, Pierre Klossowski and Walter Benjamin rediscovered Fourier. Klossowski claimed that the Marquis de Sade adumbrated "Fourier's . . . harmonist society based on the free play of passions."[31] And Benjamin, who saw Klossowski with some regularity in Paris between 1935 and 1939, evoked Kabbalah in connection with Fourier, speaking of the "meshing of passions, the intricate interaction of the passions mèchanistes with the *passion cabaliste* . . ."[32] One can hardly help, then, but recall Scholem's contemporaneous characterization of Frank's antinomianism: "It is the anarchic promiscuity of all living things."[33]

THE RECRUDESCENCE OF GNOSIS

In addition to associations with the French Revolution and the subsequent Fourieristic "free play of passions," Scholem and Klossowski liken Sade and Frank to ancient gnostics. In fact, they (simultaneously) claimed to have discovered nothing less momentous than a spontaneous rebirth of gnosis in eighteenth-century Europe. This is Klossowski on de Sade: "In the soul of this libertine great lord of the century of the Enlightenment, very old mental structures are reawakened; it is impossible not to recognize the whole ancient system of the Manichaean gnosis, the visions of Basilides, Valentinus, and especially Marcion."[34] And this is Scholem on Frank: "Indeed, to anyone familiar with the history of religion it might seem far more likely that he was dealing here with an antinomian myth from the second century composed by such nihilistic Gnostics as Carpocrates and his followers than that all this was actually taught and believed by Polish Jews living on the eve of the French Revolution."[35]

In a work that sheds light on the recent discussion, Jeffery Mehlman astutely observes that "in the construing of Sabbatianism as the historically repressed past of rationalism, Scholem's thought converges with Benjamin's."[36] I would add that Klossowski coincides with Scholem and Benjamin in identifying a sudden reeruption of the gnostic repressed. They each argued, variously, that a sudden recrudescence of gnosis uncovered antinomian norms long repressed in history.

FESTIVAL AND INVERSION

La fête est le chaos retrouvé et façonné à nouveau.
—*Roger Caillois*

Scholem claimed that Frank taught a "religious myth of nihilism," a "mythology of nihilism," while Klossowski argued that de Sade inaugurated a "utopia of evil."[37] The question that next presents itself is the following: How were such countermodernist claims reinscribed into successful histories of religion? One answer is that they operated by inversion. In Paris of the 1930s, a post-Durkheimian sociology, largely flourishing outside the groves of the academy, came to emphasize a sacred sociology, also termed the sacred of the Left Hand.[38] Its primary venue was the short-lived College of Sociology (Collège de Sociologie), where Klossowski spoke on the Marquis de Sade, and where Benjamin showed up from time to time.[39]

In this alternative sociology of religion, conventional valences were inverted more or less systematically. Perhaps its key contribution to social theory is found in the concept of transgression, best known in the now famous formulation of Georges Bataille. One motif in the study of religion that came to prominence in this sacred sociology was its transgressive reading of festival. Roger Caillois, cofounder with Bataille of the College of Sociology, author of the influential *Man and the Sacred*, and, eventually, publisher of Scholem on several occasions, epitomized the Left Hand sacred sociology in his influential "theory of celebrations": "This interval of universal confusion represented by the festival masquerades as the moment in which the whole world is abrogated. Therefore all excesses are allowed during it. Your behavior must be contrary to the rule. Everything should be back to front . . . in this way all those laws which protect the good natural and social order are systematically violated."[40] Caillois wrote his dissertation with Dumézil, from which he seemed to derive his ideas on festival.[41]

Shortly after the war, Denis de Rougemont, another leader of the College of Sociology, published *The Devil's Share*. This work was personally funded by Mary Mellon, patron of the the Eranos group and the Bollingen Foundation, which was soon to fund Scholem's writing of *Sabbatai Sevi, the Mystical Messiah*.[42] In *The Devil's Share*, de Rougemont reiterated this transgressive view of festival. "[T]he overturning of the moral laws (thou shalt kill, thou shalt steal, thou shalt bear false witness, with honor); the suspension of law; limitless expenditures; human sacrifices; disguises; processions; unleashing of collective passions; temporary disqualification of individual conflicts. I speak of a state of exception as one might say a state of siege or state of grace."[43]

Festival was thus conceived in the work of young intellectuals in Paris as the ultimate ritual, carnival as eschaton. According to this generalization, ritual as regulative practice was inverted into myth as the collapse of normative practice. By this same inversion, antinomian Historians of Religion could alchemically transmute dead ritual into living myth. Beyond the fleeting moment of festival, the very ideal human type in philosophical anthropology, according to this sacred sociology, likewise was inverted. Thus the holy man became the holy sinner; the public leader became the secret saint; the rational morality of monotheism became the transrational amorality of mysticism; and the heretic became exemplar.[44] *Nomos* was now inverted into antinomianism.

ERANOS: BEHOLDING THE KINGDOM
OF ETERNITY THROUGH THE RUINS

To live outside the law you must be honest.
—*Bob Dylan*

Henry Corbin, on his way to an Eranos meeting, once stood in the garden of Denis de Rougemont and proclaimed, "Heretics of the World Unite!"[45] However committed to a collective, Zionist struggle, Scholem remained an independent Historian of Religion.[46] Whether Corbin had Scholem in mind when he cried out to "Heretics" cannot be known. But when Scholem set to stating certain general reflections on religion, he did so through the most undogmatic and anticatechetical venue imaginable, the Eranos meetings. Whether or not it was "heretical," Eranos, like the College of Sociology, tended to transmute ritual into myth. Insofar as Eranos removed itself from social reality, it operated by self-conscious contrast as an insulated paradise of texts, as a veritable world navel of (so-called) spiritual hermeneutics. For this hermeneutics, historical details (so precious to Scholem) tended to imply tiny textual units rather than the smithereen increments of real ritual practice. By thus implicitly escaping social analysis to leap into textual boundlessness, they found themselves at the end of history, freed, if only "hermeneutically," from history's bonds.[47]

Gerardus van der Leeuw, at the 1949 Eranos meeting that Scholem attended, spoke of "eschatology, the myth of the impossible." Scholem, in the printed version of the lecture he delivered at the same meeting, later cited this essay.[48] Georges Bataille, friend of Benjamin and Eliade, provides a thematic link here, inasmuch as his transgressive philosophy also rested on a myth of the impossible: a vertiginous impossible, the subsuming of possibles, the "reconciling of what seems impossible to reconcile, respect for the law and violation of the law, the taboo and its transgression."[49] Yet another myth of the impossible, the eschatological overcoming of oppositions, became a foundational myth of Eranos. Perhaps the most eloquent characterization of this dizzying Eranos ideal came from Father Hugo Rahner, a repeat participant:

> What is here contained is a gift to that living round-table [Eranos], made up of men who believe that our Western civilization has broken down only in

order that it may be born anew, to the Eranos of those who dimly perceive the truth, as did Plato in his immortal seventh letter, and can behold the kingdom of eternity through the ruins. These are the men who know the comforting law of the spirit, that the demon in man is only permitted to tear down so that the angel in man with faltering hand may trace out the sources of new life.[50]

Father Rahner's dialectical dualism here poetically drives home the familiar imperative of defeating evil from within. This antinomianism, which also may be called cultural Sabbatianism, underwrote the transgressive sacred sociology of prewar Paris just as it did the History of Religions as practiced at Eranos, so fabulously successful throughout the Cold War period.[51]

CONCLUSION: CONTEXTUALIZING THE SABBATIAN PARADOX

> Benjamin was the first person I told about a very surprising discovery I had made: Sabbatian theology—that is, a messianic antinomianism that had developed within Judaism in strictly Jewish concepts.
> —*Gershom Scholem, "Paris (1927)"*

The greatest scholars require the closest study. Especially in the case of Gershom Scholem and his remarkable cohort, this shared cultural Sabbatianism demands protracted study because it rests on a "seemingly inexhaustible" paradox: redemption through sin. For Scholem and his colleagues, to be sure, such paradoxes were not examples of ultimate contradiction, or blatant violations of logic. Along with Mircea Eliade, Henry Corbin, Carl Jung, and other Eranos luminaries, Scholem subsumed the superficial contradiction of mere paradox into the higher continuities of *coincidentia oppositorum*, the coincidence of opposites, a doctrine they all employed.[52] For Scholem himself, the rational paradoxically reopens a transcendent access to the transrational, just as a higher historicism returns the historian of mysticism to the untramelled freedom at the end of history. In transtemporal terms, his dialectic ascends, like a ladder undercutting itself at every rung attained, from the pit of history all the way into that blue messianic heaven where laws of logic, historical laws, moral laws, are transvalued and made anew. For all its celestial overtones of timelessness, however, Scholem's earthly accomplishment in "Redemption through Sin" was to make this Hebrew essay so deeply a part of its concretely historical interwar moment. By investing the young field of Jewish Studies with the even younger History of Religions, he represented his day just as he successfully portrayed "tradition" in modernist monographs.

It may not be irrelevant to observe that these religious studies were not the only expressions of cultural Sabbatianism articulated in these years. Precisely the imperative to defeat evil from within was articulated by the political theologian and Kronjurist of the Third Reich, Carl Schmitt. It has been reported that, at his denazification hearing, he proudly confessed that he had intentionally immunized himself against Nazi infection: "I have drunk the Nazi bacillus, but it did not infect me!"[53] Similarly, the Italian Fascist and friend of Eliade Julius Evola claimed that we live in the last age, the epoch of the "expiration of traditional spiritual forms." Consequently, a true elite is obliged to wrestle the evil of this dark age, an imperative he called "riding the tiger."[54] Finally, the philosopher Theodor Adorno delivered this related dictum at the end of his life: "Only that which inexorably denies tradition may once again retrieve it."[55] In short, Scholem's antinomian necessity "to defeat evil from within" enjoyed a certain elective affinity not only with the College of Sociology, Eranos, and the History of Religions, but with a contemporaneous if scattered élite of postreligious intellectuals.

Because Scholem's own "inner logic" demands close critical analysis, we must not balk at understanding him as an actor in his own day. This is so, moreover, because his own historiosophy was so thoroughgoing as to be almost pantheistically exacting. He was so minutely preoccupied with the details of historical change because "history causes truth to break forth from the smallest illusions of 'development.'"[56] In fact, at the end of his life, he underscored this point: "[It is] precisely in the noninterchangable sequence of epochs that the true mystery of the deity is unveiled."[57] And so, following this "inner logic," we must see him as a member of his moment, as an active agent in the "noninterchangable sequence of epochs." Walter Benjamin summoned just such a deep historicism in his call for a history of esoteric literature: "[A]s the deeply grounded composition as an individual who, from inner compulsion, portrays less a historical evolution than a constantly renewed, primal upsurge of esoteric poetry—written in such a way it would be one of those scholarly confessions that can be counted in every century."[58]

CHAPTER 15

On the Suspension of the Ethical

THE FUNCTION OF ETHICS IN
THE "HISTORY OF RELIGIONS"

There is little explicit discussion of ethics in the work of Scholem, Corbin, and Eliade. For Eliade and Corbin the *ontical* effectively replaced the *ethical* at the center of intellectual concern. Scholem certainly wrote more directly on ethics than did his two friends.[1] But to the extent that he replaced, in effect, *mitzvot* (commandments) and *Halakha* (Jewish law) with "the dialectics of continuity and revolt" as the driving force of Jewish history, he may be said to have deethicized Judaism.[2] If, as I have tried to show in the preceding chapters, the aesthetic was far more fully developed than the ethical in their work, then I now conclude that this replacement significantly challenges our understanding of their theory of religion. It is necessary, therefore, in the present context, to pursue further this perplexing deethicizing in the History of Religions. To some observers, inside and outside the academy, Corbin's Islam and Scholem's Judaism—monotheisms without religious law at their centers—were tantamount not merely to heresy but to a seemingly willful perversity. I suggest no such thing. But I do think that their revisionism must be identified and worked through as such, if we are to progress in the critical study of religion. These Historians of Religion effectively suspended ethics in favor of ontic depths, of this there is little question. It is almost a truism, but perhaps a necessary one, to insist, at this point, that we can't move beyond them until we work through them.

TELEOLOGICAL SUSPENSION OF THE ETHICAL

One trajectory toward their transvaluation of monotheistic values ran through the interest in Soren Kierkegaard, which flourished during their early years. Kierkegaard's famous question "Is There Such a Thing as a Teleological Suspension of the Ethical?" was of lively interest to their generation.[3] The intellectual lineage running from Hamann through Kierkegaard was powerfully influential on Corbin and Scholem, and to a lesser extent on Eliade. Martin Buber—perhaps the best-known Jewish proponent of "existentialism"—wrote an essay titled "On the Suspension of the Ethical."[4] The Kierkegaardian "exception" so important to early Heidegger, to Shestov, to Schmitt, eventually led to Corbin's (and Baeck's) evocation of the phrase "*Individuum est ineffabile.*"[5] Proclaimed as a godfather, so to speak, of so-called existentialist philosophy, Kierkegaard might seem likely to have been rejected by Scholem and Eliade, avowed opponents to existentialism in the 1950s.[6] He was not. Corbin could seem still to embrace "existential phenomenology" at the end of his life, when he identified it with the "Imago Templi."[7]

"GOD IS DEAD"

> It is only the spiritual tragedies of Goethe's *Faust* and Nietzsche's *Zarathustra* which make the first glimmerings of the break-through of a total experience (*Ganzheitserlebnis*) in our Western hemisphere.
> —*Carl Jung*

The Nietzschean avant-garde currents that ran through Ascona, to be sure, had poured into that town before Eranos was initiated in 1933.[8] Ascona was, as Martin Green put it, where "the counterculture began."[9] The young Historians of Religion were unmistakably drawn to the Dionysian pole, the ecstatic mode favored by the Asconan bohemians, in conscious opposition to the Apollonian demeanor typical of the contemporaneous university, the indisputable bête noire of the avant-garde.

Eventually, the Historians of Religion claimed that Nietzsche's cry "God is Dead" had been anticipated in the histories of their respective religious traditions.[10] Scholem, for example, found the death of God adumbrated in the legend of the Golem. "It is indeed significant that Nietzsche's famous cry 'God is dead,' would have gone up first in a Kabbalistic text warning against the making of a Golem and linking the death of God to the realization of the idea of the Golem."[11] Corbin found the death of God, quite similarly, in the fourteenth-century Sufi al-Semnani. "One could say that the moral danger described by Semnani on both sides is the very same situation with which the West came face to face when Nietzsche cried out: 'God is dead.'"[12] And Eliade could say much the same about prehistoric religion. "In some respects it could be said that the *deus otiosus* is the first example of the 'death of God' that Nietzsche so frenziedly proclaimed."[13] They each in their own way assumed the "Death of God" not only as a moment in European intellectual history but also as a marker in a cosmic dialectic.

Corbin's use of Nietzsche, in particular, was a violently creative mis-reading, or overreading.[14] The Islamicist repeatedly called upon the ex-ample of Nietszche.[15] At the beginning of his discussion of "History of Religion and Cultural Renewal," Eliade likewise adduced the example of Nietzsche, who, he proclaimed, should guide the History of Religion. "It is rather *the example of [Nietzsche's] freedom of expression* that should be underlined."[16] Eliade spoke frequently of Nietzsche in this exalted lan-guage, treating the philosopher as a visionary or a poet, evoking "only great poets, or visionaries like Nietzsche."[17] "The example of Nietzsche ought to encourage and, at the same time, guide the historian of reli-gions."[18] But Eliade revealed little content behind his rhetorical enthusi-asm, as if Nietzsche were perhaps only a revolutionary decoration for his rhetoric, with one important exception. Although he tended to downplay this influence, Eliade was beholden to Nietzsche for his famous "myth of the eternal return."[19]

Eliade and Corbin absorbed from Nietzsche not only an immediate influence, which they occasionally acknowledged, but, perhaps even more significantly, a consistently magniloquent gesture to be flouted at traditional religion. The role of Nietzsche in the work of Scholem re-mains to be explored in depth.[20] In all three cases, in any event, the "death of God," more than merely a faddish moment in postwar reli-gious discussion, was a profoundly serious issue, one that they later ar-gued already to have been anciently adumbrated in the history of reli-gions. And so, in a normative declaration in the form of a "description" of ancient Gnosis, Eliade identified an "elite . . . just like" his Yogi heroes. This identity was provided by the phrase of Nietszche: "[T]he Gnostic feels that he is freed from the laws that govern society: he is beyond good and evil."[21]

NIHILISM AS A RELIGIOUS PHENOMENON

"Nihilism," like ethics more generally, occupied a rather curious position in the History of Religions. In his penultimate lecture at Eranos, Scholem delivered a lengthy address titled "Nihilism as a Religious Phenomenon" (*Der Nihilismus als religiöses Phänomen*).[22] On only one other occasion, out of a total of nineteen Eranos lectures, had the Kabbalah scholar spo-ken on a topic in the general study of religion.[23] "Nihilism as a Religious Phenomenon," written when Scholem was seventy-six years old, has re-ceived no critical attention. For this reason, it seems warranted to provide the following translated excerpt.

Of course the elitist attitude of Nihilist groups was not just caused by this historical fact but also by the very nature of Nihilist phenomena. They presupposed a consciousness that was unattainable for the masses with which it contrasted. The enlightenment about the excesses (*Unwesen*) of things, which stood at the beginning, implied an inversion of the ruling yardsticks and norms. In that sense it belonged to the realm of the "counter-culture," as one would say today [1974].

Nihilism, which first became tangible exactly as a religious phenomenon, presupposed the firm development of positive religious structures, the establishment of value systems that claimed absolute validity. That inextricable combination of impulses which were social and beyond the social was what actually integrated them, and it is this which makes the historical impact of religions. The immense energies that went into the construction of religious structures in which experience of the world was supposed to be linked to that of transcendence did not leave any room for the deconstruction of that which was only just in the process of crystallizing. Only where these processes had fully developed their inner tendencies, and where positive revelations of the highest pretension, where rituals and sacred acts that stemmed from them had created a firm framework, only there could developments exert influence which were directed towards their deconstruction.

On the whole, the religion of history pictures the metamorphoses—sometimes slow, sometimes eruptive—in which changes and reevaluations of such traditionally affirmed systems take place. At special points of crisis, however, religious Nihilism arises with an extremely elitist accentuation. The following exposition will deal with this. By the above concept I do not mean a Nihilism regarding religion but rather a Nihilism that appears in the name of religious claims as well as with religious claims. *It recognizes the religious sphere, but radically denies the authority which it presumes to control.* It does not want affirmation of new structures in lieu of old ones, but their deconstruction. This happens not always but often in the name of mystical experience. The reason for this lies in the amorphous nature of such experience. The way of the mystic leads to a progressing dismantling of the structures of the world of experience and a building up of mystical structures which accompany the expiring of the world of natural forms on the various levels of consciousness.[24] But these mystical structures themselves are then dismantled into the Amorphous with further progress, however much they may be determined through holding on to traditional symbols from the world of light and sound. Actual mystical experience transcends all structure. It can in its infinite plasticity create or reconstitute new ones; but it can also leave it at this dismantling as in the case of the Nihilist mystics. For where the mystic realizes as the highest value the deconstruction of all form (*Gestalt*) in mystical experience he may also execute its deconstruction in the relationship to the external world. Above all, that means the deconstruction of values and of the authority that guarantees their validity.[25]

One of the most tantalizing (if perhaps presently impenetrable) aspects of Scholem's preoccupation with nihilism is the parallels it suggests with Heidegger. It may be remembered that the philosopher Rosenzweig, who himself seems to have shifted somewhat at life's end toward the thought of Heidegger, once called Scholem himself a "nihilist."[26] Eliade's rhetorical question from 1971 comes to mind: "In the last thirty years, who can honestly pretend that he did not learn anything from Heidegger?"[27] Still, as is the case with his Nietzscheanism, Scholem's intellectual relationship with the work of Heidegger, especially on the question of "nihilism" (one of Heidegger's central concerns), remains to be explored.[28] One who learned much from Heidegger, to be sure, was Henry Corbin. It is rather striking to note that shortly after Scholem's "Der Nihilismus als religiöses Phänomen" was published in the 1974 volume of the *Eranos-Jahrbuch*, Corbin published what may be read as a kind of response, "De la théologie apophatique comme antidote du nihilisme," originally delivered in Tehran in October 1977.[29]

When Scholem evoked the mystic's "deconstruction of values," in any case, he would unquestionably have intended the resonance with Nietzsche—and, it is reasonable to assume, with Heidegger as well. This is not to say, of course, that Scholem was a "nihilist," and he was most certainly not a Heideggerian. But he was engaged philosophically with issues of loss and emptiness in a postmetaphysical world. This point, this deeply ethical engagement with its postethical moment, is expressed by Scholem at almost the same time of his Nihilism essay.

> "The ethical is always self-evident." Today, when the unethical seems so self-evident, does the Bible still address us with its call? And is the people of the book still able to do something with its book? It is possible that a time will come when it will fall silent? I am convinced that the existence of [Israel] depends upon the answer to this question far more decisively than it does upon the ups and downs of politics.[30]

The point here is not, then, that Scholem addressed the major philosophical issues of continental philosophy—anything else would be surprising—but that "nihilism as a religious phenomemon," in the thought of these Historians of Religions, has not received the attention it deserves. The History of Religions, as epitomized at Eranos, I suggest, will not be understood in historical perspective until such attention duly is paid.

A comparison illuminating this discourse on nihilism is that of French historian of religions Henri-Charles Puech (1902–1986).[31] Corbin published his first major articles, and a number of lesser pieces, in the journal edited by Puech, *Recherches philosophiques*.[32] At the very end of his life, Corbin still remembered this journal fondly with the praise, "Nous n'avons plus rien d'équivalent de nos jours."[33] Puech eventually became a world authority on Manichaeism and gnosticism, contributing lectures at Eranos on these themes.[34] In the transitional decade from 1945 to 1955, when an unemployed Eliade lived in Paris, Puech aided the Romanian refugee with contacts and publication invitations.[35] In fact, he solicited and published one of Eliade's first postwar articles.[36] After the war he became the editor of the venerable *Revue de l'histoire des religions*, in which venue he published Corbin, Scholem, and Eliade.[37] Scholem, most notably, published a lengthy three-part article on Polish Sabbatianism in that journal.[38] The trio returned the favor when they each contributed an article to his *Festschrift*.[39] Eventually, at the end of his life, Eliade cited Puech a final time. In a telling footnote from his treatment of ancient gnosticism in his *History of Religious Ideas*, Eliade invoked Puech on the "inner freedom obtained by gnosis [which] enables him to comport himself freely and to act as he pleases."

> More than a critique or a refutation, we have here a revolt . . . obstinate, violent, of vast scope and grave consequences; against the human condition, existence, God himself. It can lead equally well to imagining a final event that will be an *eversio, revolutio*—an overturning and reversal of the present situation, reciprocal substitution of left and right, outer and inner, higher and lower—or to nihilism.[40]

THE "EXCEPTION": COUNTERMODERNISM AS ANTINOMIANISM

> [T]he secret gives one the position of exception.
> —*Georg Simmel*

Nihilistic mysticism, I suggest, functioned for the trio's History of Religions as a kind of ethic—or, perhaps, antiethic. Ethics, characteristic of the forms (*Gestalten*) that make up the social world, break down when this world is deconstructed (*Gestaltlos*) in mystical experience. The mystic, reduced in this way to formlessness, anticipated in person the purification required for the incipient perfection of this world. This ideal type, the holy sinner, thus sinned to actuate today that coming world. An exception to the rules binding the rest of us, this gnostic lives in a state of grace, or perfection, by recognizing his own "perfect nature." An ethics of the exceptional, in this sense, was perhaps the only ethics actively cultivated by the Historians of Religion.

The French sociological school of Caillois, de Rougemont, and Bataille had tried in the late 1930s to establish this ideal in terms of religious sociology. In *The Devil's Share*, Denis de Rougemont reiterated their proudly transgressive view of the exception, in his evocation of the release experienced in wartime. "[T]he overturning of the moral laws (thou shalt kill, thou shalt steal, thou shalt bear false witness, with honor); the suspension of law; limitless expenditures; human sacrifices; disguises; processions; unleashing of collective passions; temporary disqualification of individual conflicts. I speak of a state of exception as one might say a state of siege or state of grace."[41]

Carl Schmitt's related principle is well known in political theory. "Sovereign is he who decides on the state of exception (*Ausnahmezustand*)."[42]

> The exception can be more important . . . than the rule, not because of a romantic irony for the paradox, but because the seriousness of an insight goes deeper than the clear generalizations inferred from what ordinarily repeats itself. The exception is more interesting than the rule. The rule proves nothing; the exception proves everything; it confirms not only the rule but its existence, which derives only from the exception.[43]

Richard Wolin notes that Carl Schmitt's partisanship for the moment of absolute decision, which can only emerge once conditions of political normalcy have been suspended in the *Ausnahmezustand*, represents a transposition of Kierkegaard's "teleological suspension of the ethical" from the moral to the political sphere.[44] Scholem's notion of Sabbatai Zevi as worldhistorical exception, in this light, appears crucially ambiguous.[45] Scholem seemed to have used the false messiah—or rather, as he preferred, "the *mystical* messiah"—as an *exception* in the sense that an "exception to the rule" implies an anomaly that doesn't count. He also, however, seemed to evoke a Sabbatian *exception* in the sense of "an exceptional person" as an anomaly above the rules conventionally governing social behavior.

The "exception" thus variously served the Historians of Religions as an Archimedean point for a cartographer off the map; or a sovereign; or a phenomenologist. The observer is excepted, by definition, from the demands incumbent on the believers being observed. Such, it would seem, was the purport of phenomenological *epoche*. And so too, analogously, was the messianic *epoche* one big exception to the rules of the present era. In this sense, phenomenological *epoche* inclined, slightly, heliotropically, toward the messianic *epoche*. The exception, as ultimately understood among the Historians of Religion, implied not merely an exceptional role played in social life but—and this is what made Eranos rhetoric remarkable in this regard—*the exception also is everyone*. The reader, as any modern person, is by definition excepted from traditional interdictions.[46] This latter appeal accounts, at least in part, for the popularity of the History of Religions among seekers of a certain sort.

Such antinomianism might seem virtually to define modernity, the era in which traditional restraints are loosened. However, the antinomianism of the Historians of Religion was not characteristically modernist, for at least two reasons. First, it was opposed to positivist, technological, and rationalist "progress," standing instead obstinately in favor of "tradition." It saw itself, moreover, as "free," by contrast to "most moderns," who are implicitly castigated as being restricted by conventional belief and practice. Antinomianism thus defined, however, also is not identical with *anti*modernism. This version might better be called countermodernism, because it does not linearly position itself against modern mores. Rather, it dove into modernity in order to overcome it. Countermodernism is holy sinning, religious secularity, sanctified perversity. It thus usually inclined toward the gnostic inasmuch as it shared the (putative) gnostic worldpicture of the fallen world which hides within itself the sparks of its own redemption. Such self-styled gnosis sought to redeem an absurd world by pitting its own tools of existential violence against it, for its own good.[47]

RESPONSES TO JOB

The Historian of Religion R. J. Zwi Werblowsky translated into English Scholem's monumental *Sabbatai Sevi, the Mystical Messiah*.[48] Werblowsky's first book, *Lucifer and Prometheus*, bore an introduction by Jung.[49] This study appeared at a time when Werblowsky was a Jungian student in Switzerland, and when he was also counseling Jung on the study of Kabbalah. Werblowsky originally opposed Scholem's theory of Sabbatai Zevi, but then changed his mind and translated this masterpiece into English.[50] Of particular relevance here is the focus on the Luciferian element in Werblowsky's early work. Such a "sympathy for the devil" likewise was much emphasized in Jung's contemporaneous assault on the God of the Hebrew Bible, *Response to Job* (*Antwort auf Hiob*).[51]

Henry Corbin passionately cherished his interaction with the Jung of *Response to Job*. It seemed to coincide in his mind with his ascension to Eranos: "[C]'est 'en Eranos' que le pèlerin venu de l'Iran devait rencontrer celui qui par sa 'Réponse à Job' lui fit comprendre la réponse qu'il rapportait en lui-même de l'Iran. Le chemin vers l'éternelle Sophia. Que C. G. Jung en soit remercié."[52] Corbin wrote an extraordinarily effusive review of *Response to Job*.[53] This review elicited a letter from Jung in which he said that Corbin was the only one of hundreds of reviewers who understood him.[54] Eliade likewise stepped onto the side of Jung in this heated controversy over his strange book. In 1952, Eliade interviewed Jung for the Parisian journal *Combat*.[55] He seemed to have taken his cue from Corbin, who had published his audaciously adulatory review of *Response to Job*. Eliade's equally adulatory essay "Jung et l'Alchimie" called Jung's work a "revelation." For this almost sycophantic praise he cited Corbin's "Sophia éternelle" in corroboration.[56] Eliade concluded that *coincidentia oppositorum* was a central mystery for Jung and that "surtout dans la *Réponse à Job*, Jung a montré que le même mystère constitue le paradoxe central du Christianisme."[57] Both Eliade and Corbin, then, agreed with Jung, when he read Job as a kind of primordial scandal in heaven. "An unusual scandal was blowing up in the realm of metaphysics, with supposedly devastating consequences, and nobody was ready with a saving formula which could rescue the monotheistic conception of God from disaster."[58] Corbin agreed strongly with Jung but suggested (favorably) that the scandal was in *Response to Job* "ce livre, magnifiquement scandeleux."[59] And Scholem too responded similarly: "Il est assez scandaleux, ce livre."[60]

Eliade, however, reported that Scholem also took it lightly. "Scholem, somewhat in jest, said that Jung had tried to psychoanalyze Yahweh!"[61] Scholem himself, in fact, seemed to echo Jung's claim that an "unusual scandal was blowing up in the realm of metaphysics," when he remarked that a "tremendous agitation that came into the world with the *Book of Job* and its daring questioning."[62] This may be a particularly significant parallel, especially given the technical usage to which Scholem put the term "daring."[63] Job became, for Scholem, first in the pantheon of revolutionary spirits daringly driving the dialectic of Jewish history. "I advise you to begin any inquiry into Kafka with the Book of Job, or at least with a discussion of the possibility of divine judgement, which I regard as the sole subject of Kafka's production."[64] Job had anticipated the predicament of religion in modern society. "Our position has been measured/ On Job's scales with great precision."[65] It may not have been accidental, finally, that Scholem's only sustained treatment of ethics, "On Sin and Punishment: Some Remarks concerning Biblical and Rabbinical Ethics," published in Eliade's *Festschrift, Myths and Symbols*, addressed Job's problem at some length.[66] We know unquestionably that Scholem considered his Job verses to be his central statement on theistic ethic. This is confirmed in a letter he wrote to George Lichtheim.[67]

Just as Scholem never distanced himself from his Job poem, Jung never changed his mind about *Response to Job*.[68] In the context of so much passionate thought dedicated to Jung's *Response to Job*, Martin Buber's anguished assault on this book stands out.[69] Jung's petulant response to Buber only compounded the injury with additional insult.[70] Jung claimed in his response to Buber that the composition of his book had been motivated in part by "mass murder . . . which engulfed . . . major parts of Europe."[71] But, unsuprisingly, insofar as *Response to Job* constituted an attack on the Jewish God so shortly after the Shoah, Jung's insistence that the book attempted empirically to explain that catastrophe shocked Buber. The Buber-Jung controversy leads beyond the present inquiry.[72] This much may be relevant in this context, however. For Jung to place God in the prosecutorial docket—writing in German less than a decade after Auschwitz, seeming to blame the Jewish God for that event—may now appear to unprejudiced readers as an act of exquisite disregard for Jewish sensibilities.[73] Such offense may have stimulated Buber's response. What is relevant here is that, with *Response to Job*, the authority of the One God, the issue of the book of Job, became a point of renewed modern contestation. At stake, in short, was the very ethical substance of monotheistic revelation. Corbin, Eliade, and Scholem entered this conversation each with his own passionate intensity.

MORAL AUTHORITY WITHOUT
ETHICAL MONOTHEISM

Monotheism was a central issue, a fiercely contested issue, to Gershom Scholem, Henry Corbin, and Mircea Eliade, internationally influential students of Judaism and Islam, respectively and a world-famous exponent of "cosmic" Christianity. The Eranos version of gnosis, as I have outlined it in the preceding chapters, deflected discussion of monotheism away from the unequivocally commanding ethical voice associated with the Sinaitic revolution.[74] Instead, they swerved toward primal scenes in Torah, those which most problematized the centrality of ethics in monotheism, especially Abraham's Binding of Isaac (*Akeda*) and Job's questioning of God. The collective reception of divine commandments, in this way, was deemphasized in favor of an individual gnostic encounter with a *theophany*. This already distant disconnection from Kant's harmony of reason and ethics further drove the Historians of Religion all the more so to stress the autonomous "reality" of "religious experience."[75] No longer was the commanding voice of a lawgiver being experienced; rather, it was a sheer *Tremendum*, a hierophany beyond ethics or reason.

By rejecting any available culture critique that was predicated on a moral system—whether neo-Kantianism, traditional law, social theory, psychoanalysis, or Marxism—the Eranos scholars were left with Abrahamic scriptures that could no longer mean what they said. Their form of "pure" religiosity, in other words, ironically expressed an ambivalent attitude to the monotheistic message.[76] They rejected the masters of suspicion, especially Marx, Freud, and Durkheim. Yet they themselves remained positioned in their own ironic posture, implying as they did a religious authority, but one esoterically occulted out of reach of ordinary believers—which elevation, it might seem, would only raise suspicions. Perhaps this wasn't so ironic. They asserted, indirectly against Weber, that the mystic's intrinsically anarchical "experience" was meant to replace the structures of ethics as the driving force of developing history. Therefore, they were forced into two positions not entirely compatible with one another: to deny scripture ethical authority by imploding its infinity of meanings inside a pleromatic godhead or to deny to moral critics of religions (Kant, Durkheim, Freud, Marx) any authoritative understanding by veiling ultimacy behind that presumptive infinity of meanings. In this way, ironically, they doubly denied the centrality of monotheistic ethics. They implicitly denied it as binding commandment in the first place and then explicitly denied it as a suasive modernist argument as well. Their program, then, was consistent neither with traditionalist monotheistic doctinalism nor with modernist unmasking of tradition. Perhaps for this reason it was also, necessarily, indirect in its expression.

Social theory, for Émile Durkheim, unquestionably must be a moral science.[77] While Eliade appropriated the bipolarity of "sacred/profane" from the French Durkheimians, he jettisoned its seemingly essential moral framework. The Eranos professors, more generally, abandoned both the primacy of conventional politics and ethics and the Durkheimian or Weberian reflection on moral development or social evolution. They concentrated their focus, instead, on a myth of origins; the play of impersonal ontological symbols; a magnification of the self as Perfect Nature or Angelic Self. Deethicized abstractions such as these, occupying the entirety of purview, required full-time diversion; they implied a paradisal possibility of soul soaked to the point of sateity; they spoke to satisfaction's overflow. There was, in other words, no *need* here. Or, rather, the one primary need they posited by contrast to Durkheim's social needs or Freud's psychological needs was an *ontological need*.[78]

This reading, however, is perhaps only half the story. As Scholem once adjured us (in a different context), "[W]e ourselves need to worry about both sides of the coin."[79] The other side of the coin is this: Scholem himself insisted that his *aliya* (immigration to Israel; return from exile) was an act not political but ethical.[80] Eliade and Corbin suggested something similar about their respective "exiles." The seeming transcendence of conventional ethics at Eranos, then, may only be, from their perspective, a matter of perspective. Their ethical choice took place, they would say, on another plane, that of ontology. From the point of view of the Historians of Religion, conventional—one might, in this context, legitimately say "bourgeois"—ethics had been immolated, reconfigured, in the horrific crises of our time. These men had felt themselves called upon to make, and had presumably made, "higher" or "deeper" ethical choices. But those "heights"—or "depths"—are hidden, it would seem, from the casual observer, much less from the historian of the History of Religions. They remain hidden in the "depths of Being."

THE APPARENT ABSENCE OF ETHICS AT ERANOS

> You can never know who these highest bearers of
> moral standards are.
>
> —*Gershom Scholem*

The foundation of this ethical exceptionalism, I have suggested, was occultated in symbols; secured inside a godhead of transmoral infinity. This godhead, accessible by means of gnostic "knowledge," esoterically was described in terms of symbols, that is, mediatory manifestations or identifiable hypostases. For Scholem these symbols were *sefirot*; for Corbin they were *Angels*; for Eliade they are *hierophanies*. Two subsidiary moves were shared by this disparate trio. First, all three suggested that such symbology was somehow primary in the meaning of their traditions. Second, the three of them encouraged these symbolic secrets as salutary study for otherwise debased moderns. These inner lineaments of the divine life were then rendered appealingly accessible in paperback editions. Thus each Historian of Religion, one way or another, recommended an esoteric rejuvenation for the spiritual depletion of his times. The cure is to come from a depth (or height) experience, as insight into ontological essence, and not in any kind of ethical action per se. Ethics, *it would seem*, was suspended at Eranos. But they knew, I think, that this was a very dangerous formulation. How could they not? As Scholem admitted, "[T]he act of leaving the confessional realm . . . for the bright light of world history involved a certain challenge which also entailed dangers. . . . It demanded the ethical courage to undertake dangers."[81]

Conclusion

> We know that genius is incomprehensible and un-
> accountable and it should therefore not be called
> upon as an explanation until every other solution
> has failed.
>
> —*Sigmund Freud*

HISTORY AFTER "HISTORY OF RELIGIONS"

There are many contexts into which one can place the amazingly successful studies of religion authored by the Historians of Religions, over the
course of careers spanning two generations, straddling the most dramatic
decades of this century. I have only traced here a few of those contexts,
the turn to myth in Weimar thought, Paris in the thirties, Christian
Kabbalah, Heidegger, Jung, fictional androgynes, Nietzsche, Schelling,
Goethe, Hamann, Kierkegaard, proud and tragic nationalisms, and so on.
These influences were integrated distinctively each into their own system,
none really quite resembling the others. Each was an *individuated* History of Religions, to misapply an idea from Jung.

But one idea that they shared, the idea represented by their loyal and
acclaimed attendance at Jung's Ascona, was an idea about the study of
religion. This was a perplexingly self-effacing idea that seemed, on the
face of it, to turn away from acclaim, into the ordinary activity of the
working scholar. They each, I might say with some affection, struggled
heroically within the constraints of scholarly rigors. And they did so as
integral men, that is, writers determined to transcend disciplinary limitations, in order to articulate a modern study of religion worthy of world
respect. To do so they looked everywhere. They looked to poetry, history,
philosophy, to symbol, to aesthetics, perhaps even to the depths of transpersonal vision. They sought to create a world-class study of religion, one
capable of standing (at the least) on par with the other forms of knowledge.

They sought to return religion to its original splendor, no less. But
they did so through a dangerous trade-off. To make sense of religion they
felt it necessary to abandon other forms of knowledge, to leave behind
the many inadequate modes of rationality, in favor of symbols and myths,
those truly privileged expressions of the spirit. The problem I want now
to explore, by way of conclusion, is this abandonment. We students of

religion need now to consider the consequences of an idea of religion that may eloquently preach to the converted but may not exploit the vaster range of resources that reason provides us. The greatest scholars demand the closest study, to be sure. But religion demands the greatest study of all: one that is required neither to privilege the transrational nor to submit to a supremacy beyond ethics. To stay within the limits of human knowledge, not to speak of the limits of human dignity, that is the difficult challenge. It remains almost impossible, finally, to imagine that we critical students of religion can meet that challenge by surrendering to theophany, theosophy, or even theology. Without holding on to the first and last traces of the past available to us, the texts of history, we break the chain connecting us to the living past. This past was not crowded with mystics, but rather with detailed practices and personalities of all types. Remaining traces of those ancestors are our only evidence, the stuff that provides our purpose, and to it we must yield and then yield again. The history of religions, I conclude, must end up being a historical study or it may be no study at all.

"RELIGION" AFTER THE "HISTORY OF RELIGIONS"

By setting them in their contexts, I have not tried to reduce the great men's greatness. But I am concerned to reflect seriously on the History of Religions as conceived by its greatest minds. That they were influenced is no shame. Their achievements cannot be reduced to autobiography, but neither can their greatness be limited to their monographs. My project has been to see them integrally, as the cultural giants they were. Only thus can we honestly locate the rise and decline of History of Religions in its time.

The present study, after all, emerges out of a mildly momentous transition in Religious Studies. It is not merely that History of Religions (as defined by the figures under study here) is on the decline in Religious Studies, though that seems certainly the situation. But the expanding universe of knowledge has itself simultaneously shifted, relocating the place of History of Religions in the general fields of knowledge.[1] For another thing, the so-called New Age is a phenomenon entirely outside the academy, and it is the New Age to which much of the spirit of History of Religions has fled. This spirit has also run, almost paradoxically, to a renewed traditionalism within so-called mainstream religions. Thus, interdisciplinarity within the academy and new religious movements and retraditionalization outside the academy have absorbed the energies if not the substance of History of Religions. These shifts help locate its brief centrality in Religious Studies. Perhaps of all its continuing influences, however, it may be most continuingly influential in the arts. History of Religions, I have tried to show, lies squarely on the Arts side of the Arts and Sciences in the academy. Moreover, it has also claimed the romantic side of the classical/romantic dichotomy in the Arts. It is not surprising, then, that much of its legacy is now outside the academy, especially in the world of artists.

It is imperative, finally, to locate the History of Religions in the disciplines at large. The History of Religions in the history of thought somewhat follows the career of what is generally called "Continental Philosophy." Thus, today, just as "Continental Philosophy" is increasingly marginalized in North American philosophy departments, so too is "History of Religions" finding itself on the margins of Religion departments. One well-rehearsed reason for this change is usually attributed to the normative claims made by the History of Religions. These universalizing claims made by the History of Religions were unique in the university. More so than perhaps any other discipline, here the subject and the object of study were confused, conflated, confounded. Corbin, for example, demanded that he himself was the proper object of inquiry. This, he asserted, constituted a properly "traditional" claim. Studying the form, content, and function of History of Religions, however, does not and probably cannot tell the present student how or, more important, *why* this discipline took such a high road to its own noble isolation. But the study of its historical context, I suggest, may yield some insight into this interesting question. After all, as I have tried to show, these scholars were opposed, sometimes quite vehemently, to the regnant intellectual culture of the academy. At the same time, they succeeded in it, as much as one could hope to succeed. Out of this interesting irony the present volume has taken its inspiration.

AGAINST MYSTOCENTRISM

Eranos tended to inherit from the traditions under study a *mystocentric* conception of religion. For example, the historiography made conventional by Corbin, which accepts Ibn al-ʿArabi's theosophical breakthrough as a great step forward, tacitly privileges "Akbarian" gnosis as pinnacle, or quintessence, of the entirety of Islam as a religion.[2] The essence of religion thus is assumed to be found in religious experience; by a process of concentric essences, the essential kind of religious experience in turn is seen to be mystical experience.[3] This is, in effect, an inheritance from Ibn ʿArabi himself. The problem is not that, in this way, we take the tradition as a guide; the problem is that we do so uncritically. However, as is well known, a critical history of Sufism remains lacking.[4] Aside from the obviously absent spadework, this lacuna is more fundamentally due to the failure of a properly critical approach to mysticism as such. In the case of Ibn ʿArabi, it seems altogether plausible, if not imperative, to study him in all possible contexts. Following the model of a pioneer like Michel de Certeau, one can hope for a History of Religions inquiry into mysticism that is integrated with all kinds of inquiries—sociological, psychological, historical, theological.[5] Ibn ʿArabi is too important to be left to a scholasticism, however esoterically inspired.

The dominance of mysticism in the History of Religions, more generally, remains regnant (not only genealogically) throughout the study of religion. This is markedly the case in the study of Islam as a religion. The study of Islam as a religion, it should be recalled, has been dominated by students of mystical Islam, especially but not exclusively by non-American or emigrant scholars. Massignon and Corbin, Schimmel and Nasr, have provided the lead conceptions of Islam as something "religious."[6] According to this conception, what is "really religious," what is a "religious reality," what is distinctively and essentially "religious" as opposed to being something, say, economic or psychological, is something that turns out to fall under the rubric of mysticism.

"Religious reality," not surprisingly, makes mostly mystical sense. We study, however, only texts and contexts. As Jonathan Z. Smith has shown effectively, there are no "religious phenomena" available to the classroom; only epiphenomena.[7] The assertion of a distinctive sacred realm of reality, alas, is best left to metaphysics.[8] Such a realm is said by exponents of the "autonomy of religion" to be irreducible to any context, inexplicable other than autonomously, in terms of itself alone. But, again, this is itself wholly a metaphysical or ideological claim, hardly one healthily to be urged on innocent students. So we cannot resort to the "autonomy" of "religious reality" of Islam to elucidate it as a "religion." What then distinguishes it, and what does it share with others?

It may be apparent that I am concerned for the fate of the study of religion restricted to the visionary, the exceptionalist preoccupation with the special case of enlightenment. Can *Homo religiosus* be only an illumined one? Clearly not. If History of Religions is to remain a broadly communicable intellectual operation, we teachers should resist mystocentrism, with its Self-centered privileging of the esoteric. Insofar as scholars such as Corbin persuasively seem to have been poetically accurate inheritors of indigenous and other esoteric interpretations, they may continue to guide some students through those rarified spheres. In an increasingly scientistic academy, ever more inimical to those realms they plumbed, esotericists sometimes have served as inspiring antagonists to what they portrayed as "the crisis of the modern world."[9] But have they provided a wide enough program for *postmodern* History of Religions to proceed and thrive inside, as our beleaguered discipline muddles through the first years of the millennium? I am concerned that they have not done so. That is why I have tried to demonstrate the inadequacies of esotericism as a primary device in the teaching of religion. Corbin, for example, evasively proposed all manner of influence even as he occultated these influences to the sphere of the unobservable.[10] But we must be able to see the history we study and we must make it openly available to others.[11] We must encompass the esoteric in our studies, but we also must find out for ourselves what *all* sorts of believers have done *as believers, in the public life of believers.*

NOTES TOWARD A CRITIQUE OF ERANOS

A motivating notion impelling the present work, therefore, is the de-reification of secrets. That is, while one must naturally assume that the world of esoterism was a world of secrets, it does not follow that there was a discernible essence to those secrets.[12] In other words, I assume the enormous importance of presumptive secrets in the lives of the mystics studied by the Historians of Religion. I do not suppose, however, that a specifiable content to those secrets can be identified today. There should be no "core" or "essence" to the "hidden wisdom"—no "big secret"— that the historian seeks. Rather, there was a social process in which this assumption, so to speak, loomed large as a cumulonimbus cloud, and whose overcasting effects accordingly must be registered. These claims for secrecy can be traced.[13]

The problem with a gnostic History of Religions is that it imposes patterns on the past that were never (demonstrably) there in order to draw lessons for a present that isn't (demonstrably) here. This ahistorical recycling, this eternal return of the same, suggests a gnosis arrogated to the historian by an a priori disgust with modernity, not by research into previous reality. The presumption of such world-rejection-as-history is *insight into totality*—surely an unacceptable assumption for the historian to claim.[14] The historian lights historicity no more than the lightning bug produces lightning, to vary a phrase from Alfred North Whitehead.[15] The light shed by historians is not nothing but it is certainly not revelatory. At most, its lamp lights an infinitesimal patch. There may be more light, but not for us historians to bestow. We are limited, fallible—not all-too-human, but human only.

As Cold War Sages par excellence, Scholem, Corbin, and Eliade erected a seemingly unassailable edifice of authority; but now, after 1989, we know that even the most imperious of walls fall down. My present interest, however, lies less in the iconoclastic demolition of walls, or the minute correction of particulars—on which generations of Ph.D.'s will labor—than in the *History of Religions as regulative idea*. They embodied the Idea of Real Authority, the Idea of Direct Apprehension of Symbols of the Divine. But Map is not Territory and History of Religions cannot be Religion.[16] Rather, it represents the Idea of Religion, the Idea of the Sacred, the nostalgic Idea of the Holy.[17]

But they had one thing in common, a thing signified by their Eranos participation. And that was that they all developed a theory of *religion after religion*. The present project, however, is not determined to reveal their "real" religious identities. Besides being indiscreet, the answer to that question is in any event imponderable. Rather, it was their apparently postreligious theory of religion that matters here. And if the traditional myths and symbols of which they wrote were not demonstrably central to "religion," then we are left with the greatest Historians of Religion writing, as it were, against the grain. Not that that conclusion would diminish their accomplishments. This book has not been a critique of their selectivity, in any event, so much as a drive toward clarification of their totality. The clarity sought in the foregoing essays may be nothing more than orienteering, trying to locate them in the larger world of thought. To do so is not to judge the work by the lives. Rather, it is to clarify the role played by contemporaneous forms of authority in their hermeneutics of the past.

They were outstandingly authoritative in their own fields, for obviously good reasons. They were also, furthermore, the crossover success stories of their day. That is, they spoke broadly across disciplinary boundaries to a general audience. In fact, their reception crossed disciplines, religions, and gender and political differences. The Archimedean point that gave them such leverage uncannily rested outside the ordinary planet of discourse. Symbolism may in fact alone be so alien, so foreign-yet-familiar, that it provides this point. Symbolism, perhaps. But when we come to myth, that's another story. The other story, of course, is the use of myth to make meaning for universal history. And it is here that the "religious dimension," properly speaking, also becomes problematic. I do not propose that the History of Religions must demystify myth. But their depreciation of society, social theory, thinking on society, demanded myth and symbol—what Corbin called the *imaginal*—to be the exclusive locus of real religious meaning. And that, I conclude, brings us to the deepest internal contradiction in their *religion after religion*.

That contradiction emanates from "theogonic process," the fabulous *imaginal* dialectic by which human history is seen theosophically as unfolding inside cosmic process. This theosophy allowed the three Historians of Religions to write academic history while retaining religious significance, which proved to be inspiring for many readers. But it also—

and here's the rub—tended to eradicate social difference. To take up theogonic process, history as the unfolding of a great myth, to take this grandiosity on its own terms, as they insisted, must also be to diminish the little differences seemingly so little when seen from such a height. But close analysis of context tells the historian that differences are never humanly little. Myth, in short, belittles difference; it builds on the drive, in fact, to close the gap of contradictions, to tell one story and not two.

Coincidentia oppositorum is the magnetic pole attracting myth because the obdurate contradictions of the given seem, to the seeker of totality, never to be sufficiently coherent. But I will not conclude that myth is a wish fulfillment for overcoming painful oppositions; though it does, of course, perform that function. To return to society, to return to difference, the Historian of Religion need not necessarily give up the consolations of myth and symbol, *coincidentia oppositorum* and theosophy. But they must be brought back to society, challenged with difference, put to the test of living otherness. To bring history back in, to historicize religion, is not to denude it of mystery, much less to rob it of supernatural authority. But the historian of religion has, finally, a responsibility to historical reality.

Many so-called secular readers, especially those in arts and psychology, as well as those commited to national identity building, have looked to *religion after religion* as a path to a kind of point outside opposition, from which promontory they could bring their complexities into coherence. This may be why the study of the New Age and of new religious movements, in a final irony, is so necessary for understanding *religion after religion*. Jung, who provided much of the rhetorical strategy, is the godfather of this secular esoterism.[18] And the New Age movement, predicated on the creative imagination, draws especially on those in the arts and the helping professions to live a new religion after "traditional" "organized" religion.

This may be the final rub. If their legacy is this kind of secular syncretism, then it may be fundamentally at odds with a countervailing tendency, that toward "fundamentalisms." It is too early to tell. For we are indeed in the midst of a great turning to a greater unknown. The combat for the soul of the world, as Corbin put it, may indeed be a vast planetary struggle for control of our inheritance of symbol systems. Eliade thus conceived History of Religions as a Noah's Ark that carries all traditional symbolisms across a terrifying flood.[19] Scholem saw history in a dynamic chiaroscuro of darkness and light, as a rolling dialectic of creation and destruction.

The millennium, if it meant anything, traditionally promised future redemption. These men, remarkably, said that this eschatological *renovatio* already is realized now; or can be, at least potentially, through an immediate identification with the deepest myths of our being-in-the-world. The research represented in the present volume suggests that this incipient wholeness cannot, should not, be "realized" at the expense of historical truth, or on the backs of others. To make myth reality has too often meant the diminution of difference, the collapsing of distinctions, and therefore the evaporation of the very stuff on which all serious thought must necessarily labor. Our task as historians of religion remains the negotiation of universality and particularity. The universal potentially smothers the particular even as the particular too often obviates the universal. We rest with that opposition never. We study and we research and we publish in its light. At least in our historical practice, the *coincidentia oppositorum* does not manifest itself this side of paradise.

THE NEXT WORLD

The Historians of Religions clearly did not espouse a Weberian value-neutrality (*Wertfreiheit*).[20] In proclaiming a religion-centered study of religion—as opposed to a society-centered study or a psyche-centered study—they did not pretend that values were irrelevant to this work. But the values operative in the History of Religions were *transvalued*, to apply the appropriate idiom from Nietzsche. Jung and Heidegger, rival heirs to Nietzsche's eminence, had pioneered, respectively, a post-metaphysical reading of transvaluation.[21] In both cases readers thus found themselves routinely confounded in their encounter with a Dionysian voice that apophatically denied its own prophetic status.

Max Weber, most famously, declared the prophet *Verboten* in the classroom.[22] Heidegger, however, was another matter. He posed the question with probing directness: "Who is Nietzsche's Zarathustra? The question now is: Who is this teacher? Who is this being who appears within metaphysics at its stage of completion?"[23] One answer to Heidegger might be: the Historians of Religions. While Corbin explicitly fits this description, and Eliade does so only through a veil, Scholem was, in most of his publications, almost a perfervid historicist, and thus seemingly the antithesis of the mantic teacher. But it may be precisely here, in the extraordinary ardor of Scholem's historicism, that a clue to this dilemma may be located. That is, while Corbin was Zarathustran through and through, Scholem was the epitome of the working historian, of the philological perfectionist. And yet in his perfection of philology was his transcendence of philology, to which he himself aphoristically alluded on several occasions.[24] Here, at the point where historical inquiry and interpretation attained their happy apogee, the historian shifted, somehow, into the transhistorical. In short, Corbin presented the student with a model of sudden transcendence—to borrow a Buddhist notion—while Scholem represented the paradigm of gradualist enlightenment. The former seized on esoteric enlightenment; the latter prized the enlightenment of reason. In both cases, nonetheless, history was not an end in itself but rather a vehicle, temporary by definition, that conduced to eternity. In fact, Zarathustran or not, this tipping of history into its abysmal source was the prime paradox of the *History* of Religions in the classroom. Prophet or not, here was no ordinary teacher, but rather a "being who appears within metaphysics at its stage of completion."

By all accounts, most of the time the Historians of Religions were ordinary if gifted teachers, concentrating mightily on the texts at hand. No one has suggested that their academic charisma was manifested, at least during the years of their Eranos prestige, other than through recognizable university norms. At the same time, they layered in more than one notion of time, so that the history at hand could be felt, footnotes and all, as access to another world altogether. This particular appeal was certainly apparent in their rhetorical stance as writers. Most notably, Eliade stroked his readers with intimations of their immortality.[25] Nor was Scholem immune from flattering the history-minded reader that depths of revelation rumble, perceptibly to the attentive listener, under the modern. Together, they thereby implied to the reader that the reader's doubt is somehow also a sword of discernment—somehow a flash of antibourgeois advance—somehow something magnificently more than the passive "reading" it appears to be.[26]

The "History of Religions" by this means presented to its readers an invisible object, but one ardently to be sought. That is, the symbol systems of the mystics were retrieved and displayed as the optimal view inside the traditional divinity. This divine object, it must be said again, was absent to the reader. And so their inside view was, so to speak, a perspective from the next world. This was a world with its own history, but not the social world we know; a world always parallel to all societies, but always chronologically autonomous. It was and it is next to us. An implicit answer to the problem of the "modern," then, was thus offered from Eranos: the solution to modernity's crisis is not to change the world but to change worlds, to colonize another world, neither prior to nor subsequent to now. This solution is called, in a bold misnomer, the *History* of Religions, for, though it studies an alternative universe—Eliade's *univers imaginaire*, Corbin's *imaginal*, Scholem's *myth*—with a traceable sequence of epochs all its own, it does not obey the laws of history as established in *this* world. More precisely, Scholem saw these laws as the very means (gradually) to leave this world, while Corbin and Eliade held out the allure of a reversal of time as the vehicle (suddenly) to get to the desired other world.

The way into that next world? They agreed on an answer, with varying intensities: it passes through the wall of time. This passage meant neither return to premodern modes of society nor progress to a new society ahead. Rather, it meant bursting the bounds of personality, routing through the person into the transpersonal, where another world waits. This programmatic colonization of the next world, however, may be understood as a variant on myth itself, a kind of remythologization of the contemporary world. Here the "deeper" resources, those of myth and image, are used to appropriate the "deepest" symbologies of the past. This retrieval, with its earmarks of danger and audacity, attracted explorers of a certain kind. Ardent exploration bore the appeal of a great adventure. "Likewise, the inner attitude of the adventurer, which laughs at all ethical limitations, has been universal."[27] Consummate "professionals," the Eranos professors never claimed to be adventurers. But they were, happily for their readers around the globe, colonists of the next.

RECOVERIES

We came as rebels and found ourselves to be heirs.
—*Gershom Scholem*

The greatest scholars demand the closest study. In the third millennium the Historians of Religion under discussion here will no more be replaced than religion will be undone. That their scholarly legacies have been put into question by historical changes, however, would be fatuous to dismiss. Because they were great, we must exert ourselves all the more in the effort to understand them, first in perspectives fairest to their own contexts, truest to their own era. We then may—perhaps—be capable of recovering from them something of what we need to teach the next generation of students of religion.

Accordingly, our relation to them, complex if not multiplex—must be one of *recovery*. The several senses implicit in the word *recovery* encompass several attitudes; the several significant gestures implied in the act of leaving behind, even as as one simultaneously retains, an authority of the past.

The first sense of *recovery* is that of working through it. We can first of all only effectively move beyond these authorities if we have recovered from them, in the sense of having worked through them. The present work is, if nothing else, an honest effort to recover their authority in this sense. Critique is summoned by the seriousness of the work but will itself only be serious if it has shown itself to have mastered the object of its criticism. The greatest scholars, in this sense, demand the closest study. We first must recover their work by going through it, not around it.

Recovering also means retrieving. Retrieving the fullness of the work and describing, once and for all, its real contours without sentimentality or subservience. Tracing the extent of its breadth, delineating its edges, and, to the extent our capacity allows, to gauge (if not plumb) its depths. We retrieve the History of Religions to the extent that we know its scale, its limits, its parts as well as its "totality." We must then recover even its hidden parts, at least to the extent that dignity allows.

Engaging in a dialectical conversation with the past provides another sense for the notion of *recovery*.[28] *Recovery* furthermore implies recuperation—recovering *from*. Getting over it, getting over the trauma not so much of their authority per se as the trauma caused by our necessary break with their nurturing authority.

Finally, *recovery* requires rediscovering their legacy. That testament, if nothing else, claimed to honor religion's fullness and majesty, its terrors and its delights. We may continue, we will no doubt continue to return to their masterworks for various kinds of edification and instruction. We will thus detain them from the centrifugal force exerted by the past. This is the meaning of recovery, too: to find and keep finding the necessary remainder, the kernel of remaining truth, of truth (as opposed to untruth) remaining in the past.

These recoveries inevitably bring to our attention a double message. The History of Religions, one may conclude, taught and still teaches us ways to engage the perennial mystery in religion. Today we see this mystery fully in tension with, being tested by, the deep complexity of reality itself. Precisely in this contestation between tradition and its critique we continue to seek the stimulus appropriate for further study. Our new research, our new synthesis, may then deserve to be called History of Religions. This dialectic, of course, indicates only that we too, we students of religion in the twenty-first century, are continuing where Mircea Eliade, Henry Corbin, and Gershom Scholem left off. We too are finding our generation's own distinctive means to make sense of religion; to locate religious reality in the context of the larger organization of knowledge; even to pit history against the transcendent, again. This, given what we have learned from the past, the distant as well as the immediate past, may be just enough to move ahead, if only on the shoulders of giants.

UNCONCLUDING CODA

> We are all of us, and Eliade first of all, *would-have-been* believers; we are all religious spirits without religion.
>
> —*Emil Cioran*

Finally, I would conclude with what may seem to be an obvious point, but one that, I believe, bears more thought than it has received. *Scholem chose to be a Historian of Religions.* That is why he came to Eranos and that is why he stayed at Eranos. The significance here, if nothing else, is that he chose to write not for a parochial audience, for a community of Jews alone. However colossal and indisputable his stature as a Zionist, he chose not to write only in Hebrew, only for Israelis. Rather, he wrote in German (with translations to other languges) for a world audience, the bulk of whom were not Jewish. It seems clear enough, given the monumental efforts he certainly put into the literary felicity and philosophical cogency of his essays, that he saw this opening to the world as proud part and parcel of his Zionist self-understanding.[29] That is, he saw the "return to history" to be the great task of Zionism. A great essay, a magisterial monograph, spoke with historical potency to all honest readers and in so doing brought the soul of living Judaism to them as never before. "Through its fruitful dialectic . . . historical criticism henceforth also serves as a productive decoding of the secret writing of the past, of the great symbols of our life within history."[30] Such a philological recuperation of the Jewish past, and such an opening of that past to the contemporary nations of world, was continuous with the work of Zionism itself. In fact, to come full circle, to return to the point of the present work, it may be recalled that Scholem defined *"religio"* as a "tie to the past"— precisely when he defined the "historical consciousness" of Zionism.[31]

In this sense, Scholem could not have done so without his Eranos affinity group. These colleagues provided not merely moral support but also models of engaged scholarship, unstinting infusions of passion, world-class literary aspirations, and myriad particular means (Bollingen, Eranos, invitations, reviews, and so on) for sustaining a career at the very top of the intellectual world. Most especially, they provided a view of religion that was largely compatible with his, one that was determined to exhibit the treasures of spiritual history in their own terms, and not in the "reductionistic" terms current in the social sciences. And they all understood this common work in the History of Religions furthermore to be a religious task of a certain sort: a paradoxically unconventional kind, one often verging on the visionary and the ecstatic while not belonging to contemporary churches, synagogues, or mosques. Their guiding task— for which one might trace a wavering line back to the first Christian Kabbalists of the Renaissance—was to forge another spiritual intelligence collectively, a soteriologically vibrant conversation of like-minded intellects, a transcultural circle of intensively learned but entirely nonpracticing believers, an invisible congregation of the very few, a quiet scattered commonweal; perhaps, for all that, a *religion after religion.*

Lest I be misunderstood, I am not claiming that Scholem intended to start a new religion, or anything of the sort. But he was committed in the most profound fashion to the proposition that religion is a historical reality and as such is a living, growing, and therefore changing reality.[32] The writing of a serious history of Judaism was full of problems, he admitted, but "all have been developed here as legitimate problems when we approach them from the proper place: the renewal of the nation from within its tumultuous and tragic history."[33] He was willing, radically and daringly, to take on paradoxical partners if he felt it aided in this renewal of his nation. Whatever flaws we might now be able to identify in the History of Religions as it was practiced by these extraordinary minds, timidity before the historic challenges they faced—fear of change—was not among them. This may be, in the end, the one most foundational feature they shared. They were committed to a dynamic religion, a religion of change, a religion of growth. Not, to be sure, a religion of the new, of sheer novelty—this was properly anathema to them. And this religion of change was, for each of them in importantly different ways, less a History of Religions than a religion of history. As Scholem said of Kabbalah, it was "the secret of time-bound thought."[34] I draw this conclusion in mind of the abhorrence of conventional history espoused by Corbin and Eliade. But, as Scholem put it, a "mystical *now* [is] the dimension of time proper to the symbol."[35] In the end, then, their poetic sense of immediacy, perhaps of the *kairos*, what may be called *historicity*, pushed them creatively cresting the edge of change, insofar as they—implicitly—called to readers to take the task of understanding religion seriously and to do so *now*.[36]

One might now question the consequences of this call. But it was just as radical as it was to become authoritative, and for one good reason: because the conditions of the century they spanned were volatile and the History of Religions did not shrink from the task of response. Contemporary history, in this dynamic sense, was their religious business. I might conclude, at risk of portentousness—a risk solicited, I think, by the fact of their monumentality—that *religion after religion* intended to render the century's history aware of itself. This they did, if only in the language of symbols. *Religion after religion* self-reflexively symbolized this diminishing era, connected to the chain of tradition in precise proportion to its snapping link after link in that chain.[37] To make irreligion religious again, they felt, one can have no honest choice in our secular century but thus to pull on the chain till it breaks, in order, after the apocalypse, for the next generation to rediscover the meaning of their cherished paradox: that the broken tradition itself still functions as a link, and so on, into the undiminishable.

Abbreviations Used in the Notes

Henry Corbin

Avicenna	*Avicenna and the Visionary Recital.* Translated by Willard R. Trask. Irving, Tex.: Spring Publications, 1980.
CI	*Creative Imagination in the Sufism of Ibn ʿArabi.* Translated by Ralph Manheim. 1969. Reprint, Princeton, N.J.: Princeton University Press, 1981.
HIP	*History of Islamic Philosophy.* Translated by Liadain Sherrard with the assistance of Philip Sherrard. London: Kegan Paul, 1993.
MLIS	*The Man of Light in Iranian Sufism.* Translated by Nancy Pearson. Boulder, Colo.: Shambhala, 1978; distributed in U.S. by Random House.
Paradoxe	*Le paradoxe du monotheisme.* Paris: l'Herne, 1981.
SBCE	*Spiritual Body and Celestial Earth: From Mazdean Iran to Shiʾite Iran.* Translated by Nancy Pearson. Princeton, N.J.: Princeton University Press, 1977.
SEI	*Swedenborg and Esoteric Islam.* Translated by Leonard Fox. West Chester, Pa.: Swedenborg Foundation, 1995.
TC	*Temple and Contemplation.* Translated by Philip Sherrard with the assistance of Liadain Sherrard. London: KPI in association with Islamic Publications, 1986.
VM	*The Voyage and the Messenger: Iran and Philosophy.* Translated by Joseph Rowe. Berkeley, Calif.: North Atlantic Books, 1998.

Mircea Eliade

A I	*Autobiography: Journey East, Journey West: 1907–1937*, Vol. 1. Translated by Mac Linscott Ricketts. 1st ed. San Francisco: Harper and Row, 1981.
A II	*Autobiography: Exile's Odyssey: 1938–1969*, Vol. 2. Translated by Mac Linscott Ricketts. Chicago: University of Chicago Press, 1988.
CH	*Cosmos and History: The Myth of the Eternal Return.* Translated by W. Trask. 1954. Reprint, New York: Harper/Bollingen, 1959.
FC	*The Forge and Crucible: The Origins and Structure of Alchemy.* Translated by Stephen Corrin. 1962. Reprint, New York: Harper and Row, 1971.
HRI 1	*History of Religious Ideas: From the Stone Age to the Eleusinian Mysteries*, Vol. 1. Translated by W. Trask. Chicago: University of Chicago Press, 1978.

HRI 2 — *History of Religious Ideas: From Gautama Buddha to the Triumph of Christianity*, Vol. 2. Translated by W. Trask. Chicago: University of Chicago Press, 1982.

HRI 3 — *The History of Religious Ideas: From Muhammad to the Age of the Reforms*, Vol. 3. Translated by A. Hiltebeitel and D. Apostolos-Cappadona. Chicago: University of Chicago Press, 1986.

IM — *Imagination and Meaning: The Scholarly and Literary Worlds of Mircea Eliade*. Edited by Norman J. Girardot and Mac Linscott Ricketts. New York: Seabury Press, 1982.

IS — *Images and Symbols: Studies in Religious Symbolism*. Translated by P. Mairet. 1961. Reprint, New York: Sheed and Ward, 1969.

J I — *Journal I, 1945–1955*. Translated from the Romanian by Mac Linscott Ricketts. Chicago: University of Chicago Press, 1990.

J II — *Journal II, 1957–1969*. Translated from the French by Fred H. Johnson, Jr. Chicago: University of Chicago Press, 1989.

J III — *Journal III, 1970–1978*. Translated from the French by Teresa Lavender Fagan. Chicago: University of Chicago Press, 1989.

J IV — *Journal IV, 1979–1985*. Translated from the Romanian by Mac Linscott Ricketts. Chicago: University of Chicago Press, 1990.

MDM — *Myths, Dreams and Mysteries: The Encounter Between Contemporary Faiths and Archaic Realities*. Translated by P. Mairet. 1960. Reprint, New York: Harper and Row, 1967.

MR — *Myth and Reality*. Translated by W. Trask. 1963. Reprint, New York: Harper and Row, 1968.

OL — *Ordeal by Labyrinth: Conversations with Claude-Henri Rocquet: with an Essay on Brancusi and Mythology*. Translated by D. Coltman. Chicago: University of Chicago Press, 1982.

OWCF — *Occultism, Witchcraft and Cultural Fashions: Essays in Comparative Religions*. Chicago: University of Chicago Press, 1976.

PCR — *Patterns in Comparative Religion*. Translated by R. Sheed. London: Sheed and Ward, 1958.

Q — *The Quest: History and Meaning in Religion*. Chicago: University of Chicago Press, 1969.

R — Ricketts, Mac Linscott. *Mircea Eliade: The Romanian Roots*. 2 vols. New York: Columbia University Press, 1988.

RSI — *Rites and Symbols of Initiation: The Mysteries of Birth and Rebirth*. Translated by W. Trask. 1956 Haskell Lectures, University of Chicago. Reprint, New York: Harper and Row, 1965.

Shamanism — *Shamanism: Archaic Techniques of Ecstasy*. Translated by W. Trask. 1964. Reprint, Princeton, N.J.: Princeton/Bollingen, 1974.

SP	*The Sacred and Profane: The Nature of Religion.* Translated by W. Trask. New York: Harcourt Brace, 1959.
SSA	*Symbolism, the Sacred, and the Arts.* Edited by Diane Apostolos-Cappadona. New York: Crossroad, 1988.
TO	*Two and the One.* Translated by J. M. Cohen. 1965. Reprint, 1st Harper Torchbook ed. New York: Harper and Row, 1969.
TSS	*Tales of the Sacred and the Supernatural.* Philadelphia: Westminster Press, 1981.
Yoga	*Yoga: Immortality and Freedom.* Translated by W. Trask. 1958. 2^d ed. Princeton, N.J.: Princeton/Bollingen, 1969. Reprint, 1973.
Zalmoxis	*Zalmoxis, The Vanishing God: Comparative Studies in the Religions and Folklore of Dacia and Eastern Europe.* Translated by W. Trask. Chicago: University of Chicago Press, 1972.

Gershom Scholem

Briefe I	*Gershom Scholem: Briefe Band I: 1914–1947.* Edited by Itta Shedletzky. Munich: Verlag C. H. Beck, 1995.
Briefe II	*Gershom Scholem: Briefe Band II: 1948–1970.* Edited by Thomas Sparr. Munich: Verlag C. H. Beck, 1995.
Correspondence	*The Correspondence of Walter Benjamin and Gershom Scholem, 1932–1940.* Translated from the German by Gary Smith and Andre Lefevere, with an introduction by Anson Rabinbach. New York: Schocken, 1989.
FBJ	*From Berlin to Jerusalem: Memories of My Youth.* Translated from the German by Harry Zohn. New York: Schocken, 1980.
JJC	*On Jews and Judaism in Crisis: Selected Essays.* Edited by Werner J. Dannhauser. New York: Schocken, 1976.
Kabbalah	*Kabbalah.* New York: Quadrangle/New York Times Books, 1974.
MIJ	*The Messianic Idea in Judaism and Other Essays on Jewish Spirituality.* New York: Schocken, 1971.
MSG	*The Mystical Shape of the Godhead.* Translated from the German by Joachim Neugroschel, edited and revised, according to the 1980 Hebrew edition, with the author's emendations, by Jonathan Chipman. New York: Pantheon, 1991.
MTJM	*Major Trends in Jewish Mysticism.* New York: Schocken, 1954.
OK	*Origins of the Kabbalah.* Edited by R. J. Zwi Werblowsky, translated from the German by Allan Arkush. 1st English ed., Philadelphia and Princeton, N.J.: Jewish Publication Society/Princeton University Press, 1987.
OKS	*On the Kabbalah and Its Symbolism.* Translated by Ralph Manheim. New York: Schocken, 1965.
OPJM	*On the Possibility of Jewish Mysticism in Our Time and Other Essays.* Edited and selected with an introduction by Avraham

Shapira, translated by Jonathan Chipman. Philadelphia: Jewish Publication Society, 1997.

Sabbatai Sevi   *Sabbatai Sevi, the Mystical Messiah, 1626–1676.* Translated by R. J. Zwi Werblowsky. Princeton, N.J.: Princeton University Press, 1973.

Notes

Preface and Acknowledgments

1. I spent a year and a half on a postdoctoral fellowship (in the History of Religions program and the Middle East Studies Center) at the University of Chicago. This sojourn came at the end of the life of Eliade, whom I never met. In fact, I began graduate work in Islamic Studies in the year that Corbin died (almost to the month) and I ended my postgraduate work in the year and the city of Eliade's death.

2. Of course, that may not necessarily be identical with their own self-presentation. When revelations concerning Eliade's political past came to be generally known in the early 1990s, I set out to write a monograph that explored the links between his life and his work. I abandoned that project, though I hope to return to it on another occasion.

3. All three of these men eventually published autobiographical works—at great length, in the case of Eliade, of moderate dimensions for Scholem, and only a few pages in the case of Corbin. These proportions seem almost the inverse of the exoteric dimension of their work. That they themselves presented their own lives as worthy of study invites us to do so, especially if we take them seriously. I never met any of the three, nor have I attempted to locate (with a few exceptions) their unpublished letters or works.

After this book went to press, Dr. Thomas Hakl, the author of a forthcoming history of Eranos, brought to my attention the just-published third volume of Scholem's letters (*Gershom Scholem Briefe III 1971–1982*, edited by Itta Schedletzky, Munich: Verlag C. H. Beck, 1999). Dr. Hakl also brought to my attention the letter of condolence that Scholem wrote to Corbin's wife Stella on the occasion of Corbin's passing. Given their significance to the book in hand, I quote here the following lines. "For me [Henry] was not only a friend and a fellow but a man who devoted a life to understand, to penetrate as a scholar a world as near to the one which I had devoted my own as anybody I could imagine. We were in the truest sense honest and possibly the first scholarly excavators of esoterical imagination such as Islamic and Jewish gnose. Of all speakers at the Eranos it was he to whom I felt the greatest affinity . . . He alone had that kind of inner sympathy that enabled him to light up the dark and difficult way to the mystical world which I considered essential to do really important and at the same time scholarly work in these spheres. His passing away means to me the loss of a spiritual brother." (p. 193; written in English, sent from Jerusalem on October 26, 1978).

Author's Note

1. These proportions seem almost the inverse of the exoteric dimension of their work.

256 NOTES TO AUTHOR'S NOTE

2. The most famous are the letters exchanged between Gershom Scholem and Walter Benjamin. See *Correspondence.*

3. I hasten to add that I write here autobiographically not to associate my life with theirs—*le-havdil*—but simply to provide readers with some—it is hoped—helpful framework for understanding these essays.

4. Immersion in their work has led me occasionally to notice quite precise "parallels" that are, in the end, rather insubstantial. For example, Scholem ended his 1953 Eranos lecture, and subsequently his collection *On the Kabbalah and Its Symbolism*, with the following sentence. "But the historian's task ends where the psychologist's begins." *OKS*, 204. Eliade, who also lectured at the 1953 meeting, wrote a few years later (the Introduction is dated April 1956) his widely read *The Sacred and the Profane*, with its concluding paragraph consisting of two sentences. "Here the considerations of the historian of religions end. Here begins the realm of problems proper to the philosopher, the psychologist, and even the theologian" *SP*, 213.

5. Reference will be made throughout this book to many studies, of considerably unequal quality, on each scholar. For general orientation see, on Scholem, David Biale, *Gershom Scholem: Kabbalah and Counter-History*, 2d ed. (Cambridge: Harvard University Press, 1982); on Corbin, Daryush Shayegan, *Henry Corbin: La topographie spirituelle de l'Islam Iranien* (Paris: Éditions de la Différance, 1990), and Christian Jambet, *La Logique des Orientaux: Henry Corbin et la science des formes* (Paris: Le Seuil, 1982); for Eliade, Shafique Keshavjee, *Mircea Eliade et la Coïncidence des opposés* (Paris: Peter Lang, 1993), Bryan S. Rennie, *Reconstructing Eliade: Making Sense of Religion* (Albany: State University of New York Press, 1996), and Mac Linscott Ricketts, *Mircea Eliade: The Romanian Roots*, 2 vols. (New York: Columbia University Press, 1988).

6. The first sustained treatment of Eranos seems to have been the special issue of the Swiss magazine *Du (Schweizerische Monatsschrift)* 4 (April 1955), which included contributions by Scholem, Corbin, and Eliade in addition to those of Jung and the other regular participants. See also Walter Robert Corti, "Vingt ans D'Eranos" *Le disque vert: C. G. Jung* (Brussels: Le disque vert, 1955), 288–97; Mircea Eliade, "Eranos," *Nimbus* 2 (1954): 57–58; Adolf Portmann, "Vom Sinn and Auftrag der Eranos-Tagungen," *Eranos-Jahrbuch* (1961): 7–28; Ira Progoff, "The Idea of Eranos," *Journal of Religion and Health* 5 (1966): 307–313; Gilbert Durand, "Le Génie du Lieu et les Heures Propices," *Eranos-Jahrbuch* 51 (1982): 243–277, Hans Heinz Holz, "Eranos—eine moderne Pseudo-Gnosis," in *Religionstheorie und Politische Theologie*, ed. Jacob Taubes (Munich: Verlag Ferd. Schöningh, 1984), 249–263; Donna J. Scott and Charles E. Scott, "Eranos and the Eranos-Jahrbücher," *Religious Studies Review* 8 (1982): 226–239; Rudolf Ritsema, "The Origins and Opus of Eranos: Reflections at the 55th Conference," *Eranos-Jahrbuch* 56 (1987): vii–xix.

Introduction

1. William McGuire, *Bollingen* (Princeton, N.J.: Princeton University Press, 1982), 146. Each wrote laudatory appreciations of Eranos. See Eliade, "Eranos," *Nimbus* 2 (1954): 57–58; Scholem, "Identifizerung und Distanz. Ein Rück-

blick," *Eranos-Jahrbuch* (1979): 463–467; and Corbin, "The Time of Eranos," in *Man and Time: Papers from the Eranos Yearbooks* (Princeton, N.J.: Princeton University Press, 1957). Along with Corbin, Eliade was the only other participant to contribute such a statement to the six-volume selection: see his "Encounters at Ascona," in *Spiritual Disciplines: Papers from the Eranos Yearbooks,* vol. 4 (New York: Pantheon, 1960), xvii–xxii.

2. The present work is not concerned with the merely biographical details of their lives. Between them they had five marriages and no children. Their social groups overlapped considerably. Lutz Niethammer has observed, in a related context, that such grouping is important for understanding the worldviews of these great thinkers: "Nearly all the main actors whose metaphors of history we are considering here met and kept in touch with one another, regardless of their political positions. They were a class-for-itself and, in the postwar period, formed a kind of underground school that cut across factional boundaries." Lutz Niethammer, in collaboration with Dirk van Laak, *Posthistoire: Has History Come to an End?* trans. Patrick Camiller (London: Verso, 1992), 59.

3. See Eliade, "A Cosmic Territorial Imperative," *Center Report*, 4, no. 2 (1971): 22–26; Eliade, "Space—Sacred and Profane," *Center Magazine* 4, no. 1 (1971): 53–54; and Scholem, "Jewish Theology Today," *Center Magazine* 7, no. 2 (1974): 57–71, reprinted as "Reflections on Jewish Theology," *JJC*, 261–297.

4. In Eliade's personal copies of the proceedings of these meetings, penciled marginalia prove his reading of these volumes. I thank Professor Jeffrey Kripal for securing these volumes for me.

5. The story is told that when Scholem's massive researches on Sabbatai Zevi were published in Hebrew in 1957, "Prime Minister Ben Gurion closed up his office and stayed in bed for five days to read through them." Steven Schwarzschild, "Gershom Scholem's Recent Writings," *Judaism* 10 (1961): 72–77, at 72.

6. Eliade's polemics against specialization and reductionism are well known. Scholem's essay on Wissenschaft des Judentums, one of his sharpest and most phlegmatic, has now been published in English in *OPJM* as "Reflections on Modern Jewish Studies." It has also been studied at some length by Peter Schäfer in "Gershom Scholem und die 'Wissenschaft des Judentums,'" *Gershom Scholem Zwischen den Disziplinen,* ed. by Peter Schäfer and Gary Smith (Frankfurt am Main: Suhrkamp, 1995), 122–157. See also Scholem's comments in "Memory and Utopia in Jewish History," also now available in English translation in *OPJM*, in which he explicitly rejects positivist, rationalistic, and Marxist explanations of religion (163–164). As for Corbin, one may cite any number of pointed comments. To take one from the end of his career. "The analyses of the *sacred*, for which we are indebted to the sociological philosophies or philosophical sociologies from the nineteenth century to the present day, strike us as being in perfect conformity with the intentions and dispensation of Pharoah." *TC*, 279, emphasis in original.

7. One gauge of their "spiritual" celebrity in the 1960s is the fact that American poet Allen Ginsberg made a pilgrimage both to Eliade (on 25 February, 1967—see *JII*, 292) and to Scholem (*JJC*, 40).

8. See the interesting letters exchanged between Benjamin and Auerbach.

9. Elias Auerbach, "Philology and *Weltliteratur*," *The Centennial Review* 13 (1969): 1–17, at 17 (translated by Maire and Edward Said). Emphasis added. The original essay was published in *Weltliteratur: Festgabe fur Fritz Strich zum 70. Geburtstag*, ed. by Walter Muschg and Emil Staiger (with Walter Henzen) (Berne, Switzerland: Franke Verlag, 1952). Auerbach too was a beneficiary of Bollingen. See McGuire, *Bollingen*, 193.

10. Compare Adorno on deprovincialization: "In America I was liberated from a naive belief in culture, acquired the ability to see culture from the outside." See Theodor W. Adorno, *Critical Models: Interventions and Catchwords*, trans. Henry W. Pickford (New York: Columbia University Press, 1998), 239.

11. *OPJM*, 152. This question is treated in more detail in chapter 2, "Toward the Origins of History of Religions: Christian Kabbalah as Inspiration and as Initiation" below.

12. *TC*, 278.

13. Lutzhammer, *Posthistoire*.

14. I hope to deal with this question elsewhere.

15. *OWCF*, 50.

16. Max Weber, *The Protestant Ethic and the Spirit of Capitalism*, trans. Talcott Parsons (New York: Scribner, 1958); Erik H. Erikson, *Young Man Luther* (New York: Norton, 1958).

17. Especially 203–233 on *Beruf*. Norman O. Brown, *Life Against Death: The Psychoanalytic Meaning of History* (Middletown, Conn.: Wesleyan University Press, 1959).

18. *MDM*, 231–245. See acknowledgements, 246, for publishing history.

19. Cited in Wolf Lepenies, *Between Literature and Science: the Rise of Sociology*, trans. R. J. Hollingdale (Cambridge: Cambridge University Press, 1988), 206.

20. Cited by Herbert Marcuse, on "On Science and Phenomenology," in *The Essential Frankfurt School Reader*, New York: Continuum, 1982), 466–477, at 467.

21. I discuss these trends in detail in chapter 7 of this book, "A Rustling in the Woods."

22. "Conclusions," *PCR*, especially at 459.

23. Throughout this book I use "History of Religions" to refer to the distinctive approach studied here. There are, of course, many great historians of religions in this century who did not adopt this approach. To make this distinction I will capitalize the History of Religions only in reference to the trio under study here.

24. For the comparison of Scholem and Corbin, see chapter 3, "Tautegorical Sublime"; for Scholem and Eliade as antinomian see chapter 4, "Coincidentia Oppositorum," chapter 15, "On the Suspension of the Ethical," and "Defeating Evil from Within"; and for Eliade and Corbin as esoterists, see throughout this volume.

25. Eliade recalled, in the months before his death, that he only lectured at Eranos "one or two times." See the last interview he granted, "Mircea Eliade. Some last thoughts about our relationship with our gods, finding the sacred in the profane, and the value of crisis in our lives, from a world-renowned historian

of religions," *Chicago* 35, no. 6 (1986): 147–151, 177–180, at 179. But he attended from 1950 into the 1960s, and thirteen of his lectures were published in *Eranos-Jahrbuch.* Corbin only missed three years between 1949 and 1976. Scholem published twenty lectures between 1949 and 1977 in *Eranos-Jahrbuch.*

26. Robert Wohl, *The Generation of 1914* (Cambridge, Mass.: Harvard University Press, 1979). This is most true of Scholem and least true of the youngest of the trio, Eliade. But Wohl's approach to this generation generally illuminates this group well.

27. There is simply no question, as I will show, that Corbin, Eliade, and Scholem each intended his writing to transcend merely academic discourse. As enemies of historicism and academic specialization, Corbin and Eliade espoused a totalism that denounced "reductionism" in violent terms. Scholem explicitly aligned himself with "historical criticism," calling himself a member of the "historical school" of Kabbalah studies. Still, even in his case, he was also a man of letters in the largest sense. While he was far more willing to accept elements of the sciences in his understanding of historical research, I shall treat his lifework here as a cultural project which transcends the distinction between arts and sciences.

28. Leo Strauss, *Persecution and the Art of Writing* (Chicago: University of Chicago Press, 1952), 22–38.

29. Corbin seemed privately to associate this dissembling with Eranos itself, in terms of a "spiritual family." In a letter to Eliade from Tehran dated 15 November 1953, he wrote: "La présence de Mme. Fróebe faisait de tout cela une réunion de famille (oh! de famille spirituelle, bien entendu, mais je n'emploierai pas ce mot-là!)." Published in *Mircea Eliade: Şi Corespondentii Săi* ed. Mircea Handoca (Bucharest: Editura Minerva, 1993), 237.

30. "Il est encore trop tôt pour la définir, mais on peut rapprocher cette nouvelle forme de création culturelle de certains (cercles) de la Renaissance italienne ou du Romantisme allemande, c'est-à-dire des (groupes) qui matérialisent, à un certain moment historique, le mouvement d'idées le plus fertile et le plus avancé," in "Les Danseurs Passent, La Danse Reste," *Du* (April 1955): 60–61. Published in English as "Eranos," *Nimbus* 2 (1954): 57–58, at 57.

31. For a discussion of the alchemical background of this idea, see Michael Löwy, *Redemption and Utopia: Jewish Libertarian Thought in Central Europe: A Study in Elective Affinity,* trans. Hope Heaney (Stanford, Calif: Stanford University Press, 1992).

32. Scholem spoke movingly on this point in his 1962 Rothschild Prize acceptance speech. "But, truth be told, I have learned far more than can be described in words from my errors." *OPJM,* 77.

33. To take one example, see the tangled publishing history of Corbin's *Avicenna and The Visionary Recital,* as detailed in his "Preface to the Edition in English," dated Paris, April 1960, v–viii (New York: Pantheon, 1960). Eliade's course of publication is even more labyrinthine.

34. At this stage of research it is too early adequately to compare their public versus private writings. Scholem complained to David Biale that "you are consistently confusing my *unhistoric reflections* with my *historic research* and its results." Cited in Peter Schäfer, "'Die Philologie der Kabbala ist nur eine Projektion auf

eine Fläche': Gershom Scholem über die wahren Absichten seines Kabbala studiums," *Jewish Studies Quarterly* 5 (1998): 1–25, at 24 n. 77. In Biale's defense, this distinction is not always clear in Scholem's corpus, although he held this line much more insistently then did Corbin or Eliade.

35. See "Mircea Eliade," in *Cahier l'Herne Mircea Eliade*, ed. C. Tacou (Paris: l'Herne, 1978), 270. This is Corbin's effusive statement to this effect, written at the very end of his life, as a submission to a volume in honor of Eliade.

36. As asserted by Joseph Dan in *MSG*, 7.

37. Corbin thanked the Bollingen Foundation for helping recover "certain aspects of a free spirituality . . . so to speak, a lost continent that must be reconquered." *Avicenna*, viii.

38. Both his letters and his public statements bear this out. His most significant statement is his touching farewell address at Eranos, "Identification und Distanz."

39. *OPJM*, 24.

40. *MTJM*, 6. For Scholem as a Historian of Religions, see my discussion in "A Rustling in the Woods." For now, it may be observed that Scholem had a keen and developed interest in interreligious comparison. To take just two examples, he provides a detailed overview of Christian millenarianism in *Sabbatai Sevi*, 93–102, and an important if brief comparison of Kabbalah and Tantric Yoga in *MSG*, 194–196.

41. Scholem, "Betrachtungen eines Kabbala-Forschers," *Du* (April 1955): 64–65.

42. Scholem, "Reflections on Modern Jewish Studies (1944)," in *OPJM*, 68–69.

43. *OK*, 203.

44. Ibid.

45. For the historiographic context, see David N. Myers, *Reinventing the Jewish Past: European Jewish Intellectuals and the Zionist Return to History* (New-York: Oxford University Press, 1995).

46. *FBJ*, 60–95.

47. "Irving Howe Interviews Gershom Scholem. The Only Thing in My Life I Have Never Doubted Is the Existence of God," *Present Tense*, 8/1 (1980), 53–57, at 56–57. In a poignant lecture delivered in Zurich follwing the Six Day War, Scholem called unequivocally for peace. "Our people has proven that it knows how to fight. How sad the state of a world in which such a proof has brought us more respect and prestige than the application of those peaceful qualities for the sake of whose cultivation the Jewish state was founded and intended." "A Lecture about Israel (1967)," *OPJM*, 37.

48. Corbin, "Mircea Eliade," 270.

49. *RSI*, 126–127. Some repetition may be found in Eliade's later essay on initiation, included in *The Quest*, 122. Eliade also alluded to the Fedeli in *Rites and Symbols*, 165, n. 53.

50. Antoine Faivre, "Ancient and Medieval Sources of Modern Esoteric Movements," in *Modern Esoteric Spirituality*, ed. Antoine Faivre and Jacob Needleman (New York: Crossroad, 1992), 34.

51. See *CI*, s.v. "Valli" and s.v. "Fedele." Corbin also treated Valli's theory with high approbation in the concluding pages of *Avicenna*, 267–269. See

also Corbin, "Mysticism and Humor," *Spring. An Annual of Archetypal Psychology and Jungian Thought* (1973): 24–35, at 32.

52. *TC*, 348. Faivre served with Eliade as an invited participant at Corbin's Université de St. Jean de Jerusalem. It seems reasonable to suggest that they saw this "university"—if not Eranos—as a contemporary expression of the Fedeli d'Amore.

53. Julius Evola, "Dante and the Loves's Lieges as a Ghibelline Militia," *The Mystery of the Grail: Initiation and Magic in the Quest for the Spirit*, trans. Guido Stucco (Rochester, Vt.: Inner Traditions, 1997), 144–149.

54. *L'Idea Deforme: Interpretazioni esoteriche di Dante*, ed. Maria Pia Pozzato (Milan: Bompiani, 1989). See especially the essay by Maria Pia Pozzato, "Luigi Valli e la Setta die 'Fedeli d'Amore," 147–191, and the introduction by Umberto Eco.

55. For a sustained discussion in Evola, see appendix 2, "Shaktism and the Worshippers of Love," in *The Yoga of Power*, trans. Guido Stucco (Rochester, Vt.: Inner Traditions, 1992), 205–209. This book influenced Eliade's work on Yoga. Evola also treated the Fedeli extensively in "Dante and the Loves's Lieges as a Ghibelline Militia," 144–149.

56. Luigi Valli, *Il linguaggio secreto di Dante e dei "fedeli d'amore"* (Genoa: Dioscuri, 1988).

57. René Guénon, "Le langage secret de Dante et des 'Fedeles d'Amour," *Voile d'Isis* 110 (1919). Guénon's fullest treatment was *L'Esoterisme de Dante* (Paris, 1925), now translated by C. B. Bethell into English as *The Esoterism of Dante* (Ghent N.Y.: Sophia Perennis et Universalis, 1996). Both Valli and Guénon seemed to derive their theories, in turn, from Aroux.

58. *The Portable Jung*, ed. Joseph Campbell (New York: Penguin, 1976), 419 n. 165. Jung cited there "De Geheimsprache Dantes und der Fedeli d'Amore," *Europäische Revue* (Berlin), VI Jahrgang: I Halbband (January–June 1930): 92–112. It may be noted that Evola also published in *Europäische Revue* in this period.

59. Titus Burckhardt, *Alchemy*, (Baltimore: Penguin, 1986), 144, citing Evola's *Metaphysics of Sex* (Rochester, Vt.: Inner Traditions, 1983). A more recent example would be the bizarre uses of the Fedeli d'Amore in the neo-Nazi mysticism of Miguel Serrano, in *Nos: Book of Resurrection* (London: Routledge and Kegan Paul, 1984). Serrano, a Chilean diplomat, wrote a widely read book about his meetings with Hermann Hesse and C. G. Jung in the 1960s.

60. *OL*, 80.

61. Ibid., emphasis added.

62. *SSA*, 64.

63. *J III*, 162, emphasis added.

64. Eliade, "Against Despair [January–February 1950]," *Romanian Review* 2, nos. 3–4 (1996): 20–22, at 21, emphasis added.

65. Wasserstrom, "Eliade and Evola."

66. *MR*, 202, emphasis added. Originally a review, from 1956, of a work on myth by Jan de Vries. See the comments on de Vries by the former student of Eliade, Kees Bolle. Kees Bolle, "Reply to Jerome Long," *Epoche: UCLA Journal for the History of Religions* 15 (1987): 97–105, at 100.

67. *Le Combat pour l'âme de monde: Urgence de la sophiologie: Cahiers de l'Université Saint Jean de Jérusalem* 6 (1979).

68. From those who knew them, I understand that Scholem was, in person, rather acerbic, while Eliade was gentle.

69. Feyridoun Hoveyda, "Henry Corbin, l'Architecte de l'invisible," *La Nouvelle Revue Française* 312 (January 1979): 30–47.

70. Corbin, "Mircea Eliade," 271.

71. See Scholem's 1946 reflections on humanism in *OPJM*, 164–165.

72. At the present stage of research, we have no evidence of what Scholem knew of Eliade's fascist activities with the Iron Guard. However, to extrapolate from his reaction to the case of Jung, it appears that he would not have said anything about it publicly. Scholem certainly knew that Jung was anti-Semitic and perhaps had flirted with the Nazis. This is made explicit in his German language letter (from Jerusalem, 8 December 1964) to Jung's associate, Aniela Jaffé.

My dear Mrs. Jaffe,
Thank you very much for sending me the records about Jung during the Nazi era. . . . I am very skeptical. I do not think that someone here in Israel or in America will publish these records in their present shape. It may be possible for you to publish them in a journal in Switzerland or in Germany. What is unsatisfying in your analysis is the insufficient (at least it seems so to me) analysis of Jung's essays which are impregnated with harsher and further-reaching quotations than the ones you cite. Presumably a complete analysis of the whole texts would have to be done; at least those which are predominantly seen to be anti-Jewish or the actually anti-Jewish remarks in those essays. Furthermore I must assume that besides the essays in the German journal, there must be further remarks by Jung on this topic, be it in print, be it in letters or verbal ones, since he formally retreated from the International Society and the editorial board of the *Zentralblatt* only in 1940. The whole of the problematic issue does not seem to me to be exhausted. The essay "Wotan" that you refer to has a very ambivalent attitude and has been, as far as I know, been understood by some readers totally differently, not really as a criticism of Nazism. This too would require sharp analysis.

Briefe II, 117–118. Even with this knowledge, Scholem continued to attend Eranos, and he never denounced Jung. One can assume, I think, that his discretion in relation to Jung would have—and apparently did—extend to Eliade.

73. McGuire, *Bollingen*, 150.

Chapter 1
Eranos and the "History of Religions"

1. Joseph Dan, "Gershom Scholem: Between Mysticism and Scholarship," *The Germanic Review* 72 (1997): 4–23, at 13, emphasis added. The German version is "Gershom Scholem—Mystiker oder Geschichtsschreiber des Mystischen?" in *Gershom Scholem Zwischen den Disziplinen*, ed. Peter Schäfer and Gary Smith (Frankfurt am Main: Suhrkamp, 1995), 32–70. Alexander Altmann similarly observed the significance of Eranos in Scholem's corpus. "No doubt, the Eranos

lectures represent the ripe fruit of his life-long study of Jewish (and non-Jewish) mysticism, of the history of religion, of literature and philosophy." "Gershom Scholem 1897–1982," *Proceedings of the American Academy of Jewish Research* 51 (1984): 1–14, at 14.

2. A letter to Zalman Schocken, 1937, cited in Biale, *Gershom Scholem*, 31. Biale translates "Schafpelz des Philologen" in this letter as "the hat of the phi-lologian," though it also carries the sense of "in sheep's clothing." See the impor-tant discussion by Schäfer, "Die Philologie." Schäfer's work is an eminent exem-plar of the new Scholem scholarship, which is revealing subtle developments in Scholem's thought, by means of careful archival research.

3. "Prologue" to *SBCE*, xxiv.

4. Mircea Eliade, "Initiation et Monde Moderne," *Travaux de Villard de Hon-necourt* 1 (1980): 21–27.

5. Eliade's ambivalence toward anthropology might seem to be the exception that makes this rule. Although he borrowed heavily from the "data" provided by working anthropologists, he was otherwise ardently opposed to almost all forms of conventional anthropological explanation.

6. Goodenough, "The Mystical Value of Scholarship," *The Crozer Quarterly* 22 (1945): 221–225. Goodenough was later to be published in the Bollingen series.

7. Jaroslav Pelikan, "Scholarship: A Sacred Vocation," *Scholarly Publishing* (October 1984): 3–22.

8. See Schäfer, "Die Philologie," for the most carefully nuanced discussion of the "tension between distance and identification" in Scholem's historical re-search.

9. Now reprinted in *OPJM*, 75–80.

10. Of the many effective critiques of Eliade's scholarship, I would point out Edmund Leach, "Sermons from a Man on a Ladder," *New York Review of Books* 7 (20 October 1966). For an example of a critique from a disciplinary perspective, see Richard Gombrich, "Eliade on Buddhism," *Religious Studies* 10 (1974): 225–231.

11. Corbin, "The Time of Eranos," xx, emphasis added.

12. *OPJM*, 23, emphasis added.

13. "Phenomenology of religion" has fallen into some desuetude. For an at-tempt to reconstruct it, see Sumner B. Twiss and Walter H. Conser, *Experience of the Sacred: Readings in the Phenomenology of Religion* (Hanover, N.H.: University Press of New England, 1992). See, more generally, Douglas Allen, "Phenomenol-ogy of Religion," in *The Encyclopedia of Religion* (New York: Macmillan, 1987), 11: 272–285.

14. Eliade, "History of Religions and a New Humanism," *History of Religions* 1 (1961): 1–8, revised and expanded in *Q,* 1–11.

15. *Q,* 8. In a companion essay, he almost repeats this sentiment, claiming that "many scholars are searching for a broader perspective in which the two meth-odological approaches could be integrated" 36.

16. *FBJ*, 97.

17. Ibid., 118.

18. Scholem, "Franz Rosenzweig's Star of Redemption," now reprinted in *OPJM*, at 201.

19. Scholem, "Opening Address," in *Types of Redemption: Contributions to the Theme of the Study-Conference Held in Jerusalem, 14th to 19th July 1968*, ed. R. J. Zwi Werblowsky and D. Jouco Bleeker (Leiden: E. J. Brill, 1970), 5–12, at 7.

20. Ibid., 7–8.

21. *OKS*, 2.

22. Altmann, "Gershom Scholem 1897–1982."

23. Elliot R. Wolfson, "Review of *On the Mystical Shape of the Godhead: Basic Concepts in Kabbalah* by Gershom Scholem," *The Journal of Religion* 73 (1993): 655–657.

24. Moshe Idel, "Rabbinism and Kabbalism: Gershom Scholem's Phenomenology of Judaism," in *Modern Judaism* 11 (1991): 281–293.

25. See section on nihilism in chapter 15, "Suspension of the Ethical," in this book.

26. David Biale, "Gershom Scholem's Ten Unhistorical Aphorisms on Kabbalah: Text and Commentary," *Modern Judaism* 5 (1985): 67–95.

27. Corbin, "From the Gnosis of Antiquity to Ismaili Gnosis," in *Cyclical Time and Ismaili Gnosis* (London: Kegan Paul International, 1983).

28. *Avicenna*, 27.

29. Scholem, "Who is a Jew?" in *Central Conference of American Rabbis* 80 (1970): 134. This characterization is movingly reiterated in "Kabbalah and Historical Criticism," his Rothschild Prize acceptance speech.

30. See chapter 3, "The Tautegorical Sublime," of this book.

31. Corbin's fullest discussion of phenomenology is found in his long review of Gerda Walther, in *Revue de l'Histoire des Religions* (January/March 1958): 92–101.

32. *Avicenna*, vi. Corbin speaks in the first person plural here.

33. *MLIS*, 144 , the final paragraph of the book. And see the same volume, 32, on Van der Leeuw, who cites Wagner. Also see *Avicenna*, 16, 17 (and s.v. "phenomenology"), 27, 51, and major conclusions 266, 268, 270. Also, *TC*, s.v, see especially 338, 341, 350, 355 n. 230.

34. Corbin, *En Islam Iranien* (1971–72), 1:19, as translated and utilized by H. Algar in "The Study of Islam: The Work of Henry Corbin," *Religious Studies Review* 6, no. 2 (1980): 85–90, at 90.

35. Corbin, "Divine Epiphany and Spiritual Birth in Ismailian Gnosis," in *Man and Transformation*, ed. Joseph Campbell (New York: Pantheon, 1964), 69–161.

36. Corbin, "Force of Traditional Philosophy in Iran" (lecture delivered in Tehran, 13 November 1967); trans. in *Studies in Comparative Religion* 2 (1968): 12–26, at 18 n. 1 (no translator indicated).

37. *HIP*, 275.

38. On the *Urphänomenon* in Goethe, see Vernon Pratt and Isis Brook, "Goethe's *Archetype* and the Romantic Concept of the Self," *Studies in History and Philosophy of Science* 27 (1996): 351–365.

39. *SEI*, 31. See also in the same volume, cited in chapter 5, "Symbols and Symbolizing," in the present volume. It is instructive to compare Scholem's criticism of Buber's use of *Urphänomen*. See *JJC*, 273.

40. *HIP*, 23.

41. Corbin, "The Visionary Dream in Islamic Spirituality," in *The Dream and Human Societies*, ed. G. E. von Grunebaum and Roger Caillois (Berkeley and Los Angeles: University of California Press, 1966), 381–409, at 403.

42. Jung, "American Eranos Volume: Introduction," *Spring: An Annual of Archetypal Psychology and Jungian Thought* (1984): 57–59, at 58. This text was never published in his lifetime.

43. For the coinage of "dialectical imagination," see Norman O. Brown, *Life Against Death: The Psychoanalytic Meaning of History* (Middletown, Conn.: Wesleyan University Press, 1959), 319. This coinage is not to be confused with that of Martin Jay, *The Dialectical Imagination: A History of the Frankfurt School and the Institute of Social Research, 1923–1950* (Boston: Little, Brown, 1973).

44. *J II*, (1 October 1965), 268 (emphasis in original). See also the preface to his final masterwork: "I have discussed the dialectic of the sacred and its morphology in earlier publications." *HRI*, 1, xiii.

45. Corbin, "La Théologie dialectique et l'histoire," *Recherches philosophiques* 3 (1934): 250–284.

46. "Prelude to the Second Edition," *SBCE*, xix.

47. *MTJM*, 218.

48. *FBJ*, 166.

49. "Religious reality" thus was posited to be a reality beyond the Kantian triads:

ethics	law	the good
aesthetics	art	the beautiful
logic	science	the true

50. Perhaps the most striking example in Corbin's work is found in the final paragraphs of *SEI*. Here the Islamicist invokes Schleiermacher in the most stirring terms. "If the grand task of a general theology of religions was ever foreseen, it was surely by the great Protestant theologian of German romanticism, Schleiermacher, himself a master of hermeneutics." *SEI*, 133. After citing Schleiermacher in this regard, he concludes his essay with the following proclamation. "This page of Schleiermacher could be the charter of all future comparative spiritual hermeneutics." *SEI*, 134. Schleiermacher was responsible for the appointment of Jung's grandfather to a chair at Basel University. See Frank McLynn, *Carl Gustav Jung* (New York: St. Martin's Press, 1996), 6.

51. His classic discussion is "Religious Authority and Mysticism" in *OKS*.

52. Title of a painting by surrealist Yves Tanguy (1933), now at the Seattle Art Museum.

53. See chapter 6, "Aesthetic Solutions," and chapter 5, "On Symbols and Symbolizing," in this book.

54. See the two collections edited by Robert Segal: *The Allure of Gnosticism* (Chicago: Open Court, 1995) and *The Gnostic Jung*, selected and introduced by Robert A. Segal (Princeton, N.J.: Princeton University Press, 1992).

55. Corbin, "The Time of Eranos," xiv.

56. These are the two central characteristics of Gnosticism, as identified by Kurt Rudolph, *Gnosis: The Nature and History of Gnosticism* trans. and ed. Robert McLachlan Wilson (San Francisco: Harper and Row, 1983).

57. *OL*, 19.

58. Scholem, "Judaism and Gnosticism," in Dartmouth College Comparative Studies Center, Report of the 1965–1966 Seminar on *Religions in Antiquity*, ed. Jacob Neusner (Hanover N.H., September 1966), 6 of Scholem's discussion.

59. Corbin, "From the Gnosis."

60. Among those who heard Corbin's call were Avens, *The New Gnosis: Heidegger, Hillman and Angels* (Dallas: Spring, 1984); David L. Miller, *The New Polytheism: Rebirth of the Gods and Goddesses* (Dallas: Spring, 1981); and Gilbert Durand, *L'Âme tigrée* (Paris: Denöel/Gonthier, 1986). The last two were repeat participants at Eranos. Avens began his career with a dissertation on Eliade, "Mircea Eliade's Conception of the Polarity 'Sacred/Profane' in Archaic Religions and in Christianity" (Ph.D. diss., Fordham University, 1970).

61. Corbin, "Eyes of Flesh and Eyes of Fire: Science and Gnosis" (opening address, June 1978, of the Université Saint Jean of Jerusalem), *Material for Thought* 8 (1980): 5–10, at 10 (no translator named).

62. And note that Scholem still cited Jonas with approbation in his final lecture at Eranos, "Nihilism as a Religious Phenomenon." See the section on nihilism in chapter 15, "The Suspension of the Ethical," in this book.

63. See the German discussion, for example, in *Gnosis und Politik* or the more recent *Weltrevolution der Seele: Ein Lese-und Arbeitsbuch der Gnosis von der Spätantike bis zur Gegenwart*, ed. Peter Sloterdijk and Thomas H. Mucho (Zürich: Artemis and Winkler, 1993), and Micha Brumlik, *Die Gnostiker: Der Traum von der Selbtserlösung des Menschen* (Frankfurt am Main: Eichborn, 1992). These were differently inspired by Carl Schmitt, a correspondent and acquaintance of Eliade. The Eliade-Schmitt letters can be found in the Nordrhein-Westfälisches Hauptstaatsarchiv Düsseldorf, Nachlass Carl Schmitt. I thank Drs. Horst Junginger, Gerd Simon, and George Leamann for locating these letters for me. For a promising new approach, see Wouter Hanegraaff, "A Dynamic Typological Approach to the Problem of 'Post-Gnostic' Gnosticism," *ARIES (Association pour la recherche et l'information sur l'ésotérisme)* 16 (1992): 5–44.

64. For Jung, see the statements made in *Nietzsche's Zarathustra: Notes of the Seminar Given in 1934–1939 by C. G. Jung* ed. James L. Jarrett (Princeton, N.J.: Princeton University Press, 1988), 2:1030 (24 June 1936). Also in 1936, Jung issued his best-known pronouncement on *Ergriffenheit* in his ambivalent response to J. W. Hauer: "Wotan," in *Civilization in Transition*, vol. 10 of *C. G. Jung: The Collected Works*, ed. by H. Read, M. Fordham, G. Adler, trans. R. F. C. Hull and others (Princeton, N.J.: Princeton University Press, 1953–1992). See also C. G. Jung, *Letters*, vol. 1, *1906–1950*, selected and ed. G. Adler, with Aniela Jaffé, trans. R. F. C. Hull and Jane A. Pratt (Princeton, N.J.: Princeton University Press, 1973), 1:211–212. For Hauer's side of the *Ergriffenheit* controversy see Margarete Dierks, *Jakob Wilhelm Hauer 1881–1962. Leben. Werk.Wirkung. Mit Einer Personalbibliographie* (Heidelberg: Verlag Lambert Schneider, 1986), 283–299, esp. 289–293.

For Scholem, see his "Identifizierung und Distanz." Adorno pointedly applies the notion of *Ergriffenheit* to Scholem: "Der objektive Gehlat dessen, woran gerade einem wie Scholem bis ins Innerste Ergriffenen alles liegen mußte, schien gefährdet durch rhetorische Insistenz auf Ergriffenheit." ("The rhetorical insistence on being stirred [*Ergriffenheit*] endangered the objective contents of that which matters in particular to someone like Scholem, who is moved [*ergriffen*] through and through.") "Gruß an Gershom G. Scholem. Zum 70. Geburtstag: 5 Dezember 1967", *Neue Zuricher Zeitung* 136, no. 5199, 3 December 1967. I thank Frederike Heuer for her translation of this difficult text.

For Heidegger's extensive use of *Ergriffenheit/Ergriefer*, see *Being and Time*, ed. (London: SCM Press, 1962), 565, s.v. "seize upon". For the usage in the Frobenius school, see A. P. Kriel, *The Legacy of Leo Frobenius* (Fort Hare, South Africa: Fort Hare University Press, 1973), 2–3, and 19. Frobenius's successor, Ad. E. Jensen, also centrally used this idea in "Spiel und Ergriffenheit," *Paideuma* 2 (1942): 124–139, and *Myth and Cult among Primitive Peoples* (Chicago: University of Chicago Press, 1963), 3–4, 53, 56. The Frobenius/Jensen usage has been powerfully critiqued by Jonathan Z. Smith, "No Need to Travel to the Indies: Judaism and the Study of Religion," in *Take Judaism for Example: Toward a Comparison of Religions*, ed. Jacob Neusner (Atlanta: Scholars Press, 1992), 224–225, and "Sacred Persistence" and "A Pearl of Great Price," both in *Imagining Religion: From Babylon to Jonestown* (Chicago: University of Chicago Press, 1988), 42–43 and 96–100 respectively.

65. A letter to Zalman Schocken, 1937, cited in Biale, *Gershom Scholem*, 31.

66. Scholem, "Identifizierung und Distanz," 466–467, emphasis added.

67. "Gruß an Gershom Scholem."

68. "De l'Iran à Eranos," in *Cahier l'Herne Henry Corbin*, ed. Christian Jambet (Paris: L'Herne, 1981), 263, emphasis in original.

69. *JJC*, 38.

70. *AI*.

71. Corbin, "The Force of Traditional Philosophy," 15.

72. *J III*, 108–109.

73. Muhsin Mahdi, "From the Manuscript Age to the Age of Printed Books," in *The Book in the Islamic World: The Written Word and Communication in the Middle East*, ed. George N. Atiyeh (Albany: State University of New York Press and Library of Congress, 1995), 67. Mahdi's observation has now been elaborated by Carl Ernst, *The Shambala Guide to Sufism* (Boston: Shambala, 1997), 215–220.

74. Scholem, "Zehn unhistorische Sätze über Kabbala," in *Gershom Scholem: Judaica 3: Studien zur jüdischen Mystik* (Frankfurt am Main: Suhrkamp Verlag, 1970) 264–272, at 265. I thank Frederike Heuer for her expert translation of this subtle text. See also Schäfer, "Die Philologie."

75. A full comparison of the theory of esoterism in Scholem and in Strauss remains to be undertaken. See for now Stephen Smith, "Gershom Scholem and Leo Strauss: Notes Toward a German-Jewish Dialogue," *Modern Judaism* 13 (1993): 209–229.

76. *OL*, 132.

77. *Illuminations*, trans. Harry Zohn (London: Collins/Fontana Books, 1970), 219–255. Corbin, by contrast, used "aura" in its more technically occultist sense, as that "which makes it possible for a spiritual master to establish a method of control by which to discriminate between suprasensory perceptions and what we would today call 'hallucinations.'" *MLIS*, 62. He began his 1972 Eranos lecture

by reference to the "physiology of the subtle body, whose every centre is both defined as a 'prophet of your being,' and characterized by a colour, an *aura*, visionary perception of which reveals to the mystic the degree of his advancement upon the spiritual way." *TC*, 1, emphasis in original.

78. Scholem, "Zehn unhistorische Sätze über Kabbala," 269.

79. Conclusion of chapter 1, *MTJM*, 39.

80. *JJC*, 48.

81. "Star of David," in *MIJ*, 257.

82. *MTJM*, 350.

83. *OPJM*, 36.

84. *J II*, 308

85. *OL*, 137.

86. Corbin, "From the Gnosis," 192.

87. *JII* (1 October 1965), 268, emphasis in original. See also "I have discussed the dialectic of the sacred and its morphology in earlier publications." Preface, *HRI* 1, xiii.

88. See chapter 2, "Christian Kabbalah," in this book.

89. Corbin, "Mircea Eliade," Champions of Eranos similarly alluded to an esoteric privilege in their evocations of the greatness of that institution. Gilbert Durand, a longtime participant at Eranos, said, "Ce n'est pas le lieu d'insister sur le rôle capital—*et discret sinon secret*!—que joua cette institution scientifique dans l'elaboration de la pensée constitutive de notre temps et de notre proche avenir scientifique ou éthique." "Eliade ou l'anthropologie profonde," in *Cahiers de l'Herne Mircea Eliade*, 33–40, at 37–38, emphasis added.

90. McGuire, *Bollingen*, 24.

91. For an important discussion of "aura" written by Scholem at the very end of his life, see "Walter Benjamin und Felix Noeggerath," in *Merkur* 393 (February, 1981): 134–169, at 168 n. 30, 350. Ernst Jünger praised Eliade's *Fragments d'un journal* (entry for 18 November 1973) with the comment, "on y retrouve indubitablement l'*aura* propre à votre personne et à votre oeuvre (l'atmosphere initiatique)" in *Soixante-dix s'efface II journal 1971–1980*, trans. H. Plard (Paris: Galimard, 1985), 144. For Eliade's use of "religious aura" see *MDM*, 17, and *SP*, 210 ("the unconscious has a religious aura").

Chapter 2
Toward the Origins of History of Religions:
Christian Kabbalah as Inspiration and Initiation

1. *PCR*, 146, citing in this connection "Cosmical Homology and Yoga," *PCR*, 147. Similarly, he cites *Mitul* on androgynization, *PCR*, 425.

2. *TO*, 80.

3. *SSA*; 139–141, emphasis in original.

4. A partial listing includes *SSA*, 139–141; *CH*, 153; *Yoga*, ("Reintegration and Freedom"), 95–100, 124; *SP*, 213; *Q*, 125; *PCR*, ("Orgy and Reintegration"), 358–359, 417, 421; *IS*, 89; *TO*, 80, 103.

5. *Traité de la réintégration* was published in an accessible edition for the first time more than two centuries after its composition. See the edition of Robert

Amadou (Paris: R. Dumas, 1974). It is unclear from which of the founders the name "Martinism" derives, though it is commonly ascribed to Saint-Martin.

6. *OWCF*, 50, emphasis added.

7. *MLIS*, 47–48. Corbin devotes a sustained discussion here to what he calls, with Eliade, "myths of reintegration." See especially 47–48.

8. Ibid., 48.

9. It is interesting to note that, of the three letters from Eliade to Corbin published in the *Cahier de l'Herne* volume dedicated to Corbin, two utilize the notion of "reintegration." *Cahier de l'Herne Henry Corbin*, 325–327.

10. See 20 September 1934 *Correspondence*, 143. A month later Scholem was still reading Saint-Martin. See 147.

11. *MTJM*, 268. On the following page, Scholem characterizes Lurianic Kabbalah with the phrase "theogonic process," which was taken from Schelling's late, "theosophical" phase.

12. *MSG*, 240.

13. Scholem, "Opening Address," in *Types of Redemption: Contributions to the Theme of the Study-Conference held in Jerusalem, 14th to 19th July 1968* (Leiden: E. J. Brill, 1970), 1–12, at 12.

14. *Kabbalah*, 200–201.

15. A point made by Andreas B. Kilcher, *Die Sprachtheorie der Kabbala als Ästhetisches Paradigma: Die Konstruktion einer ästetischen Kabbala seit der Frühen Neuzeit* (Stuttgart: Verlag J. B. Metzler, 1998), 208–209 n. 41.

16. Another example would be Abraham Yagel, who felt free to quote a Christian Kabbalist like Cornelius Agrippa. See Anne Oravetz, "Critiquing Traditions: The Mysticism of Abraham Yagel's Apocalyptic Vision" (senior thesis, Reed College, 1998). A study of the interactions between Jewish and Christian Kabbalists remains to be undertaken.

17. See Lluís Duch, "Retauracionismo católico alemán de entreguerras (1918–1939)," *Cristianesimo nella storia* (1991) 639–682, esp. 643–646, on Von Baader's politics and their reception in Germany in the years that Corbin and Scholem also embraced his ideas. The reception of Von Baader's ideas, while not on the scale of the contemporaneous revival of Schelling, was certainly registared in circles with which Scholem and Corbin were familiar. Theses were written on Von Baader in Weimar Germany by David Baumgardt, Leo Lowenthal (published in 1923, reprinted 1966–67, on which see Löwy, *Redemption and Utopia*), and Fritz Lieb. On the reception of Von Baader, see Löwy, *Redemption and Utopia*, 67–69. Von Baader also used the term "reintegration." See Eliade, *TO*, 102.

18. Christoph Schulte, "'Die Buchstaben haben . . . ihre Wurzeln oben.' Scholem und Molitor," in *Kabbala und Romantik*, ed. Eveline Goodman-Than, Gerd Mattenklott, and Christoph Schulte (Tübingen: Max Niemeyer Verlag, 1994), 143–164. Molitor made grand claims for what he himself called "Christian Kabbalah." See the revealing selections in Gérard van Rijnberk, *Martines de Pasqually: Un thaumaturge au XVIIIe siècle*, vol. 3 (reprint, Hildesheim: George Olms Verlag, 1982), 64–66.

19. Adolphe Franck, *La philosophie mystique a la fin du XVIIIe siècle* (Paris, 1866), and Paul Vulliaud, *La kabbale juive: histoire et doctrine: essai critique* (Paris: E. Nourry, 1923). Scholem reviewed Vulliaud's partial translation from the

Zohar. See "Vulliaud's Uebersetzung des Sifra Di-Zeniutha aus dem Sohar und andere neuere Literatur zur Geschichte der Kabbala," *Monatsschrift für die Wissenschaft des Judentums* 75 (1931) 347–362, 444–455. Eliade visited Vulliaud's home on 6 April 1946, and in 1951 wrote a preface for his posthumous book, *La Fin du monde*. See *J I*, 16, 147, and *A II*, 116.

20. And see especially Faivre, *Accès de l'ésotérisme occidental*, (Paris: Gallimard, 1996), 2:45–171.

21. *OKS*, 87.

22. See his discussion of contemporary Kabbalists in *JJC*. He states unequivocally in this lecture "On the Possibility of Jewish Mysticism in our Time" that there is no authentic Jewish mysticism today. See *OPJM*, 6.

23. See especially Andreas B. Kilcher, *Die Sprachtheorie der Kabbala als Ästhetisches Paradigma: Die Konstruktion einer ästetischen Kabbala seit der Frühen Neuzeit* (Stuttgart: Verlag J. B. Metzler, 1998), 251–252.

24. "[O]ne may say that there is no authentic original mysticism in our generation, whether in the Jewish people or among the nations of the world" *OPJM*, 6.

25. Delivered in the fall of 1956, these lectures were published with the subsidization of the Bollingen Foundation, and they led directly to Eliade being hired at the University of Chicago. While clearly designed for this limited objective, these lectures also were intended to reach a larger audience. "As I conceived it, the book is addressed to any nonspecialist reader interested in the spiritual history of humanity." For this information, see *RSI*, xii.

26. *J II*, 86 (6 January 1960).

27. Eliade, "Initiation et Monde Moderne," *Travaux de Villard de Honnecourt* 1 (1980): 21–27. Henry Corbin, it should be noted, was the subject of several articles in this journal. See, for example, V. F. Michel Waldberg, "Henry Corbin, Ministre de la pensée," *Travaux de Villard de Honnecourt* 3 (1981): 183–188; Gilbert Durand, "La pensée d'Henry Corbin et le Temple Maçonnique," *Travaux de Villard de Honnecourt* 3 (1981): 173–182.

28. Jean Mons (Député Grand Maître de la Grande Loge Nationale Française Vénérable Maître de Villard de Honnecourt) explained in his prefatory remarks that "la Loge organisa, dans les Salons de la Tour Eiffel, en alternance avec les exposés remarqués faits par nos Frères dans notre Grand Temple sur des sujets traditionnels, d'importantes rencontres avec *des hautes personnalités n'appartenant pas à la maçonnerie*, mais de réputation internationale, sur des thèmes généraux toujours présents à l'esprit des maçons." *Travaux de Villard de Honnecourt* 1 (1980): 15, emphasis added. He does not say whether he referred here to Eliade.

29. This is not to say that this itself was an exclusively "initiatory" session, if for no other reason than that it was broadcast over the radiowaves of France-Culture.

30. Eliade, "Initiation and the Modern World," *Q*, 112–127. This paper in turn translates "L'Initiation et le monde moderne," in *Initiation*, ed. C. J. Bleeker (Leiden: E. J. Brill, 1965), 1–14.

31. Eliade, "Initiation et Monde Moderne," 26. Eliade deals with the initiatory dimensions of reading in *RSI*, 133–135.

32. For some of Eliade's many statements on his concept of "camouflage," see

the references gathered in Rennie, *Reconstructing Eliade*, 32, 52, 57, 59, 87, 215, 217–218, 220.

33. This notion of "spiritual chivalry" itself derived from the Masonic traditions. See Faivre, *Access to Western Esotericism*, 177–199 (originally delivered at Corbin's Université St.-Jean de Jerusalem in 1984) See also Corbin, "Pour une nouvelle chevalerie," *Question De* 1 (1973): 101–115.

34. Eliade, "Some Notes on *Theosophia perennis:* Ananda K. Coomaraswamy and Henry Corbin," *History of Religions* 19 (1979): 167–176, at 173. 173, emphasis added.

35. *J III*, 201.

36. See in this chapter for his relations with René Guénon, nn. 44–71.

37. Faivre, *Access to Western Esotericism*, 41, 44. Faivre was a devotee of Corbin. Shortly after Corbin's death, Eliade met Faivre. "I am moved by his admiration and love for Henry Corbin. Tears welled up in his eyes when I pronounced Henry's name." *J IV*, 23.

38. Eliade, "Occultism and Freemasonry in Eighteenth-Century France," *History of Religions* 13 (1973): 89–91.

39. Eliade, *Commentary*, March 1966, 98.

40. *J II*, 16–17.

41. *Q,* 38 (a 1964 article reprinted in this collection in 1969).

42. *OL*, 20.

43. Interview with Delia O'Hara, *Chicago* 35, no. 6 (June 1986): 147–151, 177-180.

44. Isaiah Berlin, "The Counter-Enlightenment" in *Against the Current: Essays in the History of Ideas*, ed. Henry Hardy (London: Hogarth Press, 1979), 1–24.

45. Guénon, *Symbolism of the Cross* trans. Angus McNab (London: Luzac; 1958; reprint, 1975), 27–45.

46. Jean-Pierre Laurant, "Le problème de René Guénon ou Quelques questions posées par les rapports de sa vie et de son oeuvre," *Revue de l'Histoire des Religions* (1971): 40–70, at 44. Borella states unequivocally that "Guénon was admitted into all the organizations controlled by Papus, including the Ordre Martiniste (which refers to Martines de Pasqually)." See Jean Borella, "René Guénon and the Traditionalist School," in *Modern Esoteric Spirituality*, ed. Antoine Faivre and Jacob Needleman (New York: Crossroad, 1992), 330–358, at 331.

47. Jean-Pierre Laurant, "The Primitive Characterisitics of Nineteenth-Century Esotericism," in *Modern Esoteric Spirituality*, 277–288, at 285.

48. James Webb, *The Occult Establishment* (La Salle, Ill.: Open Court, 1976), 168.

49. Laurant, "Le problème de René Guénon," 46.

50. *R*, 2:1144.

51. Eliade, *Fragmentarium*, transl. Alain Paruit (Paris: l'Herne, 1989), 182, emphasis added.

52. *R* 2: 1214.

53. *A II*, 152.

54. *J III*, 163.

55. *J III*, 280, emphasis in original.
56. *OWCF*, 67.
57. This lecture is discussed at greater length chapter 12, "Psychoanalysis in Reverse," in this volume.
58. Ibid., 127 n. 40), emphasis added.
59. This has been documented massively in Piero di Vona, *Evola e Guénon: tradizione e civiltà* (Naples: Società editrice napoletana, 1985).
60. Eliade, "*Theosophia Perennis,*" *History of Religions* 19 (1979): 171.
61. Ibid. 169.
62. Cited in Marilyn J. Gustin, "The Nature, Role and Interpretation of Symbol in the Thought of René Guénon" (Ph.D. diss., Graduate Theological Union, Berkeley, Calif., 1987), 17. The original reads: "Puisque vous parlez d'Eliade, j'ai déjà rendu compte de plusiers travaux de lui, livres et articles, et je me propose d'en faire ressortir ce qu'il y a de bon; je dois dire que c'est a cause de ce que je sais de lui par Valsan [Michel Valsan, Romanian-French Traditionalist], qui le connait bien. Il est à peu près entièrement d'accord au fond avec les idées traditionelles, mais il n'ose pas trop le montrer dans ce qu'il écrit, car il craint de heurter les conceptions admises officiellement." This letter was originally cited in Jean Robin, *Réné Guénon témoin de la Tradition* 2d ed. (Paris: Guy Trédaniel, 1986), 10 n. 2.
63. Julius Evola, *The Hermetic Tradition: Symbols and Teachings of the Royal Art* (Rochester, Vt.: Inner Traditions), 1995, 212, emphasis added. Eliade praised this book as being an authentic representative of the 'Tradition." Thus Evola asserts that "The *Ars Regia*, or Royal Arts, witness a secret current of initiation, the virile, 'heroic' and solar character of which is beyond question." Evola, *The Mystery of the Grail: Initiation and Magic in the Quest for the Spirit* (Rochester, Vt.: Inner Traditions, 1995), 156. Eliade explicitly approved this characterization: "*La tradizione ermetica* . . . de J. Evola, livre que connait également Jung, présentait les principes et la technique de l'*ars regia* d'apres les meilleurs sources et dans un esprit rigoureux (celui de la 'tradition' même)." Mircea Eliade, "Note sur Jung et l'alchimie," in *Le Disque vert* (Paris, 1955), 97–109, at 105.
64. The use of "integral" was associated with Othmar Spann, Leopold Ziegler, and Walter Heinrich. Evola published Spann in his "Diorama filosoficio" in Farinacci's *Regime Fascista*. Heinrich was the editor of the complete works of Spann. Evola wrote a laudatory review of Heinrich in Tucci's *East and West* (1960), and also contributed the essay "Die organische Idee und die Krise unserer Zeit" to *Festschrift Walter Heinrich: Ein Beitrag zur Ganzheitsforschung* (Graz: Akademische Druck-u Verlagsansalt, 1963), 55–65. Heinrich in turn was strongly influenced by Guénon. "Integralism" is found this way on various European Web sites.
65. Julius Evola, *René Guenon (sic): A Teacher for Modern Times*, trans. G. Stucco (Edmonds Wash.: Holmes, 1994), 21, emphasis added
66. *IS*, 175, emphasis added.
67. *J I*, 26.
68. "The mystery of the Royal Art is strictly related to that of the heroic reintegration." Evola, *The Mystery of the Grail*, 152.

69. Guenon, *Études sur la Franc-Maçonnerie et le Compagnonnage* (Paris: Éditions Traditionnelles, 1965), 2: 40–41.

70. That this distinctive concatenation ultimately derives, through Guénon, from Martinist Illuminism seems genealogically sound but remains to be demonstrated in detail.

71. It lies beyond the present project to detail the relations of Eliade to Guénon. For now, see Enrico Montanari, "Eliade e Guénon," *Studi e Materiali di Storia delle Religioni* 61 (1995): 131–149. See also the important forthcoming study by Cristiano Grottanelli, "Mircea Eliade, Carl Schmitt, René Guénon 1942." I thank Professor Grottanelli for sharing his preprint with me.

72. *SP*, 189.

73. See *TC*, throughout.

74. Corbin, "Le récit d'initiation et l'hermétisme en Iran," *Eranos-Jahrbuch* 17 (1949): 127–187.

75. Ibid., 173, emphasis added.

76. Gilbert Durand, "La pensée d'Henry Corbin et le Temple Maçonnique," *Travaux de Villard de Honnecourt* 3 (1981): 173–182, at 178.

77. Christopher McIntosh, *Eliaphas Lévi and the French Occult Revival* (New York: Samuel Weiser, 1972), 25. See also, along these lines, Jean Tourniac, "Entre le Judaisme et le Christianisme: Les Marranes," *Travaux de Villard de Honnecourt*, 2d ser., 26 (1993): 127–156.

78. *Tableau*, cited in Joanna Hubbs, "An Analysis of Martinism in the Last Quarter of the Eighteenth Century" (Ph.D. diss., University of Washington, 1971), 204.

79. *Paradoxe*, emphasis added.

80. *SBCE*, xiv, emphasis added.

81. Recent research is now concentrating on the Kabbalah of conversos like Abraham Miguel Cardoso (1627–1706), a leading propagandist for Sabbatai Zevi who found a means to articulate a kind of Christian Kabbalah within Judaism. See Bruce Rosenstock, "Abraham Miguel Cardoso's Messianism: A Reappraisal," *Association for Jewish Studies Review* 23 (1998): 63–105; Elliot R. Wolfson, "Constructions of the Shekhinah in the Messianic Theosophy of Abraham Cardoso With an Annotated Edition of *Derush ha-Shekhinah*," *Kabbalah: Journal for the Study of Jewish Mystical Texts* 3 (1998): 11–143. Cardoso, a Portuguese Jew, developed a Jewish Kabbalah that theosophically approaches Christianity in order to redeem it from within. So too, it would seem, did Martines, Pasqually de Martines, a Portuguese Jew who developed a Kabbalah approaching Christianity—only even more explicitly. See also Scholem's entry on Cardoso in the *Encyclopedia Judaica*, reprinted in *Kabbalah*, 396–400.

82. Cited approvingly both within and outside the initiatic schools. See Guénon, *Études sur la Franc-maçonnerie*, 2:69, and van Rijnberk, *Pasqually de Martines*, 1:17.

83. Three useful works on Christian Kabbalah appeared in 1998: Joseph Dan, ed., *Christian Kabbalah* (Cambridge: Harvard University Press, 1998); Philip Beitchman, *Alchemy of the Word: Cabala of the Renaissance*, (Albany: State University of New York Press, Albany, 1998); and especially Andreas B. Kilcher, *Die Sprachtheorie der Kabbala als Ästhetisches Paradigma: Die Konstruktion einer äs-*

tetischen Kabbala seit der Frühen Neuzeit (Stuttgart: Verlag J. B. Metzler, 1998). These works each contain extensive, current bibliographies on Christian Kabbalah.

84. Eliade, "Occultism and Freemasonry in Eighteenth-Century Europe," 91.

Chapter 3
Tautegorical Sublime: Gershom Scholem and Henry Corbin in Conversation

1. A version of this chapter was delivered as a lecture at Harvard University on 7 April 1998. I thank Kambiz GhaneaBassiri and Patrice Brodeur for the invitation.

2. They first corresponded in 1937, and, as they both noted in an exchange of letters in 1973, they had first met twenty-five years before that date, in 1948.

3. Ralph Manheim. Manheim was also editor of the six-volume selection of works from Eranos, edited by Joseph Campbell for the Bollingen series.

4. *Cahier de l'Herne Henry Corbin*, 322.

5. By the 1920s, Fritz Lieb (1892–1970) was an established scholar of Pietism and Romanticism, including Weigel and Hamann, writers also favored by his friend Corbin. Corbin was a close colleague of "mon cher Lieb" during the period of their shared Barthianism (1932–1936). See "Post-Scriptum biographique" in *Cahier de l'Herne Henry Corbin*, 43. Scholem describes Benjamin's relations with Lieb in *Walter Benjamin: The Story of a Friendship* (London: Faber and Faber, 1981), 206–207, 213. For more on this friendship, see Chryssoula Kambas, "Wider den 'Geist der Zeit,' Die anti-faschichstische Politik Fritz Liebs und Walter Benjamins," *Der Fürst dieser Welt*, (ed.) Jacob Taubes (Münich: W. Fink Schöningh, 1985). Lieb eventually dedicated his Weigel study to Shestov and Benjamin: *Sophie und Historia: Aufsätze zur östlichen und westlichen Geistes- und Theologiegeschichte*, ed. M. Rohkraemer (Zurich: EVZ-Verlag, 1962). For Corbin's use of Weigel, see for example *TC*, 256–257.

6. On 20 June 1934, Scholem wrote to Benjamin regarding Shestov: "I think very highly of the man." On 2 March 1939, he wrote again to Benjamin, "But you are right, at any rate, when you call his style magnificent." From *Correspondence*, 118, 246.

7. Examples could be multiplied if one looks at the 1930s. Corbin and Kojéve translated Hendrik de Man's *The Socialist Idea*. De Man for a time taught in Frankfurt alongside friends of Scholem, including Paul Tillich and Martin Buber. For De Man in this period, see Zeev Sternhell, *Neither Right nor Left: Fascist Ideology in France* trans. D. Maisel. (Princeton, N.J.: Princeton University Press, 1986), 119–141. Kojéve would become friends with other friends of Scholem, most importantly with Leo Strauss. Yet another example would be Pierre Klossowski. He was friends of both Corbin and Benjamin. All this is to indicate that Scholem and Corbin traveled in some of the same circles. For an introduction to these contexts in the 1930s, see chapter 14 of this book, "Defeating Evil from Within."

8. *Cahier de l'Herne Henry Corbin*, 323. The letter is dated 17 June 1973.

9. There is no small irony in the fact that Corbin, in this same letter, pro-

claimed his intention to visit Israel, but never made it. Whether the parallel occurred to Scholem cannot be known, but it is hard not to think here of Walter
Benjamin, another intimate of Scholem's, whose repeatedly announced intention
to visit Scholem in Jerusalem was never fulfilled.

10. Scholem, "Identifizierung und Distanz," 466.

11. Nils Roemer, "'Breaching the Walls of Captivity': Gershom Scholem's
Studies of Jewish Mysticism," *The Germanic Review* 72 (1997): 23–41, at 31.

12. These influences are documented in the present volume. See especially
chapter 5, "On Symbols and Symbolizing."

13. These lectures are published as *Hamann, philosophe du luthéranisme* (Paris:
Berg, 1985). For Pierre Klossowski's admiration for Corbin's translation of Ham-
ann's *Aesthetica in Nuce*, see Jeffrey Mehlman, "Literature and Hospitality:
Klossowski's Hamann," *Studies in Romanticism* 22 (1983): 329–347, at 333.
This latter text also had a profound effect on Scholem.

14. Muhsin Mahdi, "Orientalism and the Study of Islamic Philosophy," *Journal of Islamic Studies* 1 (1990): 73–98, at 92.

15. Michel Löwy, "Figures of Romantic Anti Capitalism," *New German Critique* 32 (1984): 42–93. This argument is elaborated by Löwy in his later volume
Redemption and Utopia. In a December 1979 interview with Löwy Scholem disavowed Biale's theory that Romanticism was formative for him. Löwy, *Redemption and Utopia*, 217 n. 44. Löwy's treatment, especially page 61 (with quote
from Biale), stresses Romanticism as "crucial."

16. See "On Romanticism and the Study of Religion," *Annals of Scholarship* 6
(1989): 363–382.

17. *FBJ*, 103–104.

18. On Leo Baeck at Keyserling's School of Wisdom in the 1920s along with
Jung, see Alexander Altmann, "Leo Baeck and the Jewish Mystical Tradition,"
Essays in Jewish Intellectual History (Hanover, N.H.: University Press of New
England, 1981), 302. Biale notes in *Gershom Scholem* that Gershom Scholem
takes "Romantic Religion" from Leo Baeck (44). See more generally *Kabbala
und Romantik*, ed. E. Goodman-Thau, G. Mattenklott, and C. Schulte (Tübingen:
Niemeyer, 1994).

19. Scholem, "Mysticism and Society," *Diogenes* 58 (1967): 1–24, at 8.

20. Baeck was first at Eranos, and he convinced Gershom Scholem that it was
acceptable to attend. *Bollingen*, 153, and Aniela Jaffé, *From the Life and Work of
C. G. Jung* (New York: Harper and Row, 1971). I discuss Scholem's relations
with Jung in chapter 12, "Psychoanalysis in Reverse."

21. *MTJM*, 405 n. 109.

22. Not to be confused with the proto–New Age quackery of Madame
Blavatsky.

23. "The Visionary Dream in Islamic Spirituality," in *The Dream and Human
Societies* ed. G. E. Von Grunebaum and Roger Caillois (Berkeley and Los Angeles: University of California Press, 1966), 381–409, at 401. Scholem's comment is found in *MSG*, 87.

24. *MSG*, 87.

25. Jung, *Response to Job* in *The Portable Jung*, ed. Joseph Campbell (New
York: Viking, 1975) at 550.

26. Corbin, "The Dramatic Element Common to the Gnostic Cosmogonies of the Religions of the Book," *Studies in Comparative Religion* 14 (1980): 199–221, at 200, no translator indicated.

27. Ernst Benz, "Theogony and the Transformation of Man in Friedrich Wilhelm Joseph Schelling," in *Man and Transformation* ed. Joseph Campbell (New York: Pantheon, 1964), 203–250, at 245.

28. Adorno, "Salute to Gershom G. Scholem to his 70th birthday: 5 December 1967," trans. Frederike Heuer (emphasis added). Was Adorno thinking here, in fact, of *Schelling's* "theogonic process?" In any event, Scholem responded warmly and revealingly to Adorno's tribute:

> I read your musings with the highest diligence, those from 30 years ago which weren't bad at all either, as well as the present ones. That you commend my insolemnity so much was especially delightful—it is precious to me. I suppose it corresponds to your dialectical attitude when I say that I do not just have a soft spot for the heterodox but also a lot for the orthodox, and large parts of my writing are devoted to the attempt of establishing the connections between these two spheres in a dialectical manner. For although you are right when mentioning that I have had quite a bit to say about the secularization of mysticism and, going further, religion; but apart from this it should not be left unsaid that I do not hold secularization itself to be something final but rather something undergoing constant change. You know very well that I am anything but an atheist, and that my religious conviction is very closely linked to my historic insights. You yourself hint at it in a later sentence. (Letter from Jerusalem, 8 December 1967, in *Briefe II*, 191–192)

I thank Werner Brandl for help with the German text. It may be noted, finally, that Adorno addressed this point in the conclusion of his radio lecture "Why Still Philosophy?" in 1962. "What wants nothing to do with the trajectory of history belongs all the more truly to it. History promises salvation and offers the possibility of hope only to the concept whose movements follows history's path to the very extreme." *Critical Models: Interventions and Catchwords*, trans. Henry W. Pickford (New York: Columbia University Press, 1998), 17.

29. Benz, "Theogony."

30. James Merrill, *Life*, December 1988, 90.

31. See the fundamental discussion by Ernst Cassirer, *Philosophy of Symbolic Forms*, vol. 2 (New Haven, Conn.: Yale University Press, 1955).

32. "Prelude to the Second Edition," *SBCE*, xii. For Schelling's conception of narrative philosophy, see Marc Maesschalck, "Les *Weltalter* de Schelling: un essai de philosophie narrative," *Laval théologique et philosophique* 46 (1990): 131–148, at 142–145.

33. The same year, it is perhaps instructive to observe, Scholem delivered his "der Nihilismus als religiöses Phänomen." For a partial translation of this lecture, see chapter 15, "On the Suspension of the Ethical," in this book.

34. *TC*, 267.

35. Ibid. 308, emphasis in original. See also 305, where he ascribes tautegory to Philo.

36. Corbin writes in "Towards a Chart of the Imaginal," *Temenos*, (1980): 23–36 at 30:

Either way it is the idea of Theophany which is dominant, making itself evident by its own nature and of necessity between the intellectual and the sensible, and what is denoted as Sophia, as the "Soul of the World," is at the same time the *imaginal* locus and the organ of this Theophany. It is at once the necessary mediatrix, the *Deus revelatus*, between pure Divinity, forever concealed, beyond our reach, and man's world. This is what we have in another place called the "paradox of monotheism" and it is a constant theme in all those doctrines in the "religions of the book" which are in one way or another related to the Kabbala.

37. *SEI*, 107.

38. Cited in Hamid Dabashi, *Authority in Islam* (New Brunswick, N.J.: Transaction Publishers, 1989), 116.

39. *SEI*, 107, emphasis added.

40. Scholem's, "Zehn unhistorische Sätze über Kabbala," 269.

41. On the trope of transparency, see chapter 6, "On Symbols and Symbolizing," in this book.

42. *OPJM*, 112.

43. For Corbin, "legalism" was the enemy of "spiritualism": "Si l'on a vraiment compris de quoi il ságit et ce qui est en cause, on ne reste pas neutre devant la choiz entre l'Islam légalítaire et l'Islam spiritual." "De 'l'histoire," 150. It may have been that he meant by this a choice between Sunni and Shi'i Islam.

44. See the remarkable letters concerning Scholem sent by Joseph Weiss to Sarah Heller-Wilensky, "Joseph Weiss. Letters to Ora," in *Hasidism Reappraised*, ed. Ada Rapoport-Albert (London: Littman Library, 1997), 10–45.

45. Joseph Weiss, "Gerhard Scholem—Fifty Years," *Yedioth hayom* (Daily News) (Tel Aviv), 5 December 1947. The Hebrew original and German translation are found in *Briefe II*, 458–460. For a discussion of this text, see Schäfer, "Die Philologie," 22–23. I am pleased to thank Werner Brandl for his help with this German text.

46. See note 44.

47. *CH*, 117.

48. Corbin, "Transcendental et existential," *Travaux du Ixe Congrès international de philosophie (Congrès Descartes)* (Paris: Hermann, 1937), 24–31.

49. *CH*, 156 n. 12.

50. On the testimony of his student Joseph Weiss, he "likes to mock at existential philology." See "Gershom Scholem Fifty Years" in *Briefe I*, 458–460. See also *OPJM*, 79. He makes similar criticisms in his Rothschild Prize acceptance speech, "Kabbalah and Historical Criticism," *OPJM*, 75–80.

51. *MIJ*, 231, 236. There are ironies here. For one, it was Buber and not Scholem who spoke out against Jung's "jargon of authenticity," just as his friend Adorno had against Heidegger. See Adorno, *The Jargon of Authenticity*, trans. Knut Tarnowski and Fredric Will (Evanston, Il.: Northwestern University Press, 1973). Buber's critique is found in "Religion and Modern Thinking," in *Eclipse of God: Studies in the Relation Between Religion and Philosophy* (New York: Har-

per and Row, 1957), 63–93. And Scholem was quite fond of Shestov, generally considered to be an "existentialist."

52. Scholem, "Reflections on Jewish Theology." See throughout, but especially *JJC*, 279.

53. Scholem, "Kabbalah and Historical Criticism," reprinted in *OPJM*, 75–80.

54. *MIJ*, 35.

55. *OPJM*, 112.

56. Corbin, "The Force of Traditional Philosophy in Iran Today," 21.

57. It was Eliade, close to philosophical and artistic circles in Paris, who perhaps most sharply addressed "existentialism," at the conclusion of *SP*, 210. He was one who, given his debt to Heidegger perhaps, saw a religious value in "existentialism." He emphasized this point also in *Cosmos and History*, but from the angle that "the East" was itself setting out from "a sort of 'existentialism.' " 158.

58. *JJC*, 22.

59. Henry Corbin, *The Concept of Cooperative Philosophy*, trans. Peter Russell (Ipswich, U.K.: Golgonooza Press, 1981), 7.

60. *TC*, 257.

61. *JJC*, 46.

62. Scholem, "Opening Address," in *Types of Redemption: Contributions to the Theme of the Study-Conference held in Jerusalem, 14th to 19th July 1968* (Leiden: E. J. Brill, 1970), 1–12, at 11.

63. *TO*, 205, emphasis added. Elsewhere, with greater apodictic force, Eliade asserted that "All symbolism of transcendence is paradoxical, impossible to conceive at the profane level." *IS*, 83.

64. Karl Löwith, "A Jewish Theology of Secular History Is Indeed a Possibility and Even a Necessity," *Meaning in History* (Chicago: University of Chicago Press, 1949), 196.

65. *MIJ*, 49–78.

66. Ibid., 77.

67. *OPJM*, 34.

68. *MTJM*, 293.

69. *MIJ*, 141, the final words of the essay.

70. *MIJ*, 255.

71. Corbin, *Hamann, philosophe du luthéranisme* (Paris: Berg International, 1985), 82.

72. Corbin, *Le paradoxe du monothéisme* (Paris: Éditions de l'Herne, 1981).

73. Corbin does not cite Jung or Heidegger in this late essay. But, as I try to show elsewhere in the present volume, they provided psychological and philosophical underpinning to the esoterism of his last writings. In his final autobiographical statement, he wrote of them at some length, carefully qualifying their respective influences on him. See "Post-Scriptum biographique," 41, 48.

74. See chapter 4, "Coincidentia oppositorum," in this book.

75. In Israel, Martin Buber, R. J. Zwi Werblowsky, and Guy G. Stroumsa have also taught comparative religion. Still, as Stroumsa notes, at the Hebrew University, even now, "there is no single course on *Judaism as a religion* offered within the entire Institute of Jewish Studies." "Buber as an Historian of Religion: Presence, not Gnosis," *Archives de Sciences Sociales des Religions* 101 (1998): 87–105, at 104. See also Stroumsa, "Hebrew Humanism Revisited: Jewish Studies and

Humanistic Education in Israel," *Jewish Studies Quaterly* 3 (1996): 123–135. I thank Professor Stroumsa for sharing these studies with me.

76. *OKS*, 11.

77. "Revelation and Tradition" in *MIJ*, 284.

78. *MTJM*, 204.

79. Corbin, "Trois entretiens sur l'histoire spirituelle de l'Iran," *Le Monde Non-Chrétien* 43–44 (1957): 179–199, at 185.

80. Corbin, "The Meaning of the Imam," in *Shi'ism*, ed. Seyyed Hossein Nasr (Albany, N.Y.: State University of New York Press, 1988), 177.

81. Scholem, letter from Jerusalem dated 5 April 1973, translated to French by Yvonne Gibert in *Cahier l'Herne Henry Corbin* 323, my translation from French here.

82. One finds it identified also by Jonathan Z. Smith, in his wry commentary on the school led by his Chicago colleague Mircea Eliade. Smith points to the odd sort of tautology that was once claimed by Chicago's History of Religions field: "It is the contention of the discipline of History of Religions that a valid case can be made for the interpretation of transcendence as transcendence. . .a quixotic repetition of the notion exemplified by Borges's Pierre Menard that a word can only be translated into itself." Jonathan Z. Smith, "Are Theological and Religious Studies Compatible?" *Bulletin* 26, no. 3 (1997): 60–61, at 61. Smith cites here from the "Announcements: The Divinity School, University of Chicago," 1960–1961. Smith may also have had in mind contemporaneous statements made by Eliade. For example, in the Preface to *Myths, Dreams and Mysteries*, the English translation of which was published in 1960, Eliade wrote that the "myth defines itself by its own mode of being." *MDM*, 14.

Chapter 4
Coincendentia Oppositorum: An Essay

1. Shafique Keshavjee, *Mircea Eliade et la coïncidence des opposés ou l'existence en duel* (Berne: Peter Lang, 1993), 227–443.

2. Claude Lévi-Strauss, *Structural Anthropology*, trans. Claire Jacobson and Brooke Grundfest (Garden City, N.Y.: Anchor, 1967), 29–54, 128–161.

3. Catherine Bell, *Ritual Theory, Ritual Practice* (New York: Oxford University Press, 1992), 101–107.

4. Niels Bohr, "The Rhetoric of Reaction: Two Years Later," *Government and Opposition* 28 no. 3 (1993): 292–231, at 305. See also M. H. F. Wilkins, "Complementarity and the Union of Opposites," in *Quantum Implications: Essays in honour of David Bohm*, ed. B. J. Hiley and F. David Peat (London: RKP, 1987), 338–360.

5. Theodor Adorno and Max Horkheimer, *Dialectic of Enlightenment*, trans. by John Cumming (New York: Continuum, 1972; reprint 1989), 82.

6. Joseph Campbell, *The Mythic Image* (Princeton, N.J.: Princton University Press, 1990).

7. See the studies in *Not Yet: Reconsidering Ernst Bloch*, ed. Jamie Owen and Tom Moylan (London: Verso, 1997).

8. For an example of the popular use of *coincidentia oppositorum*, see Thomas Merton, *Mystics and Zen Masters* (New York: Dell, 1967) 290 n. 14.

9. *TO*, 80–81.

10. Eliade provided no reliable points of reference for the background of the phrase. He gave no indication, for example, that he was drawing on the example of René Guénon when he positioned this idea: *Symbolism of the Cross*, trans. Angus Macnab (London: Luzac, 1975), chapter 6, "The Union of Complements," 27–31, and Chapter 7, "The Resolution of Opposites," 32–41.

11. For more on *coincidentia oppositorum* in the baroque see Frank J. Warnke, *Versions of the Baroque: European Literature in the Seventeenth Century* (New Haven, Conn.: Yale University Press, 1985) 92.

12. Ronald Gregor Smith, *J. G. Hamann: A Study in Christian Existentialism* (New York: Harper, 1960), 47 and 47 n. 2. See also Rainer Röhricht, "Johann Georg Hamann und Nikolaus von Kues," in *Johann Georg Hamann: Acta des Internationalen Hamann-Colloquiums in Lüneburg 1976*, ed. Bernard Gugek (Frankfurt-am-Main: Vittorio Klosterman, 1979), 277–288.

13. Smith, *J. G. Hamann*, 47, though Hamann thinks it is from Giordano Bruno; see n. 2. For more of the influence of Hamann and Cusa, see chapter 5, "On Symbols and Symbolizing," in this book.

14. *Nietzsche's Zarathrustra*, vol. 2, especially 1029–1030, in connection with *Ergriffenheit* and "mob psychology." This passage is discussed more fully in chapter 9, "The Idea of Incognito: Authority and Its Occultation According to Henry Corbin" in this book.

15. Jung, "Answer to Job," 520; *Memories, Dreams, Reflections*, recorded and ed. Aniela Jaffé, trans. Richard and Clara Winston (New York: Vintage 1963), "Late Thoughts" [Part I] s.v. "complexio oppositorum" and "conjunctio," esp. 327–342.

16. Eliade, "Jung ou la response á Job," in *Cahier de l'Herne Mircea Eliade*, 253.

17. Campbell, Introduction to *The Portable Jung*, xxx.

18. Walter Corti, "Vingt ans d'Eranos," in *Le Disque Vert: C. G. Jung*, 294. Corti edited the *Du* magazine tribute to Eranos. *Du (Schweizerische Monatsschrift)* 4 (April 1955).

19. *MTJM*, 13.

20. *OK*, 312. Amos Goldreich has argued for the impact of Isma'ili conceptions of the Godhead in the notion of *ahdut shava*, "the highest realm within the Godhead," which Scholem terms "indistinct unity." Wilensky also notes that the doctrine of "first created being" must be investigated in regard to the analogous Isma'ili doctrine. See S. H. Wilensky, "On the 'First Created Thing' in the Origins of Kabbalah and Its Philosophical Sources" in *Studies in Jewish Thought*, ed. S. H. Wilensky and M. Idee (Magnes Press: Jerusalem, 1989) [In Hebrew]; and Amos Goldreich, "From Teachings of the *Iyyun* Circle: More on the Possible Sources of 'Ha-Ahdut Ha-Shava'," *Jerusalem Studies in Jewish Thought* VI (1987) 141–156 [In Hebrew].

21. Cited in Sara Sviri, "Does God Pray? A Judaeo-Islamic Tradition in the Light of Analytical Psychology," *European Judaism* 25, no. 1 (1992): 48–55, at 54.

22. David Biale, *Gershom Scholem*, 88. For other treatments of *coincidentia oppositorum* in Kabbalah see Joseph Dan, "The Paradox of Uniting with the Supreme Negation," review of *Unity of Opposites: The Mystical Theosophy of Habad*,

by Rachel Elior, *Tarbitz* 62 no.1 (1992). See also Philip Jay Bentley, "Uncertainty and Unity: Paradox and Truth," *Judaism* 33 (1984): 191–201; Daniel Matt, "Ayin," in *Essential Papers in Kabbalah*, ed. Lawerence Fine (New York: New York University Press, 1995) 80–81 and nn. 64–66.

23. See what is perhaps his single most important essay, at least for the present inquiry: "Religious Authority and Mysticism," in *OKS*, 5–32.

24. *MIJ*, 297.

25. At 82 in *Hamann, philosophe du luthéranisme*, cited by Daryush Shayegan in *Henry Corbin: La topographie spirituelle de l'Islam Iranien* (Paris: l'Herne, 1990), 41.

26. *SBCE*, 80, emphasis in original.

27. Ibid., 100, emphasis in original. See also 142, 324 n. 55.

28. *TC*, 375–376. Other places in his corpus where he addresses this topic include *Avicenna*, 152, 201–203, 215, 376; *MLIS*, 47, and where he positions himself contra Eliade, 50.

29. *CI*, 209–215.

30. Ibid, 188. See also 272, 273, 279 on the *Ka'aba* Vision.

31. S. A. Q. Husaini, *The Pantheistic Monism of Ibn AL 'Arabi* (Lahore: Sh. Muhammad Ashraf, 1970) 194, citing *Futuhat*, 4: 251.

32. Further on *coincidentia oppositorum* in Sufism, see Denis Gril, "Adab and Revelation," in *Muhyiddin Ibn 'Arabi: A Commemorative Volume*, ed. Stephen Hirtenstein and Michael Tiernan (Shaftesbury, U.K.: Element, 1993), 249. See also Michel Chodkiewicz, *An Ocean Without Shore: Ibn al'Arabi, the Book, and the Law*, trans. from the French by David Streight (Albany: State University of New York Press, 1993), 28; R. W. J. Austin, Introduction to *Ibn al'Arabi: The Bezels of Wisdom*, trans. R. J. W. Austin, (New York: Paulist Press, 1980), 19. See also Toshihiko Izutsu, "Paradox of Light and Darkness in the *Garden of Mystery* of Shabestari" in *Anagogic Qualities of Literature*, ed. J. Strelka (University Park: Pennsylvania State University Press, 1971), 288–307; Anne Marie Schimmel, *Mystical Dimensions of Islam* (Chapel Hill: University of North Carolina Press, 1975), 198; Sviri, "Does God Pray?" 48–55; Michael Sells, *Mystical Languages of Unsaying* (Chicago: University of Chicago Press, 1994), 21.

33. Franz Rosenthal, "Ibn 'Arabi Between 'Philosophy' and 'Mysticism,'" *Oriens* (1988): 1–35, at 35.

34. Denis de Rougemont, "Der Neu Geknüpfte Gordische Knoten," *Antaios* 1 (1959): 393–396.

35. McGuire, *Bollingen*, 76–79.

36. It was translated by Willard Trask, translator of his *Cosmos and History, Yoga* and *Shamanism*, as well as Corbin's *Avicenna and the Visionary Recital*. Also, Eliade and Scholem served on the board of editors of Anshen's parallel series, "Religious Perspectives."

37. de Rougemont, *Man's Western Quest: The Principles of Civilization* (New York: Harper and Row, 1957), 3.

38. Ibid. 115–118.

39. Ibid. 115, emphasis in original.

40. Sviri, "Does God Pray?" 49.

41. Quoted in ibid., 50.

42. Steven Schwarzschild, "Theologico-Political Basis of Liberal Christian-

Jewish Relations in Modernity," in *Das deutsche Judentum und die Liberalismus/ German Jewry and Liberalism* (Koenigswinter: Fr.-Naumann-Stiftung, 1986), 70–95, at 79.

43. Moshe Schwarcz, "Religious Currents and General Culture," *Leo Baeck Institute Yearbook* 16 (1971): 3–17, at 8.

44. Tzvetan Todorov, *Theories of the Symbol*, trans. Catherine Porter (Ithaca, N.Y.: Cornell University Press, 1982), 209. For the notion of tautegory, see chapter 3, "Tautegorical Sublime," in this book.

45. *Set in Motion: Essays, Inteviews, & Dialogues*, ed. Zofia Burr (Ann Arbor: University of Michigan Press, 1996), 13.

46. Roman Jakobson, "What is Poetry?" *Studies in Verbal Art* (Ann Arbor: University of Michigan Press, 1971), 20–32.

47. Umberto Eco, "At the Roots of the Modern Concept of Symbol," *Social Research* 52, no. 2 (1985): 398–399. Along the same lines, see his Tanner lecture, "Interpretation and Overinterpretation: World, History, Texts," in *The Tanner Lectures on Human Values XII*, ed. Grethe B. Peterson (Salt Lake City: University of Utah Press, 1991), 141–203.

48. Eco, "Interpretation and Overinterpretation," 151.

49. Cited in James Webb, *The Occult Establishment* (La Salle, Il.: Open Court, 1976), 427.

50. *The New Science of Giambattista Vico*, trans. T. G. Bergin and M. H. Fisch (Ithaca, N.Y.: Cornell University Press, 1968), 78.

51. Robert Sayre and Michel Löwy, "Figures of Romantic Anti-Capitalism," *New German Critique* 32 (1984): 43.

52. Armin Mohler, "Das Buch 'Die Konservative Revolution in Deutschland,' Drei Jahrzehnte Später," *Revue d'Allemagne* 14, no. 1 (January/March 1982): 161–164, at 164, esp. the section titled "Kulturpessimisme, Révolution Conservatrice et Modernité."

53. Pierre Bourdieu, *The Political Ontology of Martin Heidegger*, trans. Peter Collier (Stanford, Calif.: Stanford University Press, 1991), 62, emphasis in orignal.

54. Ibid., 31.

55. Theodor Adorno, Leo Lowenthal, and Paul W. Massing, "Anti-Semitism and Fascist Propaganda," in *Anti-Semitism: A Social Disease*, ed. Ernst Simmel. (New York: International Universities Press, 1946), 137.

56. Saul Friedländer,"The Road to Vichy." review of *Neither Right nor Left: Fascist Ideology in France*, by Zeev Sternhell, translated by David Maisel, *The New Republic* (15 December 1986), 26–33.

57. Friedländer, "The Road to Vichy," 27.

58. Saul Friedländer, *Reflections of Nazism: An Essay on Kitsch and Death*, trans. Thomas Weyr (New York: Harper and Row, 1984), 131.

59. Friedländer, *Reflections*, 135–136.

60. George Mosse, *Masses and Men: Nationalist and Fascist Perceptions of Reality* (Detroit: Wayne State University Press, 1987), 74–75.

61. Jeffrey Herf, *Reactionary Modernism: Technology, Culture, and Politics in Weimar and the Third Reich* (Cambridge: Cambridge University Press, 1984; reprint, 1987).

62. Evola, *Explorations: Homme et Problémes*, trans. Philippe Baillet (Puiseaux: Pardès, 1989), 143.

63. Louis Pauwels and Jacques Bergier, *Impossible Possibilities*, trans. Andrew White (New York: Stein and Day, 1971).

64. Pierrre Bourdieu, *The Political Ontology of Martin Heidegger* (Stanford, Calif.: Stanford University Press, 1991), 62, emphasis in original.

65. Denis Hollier, "On Equivocation (Between Literature and Politics," *October* 55, 1990: 3–22.

66. For examples of Eliade's use of *felix culpa* at the end of his life, see *JIV*, 104, 142.

67. Hans Jonas, "The Concept of God after Auschwitz," in *Echoes from the Holocaust: Philosophical Reflections on a Dark Time*, ed. Alan Rosenberg and Gerald Myers, (Philadelphia: Temple University Press, 1988), 294.

68. Primo Levi, *Survival in Auschwitz: The Nazi Assault on Humanity*, trans. from the Italian by Stuart Woolf (New York: Simon and Schuster, 1996), 87–88.

69. Kracauer, *History: The Last Things Before the Last* (New York: Columbia University Press, 1969), 202.

70. See remarks by Carl V. Schorske in *New York Review of Books*, (27 May 1993), 35–40, esp. 37 and 40 n. 32

71. Cited in Martin Bergmann, *In the Shadow of Moloch* (New York: Columbia University Press, 1992), 234. One can think of other examples. Alexander Altmann, "The God of Religion, the God of Metaphysics, and Wittgenstein's 'Language-Games,'" *Zeitschrift für Religions- und Geistesgeschichte* 39 (1987): 294.

72. Gary Lease, "The History of 'Religious' Conciousness and the Diffusion of Culture: Strategies for Surviving Dissolution," in *History, Historiography, and the History of Religions*, ed. Luther H. Martin, as a special issue of *Historical Reflections/Reflexions Historiques* 20, no. 3 (1994): 475.

73. Leszek Kolakowski, *Religion, If There Is No God—: On God, the Devil, Sin, and Other Worries of the So-called Philosophy of Religion* (New York: Oxford University Press, 1982), 144.

74. Ehud Ben Ezer interview, *Unease in Zion* ed. Ehud Ben Ezer, (New York: Quadrangle/Jerusalem Academic Press, 1974), 292.

75. John Joseph Stoudt, *Jacob Boehme: His Life and Thought* (New York: Seabury Press, 1968), 304.

76. Brown concludes by coining the term "dialectical imagination," with direct reference to *coincidentia oppositorum* in Eliade and Scholem. See *Life Against Death*, 319. Eventually, Brown applies Henry Corbin extensively. See his "Apocalypse of Islam," in *Apocalypse and/or Metamorphosis* (Berkeley: University of California Press, 1991), 69–95.

77. Brown, *Love's Body*, (New York: Vintage, 1966), 242.

78. Stanislav Lem, "*Unitas Oppositorum*: The Prose of Jorge Luis Borges," trans. Franz Rottersteiner, in *Microworlds: Writings on Science Fiction and Fantasy*, ed. Franz Rottersteiner and Helen and Kurt Wolff (San Diego: Harcourt Brace Jovanovitch, 1984), 233–242.

79. Ibid., "His literary game with its borderline meanings always begins where opposites repel one another with their inherent force; and it ends as soon as they are joined together." Ibid., 239.

80. Ibid., 240. Later he states that "on principle there can be no fantastic poetry." 241.

81. Rudolf Otto, *The Idea of the Holy*, trans. John W. Harvey (London: Oxford University Press, 1969), 107.

82. Lem, "*Unitas Oppositorum*," 242.

83. *MTJM*, 30.

84. Jürgen Habermas worries about the effects of a premature remythologizing. "The remythification of a society whose institutions are dependent on extreme rationality measurably raises the dangers already existing." "Martin Heidegger on the Publication of Lectures from the year 1935," *Graduate Faculty Philosophy Journal* 6 (1977): 155–180, at 180.

85. The alchemical image of the "black sun" is another variant on the *coincidentia oppositorum*, favored for example, by Jung.

86. For medieval conceptions of the angel reason, see Wasserstrom, *Between Muslim and Jew: The Problem of Symbiosis Under Early Islam* (Princeton, N.J.: Princeton University Press, 1995), 232–235.

87. See the fundamental study of Shlomo Pines, "The Limitations of Human Knowledge according to Al-Farabi, Ibn Bajja and Maimonides," in *Studies in the History of Jewish Thought*, ed. W. Z. Harvey and Moshe Idel (1979; reprint, Jerusalem: Magnes Press, 1992), 404–432.

88. For guidance on this question I follow Pines, "The Limitations of Human Knowledge."

89. Leo Strauss, "Freud on Moses and Monotheism," in *Jewish Philosophy and the Crisis of Modernity: Essays and Lectures in Modern Jewish Thought*, ed. Kenneth Hart Green (Albany: State University of New York Press, 1997), 285.

Chapter 5
On Symbols and Symbolizing

1. R. J. Zwi Werblowsky, "Structure and Archetype," *The Journal of the Ancient Near East Society of Columbia University* 5 (1973): 435–42, at 441.

2. *Eranos-Jahrbuch* 26 (1957).

3. For more on this topic, see chapter 13, "Uses of the Androgyne in the History of Religions," in this book.

4. "Greetings from Angelus," Gershom Scholem to Walter Benjamin, 9 September 1933, in *Correspondence*, 79–81.

5. *MTJM*, 27.

6. Scholem, "The Star of David: History of a Symbol." Originally in Hebrew in 1948, then in German in 1993, finally in English translation in *MIJ*, 257–282, at 257–258.

7. Erich Heller, *The Disinherited Mind* (Harmondsworth, England: Penguin, 1961), pp. 95–96.

8. Jung, *Psychology and Religion* (New Haven: Yale University Press, 1938; reprint, 1978), 72, emphasis in original.

9. Jung, *The Symbolic Life*, vol. 18 of *The Collected Works*, 283.

10. See E. M. Butler, *Fortunes of Faust* (Cambridge: Cambridge University Press, 1952; reprint, 1979) for a colorfully evocative description of "The Wizard of the North," (141–142). The definitive study in English is now Isaiah Berlin, *The Magus of the North: J. G. Hamann and the Origins of Modern Irrationalism* (London: John Murray, 1993). On the theory of opposites in Hamann see James C. O'Flaherty, *Johann Georg Hamann* (Bloomington, Ind.: Twayne, 1979), chaps. 4, 7. On Mendelssohn/Kant, and on "the great transformation (of Kant)" etc., see Walter Benjamin, "Program of the Coming Philosophy" (1917), in *Philosophical Forum* 15 (1983–84): 49, trans. Martin Ritter.

11. *FBJ*, 50, 113

12. Paul de Man also argued this point: Jeffrey Mehlman, "Literature and Hospitality: Klossowki's Hamann," *Studies in Romanticism* 22 (1983): 329–347, at 332.

13. 1931, in *JJC* 239–243, at 241. Also cited by Biale, *Gershom Scholem*, 136; Hannah Arendt, introduction to *Illuminations*, by Walter Benjamin (New York: Harcourt Brace and World, 1968), 37.

14. Scholem, "The Name of God and the Linguistic Theory of the Kabbalah," trans. S. Pleasance, *Diogenes* 79 (1972): 59–80 and 80 (1972), 164–194, 62 n. 1. This aperçu of Hamann is cited by Benjamin in his 1916 "On Language as Such and on the Language of Man," in *Walter Benjamin: Selected Writings, Vol.1, 1913–1926*, ed. Marcus Bullock and Michael W. Jennings (Cambridge: Harvard University Press, 1996), 67.

15. Corbin comments on Hamann and Kierkegaard in "L'humour dans son rapport avec l'historique chez Hamann et chez Kierkegaard," *Kierkegaard*, ed. Jean Brun (Paris: Obliques, 1981), 163–167. See also Mehlman on Corbin's Hamann, and on Klossowski's Hamann and Benjamin, "Literature and Hospitality," 340 n. 28, 332–333.

16. Hamman's latter-day reception, with its dark irrationalism, is characterized rather sharply by Isaiah Berlin: "This hatred and this blind irrationalism have fed the stream that has led to social and political irrationalism, particularly in Germany, in our own century, and has made for obscurantism, a revelling in darkness, the discrediting of that appeal to rational discussion in terms of principles intelligible to most men which alone can lead to an increase of knowledge, the creation of conditions for free co-operative action based on conscious acceptance of common ideals, and the promtion of the only type of progress that has ever deserved this name." Berlin, *The Magus of the North*, 121–122.

17. Marcus Bullock, "Ernst Jünger: Literature, Warfare and the Intoxication of Philosophy," *Mosaic* 19 (1986): 107–119, 113. For more on Jünger see chapter 10, "Mystic Historicities," in this book.

18. Jünger, "Total Mobilization," in *The Heidegger Controversy*, ed. Richard Wolin (Cambridge, Mass.: MIT Press, 1993), 124.

19. Martin Heidegger, "Language," *Poetry, Language, and Thought*, trans. A Hofstadter (New York: Harper and Row, 1971), 191.

20. See the discussion of his Aryanophilia in chapter 8, "Collective *Renovatio*," in this book.

21. The first translation is found in "Mysticism and Humour," *Spring* (1973). 24–34, at 27 (originally a lecture in Tehran in 1969); the second is the final sentence of "L'Ismaélisme et le symbole de la Croix," *La table ronde* 120 (1957): 122–134, at 134.

22. Corbin, "L'Ismaélisme et le symbole de la Croix," 134, emphasis in original.

23. *SBCE*, 135

24. *MLIS*, 139–144.

25. *SBCE*, 66.

26. Ibid. Corbin also invokes Goethe's unfinished "Geheimnisse" (Secrets) in *En Islam Iranien*, 4: 405 ff., and in *MLIS*, 54.

27. Corbin, *The Concept of Comparative Philosophy*, trans. Peter Russell (Ipswich: Golgonooza Press, 1981), 13.

28. *CI*, 13.

29. Scholem, conclusion, "Philosophy and Jewish Mysticism," 402.

30. Compare his comment that in *Sefer ha-Bahir*, "everything is already a symbol." *OK*, 58

31. *OK*, 448.

32. Nils Roehmer, "'Breaching the Walls of Capitivity': Gershom Scholem's Studies of Jewish Mysticism," *The Germanic Review* 72 (1997): 23–41, at 31.

33. *JJC*, 87. See Gershom Scholem, *Walter Benjamin: Story of a Friendship*, trans. Harry Zohn (Philadelphia: Jewish Publication Society, 1981), on many conversations with Benjamin about Goethe.

34. George L. Mosse, "Gershom Scholem as German Jew," *Modern Judaism* 10 (1990): 117–133, reprinted in Mosse, *Confronting the Nation: Jewish and Western Nationalism* (Hanover, N.H.: Brandeis University Press, 1993), 176–193.

35. *MIJ*, 303. I thank my colleague Katja Garloff of Reed College for locating the source of this citation, which Scholem did not reveal: "Vermächtnis," in *Johann Wolfgang Goethe Gedichte 1800–1832*, ed. Karl Eibl (Frankfurt am Main: Deutscher Klassiker Verlag, 1988), pp. 685–686.

36. *OPJM*, 22.

37. This letter is discussed more fully in chapter 12, on "Psychoanalysis in Reverse," in this book.

38. *AI*, 70.

39. Eliade, Introduction to *Australian Religion*, (London: Cornell University Press, 1973), xvii.

40. *AI*, 299–300.

41. *Q*, 122–124.

42. *J IV*, 41.

43. *AI*, 136, 257.

44. *MDM*, 32–33, emphasis added.

45. *J II*, 72.

46. *J III*, 110.

47. Ibid., 111.

48. *FC*, passim. For more on *Naturphilosophie* see chapter 10, "Mystic Historicities," in this book.

49. *R*, 2: 539.

50. *OWCF*, 47–93.

51. *TO*, 123.

52. *J II*, 316–317, emphasis in original.

53. *J IV*, 60. Although the influence of Goethe on Eliade has not been studied closely, it has been noticed by some scholars. See the additional materials gathered in Bryan Rennie, *Reconstructing Eliade*, 47 n. 1.

54. Cited by Rennie, *Reconstructing Eliade*, 48, who comments that this is "certainly similar to Mircea Eliade's notion of "hierophany," and by Natan Rotenstreich, "Symbolism and Transcendence: On Some Philosophical Aspects of Gershom Scholem's Opus," *Review of Metaphysics* 31 (1977–78): 604–614, at 605–606.

55. *SBCE*, 277 n. 45.

56. Cassirer, *Essay on Man*, 199.

57. *TO*, 199.

58. See, for a fuller discussion, chapter 7, "A Rustling in the Woods," in this book.

59. See also chapter 3, "Tautegorical Sublime," in this book.

60. "Post-Scriptum biographique," 43.

61. *HIP*, 13, 57. He also described the Hurufi sect as "an inexhaustible mine for the phenomenology of symbolic forms." 310.

62. Scholem, *Walter Benjamin,*, 21. On Benjamin on Cassirer (and Carl Schmitt), see Niethammer, *Posthistoire*, 131 n. 55.

63. "Observations on Religious Symbolism," *TO*, 190 n. 3.

64. Eliade, "Eranos," *Nimbus* 2 (1954): 57–58, at 58.

65. Susan J. Handelman, *Fragments of Redemption: Jewish Thought and Literary Theory in Benjamin, Scholem and Levinas* (Bloomington: Indiana University Press, 1991), 105, Handelman's treatment, especially 102–115, is the best available study of Scholem on the symbol. For Schweid's critique, see *Judaism and Mysticism According to Gershom Scholem: A Critical Analysis and Programmatic Discussion*, trans. David Weiner (Atlanta: Scholars Press, 1985), 43 n. 41.

66. "Following an old distinction that he took from Goethe and that Scholem adopted, Benjamin understood symbols as the opposite of allegories." David Biale, *Gershom Scholem*, 138. See 198 n. 108 for citation. For more on the background to this distinction, see Edward Allen Beach, "Allegory, Symbol or Reality," in *Potencies of God(s): Schelling's Philosophy of Mythology* (Albany: State University of New York Press, 1994), 25–47.

67. Jeffrey Mehlman, *Walter Benjamin for Children* (Chicago: University of Chicago Press, 1993), 45.

68. Handelman, *Fragments of Redemption*, 102–115, esp. 107; Biale, *Gershom Scholem*, 138.

69. See chapter 13, "Uses of the Androgyne in the History of Religions," in this book.

70. Eliade, "Observations on Religious Symbolism," *TO*, 203.

71. Paul Ricoeur, *The Symbolism of Evil*, trans. E. Buchanan (Boston: Beacon Press, 1967), 16–18; more generally all of "Speculation, Myth, and Symbol" (3–10), "Criteriology of Symbols" (10–18), and "The Symbol Gives Rise to Thought" (347–357), all in Ricoeur, *The Symbolism of Evil*.

72. Ibid., 16, emphasis in original.

73. *SEI*, 18.

74. *Avicenna*, 30. In his note 34 on this passage, he observes that this is "a question with which hermeneutics in general is now greatly concerned," at which point he cited Jean Daniélou and Gershom Scholem.

75. Corbin, "Chart of Imaginal," 29. Elsewhere he emphasizes that this results in the "death of the literal sense." (*SEI*, 61, emphasis in original).

76. Corbin, "Mysticism and Humour," 24–34, at 27.

77. *CI*, 14.

78. *MTJM*, 27.

79. Coleridge, "Statesman's Manual," cited by Michael P. Steinberg in "Walter Benjamin writes the essays 'Critique of Violence' and 'The Task of the Translator,' treating the subject of messianism he discussed with Gershom Scholem during the war," in *Yale Companion to Jewish Writing and Thought in German Culture, 1096–1996*, ed. Sander L. Gilman and Jack Zipes (New Haven: Yale University Press, 1997), 401–412, at 403.

80. Jonathan Z. Smith, "The Influence of Symbols upon Social Change: A Place on Which to Stand," in *Map is not Territory*, ed. Jonathan Z. Smith (Chicago: University of Chicago Press), 129–146, at 144.

81. *MTJM*, 132.

82. Scholem, "The Name of God and the Linguistic Theory of the Kabbalah," *Diogenes* 80 (1972): 165.

83. Scholem, *MTJM*, 27.

84. Biale, "Gershom Scholem's Ten Unhistorical Aphorisms on Kabbalah: Text and Commmentary," *Modern Judaism* 5 (1985): 67–93, at 82.

85. Ibid.

86. *HIP*, 13, emphasis in original.

87. *SEI*, 42, 61, 74, 79; *CI*, 187–204, 278.

88. *SET*, 61.

89. *CI*, 187. Elsewhere, in a 1967 Paris lecture, he emphasized the pure inwardness of the achievement. "What the ear of the heart hears is a sound and a music from beyond the tomb, which a few privileged ones have heard in this world, to the point that the opaque barriers between the worlds has become transparent to them." *VM*, 235.

90. *SP*, 117.

91. Ibid., 138.

92. Joseph Campbell, *The Hero's Journey: Joseph Campbell on his Life and Work*, ed. P. Cousineau (San Francisco: Harper and Row, 1990), 40.

93. Originally published in *Du* (April 1955, a special issue devoted to Eranos, edited by Walter Robert Corti): 29; reprinted in Jambet, *Henry Corbin, Cahier de l'Herne*, 261–263.

94. *MDM*, 355.

95. See *Jung on Active Imagination*, ed. Joan Chodorow (Princeton, N.J.: Princeton University Press, 1997).

96. *SBCE*, 11, emphasis in original.

97. *MTJM*, 27.

98. Scholem, *La mystique juive: les thèmes fondamentaux*, trans. Maurice Hayoun (Paris: Les éditions du Cerf, 1985), 14 n. 13.

99. *SBCE*, pp. 56–57. See also 71.

100. Discussed in chapter 13, "Uses of the Androgyne in the History of Religions," in this book.

101. Some of his work on symbolism was gathered in *Symbolism, the Sacred & the Arts*, ed. Diane Apostolos-Cappadona (New York: Crossroads, 1988).

102. *IS*, 12.

103. Ibid., 20.

104. *MTJM*, 38.

105. Scholem's massive study of Sabbatianism in its detailed historical setting is the great exception here.

106. See the influential essay by Paul Ricoeur which explicates this distinction, "Hermenuetics and the Critique of Ideology," in *Hermeneutics and Modern Philosophy* ed. Brice R. Wachterhauser (Albany: State University of New York Press, 1986), 300–343.

107. As Scholem stated, "There is no mysticism as such. There is only the mysticism of a particular religious system, Christian, Islamic, Jewish mysticsim and so on." *MTJM*, 6.

Chapter 6
Aesthetic Solutions

1. It lies beyond my scope to trace the prehistory of this conception. A work of fundamental importance in this connection is Andreas B. Kilcher, *Die Sprachtheorie der Kabbala als Ästhetisches Paradigma: Die Konstruktion einer ästhetischen Kabbala seit der Frühen Neuzeit*, (Stuttgart: Verlag J. B. Metzler, 1998).

2. See chapter 7, "A Rustling in the Woods," in this book.

3. This Benjaminian conception has gained considerable currency. For a balanced review of the literature on this theme, see Martin Jay, "'The Aesthetic Ideology' as Ideology: Or What Does it Mean to Aestheticize Politics?" in *Force Fields: Between Intellectual History and Cultural Critique* (New York: Routledge, 1993), 71–84. For a more general analysis of aestheticization in the political sphere, see Josef Chytry, *The Aesthetic State: A Quest in Modern German Thought* (Berkeley: University of California Press, 1989).

4. Walter Benjamin devoted an important essay to Surrealism. See "Surrealism," in Walter Benjamin, *Reflections: Essays, Aphorisms, Autobiographical Writings*, trans. Edmund Jephcott (New York: Schocken, 1986), 177–193. For the larger impact of Surrealism on Benjamin, see Margaret Cohen, *Profane Illumination: Walter Benjamin and the Paris of Surrealist Revolution* (Berkeley: University of California Press, 1993).

5. See the letters of Evola to Tzara, *Lettere di Julius Evola a Tristan Tzara (1919–1923)* (Rome: Fondazione Julius Evola, 1991).

6. For Eliade's dinner with Fondane, see *JIII*, 200–201.

7. *The Correspondence of Walter Benjamin and Gershom Scholem*, 107, 112, 117–118, 160, 163, 183, 243, 246. See also Eliade, *A II*, 106.

8. Emil Cioran, *Anathemas and Admirations* (New York: Arcade, 1991), 218–223.

9. See chapter 3 "Tautegorical Sublime," in this book.

10. Thomas Sparr, "Gershom Scholem und die moderne Literatur," *The Ger-

manic Review 72 (1997): 42–56; and Eliade, of course, widely published author of fiction, intimate of Eugene Ionescu and Constantin Brancusi, *SSA*. See also an example of Eliade's literary criticism across his career, "Sur le roman," in *Cahiers roumains d'études littéraires* 4 (1979): 4–29. Other examples include Scholem's correspondence (now published) with the literary critics Werner Kraft and Peter Szondi, not to speak of those with his close friend Benjamin and his cousin, the scholar of poetry Heri Pflaum. See Scholem's appreciation of Pflaum, "Hiram Péri (Pflaum)," in *Romanica et Occidentalia* (Jerusalem: Magnes Press, 1963), 7–11. Corbin's substantial influence may be gauged by his adaptation in the works of the best-selling James Hillman, whose post-Jungian "archetypal psychology" is predicated on a Corbinian "poetic basis of mind."

11. Robert Alter, "Scholem and Modernism," *Poetics Today* 15 (1994): 429–442; German version in *Gershom Scholem Zwischen den Disziplinen*, ed. G. Smith and P. Schäfer (Frankfurt am Main: Suhrkamp, 1995), 157–176. See more fully Robert Alter, *Necessary Angels: Tradition and Modernity in Kafka, Benjamin and Scholem* (Cambridge: Harvard University Press, 1991).

12. *OPJM*, 76–77.

13. For other materials on pre-Eranos Asconan counterculture, see Green, *Mountain of Truth*.

14. I found this reference in Richard Noll, *The Aryan Christ: The Secret Life of Carl Jung* (New York: Random House, 1997), 75. This novel, *Das grosse Wagnis*, is also discussed in Green, *Mountain of Truth*, 150–151.

15. Green, *Mountain of Truth*, 25, 39, 40–43, 47, 48, 50.

16. Corti, "Vingt ans d'Eranos," 290.

17. I thank Horst Junginger of Tübingen for securing these letters for me.

18. C. G. Jung, *The Psychology of Kundalini Yoga: Notes of the Seminar Given in 1932 by C. G. Jung* (London: Routledge, 1996).

19. Richard Noll, *The Jung Cult: Origins of a Charismatic Movement* (Princeton, N.J.: Princeton University Press, 1994).

20. Jolande Jacobi, "Eranos—vom Zuhörer aus Gesehen," *Du* (April 1955 [special issue devoted to Eranos, edited by Walter Robert Corti]): 51–57, at 52. A generation later George Steiner provided a colorful portrait of the Ascona "scene."

It was, thus, no accident that the famed Eranos-circle, that wheel of mystic ardour turning around Jung at Ascona, should pick up the scent. Soon Eliade was of the coven. And nothing is better fun than the account in Eliade's journals, notably Volume Two (1957–69), of annual meetings in the opulent setting and elegant aura of the alpine priesthood. Like many others, Gershom Scholem famously among them, Eliade was flattered, fascinated and sometimes put off by the Eranos alchemy (where, owing to Jung's sovereign role, "alchemy" can be taken almost literally). Eliade notes that the solemn lectures are delivered principally to ladies of a silver age, of august means and, preferably, social standing. He is drawn to Jung, yet wary: He observes, obliquely, the strain of conservative mysticism, even of *Führer*-politics, which the Eranos movement had cultivated in the 1930s and which persisted in the ambience of the 1950s. But here was a prestigious celebration of the very elements crucial to Eliade's complex commitments: animism, shamanism, allegory, astrological-alchemical symbolism, hellenistic and oriental iconography, kratophany, Orphism, Tantra, Eleusis, the investigation of the archetypal, geomancy, Cabbala, elements necessarily on the verge of the occult and of self-deceiving kitsch, yet seminal to dreams, to the ritual weave of culture and society, to the mystery of figuration in the arts. Where but at Ascona was this perilous, compelling stuff given the benefit of exact scholarship, frequently of the highest kind, and of a sort of Platonic-Nietzschean playful gravity? (*Times Literary Supplement*, no. 4565, 28 September-4 October 1990).

21. Gilbert Durand, "Le Génie du Lieu et les Heures Propices," in *Eranos-Jahrbuch* 51 (1982): 243–277; Rudolf Ritsema, "The Origins and Opus of Eranos: Reflections at the 55th Conference," in *Eranos-Jahrbuch* 56 (1987): vii-ixx, at ix.

22. Hans Heinz Holz, "Eranos—eine moderne Pseudo-Gnosis," in *Religionstheorie und Politische Theologie*, ed. J. Taubes (Munich: Verlag Ferdinand Schöningh, 1984), 249–263. Holz speaks of a world flight (*Weltflucht*).

23. For example, Eliade penned a version of *Iphigenia*. It was written in 1939 and published as *Iphigenia* (Valle Hermoso, Argentina: Cartea Pribegia, 1951). This publication was inaccessible to me.

24. Cynthia Ozick, "The Fourth Sparrow: The Magisterial Reach of Gershom Scholem," in *Art and Ardor* (New York: E. P. Dutton, 1983), 178. In another interview Scholem spoke of "all the philological games and masquerades at which I excell." *JJC*, 46.

25. *SEI*, 43, emphasis added.

26. Corbin, "The Dramatic Element Common to the Gnostic Cosmogonies of the Religions of the Book," *Cahiers de l'Université Saint Jean de Jérusalem* 5 (1978): 141–173. I use the (unattributed) English translation in *Studies in Comparative Religion* 14 (1980): 191–221.

27. *Avicenna*, 4, 21, emphasis in original.

28. *Shamanism*, 511, emphasis in the original.

29. *TO*, 186.

30. Ibid., 187.

31. *PCR*, 71, emphasis added.

32. Ibid.

33. *Shamanism*, 419.

34. Calinescu summarizes Eliade's theory of the spectacle, "the soteriological virtues of theater and performance. Acting, impersonating, role-playing, enacting, and re-enacting are activities that can mediate between the world of the ordinary and that of the mythical; understood spiritually, they are effective techniques of liberation from the tyrannical meaninglessness of the profane." Matei Calinescu, "The Fantastic and Its Interpretation in Mircea Eliade," *Youth Without Youth and Other Novellas*, trans. Mac Linscott Ricketts (Columbus: Ohio State University, 1988), xxxiii.

35. *IS*, 118, emphasis in original.

36. Ibid., 121.

37. *MDM*, 132, emphasis in original.

38. *OL*, 103–104.

39. Ibid., 103. Eliade's colleague Julius Evola held a similar notion of the "invisible masters." These "enigmatic personages . . . are proceeding from a dramatic, theatrical concept of the magus or initiate: as if the adept is preoccupied, above all else, with 'exhibiting,' or manifesting—in forms that will astonish, amaze, or terrify—everything within the power of heaven and earth so that all eyes will converge on him." Evola, *The Hermetic Tradition*, 214.

40. *MDM*, 134–135, emphasis in original.

41. *TO*, 91.

42. *PCR*, 72.

43. Eliade's wartime reflections on the "true ruler of the world, the Universal Monarch" (*SSA*, 146) might be compared instructively to Julius Evola's conception of the "Universal Ruler." See Evola, *The Mystery of the Grail*, 38–42.

44. Eliade, *Youth*, 198–207.

45. Ibid., 198, 274, emphasis in original.

46. Ibid., 205–206. Thanase, it may be noted, seems based on Julius Evola.

47. Eliade's Varuna is etymologically linked to the "Ur" of Evola's "idealismo magico" period, which in turn derives from Guénon's concept of the Lord of the World.

48. Gombrich, "Eliade on Buddhism," 229.

49. Chytry, *The Aesthetic State*. For History of Religions as a "total discipline," see Eliade, *Q*, 8.

50. *SSA*, 153. See J. Schnapp, *Staging Fascism: 18BL and the theater of the masses for the masses* (Stanford, Cal.: Stanford University Press, 1996), and his references (212–213, n. 12) to the fascist *Thingspiele*, the apparent inspiration for Eliade's wartime dramaturgy for the masses.

51. *OL*, 121. Elsewhere in the same volume he elaborated this point. "At all events, the shaman is an actor, insofar as certain of his practices are theatrical in their nature." 104.

52. *J II*, 15.

53. *Q*, 54–71.

54. Tantric sex, was, at once, the essential ritual and the essential myth of the vaunted *coincidentia oppositorum*, reintegration of opposites, that Eliade portrayed as the ultimate cosmic mystery. The personal payoff, so to speak, was nothing less than a resanctified sexual life. Eliade held these out to be universally desirable goals—even though, to achieve them, they must be preceded by *violent rebirth*, a "trial," an "ordeal," an "iniation"; symbolic dismemberment of the body, metamorphosis into a wild animal, frenzy, renewal of the viscera, etc. See *RIS*, 130. Elsewhere, more directly, Eliade claims that "[to] eat raw flesh . . . is extremely creative." *J II*, 92–93.

55. "Existence *in* Time is ontologically a non-existence, an unreality." From his 1952 Eranos lecture, "Indian Symbolisms of Time and Eternity." *IS*, 67, emphasis in original.

56. *TSS*, 8–9. emphasis added.

57. See Eliade's discussion in *Zalmoxis*. For such themes in the Legionary myth, see the sources in Wasserstrom, "Eliade and Evola."

58. *TSS*, 8, emphasis in original.

59. Two German-language poems by Scholem, one from the 1930s and one from 1943, are reproduced in Hebrew translation in *Gershom Scholem (1897–1982): Commemorative Exhibition on the Fifth Anniversary of his Death and the Installation of his Library at the JNUL March 1987* (Jerusalem: Jewish National and University Library, 1988), 40–41 (Hebrew section). For an important discussion of Scholem's poem to Hans Jonas, see Schäfer, "Die Philologie."

60. "To support his diagnosis Buber even resorts to a sin of my youth, committed nearly forty years ago, which consists of my once having perpetrated a poem." "Religion and Psychology: A Reply to Martin Buber," *Spring 1973*, 196–203, at 197. In fact, the poem was written when Jung was thirty-one years old. For some context to these verses see Noll, *The Aryan Christ*, 160–162.

61. *Cahier de l'Herne Henry Corbin*, 264–265.

62. Georges Dumézil, "*L'Histoire des Croyances* de Mircea Eliade," *Le Monde* 9791 (July 17, 1976), 1, 17. Diane Apostolos-Cappodona asserted that "Mircea Eliade is a poet in the fullest Heideggerian sense of the word." *SSA*, xii. While Eliade would have enjoyed this characterization, it is nonetheless ironic, given that he did not, in fact, publish any poems.

63. Their impact on poets was substantial. Their very persons, in fact, were employed by important poets in far corners of the world. For example, the eminent Polish poet Zbigniew Herbert begins his poem "Mr. Cogito on Magic" this way:

> Mircea Eliade is right
> we are—despite everything
> an advanced society
>
> magic and gnosis
> flourish as never before

Mr. Cogito: Poems, trans. John Carpenter and Bogdana Carpenter (Hopewell, N.J.: The Ecco Press, 1993), 34.
I thank Ryan Offutt for this reference.

The great Argentinean writer Jorge Luis Borges rhymed "Scholem" with "Golem" in a poem from his old age, in the following quatrain.

> The Cabbalist who officiated as divinity
> called his farfetched creature 'Golem';
> these truths are related by Scholem
> in a learned passage of his volume.

"The Golem," in *Borges: A Reader*, ed. Emir Rodriguez Monegal and Alastair Reid (New York: E.P. Dutton, 1981), 275.
For Scholem's assessment of Borges, see *FBJ*, 133. Eliade met Borges on 30 January 1968. See *J II*, 305.

Corbin had a major impact on the Black Mountain School poet Charles Olson. The angelology of Corbin was directly registered in the following lines of

Olson's masterwork, *Maximus*.
> Paradise is a person. Come into this world.
> The soul is a magnificent Angel.

Charles Olson, *The Maximus Poems*, ed. George F. Butterick (Berkeley: University of California, 1983), 240.

On this work, and Corbin's influence on Olson, see Tom Clark, *Charles Olson: The Allegory of a Poet's Life* (New York: W. W. Norton, 1991), 282–283.

64. Scholem cites Habermas as "an open-minded reader" of Walter Benjamin. See *JJC*, 231.

65. Scholem, "Der Nihilismus als religiöses Phänomen," *Eranos-Jahrbuch* 43 (1974).

66. Scholem spoke to this point in his "Candid Letter About My True Intentions in Studying Kabbalah (1937)": "Through the unique perspective of philological criticism, there has been reflected to contemporary man for the first time, in the neatest possible way, that mystical totality of Truth whose existence disappears because of its being thrust upon historical time." *OPJM*, 5. He repeated this point in rather different terms in his "Ten Unhistorical Aphorisms on Kabbala." Aphorism Nine begins with the sentence "Ganzheiten sind nur okkult tradierbar," which may be translated as, "Totalities can only be transmitted in an occult fashion." For the original see Scholem, *Judaica 3: Studien zur jüdischen Mystik* (Frankfurt am Main: Suhrkamp, 1970), 264–272, at 270. For a discussion of this passage see David Biale, "Gershom Scholem's Ten Unhistorical Aphorisms on Kabbalah: Text and Commentary," *Modern Judaism* 5 (1985): 67–95, at 86–87. Eliade's most extensive claims for "totality" are found in the title essay of *TO*, 78–125, where he argues that *coincidentia oppositorum* is "the mystery of totality." For more, see chapter 4 on "*Coincidentia oppositorum*," in this book.

67. The unreproducible masterwork, monograph as mastery, meant that an essay in the History of Religions was often overdetermined, like a good poem—or an ordinary dream. The systematic conception of the monograph, the "whole" as it were, always outweighed its details. In this sense, Scholem's famous motto—God lurks in the details—may be his vastest screen. In these monumental constructions the forest of the whole is not composed of trees but of little wholes. "God lurks in the details," to be sure, implies a philologist's purism, the credo of the ultimate particularist. But Scholem was also the most consistent and interesting in squeezing worldprocess through the needle's eye of detail, what he called "the smallest illusion of development."

68. Scholem famously defined Kabbalah as "secret doctrine" in *MTJM*, 21.

69. Corbin, "The Time of Eranos," xx, emphasis added. Corbin was almost deaf, but he was also a profound lover of music, especially as an amateur performer on the organ. For another example of his use of musical metaphors for spiritual perception, see his prologue to *SBCE*, in which he refers to "something in the nature of harmonic perception." xxviii. He returns to this point in the body of the text. 51, 54, 57, and 71.

70. Corbin, "On the Meaning of Music in Persian Mysticism," in *Temenos* 13

(1992): 49–52, at 50–51. See also "The Musical Sense of Persian Mysticism," *VM*, 231–236, for a different translation.

71. Corbin concluded his most musical essay (delivered at Eranos in 1953 and constituting the narrative text of *SBCE*) with ecstatic chords invoking Richard Strauss and Gustav Mahler (*SBCE*, 105). Elsewhere, Corbin claimed that one "cannot therefore speak of the Temple of the Grail without opening one's inner vision and hearing the musical dramas of Richard Wagner." *TC*, 368. Scholem used the symphonic metaphor to evoke the "chain of tradition": "The musician who plans a symphony has not composed it; still, he participates in significant measures in its production." *MIJ*, 297.

Chapter 7
A Rustling in the Woods: The Turn to Myth in Weimar Jewish Thought

1. Paul Tillich, "Kairos," in *The Protestant Era* (Chicago: University of Chicago Press, 1948), 32–55, at 48.

2. Albert Schweitzer, *The Decay and Restoration of Civilization* (London: Black, 1923; reprint, 1961).

3. T. S. Eliot, "*Ulysses*, Order and Myth," *The Dial* 75 (1923): 480–483.

4. For effects of the insane inflation of 1923, see *The German Inflation of 1923*, ed. Fritz Ringer (New York: Oxford University Press, 1969); Walter Benjamin, "A Tour of German Inflation," in *Reflections* (New York and London: Harcourt Brace Jovanovich, 1978), 70–76; and especially Gerald Feldman, *The Great Disorder: Politics, Economics and Society in the German Inflation, 1914–1924* (New York: Oxford University Press, 1993). Note George Steiner's "intriguing suggestion," from Elias Canetti, that "the ease of the Holocaust relates to the collapse of currency in the 1920s. . . . The same large numbers tainted with unreality the disappearance and liquidation of peoples." *In Bluebeard's Castle: Some Notes Towards the Re-definition of Culture* (London: Faber and Faber, 1971), 45. See also Canetti's vivid memories in "Inflation and Impotence, Frankfurt 1921–1924," *The Torch in my Ear* (New York: Farrar Straus Giroux, 1982), 3–55.

5. Recalled by Bergson in *Mélanges* (Paris: Presses Universitaires de France, 1972), 1340–1346; cited by Ilya Prigogine and Isabelle Stengers, *Order out of Chaos* (New York: Bantam, 1984), 294.

6. For this notion of so-called neo-Riemannian time see, for example, Wayne Hudson, *The Marxist Philosophy of Ernst Bloch* (London: Macmillan, 1982), 146–148.

7. As volume 13 of the series *Die Gesellschaft* (Frankfurt-am-Main, 1923).

8. Discussed in Löwy, *Redemption and Utopia*, 203–206. Löwy notes that Landauer's anarchism strongly affected Scholem at the time.

9. Wohl, *Generation of 1914* (Cambridge: Harvard University Press, 1979), 74.

10. Ibid., 3.

11. Discussed by Löwy, *Redemption and Utopia*, 163.

12. Canetti, *Torch in My Ear*, 49.

13. Wolfgang Schivelbusch, *Intellektuellendämmerung: Sur Lage der Frankfur-*

ter Intelligenz in den zwanziger Jahren: Die Universität. Das Freie Jüdische Lehrhaus. Die Frankfurter Zeitung. Radio Frankfurt. Der Goethe-Preis und Sigmund Freud. Das Institut für Sozialforschung (Frankfurt am Main: Insel Verlag, 1982).

14. Aby Warburg, "A Lecture on Serpent Ritual," *Journal of the Warburg and Courtauld Institute* 2 (1939): 277–292, at 292. This was his only English-language lecture to be published in the *Journal of the Warburg and Courtauld Institute.*

15. Gertrud Bing, cited by Peter Gay in *Weimar Culture. The Outsider as Insider* (New York: Harper and Row, 1968), 33.

16. George Lichtheim, *From Marx to Hegel* (New York: Seabury Press, 1971), 20.

17. Karl Löwith, *Meaning in History* (Chicago: University of Chicago Press, 1949).

18. Benjamin, "Theses on the Philosophy of History," in *Illuminations*, 263.

19. Walter Benjamin, *An Essay on Man* (New Haven, Conn.: Yale University Press, 1946).

20. Cited by Irving Wohlfarth, "On Some Jewish Motifs in Benjamin," in *The Problems of Modernity: Adorno and Benjamin*, ed. Andrew Benjamin (London, 1989), 157–215, at 164.

21. Ernst Bloch, *The Principle of Hope* (Cambridge, Mass.: MIT Press, 1986), 1:134.

22. Bloch's *Durch die Wüste* and the second edition of *Geist der Utopie* were published in 1923. See the overview of this period in Richard H. Roberts, *Hope and its Hieroglyph: A Critical Decipherment of Ernst Bloch's Principle of Hope* (Atlanta: Scholars' Press, 1990), 12–19. Ortega y Gasset published *The Theme of Our Time* in 1923, on which see Wohl, *The Generation of 1914*, 134–142. For Ortega's debt to Cohen, see Steven Schwarzschild, "The Theologico-Political Basis of Liberal Christian-Jewish Relations in Modernity," in *Das Deutsche Judentum und der Liberalismus—German Jewry and Liberalism* (Sankt Augustin: Comdok-Verlagsabteilung, 1986), 70–95, at 90. Ernst Cassirer published *Language and Myth* in that year. Martin Buber's *I and Thou*, also published in 1923, marked a watershed in his career. So too his *Lectures on Judaism:* "[Buber's] lectures of 1938 simply elaborate the argument of 1923 (indeed, one could say this about everything Buber wrote after 1923)." David Novak, "Buber's Critique of Heidegger," *Modern Judaism* 5 (1985): 125–140, at 132.

23. On Cohen's rejection of Schelling, see William Kluback, *The Legacy of Hermann Cohen* (Atlanta: Scholars Press, 1989), 58–63.

24. Of course, Cohen's original success itself may be the really surprising fact. As Moshe Schwarcz put it, "One of the most surprising phenomena in connection with Jewish thought in Germany is the conceptual subservience of all thinkers, no matter to which current in Judaism they belonged, to the philosophy of Kant," Moshe Schwarcz, "Religious Currents and General Culture," *Yearbook of the Leo Baeck Institute* 16 (1971): 3–17, at 7.

25. In fact, "[the] dichotomy for or against *Mythos* already characterized Jewish thinking (especially in the German cultural sphere) in the first decades of this century." Ze'ev Levy, "Über Franz Rosenzweigs Auffassung des Mythos," in *Der Philosoph Franz Rosenzweig (1886–1929) Bd. II. Das Neue Denken und seine Di-*

mensionen, ed. Wolfdietrich Schmied-Kowarzik (Freiburg/Munich: Verlag Karl Alber, 1988), 287–299, at 288 (my translation).

26. Wolfgang Schluchter, *The Rise of Western Rationalism: Max Weber's Developmental History* (Berkeley: University of California Press, 1981). "Ethical monotheism" was itself, it would seem, a neologism coined by German Jewish reformers, but I have been unable to identify the author of its coinage.

27. See Schwarzschild, "The Theologico-Political Basis," p. 81.

28. This view has remained persuasive for decades. See for example, Norbert Elias, "The Sociologist as a Destroyer of Myths," in *What is Sociology?* (New York: Columbia University Press, 1978), 50–70.

29. H. Stuart Hughes, *Consciousness and Society: The Reorientation of European Social Thought 1890–1930*, 2d ed. New York: Vintage, 1977).

30. Wolf Lepenies, *Between Literature and Science: The Rise of Sociology*, (Cambridge: Cambridge University Press, 1988), 292.

31. Hermann Cohen, "Deutschtum und Judentum," in *Jüdische Schriften* (Berlin: C. A. Schwetschke, 1924), 2:312. Schwarzschild angrily insisted, however, that "Cohen is often accused of some sort of fatuous historical as well as philosophical optimism. This accusation displays real psychological and conceptual insensitivity." " 'Germanism and Judaism'—Hermann Cohen's Normative Paradigm of the German-Jewish Symbiosis," in *Jews and Germans from 1860–1933: The Problematic Symbiosis*, ed. David Bronsen (Heidelberg: Carl Winter, 1979), 129–157, at 139.

32. Max Weber, *Wirtschaft und Gesellschaft*; Cohen, *Jüdische Schriften*.

33. Cited in John Raphael Staude, *Max Scheler 1874–1928: An Intellectual Portrait* (New York: Free Press, 1967), 146.

34. For studies on the relation between Judaism and myth see *The Seductiveness of Jewish Myth: Challenge or Response?* ed. S. Daniel Breslauer (Albany: State University of New York Press, 1997).

35. Paul Mendes-Flohr, " 'To Brush History Against the Grain': The Eschatology of the Frankfurt School and Ernst Bloch," *Journal of the American Academy of Religion* 51 (1983): 631–650. For more on Bloch and Cohen, see Mendes-Flohr, " 'The Stronger and the Better Jews': Jewish Theological Responses to Political Messianism in the Weimar Republic," *Jews and Messianism in the Modern Era: Metaphor and Meaning*, vol. 7 of *Studies in Contemporary Jewry*, ed. Jonathan Frankel (New York: Oxford University Press, 1991), 159–196.

36. Marianne Weber, *Max Weber, ein Lebensbild: mit 11 Tafeln und Faksimiles* (Tübingen: publisher 1926), 476, cited in Richard H. Roberts, *Hope and Its Hieroglyph: A Critical Decipherment of Ernst Bloch's Principle of Hope* (Atlanta: Scholars' Press, 1990), 8. Roberts also cites an amazing letter of Bloch to Lukács from 1911 ("Ich bin der Paraklet . . ."). n. 20. This immediacy of the messianic was sustained for some time. Between 1917 and 1919 at least three revolutions (in Russia, Bavaria, and Hungary) were partly spearheaded by Jews. As noted shortly thereafter, some Jews experienced revolution as a "collective messiah." See Paul Honigsheim from 1924, cited in Michael Löwy, "Jewish Messianism and Libertarian Utopia in Central Europe (1900–1933)," *New German Critique* 20 (1980): 105–115, at 105.

37. Roberts, *Hope and Its Hieroglyph*, 9–10.

38. The fullest treatment of the viscissitudes of Schelling in Jewish thought is Werner J. Cahnmann, "Schelling and the New Thinking of Judaism," *Proceedings of the American Academy for Jewish Research* 48 (1981): 1–56.

39. Jürgen Habermas, *Philosophical-Political Profiles* (Cambridge, Mass.: MIT Press, 1984), 61–79.

40. Published in 1917, and republished in Rosenzweig's in Franz Rosenzweig's *Kleinere Schriften* (Berlin: Schocken, 1937).

41. Cited in Cahnmann, "Schelling," 50, Compare Scholem, "In Memory of Hermann Cohen," *Modern Judaism* 5 (1985): 1–3 (dated 5 April 1918).

42. The debate over the identity of the author of the *Systemprogramm* continues. The fullest treatment of the problem is *Mythologie der Vernunft: Hegel's "Altestes Systemprogramm des deutschen Idealismus,"* ed. Christoph Jamme and Helmut Schneieder (Frankfurt am Main: Suhrkamp, 1984). Xavier Tilliette continues to defend Rosenzweig's argument for Schelling's authorship: "Rosenzweig et Schelling," in *Ebraismo Ellenismo Cristianesimo II* [*Archivio di Filosofia LIII/2–3*)] (1985): 141–152. For Rosenzweig and Schelling, see Massimo Cacciari, "Sul presupposto. Schelling e Rosenzweig," *Aut Aut* 211–212 (1986): 43–65, and, more generally, Cacciari, *L'Ange Nécessaire* (Paris: C. Bourgois, 1988).

43. Franz Rosenzweig, *The Star of Redemption*, trans. William Hallo (Boston: Beacon Press, 1972), 329. For a fine treatment of the unresolvable tension between Cohen and Rosenzweig regarding Schelling's philosophy of myth, see William Kluback, "Time and History: The Conflict between Hermann Cohen and Franz Rosenzweig," in *Der Philosoph Franz Rosenzweig (1886–1929) Bd. II*, ed. Schmied-Kowarzik, 801–813.

44. In his "New Thinking: Notes on *The Star of Redemption*," Rosenzweig chooses the Schellingian slogan "absolute empiricism" for his system: *Franz Rosenzweig: His Life and Thought*, 2d ed., Nahum N. Glatzer (New York: Schocken, 1967), 207. For the "new thinking" more generally see the comments of Karl Löwith: "The 'new thinking' was a phenomenon characterizing a whole generation deeply impressed by the bankruptcy of the bourgeois-Christian world and the emptiness of the academic routine." *Nature, History and Existentialism* (Evanston, Il.: Northwestern University Press, 1966), 53. For the "New Being" of Tillich, see *The New Being* (New York, 1955) and "The Importance of New Being for Christian Theology," originally in *Eranos-Jahrbuch* 1954, translated in *Man and Transformation: Papers from the Eranos Yearbooks 5* (New York: Pantheon, 1964), 161–179.

45. Scholem, *Walter Benjamin*, 31.

46. Ibid., 59.

47. Ibid., 61.

48. Discussed by Löwy, *Redemption and Utopia*, 101–102.

49. In the opening pages of Ernst Cassirer, *Mythical Thought* vol. 2 of *Philosophy of Symbolic Forms* (New Haven, Conn.: Yale University Press, 1955).

50. Cited by N. Tertulian, "The History of Being and Political Revolution: Reflections on a Posthumous Work of Heidegger," in *The Heidegger Case: On Philosophy and Politics*, ed. Tom Rockmore and Joseph Margolis (Philadelphia: Temple University Press, 1992), 208–231, at 209. This work was also crucial in

the development of Tillich's theology. See James Luther Adams, *Paul Tillich's Philosphy of Culture History, Science and Religion*, (New York: Schocken, 1970), 7.

51. David Farrell Krell, "Shattering: Toward a Politics of Daimonic Life," *Graduate Faculty Philosophy Journal* 14–15 (1991): 153–183. And for Rosenzweig, *Star of Redemption* (from Part I to Part II), see "Transition, Retrospect: The Chaos of the Elements," which begins, "Mythic God, plastic world, tragic man—we hold the parts in our hand. Truly we have smashed the All. . . . the unity of the All [is] shattered for us." *Star of Redemption*, 83.

52. Martin Heidegger, "Review of Ernst Cassirer's *Mythical Thought*" (1928), trans. James C. Hart and John C. Maraldo, in *The Piety of Thinking: Essays by Martin Heidegger* (Bloomington: Indiana University Press, 1976), 32–45, at 45. It should be noted that Heidegger was not entirely accurate here. Usener, for example, had already laid the groundwork, as Cassirer himself scrupulously observes in *Language and Myth* (New York: Harper, 1946), 15.

53. Schwarzschild published a précis of this unpublished work as "Franz Rosenzweig and Martin Heidegger: The German and the Jewish Turn to Ethnicism," in *Der Philosoph Franz Rosenzweig (1886–1929) Bd. II*, ed. Schmied-Kowarzik 887–889. Other convergences of these two thinkers are noted by Karl Löwith in "M. Heidegger and F. Rosenzweig or Temporality and Eternity," in *Philosophy and Phenomenological Research*, 3 (1942/1943): 53–77; and by Michael Theunissen in *The Other: Studies in the Social Ontology of Husserl, Heidegger, Sartre, and Buber* (Cambridge, Mass.: MIT Press, 1986), especially 263.

54. It also included, for example, such French Jewish scholars of religion in the 1920s as Marcel Mauss: "Il ne nous suffit pas de décrire le myth. Suivant les principes de Schelling des philosophes, nous voulons savoir quel être il traduit." Cited by M. Detienne, "Une mythologie sans illusion," *Le temps de la réflexion* 1 (1980): 29.

55. For "Civilisation" vs. "Kultur" at this time, see, for example, Albert Schweitzer, *Verfall und Wiederaufbau der Kultur* and *Kultur und Ethik*, both published in 1923. For a general orientation to the dichotomy, see Norbert Elias, "On the Sociogenesis of the Concepts 'Civilization' and 'Culture'," in *The History of Manners*, vol. 1 of *The Civilizing Process* (New York: Pantheon, 1978), 1–35.

56. For example, Rudolf Otto claimed that the primordial, prereligious *daimonic* arises from "intuitions of persons of innate prophetic powers." *Idea of the Holy*, (London: Oxford University Press, 1939), 122. It is important to remember that early sociology was still forming in the tension between literature and science. See Lepenies, *Between Literature and Science*.

57. Karl Kerényi, "Dionysus, the Cretan: Contributions to the Religious History of Europe," *Diogenes* 20 (1957): 1–21, at 13.

58. They did much to revive the moribund "primal" scenario. Max Müller, a student of Schelling, had already said, in 1885, that the "devil-savage, however, of the present anthropologist is as much as a wild creation of scientific fancy as the angel-savage of former philosophers. The true Science of Man has no room for such speculations." Reprinted as "Reflections on Savage Man," in *Ways of Understanding Religion* ed. Walter H. Capps (New York: Macmillan, 1972), 70–77, at 73. By 1965, E. E. Evans-Pritchard could flatly observe that such theories

were "for anthropologists at least, as dead as mutton, and today are chiefly of interest as specimens of the thought of their time." Cited in ibid., 127.

59. For contrasts between Benjamin and Rosenzweig on the "Revelation of Adam," see Stéphane Mosès, "Walter Benjamin and Franz Rosenzweig," *The Philosphical Forum* 15 (1983–1984): 188–206, at 198–199. For an insightful characterization of this "semiotic of the prelapsarian" and its implications, see George Steiner, "The Scandal of Revelation," in *Salmagundi* 98–99 (1993): 42–71, at 67–68.

60. Schelling, *Philosophical Lettters upon Dogmatism and Christianity*, cited in Arthur P. Mendel, *Vision and Violence* (Ann Arbor: University of Michigan Press, 1992), 139, emphasis added.

61. Boris Pasternak, "Random Thoughts" (dated 1919/1922), in *Selected Writings and Letters* (Moscow: Progress Publishers, 1990), 88. For Benjamin's corrosive rejection of such "primeval forest" scenarios, see Winfried Menninghaus, "Walter Benjamin's Theory of Myth," in *On Walter Benjamin: Critical Essays and Recollections*, ed. Gary Smith (Cambridge Mass.: MIT Press, 1991), 292–329, at 298.

62. As discussed by Richard Faber, "Einleitung: 'Pagan' und Neo-Paganismus. Versuch einer Begriffsklärung," in *Die Restauration der Götter: Antike Religion und Neo-Paganismus*, ed. Richard Faber and Renate Schlesier (Würzberg: Königshausen + Neumann, 1986), 10–26, at 15. See also Anson Rabinbach, "Introduction to Hugo Ball," in *Critique of the German Intelligentsia* (New York: Columbia University Press, 1993).

63. This was true of those non-Jewish thinkers who turned to this new orientation to immediacy: "Heidegger had baldly appropriated the *kairological*—the *kairos*, the appointed time, the "moment" (*Augenblick*) of truth and decision in *Being and Time* (§ 67a)—and kerygmatic conceptions of human existence that he had first learned from biblical Christianity, and gratuitously attributed them to the Greeks, to whom they were quite alien." In John D. Caputo, *Demythologizing Heidegger* (Bloomington: Indiana University Press, 1993), 181. Related idioms were appropriated into the notion of "decision" (*Decizion/Entschiedung*) used for the Conservative Revolution by Carl Schmitt, and by Paul Tillich in the interests of religious socialism in *The Socialist Decision* (1933; reprint, New York: Harper and Row, 1977).

64. Bloch, *The Principle of Hope*, 1:124.

65. Rosenzweig, "The New Thinking," notes (1925) on the *Star of Redemption*: Glatzer, *Franz Rosenzweig*, 196–197. For metahistorical implications, see *Star of Redemption*, 110–11 ("The Moment"). See Meinecke's final work, *Historism: The Rise of a New Historical Outlook* trans. J. E. Anderson (New York: Herder and Herder, 1972). See also Georg Scherer, "Der Augenblick im Denken Europas," in *Zeit und Mystik: der Augenblick im Denken Europas und Asiens* (Sankt Augustin: Academia Verlag, 1992), 113–128, at 126–128.

66. See the discussion Wayne Hudson, *The Marxist Philosophy of Ernst Bloch* (New York: St. Martin's Press, 1982), 148. See also, for a comparison of Benjamin and Rosenzweig on this point, Löwy, *Redemption and Utopia*, 58–59.

67. *MTJM*, 27, emphasis in original.

68. In his 1928 review of Cassirer's *Mythical Thought*, Heidegger applied the

thinking of his *Being and Time*, published just the year before, to his Jewish colleague's approach to myth. Heidegger asserted here that "all disclosed beings have the ontological feature of overwhelmingness (*mana*) . . . [and] *mana* discloses itself in a specific present 'moment of vision'" (*"Augensblicklichkeit"*). See Heidegger, "Review of Ernst Cassirer's Mythical Thought" (1928), 43. This passage is glossed in David Farrell Krell, *Daimon Life: Heidegger and Life-Philosophy* (Bloomington: Indiana University Press, 1992), 167. One also thinks of Rosenzweig's essay of 1917, "Zeit ists. Gedanken über das jüdische Bildungsproblem des Augenblicks," in *Zweistromland. Kleinere Schriften zur Religion and Philosophie* (Berline: Philo Verlag, 1926).

69. Cassirer, *Language and Myth*, 72.

70. Rosenzweig, *Star of Redemption*, 71.

71. In part due to the vogue for depicting historical development in terms of an organism's development. For generational metaphors, see Robert Wohl's admirable *The Generation of 1914*. Note that Scholem never lost the sense of his generation as a youth movement (*FBJ*, 166). For Schelling's revolutionary notion of "organism" see Karl Mannheim, "The Concept of the State as an Organism," in *Essays on Sociology and Social Psychology* (London: Routledge and Kegan Paul, 1953; reprint, 1966), 165–185. Nor did Scholem forgo his own "organicism": "his works contain numerous instances of the key terms 'organic', 'organism,' 'original,' 'sovereign,' and 'spontaneous.'" Amos Funkenstein, "Gershom Scholem: Charisma, *Kairos* and the Messianic Dialectic," *History and Memory* 4 (1992): 123–139, at 130.

72. Paul Tillich, *The Construction of the History of Religions in Schelling's Positive Philosophy: Its Presuppositions and Principles* (Lewisburg, Pa.: Bucknell University Press, 1974), 16.

73. Cited in William Kluback, *Hermann Cohen: The Challenge of a Religion of Reason*, (Chico, Calif.: Scholars Press, 1984), 63.

74. Scholem, *Walter Benjamin*, 61. Much remains to said about triadic schemes in this milieu. They were used by Cassirer, Rosenzweig, and Scholem. Behind them echoes the portentous Schelling. For some observations on triadic myth in Benjamin, see Irving Wohlfarth, "On the Messianic Structure of Walter Benjamin's Last Reflections," *Glyph* 3 (1978): 148–212, at 174–184.

75. *MTJM*, 7. This passage perhaps echoes Vico, paragraph 379, "All things are full of Jove," which in turn derived from Vergil. A further source may have been Thales of Miletus, "Everything is full of gods."

76. Cited in John Michael Krois, *Cassirer, Symbolic Forms and History* (New Haven, Conn.: Yale University Press, 1987), 86. In 1928, Heidegger reviewed Cassirer's second volume of *Philosophy of Symbolic Forms*. He seemed to agree that (in Krell's paraphrase) "the daimon is as close as the nearest rock, tree or canoe paddle . . . the daimon hovers in the reflected or refracted light of the world." David Farrell Krell, "Shattering: Towards a Politics of Daimon Life," *Graduate Faculty Philosophy Journal* 14, no. 5 (1991): 153–182, at 166.

77. Cited in H. Frederick Reisz, Jr., "The Demonic as a Principle in Tillich's Doctrine of God: Tillich and Beyond," in *Theonomy and Autonomy* ed. John J. Carey (Macon, Ga.: Mercer University Press, 1984), 135–156, at 148.

78. Paul Tillich, "The Demonic. A Contribution to the Interpretation of His-

tory" (1926), in *The Interpretation of History* (New York, Scribner's, 1936), 80. See also Reisz, "The Demonic," 138–143, for the roots of this image in Schelling.

79. Rosenzweig, "The New Thinking," in Glatzer, *Franz Rosenzweig*, 202. One sees here the concern which Benjamin called *Urgeschichte des Bedeutens* ("The original history of meaning"), a phrase that could well have been used by Cassirer. See Irving Wohlfarth, "On the Messianic Structure of Walter Benjamin's Last Reflections," *Glyph* 3 (1978): 148–212.

80. Note that Gustav Landauer, who developed a theory of "demonic depth," conceived "Revolution" as "an irruption in the world." See Löwy, "Jewish Messianism," 108, following Karl Mannheim. For *Plötzlichkeit* and the "aesthetics of horror," see Karl Heinz Bohrer, *Asthetik des Schreckens* (Munich: Carl Hanser, 1978), 334 ff., and the discussion in Richard Wolin, "Carl Schmitt. The Conservative Revolutionary Habitus and the Aesthetics of Horror," *Political Theory* 20 (1992): 424–447.

81. William Cutter, "Ghostly Hebrew, Ghastly Speech: Scholem to Rosenzweig, 1926," *Prooftexts* 10 (1990): 413–433, at 417. For more on this text see Rivka Horowitz, "Franz Rosenzweig and Gershom Scholem on Zionism and the Jewish People," in *Jewish History* 6 (1992): 99–113; Michael Brocke, "Franz Rosenzweig und Gerhard Gershom Scholem," in *Juden in der Weimarer Republik* ed. Walter Grab and Julius H. Schoeps (Stuttgart: Burg Verlag, 1986), 127–153, text at 148–150.

82. Cited, with important discussion, in Bishop, *The Dionysian Self*, 309.

83. For Jung, see for example the statements made in *Nietzsche's Zarathustra: Notes of the Seminar Given in 1934–1939 by C. G. Jung* edited by James L. Jarrett (Princeton, N.J.: Princeton University Press, 1988), 2:1030 (June 24, 1936). Also in 1936, Jung issued his best-known pronouncement on *Ergriffenheit*, in his ambivalent response to J. W. Hauer: "Wotan", in *Civilization in Transition*, vol. 10 of *Collected Works* (New York: Pantheon, 1964). See also Jung, *Letters*, 1: 211–212. For Hauer's side of the *Ergriffenheit* controversy see Margarete Dierks, *Jakob Wilhelm Hauer 1881–1962: Leben. Werk. Wirkung. Mit Einer Personalbibliographie* (Heidelberg: Verlag Lambert Schneider, 1986), pp. 283–299, esp. 289–293.

For Scholem, see his "Identifizierung und Distanz. Ein Rückblick," in *Eranos-Jahrbuch* 1979, 463–467, at 466. Adorno pointedly applies the notion of *Ergriffenheit* to Scholem: "Der objektive Gehalt dessen, woran gerade einem wie Scholem bis ins Innerste Ergriffenen alles liegen mußte, schien gefärhdet durch rhetorische Insistenz auf Ergriffenheit." ("The rhetorical insistence on being stirred (*Ergriffenheit*) endangered the objective contents of that which matters in particular to someone like Scholem, who is moved (*ergriffen*) through and through"). "Gruß an Gershom G. Scholem. Zum 70. Geburtstag: 5 Dezember 1967," in *Neue Zuricher Zeitung*, 136 no. 5199, 3 December 1967. I thank Frederike Heuer for her translation of this difficult text.

For Heidegger's extensive use of *Ergriffenheit/Ergriefer*, see *Being and Time*, 1st English ed., (London: SCM Press, 1962), 565, s.v. "seize upon." For the usage in the Frobenius school, see A. P. Kriel, *The Legacy of Leo Frobenius* (Fort Hare, South Africa: Fort Hare University Press, 1973), 2–3, and 19. Frobenius's successor, Ad. E. Jensen, also centrally used this idea: "Spiel und Ergriffenheit," *Paideuma* 2 (1942): 124–139, and *Myth and Cult among Primitive Peoples* (Chicago: University of Chicago Press, 1963), 3–4, 53, 56. The Frobenius/Jensen usage has been powerfully critiqued by Jonathan Z. Smith: "No Need to Travel to the Indies. Judaism and the Study of Religion," in *Take Judaism for Example: Toward a Comparison of Religions* ed. Jacob Neusner, (Atlanta: Scholars Press, 1992), 224–225; and "Sacred Persistence" and "A Pearl of Great Price," both in *Imagining Religion: From Babylon to Jonestown* (Chicago: University of Chicago Press, 1988), 42–43 and 96–100, respectively.

84. It should be noted, however, that even some of these revolutionaries were taken up with the idea originally. Near the end of his long life, Leo Lowenthal wittily recalled: "My first publication [in 1923] was an essay 'The Demonic. Outline of a Negative Philosophy of Religion.' It was a terribly ambitious thing, and earned me a great deal of criticism at the time from Siegfried Kracauer and Franz Rosenzweig, but also excited praise from Ernst Bloch. . . . 'The Demonic' was a mix of Marxist theory, phenomenology, psychoanalysis and religious-mystic-Jewish themes. It all seemed to go very well together." From "We Never Expected Such Fame," conversation with M. Greffath (1979) in *Critical Theory and Frankfurt Theorists: Lectures, Correspondence, Conversations*, ed. Leo Lowenthal (New Brunswick, N.J.: Transaction, 1989), 240. This dissertation was published in 1923—but before the decade was out Lowenthal had converted with his friends to a mélange of Marx and Freud. His turn to myth and the daimonic, in other words, was a brief affair, typifying its Weimar moment. "The Demonic. Outline of a Negative Philosophy of Religion," moreover, specifically concerned the reactionary Catholic theosophist Franz von Baader, colleague of Schelling and a major influence on Gershom Scholem. Arnaldo Momigliano noted that the specifically Catholic influence on Scholem's early thought has been almost entirely unappreciated. See his brilliant review, "Gershom Scholem's Autobiography," *New York Review of Books*, 18 December 1980, 37–39, reprinted in *Settimo Contributo alla Storia Degli Studi Classici e del Mondo Antico* (Rome: Edizioni di storia e letteratura, 1984), 350–359.

85. Adorno and Horkheimer *Dialectic of Enlightenment* (New York: Continuum, 1944; reprint, 1989), 15–16 and 20–21. Vico and Durkheim had both invoked the Lucretian maxim that "fear is the beginning of the gods," though Durkheim criticizes Lucretius for it.

86. Adorno, "Subject and Object," in *The Essential Frankfurt School Reader*, eds. Andrew Arato and Eike Gebhardt (New York: Continuum, 1988), 497–511, at 499. It should be noted that Cassirer, like Adorno in this passage, also locates the first spark of monotheism at this daimonic moment: "Here it is but a single step to the fundamental idea of true monotheism." *Language and Myth*, 76. Again, a certain common connection to Schelling is at work here, though the link is much more attenuated in the case of Adorno. See Klaus Baum, *Die Transzendierung des Mythos: Zur Philosophie und Äesthetik Schellings und Adornos* (Würzberg: Königshausen & Neumann, 1988). Regarding the origins of monotheism, on the other hand, they retained a (largely unacknowledged) similarity to Cohen.

Adorno, like Scholem, explicitly denied that such statements should be taken as evidence for an affinity which he might be seen to share with the archbourgeois Cassirer, but the affiliation is unmistakable. David Biale, for one, recognized Scholem's similarity to Cassirer in relation to his theory of symbolism: Biale, *Gershom Scholem*, 68. I would add other examples. Compare Scholem from 1938 with Cassirer from 1946: "The attempt to discover the *hidden life* beneath the external shapes of reality and to make visible that abyss in which the symbolic nature of all that exists reveals itself: this attempt is as important for us today as it was for those ancient mystics." *MTJM*, 38. "There is also a prophecy of the past, a revelation of its *hidden life*." Cassirer, *Essay on Man*, emphasis added.

One should not underestimate the impetus of antibourgeois passion in Scholem's denial of Cassirer's influence. After all, Scholem, in his first published essay, had defined Jewish tradition itself as "unbürgerlich." Löwy, *Redemption and Utopia*, 62. Such sentiments were common in this milieu. See the remarkable letter of Ernst Simon to Martin Buber (11.2.23), where he castigates Buber for pandering to the same audience which celebrated Hermann Cohen: "We will only half understand him—and his historic place within German Jewry not at all—unless we see what kind of people he was condemned to speak to. Who sustained his reputation among Jews in his lifetime . . .? The lazy and fat bourgeoisie of the B'nai Brith lodges." *The Letters of Martin Buber: A Life of Dialogue*, ed. Nahum N. Glatzer and Paul Mendes-Flohr and trans. R. and C. Winston and H. Zohn (Syracuse, N.Y.: Syracuse University Press, 1991), 307.

87. E. Hieronimus, *Der Traum von der Urkulturen* (Munich: Carl Friedrich von Siemens Stiflung, 1975); and *Die Restauration der Götter: Antikereligion und Neo-Paganismus* ed. Richard Faber and Renate Schlieser (Würzberg, 1986), esp. Karl-Heinz Kohl, "Naturreligion: Zur Transformationsgeschichte eines Begriff," 198–215.

88. For "life," see Krell, *Daimon Life*. For Cassirer's views in 1930, shortly after his encounter with Heidegger, see " 'Spirit' and 'Life' in Contemporary Philosophy," in *The Philosophy of Ernst Cassirer*, ed. Paul A. Schilpp (New York: Tudor, 1949).

89. Letter of 6 October, 1885, cited in Lepenies, *Between Literature and Science*, 206. For more on Yorck in the context of the milieu under discussion here, and with reference to the metaphor of "eruption," see George Lichtheim, "On the Rim of the Volcano: Heidegger, Bloch, Adorno," *Encounter* 22, no. 4 (April 1964): 98–105, at 102. Lichtheim, in his youth, was responsible for the English translation of Scholem's *Major Trends in Jewish Mysticism*.

90. *FBJ*, 166.

91. Cited in Biale, *Gershom Scholem*, 67, who notes that this was also cited by Cassirer, *Philosophie*, 2: 5.

92. Three works composed by emigrant German Jews in the United States during the Third Reich present a important follow-up to the earlier turn to myth. Adorno and Horkheimer's *Dialectic of Enlightenment* (written in Southern California) and Ernst Bloch's *the Principle of Hope* (composed largely in Cambridge, Massachusetts, from 1938 to 1947) are masterpieces in which, as the *Dialectic* epigrammatically declares, "myth is already enlightenment; and enlightenment reverts to myth." *Dialectic of Enlightenment*, xvi). Cassirer's *The Myth of the State*

(New Haven, Conn.: Yale University Press, 1946; reprint, 1973), produced at Yale during the war, likewise reflects this subsequent, disillusioned phase of the dialectic. Now *Mythos* is a darker daimon, the realized nightmare of maturity and not some youthfully dreamt anticipation of a more potent future.

93. See, preeminently, "Religious Authority and Mysticism," in *OK*, 5–32, which remains among the most important theoretical statements in the history of religions to be written in this century.

94. Adorno, "Gruß an Gershom G. Scholem." Note that in Scholem's letter to Rosenzweig in 1926, his ferocious antibourgeois loathing of "secularization" is obvious: "The ghastly gibberish which we hear spoken in the streets is exactly the faceless lingo that 'secularization' of the language will bring about; of this there cannot be any doubt!" Cutter, "Ghostly Hebrew," 417.

95. George Steiner, "The Remembrancer: Rescuing Walter Benjamin from his Acolytes," *Times Literary Supplement*, 8 October 1993. One may say that, just as Schelling espoused an "absolute empiricism," and a "higher realism," so too did Scholem argue an "ultimate disenchantment."

96. See Rosenzweig's letter of 14 November 1923 assuring Buber that Simon will get over "the great hangover from his [dreamy faith] in the power of form to save a person." *The Letters of Martin Buber*, ed. Glatzer and Mendes-Flohr, 310.

97. Alexander Altmann, "Franz Rosenzweig on History," in *Studies in Religious Philosophy and Mysticism* (Ithaca, N.Y.: Cornell University Press, 1969), 275–292, at 288.

98. Also "absolute empiricism": Glatzer, *Franz Rosenzweig*, 207. See also Isaac Heinemann, who in his introduction to the *Kuzari* saw Halevi's view of truth as "radical empiricism." 20. See *Three Jewish Philosophers. Philo: Selections, Saadyda Gaon: Book of Doctrines and Beliefs, Jehuda Halevi: Kuzari*, ed. Hans Lewy, Alexander Altmann, and Isaak Heinemann (New York: Atheneum, 1969), 20.

Chapter 8
Collective *Renovatio*

1. *CH*, 139–175. This was also the year Joseph Campbell published *Hero with a Thousand Faces*. See chapter 13, "Uses of the Androgune in the History of Religions," in this book.

2. Corbin may have been thinking here of his own 1938 translation from Heidegger's essay on Hölderlin. "C'est le temps de la *détresse*, parce que ce temps est marqué d'un double manque et d'une double négation: le "ne plus" des dieux enfuis et le "pas encore" de dieu qui va venir." *Qu'est-ce que la métaphysique?* 3d ed. (Paris: Gallimard, 1938), 251, emphasis in original.

3. *OK*, 2.

4. One may compare the question raised by Arno Mayer in *Why Did the Heavens Not Darken? The "Final Solution" in History* (New York: Pantheon, 1988).

5. Martin Heidegger, *An Introduction to Metaphysics* (New Haven, Conn.: Yale University Press, 1959), 30. This translation was made by Ralph Manheim, also the translator of Corbin and Scholem.

6. *Avicenna*, 24.

7. Ibid., 26, emphasis added.

8. Michael Williams, *Rethinking "Gnosticism": An Argument for Dismantling a Dubious Category* (Princeton, N.J.: Princeton University Press, 1996).

9. *Avicenna*, 16–28.

10. Ibid., 19. My translation.

11. Some of the literature pertaining to Eliade's involvement with Nae Ionescu (not to be confused with Eliade's friend, the celebrated playwright Eugen Io- nescu) and the Iron Guard can be found in Philippe Baillet, "Éclipse et retour de la tradition: autour de mouvement légionnaire roumain," in Claudio Mutti, *Les plumes de l'Archange: Quatre intellectuals roumains face à la Garde de Fer: Nae Ionescu, Mircea Eliade, Emil Cioran, Constantin Noica*, translated from the Ital- ian by P. Baillet (Chalons-sur-Saône: Ed. Herode, 1993), 5–35; Adriana Berger, "Mircea Eliade: Romanian Fascism and the History of Religions in the United States," in *Tainted Greatness: Antisemitism and Cultural Heroes*, ed. N. Har- rowitz (Philadelphia: Temple University Press, 1994), 51–74; Adriana Berger, "Fascism and Religion in Romania" [Review of Mircea Eliade, *Autobiography. Exile's Odyssey: 1938–1969*, vol. 2 (Chicago: University of Chicago Press, 1988) and Mac Linscott Ricketts, *Mircea Eliade: The Romanian Roots* (New York: Co- lumbia University Press, 1988)], *Annals of Scholarship* 6 (1989): 455–465; Phi- llipe Borgeaud, "Myth et histoire chez Mircea Eliade: Réflexion d'un écolier en histoire des religions," *Institut National Genovois. Annales* (1993): 33–48; Isac Chiva, "A propos de Mircea Eliade. Un téimoinage," *Le Genre humain* 26 (1992): 89–102; Radu Ioanid, *The Sword of the Archangel: Fascist Ideology in Romania*, trans. Peter Heinegg (Boulder: Eastern European Monographs; dis- tributed by Columbia University Press, 1990); Vittorio Lanternari, "Ripensando a Mircea Eliade," *La critica sociologica* 79 (1986): 67–82; Norman Manea, "Happy Guilt: Mircea Eliade, Fascism, and the Unhappy Fate of Romania," *The New Republic*, 5 August 1991), 27–36; Alfonso M. di Nola, "Mircea Eliade e l'antisemitismo," *La Ressigna mensile di Israel* (January/February 1977): 12–15; Leon Volovici, *Nationalist Ideology and Antisemitism: The Case of Romanian In- tellectuals in the 1930s*, trans. Charles Kormos (Oxford: Pergamon Press for Vidal Sassoon International Center for the Study of Antisemitism, Hebrew University of Jerusalem, 1991).

12. Theirs was a very old relationship, beginning in 1927 (*R*, 1: 1299). Evola urged the twenty-one-year-old Eliade to experiment personally with Yoga, before the latter's "Journey to the East" in 1928 (an admonition Eliade recalled fondly in 1974: see *J III*; 162). Upon returning to Romania, Eliade published a gushing evaluation of Evola's *Revolt Against the Modern World* in 1935, dubbing his Ital- ian mentor "one of the most interesting minds of the war generation," and com- paring him to Spengler, Gobineau, Chamberlain and [Alfred] Rosenberg (RR II; 849). This review is available in a French translation by Faust Bradesco, published in the first issue of the neofascist journal *Les deux etendards* (1988). I thank Leon Volovici of Jerusalem for sending me a copy of this translation. Bradesco, a propa- gandist for the Iron Guard, copublished an article in the leading journal of Holo- caust Denial, *The Journal for Historical Review*, along with Alexander Ronnett, Mircea Eliade's longtime personal dentist and doctor. For Ronnett's relation with Eliade see Ted Anton, *Eros, Magic, and the Murder of Professor Culianu*. (Evan-

ston, Il.: Northwestern University Press, 1996), 117. For the Bradesco/Ronnett joint article see "The Legionary Movement in Romania," *The Journal for Historical Review* 7, no. 2 (1986) 193–228, which begins with an editorial note to the effect that the "authors of the following article are both members of and avowed partisans of the Legionary Movement." Legionary Chief Codreanu exhorted the "New Man" to undertake violent actions, in order thereby to create Himself by eliminating the Old Man, "totally cleansed of today's vices and defects. In place of the corrupt specimen, who now dominates our political life, a new man of integrity and strong character must rise." See the chapter on "The New Man" in Alexander Ronnett's *Romanian Nationalism: The Legionary Movement* (Chicago: Loyola University Press, 1974), 7. In this same passage, the "corrupt specimen" is identified as "the Jews." This book was published in 1974, at a time when Ronnett was serving as Eliade's personal physician and dentist. A flamboyantly unrepentant Legionary, Ronnett "insisted" to an inquiring journalist that "his patient was once a prominent Guardist." See Anton, *Eros, Magic, and the Murder of Professor Culianu*, 117.

13. Jürgen Habermas, "Carl Schmitt in the Political Intellectual History of the Federal Republic," in *A Berlin Republic: Writings on Germany*, transl. Steven Rendall (Lincoln: University of Nebraska Press, 1997), 108: "[Schmitt and Heidegger] were among the 'great yea-sayers of 1933,' because both felt infinitely superior to the Nazis and wanted to 'lead the leader.' They recognized the delusionary character of their bizarre plan, but *post festum* they refused publicly to admit their guilt or even their political mistake." For an important discussion of Schmitt's relations with Eliade, see Cristiano Grottanelli, "Mircea Eliade, Carl Schmitt, René Guénon 1942," which the author graciously allowed me to study in typescript.

14. Corbin, "The Time of Eranos," xx.

15. See Michael Brenner, "From Self-Declared Messiah to Scholar of Messianism: The Recently Published Diaries Present Young Gershom Scholem in a New Light," *Jewish Social Studies* 3 (1996): 177–182.

16. For important discussions of the myth of National Regeneration, see Emilio Gentile, "The Myth of National Regeneration in Italy," in *Fascist Visions: Art and Ideology in France and Italy* (Princeton, N.J.: Princeton University Press, 1997), 25–45, and Roger Griffin, "Palingenetic Myth," in *The Nature of Fascism* (London: Routledge, 1993), 32–36.

17. In *The Jewish People Past and Present*, (New York: Jewish Encyclopedic Handbooks, 1946; reprint, 1955), 1:308–327, at 308. Reprinted in *OPJM*, 121–154, at 122 (a different translation). See *OPJM*, 121, for Hebrew versions.

18. George L. Mosse, "Gershom Scholem as German Jew," in *Confronting the Nation: Jewish and Western Nationalism* (Hanover: Brandeis University Press, 1993), 176–192, at 180.

19. He was much less vociferous in his castigations of sociology than were Corbin or Eliade, for example, who were ferocious polemicists against all so-called sociologism.

20. Löwy, *Redemption and Utopia*.

21. Scholem first learned of Frankism from Zalman Rubaschoff/Shazar: see Biale, *Gershom Scholem*, 27. Even Isaac Bashevis Singer wrote a novel with a

Frankist protagonist in the 1930s. See Chone Shmeruk, "The Frankist Novels of Isaac Bashevis Singer," *Studies in Contemporary Jewry: An Annual* 12 (1996): 118–128.

22. See Arnaldo Momigliano, *Settimo Contributo alla Storia Degli Studi Classici e del Mondo Antico* (Rome: Edizioni di storia e litteratura, 1984), 356.

23. For more on this theme, see chapter 7, "A Rustling in the Woods," in this book.

24. See the discussion of "phenomenology of religion" in chapter 1, on "Eranos and the 'History of Religions'" in this book.

25. *A II*, 65. It lies beyond my purposes to review the evidence for Eliade's involvement with the Iron Guard. For the relevant literature, see n. 11 above. The fullest treatment is now the partisan but well-documented Mutti, *Les Plumes de l'Archange*. In particular, it will be noted that Eliade apparently attempted to stand for election on an Iron Guard ticket. It may be added that Legionaries today proudly claim Eliade as one of their own, who, they say, never denied his Legionary affiliation. Such examples are conveniently accessible on the World Wide Web. To take one example, see the article "Legionarism against extremism. There is no Anti-Semitism. What does Exist is a Jewish Problem," by Zaharia Marineasa, a member of the Iron Guard. This article is found on the World Wide Web at http://www.geocities.com/Paris/Maison/1849/zmarineasa.html.

26. George L. Mosse, "Introduction: The Genesis of Fascism," in *International Fascism 1920–1945*, ed. Walter Laqueur and George L. Mosse (New York: Harper and Row, 1966), 14–27 at 21.

27. Ronnett, *Romanian Nationalism*, 7. For the relevant literature, see note 11, this chapter.

28. Ibid., 6–7.

29. Anton, *Eros, Magic, and the Murder of Professor Culianu*, 117. See "The Legionary Movement in Romania," in volume 7, number 2 of that journal (with Faust Bradesco). See also Claudio Mutti's edition of Ion Mota, *L'uomo Nuovo* (Padua: Ar, 1978).

30. *CH*, 159.

31. *PCR*, 358–359, emphasis added.

32. Saint-Martin, *Le Nouvel Homme* (Paris, 1976). For some orientation see "Martinisme" in *Dictionnaire de la Franc-Maçonnerie*, ed. Daniel Ligon (Paris: PUF, 1987), 777–781.

33. Eliade, "Occultism and Freemasonry in Eighteenth-Century France." See the conclusion of this book for some reflections on the Historians of Religions as exponents of a kind of Christian Kabbalah.

34. *TO*, 159.

35. *HIP*, 366, emphasis in original.

36. *Avicenna*, 17.

37. Corbin, "L'Iran, patrie des philosophes et des poètes," in *L'Âme de l'Iran* (Paris: Albin Michel, 1951).

38. *VM*, 34.

39. See the classic essay by H. A. R. Gibb, *Studies on the Civilization of Islam* (London: Routledge and Kegan Paul, 1969).

40. See Carl Kraeling, *Anthropos and Son of Man: a study in the religious syn-*

cretism of the Hellenistic Orient (New York: Columbia University Press, 1927), for the contemporaneous expression. The best study remains Carsten Colpe, *Die religionsgeschichtliche Schule: Darstellung und Kritik ihres Bildes vomgnostischen Erlosermythus* (Gottingen: Vandenhoeck & Ruprecht, 1961).

41. Cristiano Grottanelli, *Ideologie, Miti, Massacri: Indoeuropei di Georges Dumézil* (Palermo: Sellerio, 1993).

42. Corbin, *Les motifs zorastriens dans la philosophie de Sohrawardi* (Tehran: Publications de la Societé d'Iranologie 3, 1946).

43. Corbin, "L'Iran, patrie des philosophes et des poètes," 27–31.

44. "Post-Scriptum," 41.

45. *SBCE*, 105. A parallel is found in Eliade's reflections: "The *separation* and *integration* of symbols—these two 'methods' are as characteristic of India as of Goethe." *J II*, 103.

46. *MLIS*, 1.

47. He returned to this theme elsewhere. For example, in *Avicenna*, he discusses "the cosmic north."

48. *Avicenna*, 128.

49. *SBCE*, 70. Another revealing locus of publication was *Antaios*, edited by Mircea Eliade and Ernst Jünger, in which Corbin published "Über den zwolften Imam." *Antaios* 2 (1961): 75–92.

50. "Sophia éternelle," 290. For other examples of Corbin's use of the language of race see "Über den zwolften Imam," 79 ("des volkommenen Sohne seiner Rasse"), and *En Islam iranien*, 2: 337–338, for a remarkable disquisition on "Kouschisme."

51. It will be remembered in this connection that Jung announced in 1936 that Nietzsche's Superman, Zarathustra, was "a prophetic anticipation of a Führer." *The Symbolic Life*, 578.

52. Regarding Corbin's Aryanism, Hamid Algar properly observed that Corbin "transferred the dichotomy (Aryan = Iranian/Semite = Arab) from the biological to the spiritual plane." "The Study of Islam: The Work of Henry Corbin," *Religious Studies Review* 6 (1980): 85–91, at 89.

53. Aziz al-Azmeh similarly has observed that Corbin (along with his acolyte Nasr) attributed "gnostic metaphysics . . . to Persia—in terms almost fully reminiscent of the determinations of Aryan thought in the last century, determinations which have been transferred to other fields of enquiry." "The Articulation of Orientalism," in *Orientalism, Islam, and Islamists*, ed. Asaf Hussain, Robert Olson, Jamil Qureshi (Brattleboro, Vt.: Amana Books, 1984), 89–125, at 114. In the frank assessment of his harsh critic Algar, Corbin's hyper-Aryan version of Persia amounted to a "rarified and idiosyncratic form of spiritual colonialism." 91.

54. "A Letter by Henry Corbin," dated 9 February 1978, which serves as 'Preface" to David. L. Miller, *The New Polytheism: Rebirth of the Gods and Goddesses* [*sic*] (Dallas, Tex.: Spring, 1981), 1–7, quotation at 4, emphasis added.

55. Corbin, *Qu'est-ce que la métaphysique?* The concluding sentence of the title lecture in this collection was rendered by Corbin as: "Pourquoi, somme toute, y a-t-il de l'existant plutôt que Rien?" 44. Scholem alluded to this sentence by Heidegger in his 1974 "Reflections on Jewish Theology," when he raised once

again "the famous question of why thing existed rather than there being nothing, posed by existential philosophers from Schelling to Heidegger." *JJC*, 279.

56. Corbin, "Islamisme et Religions de L'Arabie," in *Problèmes et Méthodes d'Histoire des Religions* (Paris: Presses Universitaires de France, 1968), 135.

57. *VM*, 98.

58. "Post-Scriptum biographique," 43.

59. *VM*, 88, 214.

60. Scholem was aware of Heidegger as early as 1916. See his letter of 11 November 1916 to Walter Benjamin, in which he remarked that "Der Aufsatz über die historische Zeit von Heidegger ist sehr lächerlich und unphilosophisch." In *Gershom Scholem Tagebücher nebst Aufsätzen und Entwürfen bis 1923. I. Halbband 1913–1917*, ed. Karlfried Gründer and Freidrich Niewöhner (Frankfurt am Main: Jüdischer Verlag, 1995), 418. For subsequent exchanges between Scholem and Benjamin on Heidegger see *The Correspondence of Walter Benjamin 1910–1940*, ed. Gershom Scholem and Theodor Adorno, trans. M. R. Jacobson and E. M. Jacobson (Chicago: University of Chicago Press, 1994), 82, 168, 172, 359, 365, 372, and 571.

61. It is interesting to note that Scholem approvingly cited Altmann's 1933 "What is Jewish Theology?" in *MTJM*, 354, 26. Although he cites Altmann at this point on philosophy and Halakha, it is not irrelevant to note the explicit Heideggerian dimension of Altmann's lecture. This is another example of Scholem's knowledge of Heidegger's ideas in these years. See Alfred Ivry's collection of Altmann's early theology, *The Meaning of Jewish Existence: Theological Essays, 1930–1939*, trans. E. Ehrlich and L. H. Ehrlich (Hanover, N.H.: Brandeis University Press, 1991). Altmann returned to Heidegger in his last essay, "The 'God of Religion,' the 'God of Metaphysics' and Wittgenstein's Language-Games," in *Zeitschrift für Religions- und Geistesgeschichte* 39 (1987). An unpublished monograph by Steven Schwarzschild apparently was designed to demonstrate Heidegger's importance with regard to Rosenzweig. See also the Ph.D. dissertation of Peter Eli Gordon, "Under One Tradewind: Philosophical Expressionism in Weimar Thought from Rosenzweig to Heidegger" (University of California at Berkeley, 1997).

62. In a 1951 lecture, Corbin noted that, in Jonas' *Gnosis und Spätantiker Geist*, "methodological premises of this original and worthy effort show a strong Heideggerian influence." *VM*, 52. Hans Jonas said so himself in this book, confessing that "my generation succumbed wholesale to Heidegger." See *The Gnostic Religion*, 2d ed. ed. (Boston: Beacon Press, 1963), 337. For a discussion of "Nihilism as a Religious Phenomenon," see chapter 15, "On the Suspension of the Ethical," in this book.

63. As a token of his intimacy with Jonas in the 1930s and 1940s, see the poem Scholem wrote, which he inscribed in the copy of *MTJM* that he presented to Jonas.

64. Scholem, "Nihilism as a Religious Phenomenon."

65. Martin Heidegger, *Being and Time*, trans. John Macquarrie and Edward Robinson (London: SCM Press, 1962), 454.

66. A translation of *Was Heisst Denken?* by Fred D. Wieck and J. Glenn Gray (New York: Harper and Row, 1962).

67. Eliade, review of *Avicenne et le Récit visionnaire*, by Henry Corbin, *La Nouvelle revue française* (June 1955): 1096–99, my translation.

68. See *R*.

69. Ivan Strenski, *Four Theories of Myth in Twentieth Century History: Cassirer, Eliade, Levi-Strauss, and Malinowski* (Iowa City: University of Iowa Press, 1987), 93, 118, 122, 209 n. 32, 216 n. 62.

70. Ibid., 79, 93.

71. Ibid., 118.

72. This line of analysis has been followed by Daniel Dubuisson. See Daniel Dubuisson, *Mythologies du XXᵉ siècle: Dumézil, Lévi-Strauss, Eliade* (Villeneuve d' Ascq: Presses universitaires de Lille, 1993).

73. *SP*, 12, emphasis is in original.

74. *MDM*, 14.

75. *OL*, 75. "The Criterion group had tremendous repercussions in Bucharest. It was at one of our meetings in 1933, that existentialism, Kierkegaard, and Heidegger were discussed for the first time." Also, Strenski, 209 n. 32.

76. *OL*, 76.

77. Published in 1934, recently translated into French; republished in Romania.

78. Dennis A. Doeing, "Mircea Eliade's Spiritual and Intellectual Development from 1917 to 1940" (Ph.D. diss., University of Ottawa, 1975), 229 n. 4.

79. *CH*, 150, 152.

80. *A II*, 106.

81. Ibid., 166.

82. *MDM*, 239.

83. Ibid., 11.

84. *J II*, 200.

85. *Symposion Heidegger*, ed. G. Uscatescu (Madrid: Destin, 1971). This collection is a self-designated "Romanian hommage to Heidegger."

86. *MDM*, 49 n. 1.

87. *OWCF*, 45–46.

88. *OL*, 147.

89. Karl Löwith, *Martin Heidegger and European Nihilism*, ed. Richard Wolin, trans. Gary Steiner (New York: Columbia University Press, 1985), 38.

90. Hugo Ott, "Biographical Bases for Heidegger's 'Mentality of Disunity,'" in *The Heidegger Case*, ed. Tom Rockmore and Joseph Margolis (Philadelphia: Temple University Press, 1992), 93–113, at 106.

91. Corbin used the trope of the "planetary" at the end of his life. "If History-profanation is no more than the decadence and corruption of what was given to us originally, then we could say that in our day the disease has attained planetary dimensions." *TC*, 340. Eliade saw, similarly, that the globalization of "history" called on the History of Religions as a kind of response. "Today [1965] history is becoming truly universal for the first time, and so culture is in the process of becoming 'planetary.' . . . The history of religions can play an essential role in this effort toward a *planétisation* of culture." *Q*, 69. A decade later, Eliade was seeking "to open the Western mind and introduce a new, planetary humanism." *JII*, xii. In 1977 he was to make a related pronouncement. "At this moment in our his-

tory characterized by the "planetization" of culture, it seems to me that the History of Religions is called upon to play a privileged role." *SSA*, 155. For some reflections on Heidegger's notion of the contemporary world as that of "planetary technology," see Alan Milchman and Alan Rosenberg, "Heidegger, Planetary Technology, and the Holocaust," in *Martin Heidegger and the Holocaust*, ed. A. Milchman and A. Rosenberg (Atlantic Highlands, N.J.: Humanities Press, 1996), 215–235.

92. It may be said, for example, that Scholem shared this Heideggerian cohort what Löwith called "the *catastrophic manner of thinking* characteristic of the generation of Germans after the First World War." Löwith, *Martin Heidegger and European Nihilism*, 166, emphasis in original. Norbert Bolz calls this "philosophical extremism." See his *Auszug aus der enzauberten Welt: Philosophischer Extremismus zwischen der Weltkriegen* (Munich: Fink, 1989).

93. Wouter J. Hanegraaff engages in a useful discussion of these themes with regard to Jung in his fine work *New Age and Western Culture: Esotericism in the Mirror of Secular Thought* (Albany: State University of New York, 1998), 496–514.

94. Scholem, "Opening Address," in *Types of Redemption: Contributions to the Theme of the Study-Conference Held in Jerusalem, 14th to 19th July 1968* (Leiden: E. J. Brill, 1970), 1–12, at 11.

95. In German, *präsentische Eschatologie*. For recent application of this idea to "gnosis" see Jan Helderman in *Gnosis and Hermeticism*, ed. R. van den Broek and W. Hanegraaff (Albany, N.Y.: State University of New York Press, 1998), 68 n. 32.

96. For more on these themes, see chapter 13, "Uses of the Androgyne in the History of Religions," in this book.

97. Campbell, *Hero With A Thousand Faces*, first published by the Bollingen Foundation in 1949. I use the fifteenth printing, May 1971 (New York: World Co., 1971). The book had sold 200,000 copies by 1982, continuing at a rate of 10,000 copies per year. McGuire, *Bollingen*, 142.

98. The theory derived in part from the later Schelling's "philosophy of mythology." See F. W. J. von Schelling, *The Abyss of Freedom/Ages of the World*, trans. Judith Norman (Ann Arbor: University of Michigan Press, 1997).

99. *OK*, 460–475.

100. *IS*, 62; *CH*, 114; *MR*, 61.

101. "Shi'i Hermeneutics" in *Shi'ism*, ed. S. H. Nasr (Albany: State University of New York Press), 194–202, at 195.

102. Corbin, "The Dramatic Element," 210–212. Their interest is relevant to the common origins all three Historians of Religions shared in certain forms of Christian Kabbalah.

103. Given these manifold interconnections, resemblances between Bataille's theory of "transgression" and Scholem's theory of Shabbetai Zevi as transgressive messiah, are not surprising, as noticed recently by Mehlman, *Walter Benjamin for Children*, 40–42, 44–47.

104. Corbin, "De l'histoire des religions comme problème théologique," *Monde non chrétien* 51–52 (1960): 148–149, emphasis added.

105. Hanegraaff, *New Age and Western Culture*. The divine androgyne

abounds in popular form throughout New Age Religion. An early example was the 1963 volume in a Jungian series, Alan Watts, *The Two Hands of God* (London: Century, 1963).

106. For a firm, even definitive critique of Jung on this point, see Buber, "Religion and Modern Thinking," in *Eclipse of God* (New York: Harper and Row, 1952; reprint, 1957), pp. 91–92. See chapter 15, "On the Suspension of the Ethical," in this book, for the Buber-Jung controversy.

107. *FC*, 173. For further discussion of such a version of *Naturphilosophie*, see "Mystic Historicities," below.

108. *OWCF*, 47–68.

109. Ibid., 52.

110. Ibid., 64. In the footnote, he adds that "the entire youth (counter) culture is oriented to a radical, "existential" *renovatio*." Ibid., 127 n. 37.

111. Ibid., 66.

112. For example, the reflections on "the eventual catastrophic disappearance of humanity" in his journal entry of 27 November 1961 (*J II*, 145).

113. For Scholem's "radical new freedom" see chapter 14, "Defeating Evil from Within," in this book.

Chapter 9
The Idea of Incognito: Authority and Its Occultation
According to Henry Corbin

1. An early version of this chapter was delivered as a lecture to the Comparative Religion Colloquium of the University of Washington (Seattle), January 1996. I thank colleague Professor Martin Jaffee for the invitation.

2. These included Heidegger and Schmitt and Goebbels in Germany, Evola in Italy, and Rene Guénon and Georges Bataille in France.

3. This is a theme running throughout *Paradoxe* and *Temple*.

4. Corbin, "De l'histoire des religions comme problème théologique," 148. Elsewhere Corbin similarly asserted that "the phenomenon 'Church' has remained foreign to Islam. A Sufi could never understand that he was to receive his faith and hence eternal life from anything like a Church." "Visionary Dream," 386.

5. Ibid., 148.

6. Corbin, "Post-Scriptum," pp. 40–41.

7. Corbin, "Pour l'anthropologie philosophique: une traité persan inédit de Suhrawardî d'Alep," *Recherches philosophiques* 2 (1933): 371–423.

8. Corbin, *Qu'est- ce la métaphysique?*

9. *L'Idée socialiste* (Paris: B. Grasset, 1935).

10. Posthumously published as *Hamann, philosophe du luthéranisme* (Paris: Berg International, 1985).

11. Corbin, "Post-Scriptum biographique," 46. Corbin returns to the theme of the "discipline of the arcanum" in "Mysticism and Humor": "Only he who is worthy and able will comprehend: the others will perceive nothing. But despite all and everything *his message will have been transmitted*." 27, emphasis in original.

12. "I would be spending six years in Turkey as 'guardian' of the *Institut français d'archéologie* in Istanbul during the whole of WWII." *VM*, 91.

13. Corbin mentions meeting in Istanbul the Romanians Brinzeu and de Cei (otherwise unidentified) in his tribute to Eliade, in *Cahier de l'Herne/Mircea Eliade*. Jean Beaufret, another disciple of Heidegger, met with Corbin in 1945 "chez un Roumain, ancien élève de Heidegger." See Frédéric de Towarnicki, *À la rencontre de Heidegger: Souveniers d'un messager de la Forêt-noire* (Paris: Gallimard, 1993), 261. This may have been O. Vuia, whom Eliade meets in July 1946. Vuia had spent the previous six years as a student of Heidegger in Freiburg. See *JI*, 19. Corbin also worked with the German orientalist Helmutt Ritter while in Istanbul. See Charles-Henri de Fouchécour, "Henry Corbin (1903–1978)," *Journal Asiatique* 267 (1979): 231–237, at 234.

14. *TC*, 84–85.

15. Corbin, "Post-Scriptum," 46.

16. A sixth theme, *Aryanism*, is dealt with in chapter 8, "Collective *Renovatio*," in this book. His eschatology is treated in chapter 11, "The Chiliastic Practice of Islamic Studies According to Henry Corbin."

17. This latter-period esoterism is perhaps best reflected in his initiative to found l'Université Saint Jean de Jerusalem. This private colloquium, dedicated to the western occult sciences, published a series of annual proceedings until his death. These proceedings were published as *Cahiers de l'Université Saint Jean de Jérusalem*. Mircea Eliade, one of the collaborators in this endeavor, called it "a new type of university . . . [following] the model of Eranos." See Eliade, "Some Notes on *Theosophia perennis*," 173.

Thanks to the generosity of Professor Jeffrey Kripal of Westminster College, I possess Eliade's copies of volumes 2, 3, and 4 of these *Cahiers*, which survived the catastrophic burning of his library (on this event, see Wendy Doniger's introduction to the Eliade *J IV*). In each of these volumes, Eliade is listed as an active participant. Eliade's marginalia in his personal copies reveal a close reading of Corbin's contributions. These facts are noted here for the light they shed on "Some Notes on *Theosophia perennis*." In this review-essay, which devotes almost four pages to the Université St.-Jean de Jerusalem, Eliade does not tell the reader that he himself was a participant. But he does conclude his remarks with the following observation. "What interests the historian of religions the most is the resurgence of a certain esoteric tradition among a number of European scholars and thinkers who represent many illustrious universities." (176).

18. Corbin, *TC*, 388.

19. Ibid., 280.

20. Corbin, "Eyes of Flesh," 9.

21. Corbin, "Imago Templi," *TC*, 264.

22. Corbin, introduction to David L. Miller, *The New Polytheism*, 2d ed. (Dallas: Spring, 1981), 2. This theme runs throughout *Paradoxe*. On the theme of *Katastrophe* in Jung, see Bishop, *The Dionysian Self*, 314–315.

23. Corbin, "Divine Epiphany," 158. For general orientation in his angelology see Henry Corbin, *L'Homme et son Ange* (Paris: Fayard, 1983).

24. Corbin, "Mundus Imaginalis."

25. Corbin, "Visionary Dream," 406, emphasis in original.

26. Corbin, See also "A Theory of Visionary Knowledge," (written in 1977), *VM*, 117–135.

27. James Hillman, *Re-Visioning Psychology* (New York: Harper and Row, 1975).

28. Corbin, "De la philosophie prophétique," 49–56.

29. Louis Massignon, *The Passion of Al-Hallaj: Mystic and Martyr of Islam*, 4 vol., trans. Herbert Mason (Princeton, N.J.: Princeton University Press, 1982).

30. On this point he repeatedly cited Eugenio D'Ors's wartime *bon mot* to the effect that "Zoroastrian religion is translated into a sort of order of chivalry." Henry Corbin, "Cyclical Time in Mazdaism and Ismailism," in *Man and Time: Papers from the Eranos Yearbooks* ed. Joseph Campbell (New York: Pantheon, 1957) 3:115–173, and "For the Concept of Irano-Islamic Philosophy," *The Philosophical Forum* 4 (Fall 1972): 114–123.

31. *SBCE*, 72. This spiritual north was a key term for Corbin at least since the time of his "revelation" by a lake in "the forest in the North." See also "Pour une nouvelle chevalrie," *Question de* 1 (1973): 101–115.

32. *TC*, 368.

33. Corbin reviewed Van der Leeuw's *Phänomenologie der Religion* in 1933. See *Revue critique* (1934), 486–489. In his 1948 lecture on "Iranian Studies and Comparative Religion" he called van der Leeuw's *Religion in Essence and Manifestation* a "considerable book abounding in subtle analyses." *VM*, 16.

34. *MLIS*, 32, emphasis added. Corbin similarly evoked Richard Strauss, composer of *Also Sprach Zarathustra* (1864–1949): *SBCE*, 105. See also Steven Aschheim, *The Nietzsche Legacy in Germany* (Berkeley: University of California, 1992), 31–32.

35. *VM*, 220–221.

36. "[The imamate] is a kingship that by its very essence implies neither the necessity nor even the idea of temporal political success, still less the idea that majorities are always right" Corbin, *Shi'ism: Doctrines, Thought, and Spirituality*, 179.

37. Cited by Joscelyn Godwin in *Arktos: The Polar Myth in Science, Symbolism, and Nazi Survival* (Grand Rapids Mich.: Phanes Press, 1993), 170. Despite its strange-sounding title, this book contains an indispensable discussion of the occult theory of the "pole" central to Corbin's work. See especially *MLIS*, 1–14.

38. Corbin, "Pour une nouvelle chevalrie," 101–115.

39. One contribution, "The Tradition of Sacred Kingship in Iran," put the Aryan case quite succinctly: "[The] descent of the kingly principle in solar garb forms one of the pivots on which turns the national tradition of Iranians of all times. We would like to believe that the very title *Aryamehr* (Old Persian *Aryamithra*, 'Sun [or Friend] of the Aryan Community') assumed by Mohammed Reza Shah to characterize his sovereignty, is a living reminder of this remote and venerable conception, never obliterated in the popular memory of the Iranians." Pio Filippani-Ronconi, "The Tradition of Sacred Kingship in Iran," in *Iran under the Pahlavis*, ed. George Lenczowski (Stanford Calif.: Hoover Institution Press, 1978), 51–83, at 57.

On the motif of "spiritual kingship" in Corbin, see for example Charles Adams's translation of a section of *En Islam Iranien*, printed in *Shiism: Doctrines, Thought and Spirituality*, 179. For Corbin's further reflections at the Persepolis event, see the epilogue to "The Realism and Symbolism of Colours," reprinted in *TC*, 50–54.

40. "Comment concevois la philosophie comparée?" *Sophia Perennis: The Bulletin of the Imperial Iranian Academy of Philosophy* 1, no. 1 (1975): 9–35. Among

other locations, this manifesto, originally a lecture before the Faculty of Letters University of Tehran (December 1974) was translated and published as a pamplet (Upswich, U.K.: Golgonooza Press, 1981) under the title, *The Concept of Comparative Philosophy*.

41. Corbin, *Philosophie iranienne et philosophie comparée* (Paris: Éditions Buchet/Chastel, 1985).

42. See the Shahbanou's statement which follows Corbin rather closely. "Message of Her Imperial Majesty Empress Farah Pahlavi, Shahbanou of Iran," *Sophia Perennis* 1, no. 2: 7–9.

43. R. K. Karanjia, *The Mind of a Monarch* (London: George Allen and Unwin, 1977). Compare the interview with Oriana Fallaci dated October 1973. Not only had 'Ali come to him in a vision, but "[m]y visions were miracles which saved the country." William S. Hoffman, *Paul Mellon: Portrait of an Oil Baron* (Chicago: Follett, 1974), 93.

44. Karanjia, *The Mind of a Monarch*, 102–103.

45. Feyridoun Hoveyda, "L'Architect de l'invisable," *Nouvelle Revue Francaise* 32 (1 January 1979). The many honors Corbin received in Iran include Commandeur de l'ordre impérial d'Iran et de l'ordre de la Couronne d'Iran, Docteur honoris causa de l'université de Téhéran, Médaille de la reconnaissance du ministére iranien de l'Education nationale, Professeur honoraire de l'université de Mashhad. "Corbin, Henry," *Who's Who in France 1975–1976* (Paris: Éditions Jacques Lafitte, 1976), 474.

46. "Corbin has also been an important channel through which some men of action in various positions of responsiblity in Persia have been drawn to the study of the writings of their own great sages and seers. One of the foremost of this group is the Prime Minister, Amir Abbas Hoveyda, who has known Corbin since his own student days in Paris and who is an avid reader of Corbin's works. In fact, it was with this encouragement and help that the Imperial Iranian Academy of Philosophy was able to make possible the continued presence of Corbin in Persia even after his official retirement." Nasr, "The Life and Works of the Occidental Exile in Quest of the Orient of Light," *Sophia Perennis* 3 (1977): 88–106, at 106.

47. Asadollah Alam, *The Shah and I: The Confidential Diary of Iran's Royal Court, 1969–1977*, trans. A. Alikhani and N. Vincent (New York: St. Martin's Press, 1991), describes the Shah's response to the report by Nasr that his students were "poor and a great number of them fanatical Moslems" (entry for Wednesday November 29, 1972). Note that Nasr has more recently published *A Moslem Students Guide*. For Nasr's role in support to the Shah in the waning days of the regime, see the revealing entries in Parviz C. Radji, *In the Service of the Peacock Throne: The Diaries of the Shah's Last Ambassador to London* (London: Hamish Hamilton, 1983), entries for 7–12 December 1977.

48. Much of the present critique was adumbrated by Hamid Algar in "The Study of Islam: The Work of Henry Corbin," *Religious Studies Review* 6 (1980): 85–91. Thus, for example, I agree with Algar that "It remains, however, a fact of some significance that his particular vision of 'Iranian Islam' corresponded nicely to the cultural policies of the Pahlavi regime" (90).

49. Corbin, *En Islam iranien: Aspects spirituels et philosophiques*.

50. Corbin, *HIP*, 363.

51. See Mellon's brilliantly polished *Reflections in a Silver Spoon: A Memoir* (New York: William Morrow, 1992). See also Hoffman, *Paul Mellon*.

52. As a self-styled traditionalist, Corbin would have understood the quasi-medieval trappings of such patronage, which were the ordinary working realities for the mystics he championed.

53. A second example from the 1930s is found in the minutes of the Collège de Sociologie. In February 1939, they promulgated a questionnaire titled "Inquiry: On Spiritual Directors." Corbin was close to various members of the College at the time, paricularly to Pierre Klossowski.

54. See the discussion on *Ergriffenheit* in chapter 7, "A Rustling in the Woods," in this book.

55. Jung, *Nietzsche's Zarathustra*, 2:1030. See the brief but penetrating remarks on these seminars by Aschheim, *Nietzsche's Legacy*, 258–262. See also Jung's notorious remarks in "Wotan": "[A] god has taken possession of the Germans, and their house is filled with a 'mighty rushing wind.'" (*Collected Works*, 10: 389). That Jung was alluding to Hitler here was made unmistakable a year and half later, in October 1938, when he delivered the following pronouncement: "And all these symbols together of a Third Reich led by its prophet under the banners of wind and storm and whirling vortices point to a mass movement which is to sweep the German people in a hurricane of unreasoning emotion on and on to a destiny which perhaps none but the seer, the prophet, the Führer himself can foretell—and perhaps, not even he. "Diagnosing the Dictators," *C. G. Jung Speaking: Interviews and Encounters* ed. William McGuire and R. F. C. Hull (Princeton, N.J.: Princeton University Press, 1978), 118.

56. "De 'Iran à Eranos," in *Cahier de l'Herne Henry Corbin*, 263. In this same paragraph he calls down a descent of the Valkyries once again.

57. Jung, *Nietzsche's Zarathustra*, 1031. Jung elsewhere warmly praises Catholic "*directeurs de conscience.*"

58. See the letter to her, dated 24 September 1945. It includes the following passage:

> You have probably heard the absurd rumor that I am a Nazi. This rumor had been started by the Freudian Jews in America. This hatred of myself went as far as India, where I found falsified photos of mine in the Psychological Seminar of Calcutta University. It was a photo retouched in such a way as to make me appear as an ugly Jew with a pince-nez! These photos came from Vienna! This rumor has been spread over the whole world. Even with us it has been picked up with such alacrity, that I am forced to publish all the things I have written about Germany. It is however difficult to mention the antichristianism of the Jews after the horrible things that have happened in Germany. But Jews are not so damned innocent after all. The rôle played by the intellectual Jews in pre-war Germany would be an interesting object of investigation. (Andrew Samuels, "New Material Concerning Jung, Anti-Semitism and the Nazis," *Journal of Analytical Psychology* 38 [1993]: 463–470, at 469).

For Jung on Jews as "super-intellectuals," see *Memories, Dreams, Reflections*, 326, and Bishop, *The Dionysian Self*, 361.

59. A monument to the intimacy of projects shared by Mellon and Jung is to

be found in the vast collection *Alchemy and the Occult: A Catalogue of Books and Manuscripts from the Collection of Paul and Mary Mellon Given to the Yale University Library*, 2 vols. (New Haven, Conn.: Yale University Press, 1968), which includes such contributions as a frontispiece by Jung; "The Influence of Alchemy on the Work of C. G. Jung," by Aniela Jaffé (xv–xxxiii); and "References to the Collected Work of C. G. Jung," by William McGuire (xlv–xlvii). The Bollingen Foundation provided the means (two hundred dollars per month) for Eliade to survive during his unemployment, from 1951 to 1954. See his *J I*, 199.

60. McGuire, *Bollingen*, 57, 72. That Dulles turned out hardly to be an irreproachable source on this subject is now well known. See for example, Charles Higham, *American Swastika* (Garden City, N.Y.: Doubleday, 1985), 188–191. Conversations of Dulles in Geneva in April of 1943 show his own attempted appeasement of the Nazis, in which he disparages Jews repeatedly.

61. Hoffman, *Paul Mellon*, 92–94.

62. For example by Eliade, in his obsequious interview with Jung concerning *Response to Job*: "Jung ou la réponse à Job," 250. Note that when Jung thanked Corbin for his extremely favorable review of *Response to Job*, Jung spoke of Schleiermacher as his "Spiritus Rector."

63. Take for example Corbin's lecture, "De l'histoire des religions comme problème théologique." One is fully justified, he announced in this lecture of 1959, to call Shi'ism a "religion of authority": "The 'Imam of our Time' is The Hidden Imam, 'invisible to the senses, but present in the hearts of the faithful.' This is no pontifical authority. Its figure dominates the horizon of the Shiite Spiritual as a personal guide, an interior master. Every Shiite shows an extreme probity and reserve in speaking of this theme." 148.

64. "Let us not be in too much of a hurry to speak of relativism or monism or syncretism for here we are not dealing with a philosophical point of view or with the history of religions." *CI*, 119.

65. Ibid., 81

66. Ibid, 82.

67. Ibid, 83.

68. We still have no more eloquent expression of the distinction between professor and prophet than that of Max Weber's 1919 essay, "Science as a Vocation," *From Max Weber: Essays in Sociology*, ed. H. H. Gerth and C. W. Mills (New York: Oxford University Press, 1946), 128–156.

69. Ibid., 156.

70. Here, as in other points, one can detect a certain congruity with Heidegger's thought. For the category of "danger" (*Gefahr*) in Heidegger, see John D. Caputo, *Demythologizing Heidegger* (Bloomington: Indiana University Press, 1993), 53–56, 88–89.

71. Corbin, "De l'histoire des religions comme problème théologique," 149.

72. Corbin, "Toward a Chart of the Imaginal," 31.

73. See Hollier on Bataille, "On Equivocation Between Literature and Politics," See also Wohl, *The Generation of 1914*.

74. The Traditionalist school is associated with René Guénon, who strongly influenced Eliade. While Corbin was not a follower of Guénon, his late-career esoterism is connected to Guénon's Traditionalism through a common emphasis on Martinism.

75. Umberto Eco, "Ur-Fascism," *New York Review of Books*, 22 June 1995, 12–15.

Chapter 10
Mystic Historicities

1. The term "counterhistory" has been associated with the scholarship of Amos Funkenstein. See his "Anti-Jewish Propaganda: Pagan, Medieval and Modern," *The Jerusalem Quarterly* 19 (1981): 56–72; "A Schedule for the End of the World: The Origins and Persistence of the Apocalyptic Mentality," in *Visions of Apocalypse, End or Rebirth?* ed. Saul Friedländer (New York: Holmes and Meier, 1985), 44–60; "History, Counterhistory, and Narrative," in *Probing the Limits of Representation: Nazism and the "Final Solution,"* ed. Saul Friedländer (Cambridge: Harvard University Press, 1992), 66–82, 345–350; *Perceptions of Jewish History* (Berkeley: University of California Press, 1993), 22–50.

2. Biale, *Gershom Scholem*.

3. "Prelude to the Second Edition," in *SBCE*, xvi, emphasis in original.

4. *HIP*, 63.

5. Corbin, "For the Concept of Irano-Islamic Philosophy," *The Philosophical Forum* 4 (1972): 114–123, at 121. The original, "Pour le concept de philosophie Irano-islamique," is found in *Hommage Universel I*, 251–260, at 259.

6. Corbin, *The Concept of Comparative Philosophy*, 25. For an interesting comment of Scholem on the notion of "being thrown" see *MSG*, 296 n. 51.

7. Corbin and Eliade in fact both wrote at some length on the Jewish "mystical messiah" Sabbatai Zevi. "Dramatic Element," 210–212; *HRI* 3. The counterhistorical implications of Scholem's focus on Sabbatianism have been remarked by Moshe Idel. "The overwhelming emphasis in Scholem's ouevre is on Sabbatianism. A scholar who wrote on the history and concepts of almost two thousand years of Jewish mysticism devoted nearly half of his writings to an episode that was, at first glance, historically significant for only a few decades. The qualitative issue has deep conceptual implications." "Stones in an Edifice," *The Jerusalem Report*, 28 January 1993, 48–49, at 48.

8. *CI*, 90.

9. *SEI*, 94.

10. For Corbin's debt to van der Leeuw, see chapter 9, "The Idea of Incognito," in this book. For Scholem and van der Leeuw, see *MSG*. Eliade honored the Dutch scholar many times. See for example *Q*, s.v. "Van der Leeuw, G."

11. Perhaps Eliade stated this case in its quintessential form, in *Patterns in Comparative Religion*, a work published in 1949, the first year of the period under study here. "A religious phenomenon will only be recognized as such if it is grasped at its own level, that is to say, if it is studied *as* something religious. To try to grasp the essence of such a phenomenon by means of physiology, psychology, sociology, economics, linguistics, art or any other study is false; it misses the one unique and irreducible element in it—the element of the sacred." (*PCR*, xiii, emphasis in original). More simply, and pragmatically, he asserted that "there is nothing truly real except the archetypes" (*CH*, 95).

12. *MR*, 75–91.

13. René Guénon, "Oriental Metaphysics," originally a lecture delivered at the

Sorbonne, as found in *The Sword of Gnosis: Metaphysics, Cosmology, Tradition, Symbolism* ed. Jacob Needleman (Baltimore: Penguin, 1974), 40–57, at 50. Guénon develops in this lecture his conception of "metaphysical realization" as being "the knowing of that which is, in an abiding and immutable manner, beyond all temporal succession, for all states of the being, considered under their primary aspect, abide in perfect simultaneousness in the eternal now." 48.

14. Jünger's relations with Eliade deserve a detailed study. The following may be considered apposite at this juncture. Jünger contributed an essay to *Myths and Symbols: Studies in Honor of Mircea Eliade*, ed. Joseph Kitagawa and Charles Long (Chicago: University of Chicago, 1969), with the title "Drugs and Ecstasy" (327–343). This peculiarly vivid essay begins with an epigraph drawn from Eliade's 1938 treatise on the mandrake, which concludes, "la mandragore [mandrake] est 'l'herbe de la vie et de la mort.'" 327. In his discussion in the body of the essay leading up to his own invocation of mandrake, Jünger reflects on the psychotrobic transcendence of time. "The risk that we take in using drugs consists in our shaking a fundamental pillar of existence, namely time. . . . Time appears boundless; it becomes an ocean" 340. These reflections, written at the end of a decade-long collaboration with Eliade, also came after years of Jünger's drug experimentation, including several well-recorded LSD "trips" with Albert Hofman. See Albert Hofman, *LSD, My Problem Child: Reflections on Sacred Drugs, Mysticism, and Science*, trans. Jonathan Ott (Los Angeles: J. P. Tarcher, 1983), esp. chapter 7, "Radiance with Ernst Jünger" (145–171). Eliade was well aware of these experiments, having published the Islamicist Rudolf Gelpke's "trip" protocols, also undertaken with Hofman, in "Von Fahrten in der Weltraum der Seele," *Antaios* 3 (1962): 393–411. That Jünger's experiments were well known as part of a larger attempt to overcome time is a point made by Lutz Niethammer. "For half a century, Ernst Jünger devoted himself to such escapes from time and reported on them in journals, essays, and first-person novels." *Posthistoire: Has History Come to an End?* trans. Patrick Camiller (London: Verso, 1992), 26. That Eliade and Jünger shared a certain view of myth and symbol as conducive to a transcendence of time is made unequivocal in their manifesto opening *Antaios*, carrying the title "Antaios. Magazine for a Free World: A Program." Jünger, *Essays VIII. Ad Hoc* (Stuttgart: Klett-Cotta, 1978), 167–168. *Mythos*, they proclaimed, "on a principle which is unalterable, allows for the firmness of vantage points. The vantage points shall at the same time be heightened: i.e. it shall reveal not only a view of the sealed off past but also present events . . . and above and beyond this the possibilities of the future." 167,

15. See Peter Koslowski, "Die Rükkehr des Titanen Mensch zur Erde und des Ende der 'Geschichte.' Jünger's Essay *An die Zeitmauer*. (1959)," in *Ernst Jünger im 20. Jahrhundert*, ed. H. H. Müller and H. Segeberg (Munich: Wilhelm Fink Verlag, 1995).

16. Eliade, "The Sacred in the Secular World," *Cultural Hermeneutics* 1 (1973): 101–113, at 105. The transcendence of historical time is his key to retrieving the sacred today: "What we refer to as creative acts in a religious sense are precisely individual discoveries of the other dimension . . . All of them involve a going out of self into a world of a different time, a synchronic scheme that makes the past and future equally valuable with the present." 112.

17. *IS*, 57–92.
18. Ibid., 81, 82, 90.
19. *Yoga*, 363.
20. *CI*, 35.
21. See the discussion of prophetic philosophy in chapter 9 chapter "The Idea of the Incognito," in this book.
22. *CI*, 119, emphasis added.
23. Ibid, 90–91.
24. Ibid., 275–276.
25. Corbin, "The Time of Eranos," xvii.
26. *CI*, 238.
27. *Avicenna*, 17.
28. Ibid.
29. *VM*, 57–58, emphasis in original.
30. *MIJ*, 282–303.
31. Ibid., 285.
32. Ibid., 289.
33. Eliade, *Myths and Symbols*, 177. Scholem seems here to rule out the "experience" of "timelessness" championed by Eliade.
34. This is observed despite Eliade's claims to be preparing the ground for philosophy. For example, in his programmatic lecture from 1968, "The Sacred in the Secular World," he announced that "I consider this kind of history of religion to be a kind of prolegomenon or introduction to a new type of philosophy" (p. 107). Eliade considered Corbin to have been always a philosopher, one who "n'a pas consenti à sacrificer sa vocation première de philosophe." See Eliade's review of Corbin's *Avicenna et le Récit visionnaire*, in *La nouvelle revue française* (June 1955): 1096–1099 at 1096.
35. It may be recalled that the book published in English as *Cosmos and History: The Myth of the Eternal Return* was first published as *Le mythe de l'eternal retour*. Eliade considered it to be a kind of "introduction to a Philosophy of History." *CH*, xi.
36. *CI*, 182.
37. Ibid., 215. He insists that "there is no place in Ibn 'Arabi's thinking for a *creatio ex nihilo*." 200.
38. Corbin, *Paradoxe*, 199 (emphasis in original).
39. *MTJM*, 25.
40. Scholem, "Schöpfung aus Nichts und Selbstverschränkung Gottes," *Eranos Jahrbuch* 25 (1956): 87–119, reprinted in *Über einige Grundbegriffe des Judentums* (Frankfurt am Main: Suhrkamp, 1977), 952, and translated into French by Maurice-Ruben Hayoun as "La création à partir du néant et l'auto-contraction de Dieu," in *De la création du monde jusqu'à Varsovie* (Paris: Les Éditions du Cerf, 1990), 31–59. See the interesting observations on *creatio ex nihilo* in Jürgen Habermas, "Gershom Scholem: The Torah in Disguise," *Philosophical-Political Profiles*, trans. Frederick G. Lawrence (Cambridge, Mass.: MIT Press, 1983), 206–207.
41. Throughout his corpus, but usually associated with *CH*.
42. Antoine Faivre, an esoterist at times associated with Eliade and Corbin, has

provided some useful introductions to *Naturphilosophie* (from an esoteric perspective, naturally) in his *Access to Western Esotericism* (Albany: State University of New York Press, 1994), and *Accès de l'ésotérisme occidental II* (Paris: Gallimard, 1996).

43. He treated the idea in various places. See for example the discussion in *MLIS*, 13–25.

44. *OKS*, 117, emphasis in original. The phrase "fulfilled time" Scholem attributes to van der Leeuw's lecture published in *Eranos Jahrbuch* 27 (1949): 27–28.

45. *MSG*, 273, at the conclusion of the essay "Tselem."

46. *Mélanges offerts à Henry Corbin*, ed. Seyyed Hossein Nasr (Tehran: 1977), 665–670, at 670 n. 3.

47. "We are indebted to Henry Corbin for his valuable studies of the 'perfected nature.'" *MSG*, 256.

48. This point is explicated in chapter 13, "Uses of the Androgyne in the History of Religion," in this book.

49. For an extended discussion of *homo Maximus* in Corbin, see *SEI*, 49–52. Eliade wrote a short story titled "Le Macranthrope," *Cahiers de l'Est* 2 (1975): 5–25. Scholem's most extensive treatment was "Die mystische Gestalt der Gottheit in der Kabbala," *Eranos-Jahrbuch* 29 (1960), trans. Jonathan Chipman as the title essay in *MSG*, 15–56.

50. For bibliographical orientation into *Naturphilosophie*, see Faivre, *Access to Western Esotericism*, 331–333.

51. *SP*, 116–162. In 1966, Eliade contributed a review of Scholem's *OKS* to *Commentary* magazine with the title "Cosmic Religion." "We witness how Judaism successfully recovered some of the 'cosmic sacrality' which seemed to have been irremediably lost after the rabbinical reforms." *Commentary*, March 1966, 96–98, at 98. In his journal he added, "I must [one day] return to this theme: in the Kabbala we have to do with a new, real creation of the Judaic religious genius, due to the need to recover a part of the cosmic religiosity smothered and persecuted as much by the prophets as by the later Talmudic rigorists." *J II*, 266.

52. *J II*, 101.

53. *Yoga*, 287.

54. Eliade, "*Homo Faber* and *Homo Religiosus*," in *The History of Religions: Retrospect and Prospect*, ed. Joseph M. Kitagawa (New York: Macmillan, 1985), 1–12, at 6.

55. Ibid., 11.

56. *JJC*, 277.

57. *MSG*, 37.

58. *JJC*, 278.

59. Ibid., 297, emphasis added.

60. Ibid., 290.

61. *SEI*, 110.

62. *JJC*, 297.

63. Scholem, "Opening Address" in *Types of Redemption*, 1–12, at 11.

64. *SEI*, 97.

65. *CI*, 354 n. 41. Repeated in *SEI*, 134 n. 4.

66. *TC*, 338, emphasis in original.
67. For a more complete discussion of the phenomenology of religions, see chapter 1, "Eranos and the 'History of Religions,'" in this book.
68. See chapter 9, "The Idea of Incognito," in this book.
69. *TC*, 350, emphasis in original.
70. *OKS*, 96.
71. *Kabbalah* (reprinting the article "Kabbalah and Pantheism" from the *Encyclopedia Judaica*), 149.
72. *JJC*, 197.
73. *CH*, 139–175.
74. *OPJM*, 113.
75. Niethammer, *Posthistoire*.
76. This was prior to his encounter with Jung's sense of archetypes.
77. *SP*, 202, emphasis in original.
78. *OKS*, 474, emphasis added.
79. Corbin, "Toward a Chart of the Imaginal," 30.
80. *IS*, 164, 169, emphasis in original.
81. Corbin, *TC*, 196, emphasis in original. Elsewhere Corbin put it rather more directly, speaking of "entering, passing *into the interior*, of finding oneself, paradoxically, *outside* . . . since by means of *interpretation*, one has *departed* from that *external* reality." *SEI*, p. 6, emphasis in original.
82. *OKS*, 28.
83. "Today we are beginning to realize that what is called 'initiation' coexists with the human condition, *that every existence* is made up of an unbroken series of 'ordeals,' 'deaths,' and 'resurrections,' whatever be the terms that modern language uses to express these originally religious experiences." *MR*, 202, emphasis added. For Eliade, initiatory or mystical death functioned as a kind of universal passkey into salvation.
84. *Shamanism*, 486.

Chapter 11
The Chiliastic Practice of Islamic Studies According to Henry Corbin

1. I do not question his accomplishments as energetic editor, translator, and the like. One cannot gainsay his achievements in founding and directing the Bibliothèque Iranienne series, to take one example.
2. He uses this term in a number of places, perhaps most prominent among them in the long Eranos lecture of 1962, "De la Philosophie Prophetique." For more discussion of this point, see chapter 8, "Collective *Renovatio*," in this book.
3. Faivre, *Access to Western Esoterism*, is typical of the high honors presently accorded Corbin in the esoterist community. See s.v. "Corbin, Henry."
4. I would point out Christian Jambet, *La Logique des Orientaux: Henry Corbin et la science des formes*, and Daryush Shayegan, *Henry Corbin: La Topographie Spirituelle de l'Islam Iranien*.
5. I have presented the documentation in the "Aryanism" section of chapter 4, "The Idea of Incognito," in this book.
6. Corbin, "Divine Epiphany and Spiritual Birth," 158–159.

7. "The Dramatic Element," 212.

8. Löwith, *Martin Heidegger and European Nihilism*, 225.

9. It appeared in *Recherches philosophiques* 3 (1933): 250–284. While the entire article probes issues concerning of the end of time, Corbin deals directly with eschatology in the section titled "Le temps propre de l'existence et l'*Eschaton*," pp. 261–274.

10. Ibid., 255.

11. The best introduction to the concept of decisionism is the important essay of Karl Löwith, "The Occasional Decisionism of Carl Schmitt" (including a valuable, relevant Postscript, "On Martin Heidegger's Political Decisionism and Friedrich Gogarten's Theological Decisionism"), in *Martin Heidegger and European Nihilism*, ed. Wolin, trans. Smith 137–173. The original essay appeared in 1935. I take this occasion to thank Richard Wolin for sending me a copy of this most useful volume.

12. Corbin, "Hymnes Manichéens," *Yggdrasill: Bulletin mensuel de la poésie en France et à l'Etranger* 4–5 (July–August 1937): 54–55, emphasis in original. I thank Peter Eli Gordon for sending a copy of this rare article from Paris.

13. Denis de Rougemont, "Hérétiques de toutes les religions, unissez-vous," in *Mélanges offerts à Henry Corbin*, ed. Nasr, 539–547.

14. Ibid., 541, emphasis in original.

15. *PCR*, 450, italics added. Eliade made a committment to *decisive and unwavering choice*. He employed decisionist idiom in his explicitly Christian utterances: "For the true Christian . . . can no longer repudiate History but neither can he accept it all. He has continually to *choose* . . . the event which *for him* may be charged with saving significance." *MDM*, 153, emphasis in original.

16. Corbin, "For the Concept of Irano-Islamic Philosophy," 119.

17. Corbin, "Allocution d'Ouverture," *Colloque Berdiaev* (Sorbonne, 12 April 1975) (Paris: Institut d'études slaves, 1978), 47–50, at 49, emphasis added.

18. In his final address to his own private college, l'Université St. Jean de Jérusalem, he called to his listeners to become gnostics "with eyes of fire." "To open 'the eyes of fire' is to go beyond all false and vain opposition between believing and knowing, between thinking and being, between knowledge and love, between the God of the prophets and the God of the philosophers." "Eyes of Flesh and Eyes of Fire. Science and Gnosis," *Material for Thought* 8 (1980): 5–10 (no translator indicated). This talk was originally delivered as the opening address of the June 1978 convocation of l'Université St. Jean de Jérusalem. See Corbin, "L'évangile de Barnabé et la prophétologie islamique," *Cahiers de l'université Saint Jean de Jérusalem* 3 (1977): 169–212. For a more extensive treatment, see his "Harmonia Abrahamica," preface to Luigi Cirillo, *Évangile de Barnabé: Recherches sur la composition et l'origine* (Paris: Éditions Beauchesne, 1977), 5–17.

19. Corbin, "The Force of Traditional Philosophy in Iran Today," *Studies in Comparative Religion* 2 (1968): 12–26, at 26 (no translator indicated).

20. See for example his philosophical manifesto, *The Concept of Comparative Philosophy*, trans. Peter Russell (Ipswich, U.K.: Golgonooza Press, 1981).

21. Corbin, "Theologoumena Iranica," *Studia Islamica* 5 (1976): 225–235, at 235.

22. When Corbin was studying in the 1920s, Henri Bergson's theory of duration was perhaps the most influential philosophy of its day, though by that time past its prime. For Corbin's theory of time, see chapter 10, "Mystic Historicities," in this book.

23. Corbin, "The Time of Eranos," xvii, emphasis in original.

24. There may be no more consistent theme in his work, from 1932 to 1978, than his antihistoricism. The following is typical and can be multiplied by dozens of similar statements: "We can say no more here, except that the categories of historicism are completely inappropriate for the understanding of the truths that are at issue here." "The Isma'ili Response to the Polemic of Ghazali," in *Isma'ili Contributions to Islamic Culture*, ed. Seyyed Hossein Nasr (Tehran: Imperial Iranian Academy of Philosophy, 1977), 67–95, at 96 n. 8. Perhaps his most sustained discussion of antihistoricism is found in the section titled "How do we extricate ourselves from historicism?" in *The Concept of Comparative Philosophy*, 6–16.

25. Corbin, "The Time of Eranos," xvii, emphasis in original.

26. *TC*, 185, emphasis added.

27. For " 'the theology of the history of religions,' the idea of which was first put forward by Mircea Eliade," see *CI*, 352 n. 15.

28. *TC*, 280 n. 33. Corbin prefaces this digression with the comment that Eliade "initiates an entire inquiry into the question raised here."

29. For example, Theodore of Mopsuestia identified Ahriman with Satan. As Cumont commented, "[I]n fact, they are practically the same figure under different names. It is generally admitted that Judaism took the notion of an adversary of god from the Mazdeans." *Oriental Religions* (New York: Dover, 1956), 153.

30. Jung claimed to be purely an inductive empiricist, asserting that he did no more than to describe observable psychological law. But his pseudo-empiricism was doctrine in a doctor's gown. He applies the notion of "psychological law" twice in his crucial exposition of Antichrist, in "Aion," in *Psyche and Symbol*, ed. Violet S. de Laszlo (Garden City, N.Y.: Doubleday, Anchor, 1958), 40 and 41. For a more detailed discussion of *Response to Job*, see chapter 15 "On the Suspension of the Ethical," in this book.

31. Joseph Campbell, *Masks of God* (New York: Penguin), 1976).

32. For more on *The Myth of Reintegration* see chapter 13, "Uses of the Androgyne," in this book.

33. McGuire, *Bollingen*, 76–79.

34. Denis de Rougemont, *The Devil's Share*, trans. Haakan Chevalier (New York: Pantheon, 1944), 21–22.

35. For more on de Rougemont, see chapter 14, "Defeating Evil from Within," in this book.

36. Corbin, *Paradoxe*, 205.

37. Corbin, "Cyclical Time," 134, 157.

38. Corbin, *TC*, 388.

39. Ibid., 264. Just eight months before his death, he restated this emphasis in his favorite Heideggerian fashion: "To confuse Being with being is the metaphysical catastrophe." Introduction to Miller, *A New Polytheism*, 2. This theme runs throughout *Paradoxe*. For background to this hyperbolic conception in Corbin's

deutschophilic youth, consider Löwith's sharp perceptions of "the *catastrophic manner of thinking* characteristic of the generation of Germans after the First World War," in *Martin Heidegger and European Nihilism*, 166.

40. "Sabian Temple," in *TC*, 161.

41. Corbin, *The Concept of Comparative Philosophy*, 28.

42. Corbin, *Paradoxe*, 187.

43. Corbin espoused a kind of anarchism, the secretly disruptive act of which signals simultaneously the return to a presumptive original order. Joseph Pieper analogously cited Ernst Jünger: "Nihilism is differentiated from anarchism by bearing a certain relationship to order, and therefore it is better disguised and harder to discern—this penetrating observation of Ernst Jünger's [Pieper continued] has an eschatological bearing." "The Reign of Antichrist," in *Selection I*, ed. Cecily Hastings and Donald Nicholl (London: Sheed and Ward, 1953), 207.

44. Charlotte Klein, *Anti-Judaism in Christian Theology*, trans. Edward Quinn (Philadelphia: Fortress Press, 1978), esp. "Law and Legalistic Piety," 39–67.

45. Hans Jonas, "Response by Hans Jonas," in *The Bible in Modern Scholarship; Papers Read at the 100th Meeting of the Society of Biblical Literature, December 28–30, 1964* ed. J. Philip Hyatt (Nashville, Tenn.: Abingdon Press, 1965). "[T]he nature of the relation of Gnosticism to Judaism—in itself an undeniable fact—is defined by the *anti-Jewish animus* with which it is saturated. 'The greatest case of metaphysical antisemitism!' exclaimed Scholem once when we talked about these matters soon after the appearance of my first volume on Gnosis: that was in the thirties (and in Jerusalem) when one was very much alive to this aspect of things." Hans Jonas, Corbin quoted Scholem on this point, agreed that "many gnostic currents of the first centuries were militantly hostile to the God of the Bible, in a manner resembling what G. Scholem describes as a 'metaphysical anti-semitism.'" "The Dramatic Element Common to the Gnostic Cosmogonies of the Religions of the Book," *Studies in Comparative Religion* 14 (1980): 199–221, at 210 (no translator indicated).

46. It may be observed without prejudice, at least, that several of his friends and influences have been accused of various degrees of anti-Judaism, including Carl Jung, Martin Heidegger, and Mircea Eliade; or, more precisely, of holding negative views concerning Jews which have some bearing on their theories of religion. Denis de Rougemont was another; de Rougemont wrote the essay "Vocation et Destin d'Israël" at the very time that he and Corbin were cofounding their "little review of religious thought." In these explicitly Barthian reflections, he did not restrict himself to purely theological observations but extended himself to sociopolitical judgments.

Le spiritualisme transcendant des Juifs d'Orient, au contact des coutumes occidentales, se mue peu à peu en son contraire exacte: c'est le materérialisme jouisseur et cynique que les nazis reprochent aux Juifs allemands capitalistes, avec d'autant plus d'amertume que cette attitude provocante fut souvent prise à l'étranger pour un trait ce caractère germanique. Mais c'est aussi l'intellectualisme stérilisant, l'esprit d'abstraction inhumanine et chimérique, au surplus troublé de sentimentalisme, que l'on dénonce à droite chez les auteurs d'origine juive, mais qui ont cessé de croire à la mission de leur peuple, et qui exercent désormais à vide les facultés psychologiques fortement développées dans leur race par des siècles d'attente de l'invisible. *Les Juifs* (Paris: Librairie Plon, 1937, 158).

I discuss more fully the issue of Corbin's treatment of Judaism in chapter 3, "Tautegorical Sublime. Gerhsom Scholem and Henry Corbin in Conversation," in this book.

47. Letter from Jung to Corbin, dated 4 May 1953, printed in *Cahier de l'Herne Henry Corbin*, 328.

48. This is not to agree that such an assertion means anything. In his review of Harold Bloom's *Shakespeare: The Invention of the Human*, Anthony Lane deflates Bloom's elevated style. "Life must be true to Shakespeare if personality is to have value, is to *be* value. If you can tell me what, if anything, that sentence means, I'll buy you a drink." *The New Yorker*, (19 October 1998), 84. Bloom, not incidentally, is responsible for a work profoundly indebted to Corbin. See *Omens of Millennium: The Gnosis of Angels, Dreams and Resurrection* (New York: Riverhead Books, 1996).

49. Corbin, "The Force of Irano-Islamic Philosophy," 25.

50. Roger Arnaldez, "Henry Corbin et le christianisme," *Études* 355 (1981): 627–638. There seems little doubt, in any event, that Corbin wished to signal his initiation, whether or not that act itself can ever be "documented." Two months before his death, calling on all visionaries with "eyes of fire," he spoke one last time of the timeless "combat for the soul of the world": "Il y aurait même à reprendre les choses au *niveau des religions initiatiques contemporaines* encore des débuts du christianisme." *Le Combat Pour l'Âme du Monde: Urgence de la Sophiologie*, Cahiers de l'Université Saint Jean de Jerusalem (Paris: Berg, 1980), 11–15, at 15, emphasis added. It may be noted that the "auditeurs" for this 1978 session of l'Université Saint Jean de Jerusalem included twenty-three men and no women. The two participants from the United States were David L. Miller and Mircea Eliade.

51. Note that de Rougemont's religio-political philosophy was known as Personalism. In one of his final essays, "De la théologie apophatique comme antidote du nihilisme," delivered in Tehran in October 1977, Corbin devoted a section to "Théologie apophatique et personnalisme," *Paradoxe*, 194–201.

52. Löwith, *Martin Heidegger and European Nihilism*, 133, emphasis in the original. As early as 1930, in Marburg, Löwith and Corbin enjoyed "de grands entretiens sur Hamann et les courant qui se rattachent à son œuvre." "PostScriptum biographique," 43. They shared their love of Hamann, of course, with their mutual master, Heidegger.

53. Corbin, "Trois entretiens sur l'histoire spirituelle de l'Iran," *Le monde non chrétien* 43–44 (1957): 179–199. These remarks originated as interviews "radiodiffusés au printemps 1957, au cours d'un cycle réservé à l'Iran par l'émission 'Culture française.'"

54. These esoteric influences on Corbin's might imply an initiatic connection.

55. Corbin, "Trois entretiens sur l'histoire spirituelle de l'Iran," 199.

56. One reading of these words ought perhaps to be registered: it may have been that on some level Henry Corbin hoped that *he himself* would become that "Quatrième Maître."

Chapter 12
Psychoanalysis in Reverse

1. Wouter Hanegraaff sharply analyzes Jung and what he calls "the psychologization of religion" in his *New Age Religion and Western Culture*, 496–512.

2. See Martin Jay, *Adorno* (Cambridge: Harvard University Press, 1984), 122.

3. 1956 preface to *MDM*, 20.

4. Ibid., 232.

5. *Q,* 126.

6. Ibid.

7. *MDM*, 152.

8. *J II*, 229.

9. *A II*, 152, emphasis added.

10. *MDM*, 150, emphasis in original.

11. Ibid., 151.

12. *IS*, 35.

13. Ibid., 12–16.

14. Jung's antipathy toward Freud and psychoanalysis found resonant parallels in Guénon, Evola, and Eliade. René Guénon set the tone: "Why it is that the principal representatives of the new tendencies, like Einstein in physics, Bergson in philosophy, Freud in psychology, and many others of less importance, are almost all of Jewish origin, unless it be because there is something involved that is closely bound up with the "maleficent" and dissolving aspect of nomadism when it is deviated, and because that aspect must inevitably predominate in Jews detached from their tradition?" René Guénon, *The Reign of Quantity and the Signs of the Times*, trans. Lord Northbourne (Baltimore: Penguin, 1972), 355.

15. *IS*, 14–15.

16. Ibid., 15–16, 23.

17. Ibid., 37.

18. *OWCF*, 32.

19. *IS*, 89 n. 24.

20. Ibid., 30.

21. *MDM*, 53.

22. In *Cosmos and History*, he studies the biblical view of time and myth, of which he says, "[W]e are dealing with the conception of an 'elite' who interpret contemporary history by means of a myth. . . . [For a hypercritical modern, this] might represent a labored invention on the part of a Hebraic minority." *CH*, 38. As if to contradict his rather tepid disclaimer that this particular analysis is not his own, Eliade goes on to explicate his view: "But it must not be forgotten that these Messianic conceptions are the exclusive creation of a religious elite. For many centuries, this elite undertook the religious education of the people of Israel, without always being successful in eradicating the traditional Paleo-Oriental granting of value to life and history." *CH*, 107. And from this point he continues

to explicate the innovative, but epocally detrimental, "historization" of the "Isra-elitic elites" (110) and the "Judaic elites" (111). "Thus, for the first time, the prophets placed a value on history . . . the Hebrew were the first to discover the meaning of history" ((104). While this discussion is pointed but still oddly mud-died in *Cosmos and History*, it is made amply clear in subsequent works. Underly-ing his critique, in short, is a antimodernist, devolutionist view of history, in which demythologizing leads to demystification, which in turn leads to seculari-zation, the nadir of profane existence, nonbeing as such. And the initial innova-tions toward this dark end, in Eliade's view, were those of the Hebrew prophets: "secularization [may be considered] a continuation of demythologizing, which is itself a late prolongation of the prophets' struggle to empty the Cosmos and cosmic life of the sacred." *Q*, preface, unpaginated. Thus can Eliade conclude that "Judaization" is equivalent to "historicization." *MR*, 170. All this is taken as a given: "As for Judaism, the great 'demythization' performed by the prophets has long been known." *MR*, 147. And what has been known for so long? "But never was cosmic religiosity so savagely attacked. The prophets succeeded in emptying nature of any divine presence." *HRI 2*, 354. For more on his claim that Hebrew prophets, and later, "Talmudic rigorists" "smothered" "cosmic religion" see the examples in chapter 10, "Mystic Historicities," in this book. Finally, it may be observed that the section of his final masterwork, *History of Religious Ideas*, pro-duced in his last decade, dealing with the Hebrew prophets, once more repeated these assertions. *HRI 1*, 354–356.

23. *A I*, 233, emphasis in original. The "*single* royal road" Eliade elsewhere characterized as "provincialism." The aspersion of "*provincialism*" is one of his more frequent characterizations of Judaism. This comprises, without much ques-tion, a variant on the classical anti-Jewish calumny of "*exclusivism*." Not uncom-monly, in fact, he uses that loaded term itself. He thus speaks of "the exclusive character of the Revelation" (*HRI 2*, 256), which is "*limited to the Jewish people . . . exclusively*" (*HRI 2*, 275, emphasis in original). "We have found, among the Jews, the *true* religion of Jahveh." *MDM*, 149, emphasis in original. Jahweh rep-resents a process in which an Evil that had been universal "is thenceforth isolated, personified and invested with a specific and exclusive function." *HRI 2*, 270. Israelite prophets extend this exclusivism: "Yet the prophets lay claim to the purest Yahwism" (*HRI* I: 186). Little changes in this connection: the early Chris-tian community, as a practicing Judaism, "was characterized by its exclusive attachment to observance of the Jewish Law." *HRI 2*, 534. Thus, this "Judaeo-Christianity" constituted a "fossilization" and an "immobility." *HRI 2*, 534. In-sofar as Judaism may be said to be universal at all, it is not obedience to the Law, but faith in Jesus that "was the fulfillment of Jewish religious universalism; for, by virtue of the Christian Messiah, the 'people of God' could accomplish the univer-sal reconciliation . . . and prepare the renewal of the world, the 'New Creation.'" *HRI 2*, 535. Whenever this "Jewish" provincialism recurs, Eliade takes pains to label it as such. In a late discussion of his *bête noire*, Marxism, he considers it as a false universalism: "That is what I call 'mythological provincialism.'" *J II* 129.

The religion of Judaism (and, by extension, Judeo-Marxism) is provincial, and thus merely of *limited applicability* insofar as "[i]t is the specific vocation of all religious universalism to go beyond provincialism." *HRI 2*, 404. "[T]he strict and apologetic understanding of the Torah . . . was irreconcilable with the universal eschatological proclamation of the Gospels." *HRI 2*, 513. "For, to the non-Christian, one question occurs first of all: how can a local history—that of the Jewish people and the first Judaeo-Christian communities—how can this claim to become the pattern for all divine manifestation in concrete, historical Time?" *IS*, 168. After all, "[f]rom a certain point of view, any local history is in danger of provincialism." *RSI*, 114. "[P]rovincialism tending, in the end, to monotony and sterility." *IS*, 118.

24. Dennis A. Doeing, "Mircea Eliade's Spiritual and Intellectual Development from 1917 to 1940" (Ph.D. diss., University of Ottawa, 1975), 208.

25. *IS*, 120.

26. *A I*, 233, emphasis in original.

27. *Q*, 62.

28. *PCR*, xiii.

29. Ibid., 31.

30. *Q*, 50, emphasis added.

31. *J III*, 156–157.

32. *MR*, 76–79.

33. *CH*, viii–ix.

34. *Individuation* is used throughout *Avicenna*; see the index, s.v. "individuation." For other terms, see *archetype*: *CI*, 59 (Khidr), *CI*, 267; *companion archetype*: *TC*, 4, 8, 10, 164–165, *SEI*, 38; *mandala*: *CI*, 94–95, *SEI*, 31; *quaternity*: *CI*, 163, 341 n. 53, *TC*, 17–18; *shadow*: *CI*, 191, *MLIS*, passim; *active imagination*, *CI*, 242, *SI*, 15; *Self*: *CI*, 94–95; *synchronicity*: *CI*, 303, n. 27; and *animus/anima*: *SEI*, 46. For *coincidentia oppositorum* see chapter 4 in this book.

35. Corbin, "The Imams and the Imamate," in *Shi'ism: Doctrines, Thought and Spirituality*, ed. Nasr, Dabashi, and Nasr, 176.

36. *SBCE*. vii–xix.

37. Corbin, "De l'Iran à Eranos," in *Cahiers l'Herne, Henry Corbin*, 262.

38. Eliade did the same in his *History of Religious Ideas*.

39. See Hanegraaff's discussion of Jung as an esoterist himself, in *New Age Religion and Western Culture*,

40. Corbin, "Post-Scriptum," 48. This statement provides a detailed nuancing of his relation to the Jungian system.

41. Hillman, *Re-Visioning Psychology*.

42. His relationship to Jungian thought, however, has yet to be clarified.

43. *JJC*, 29.

44. *MSG*, 6.

45. *JJC*, 190.

46. In reference to the "genius of Kafka, Simmel, Freud or Walter Benjamin." Ibid., 87.

47. As "anarchy in every human soul": *MIJ*, 109; "libidinal forces": *MIJ*, 112; "the more primitive region of the soul": *MTJM*, 315; "the darker aspects": *OKS*, 157; "instincts of anarchy": *MIJ*, 109.

48. *MIJ*, 89.

49. He called Jakob Frank "the most hideous and uncanny figure in the whole history of Jewish Messianism." *MTJM*, 308.

50. *Sabbatai Sevi*, 126–128.

51. *OKS*, 23.

52. Similarly, in *Sabbatai Sevi*, a work of his middle years, Scholem interpreted the interpreting angel (*maggid*) as a product of the unconscious (82, 209). Cited by Elliot R. Wolfson in "Construction of the Shekhinah in the Messianic Theosophy of Abraham Cardoso with an Annotated Edition of *Derush ha-Shekhinah*," *Kabbalah: Journal for the Study of Jewish Mystical Texts* 3 (1998): 11–94, at 16 n. 12. I thank Elliot R. Wolfson for sending an offprint of this article to me.

53. *MSG*, 139, 195, 293. Scholem's original paper, "The Unconscious and the concept of *Kadmut ha-Sekhel* in Hasidic Literature," originally published in 1944, was reprinted in *Devarim be-Go* (Tel Aviv: Am Oved, 1976), 2:351–360.

54. *MSG*, 139.

55. *MIJ*, 18.

56. See chapter 1, "Eranos and the 'History of Religions,'" in this book.

57. McGuire, *Bollingen*, 153.

58. *MTJM*, 293.

59. *OKS*, 103, 112.

60. Scholem, "Three Types of Jewish Piety," *Eranos-Jahrbuch* 38 (1969): 331–348, reprinted in *Eranos Lectures 3, Jewish and Gnostic Man* (Dallas: Spring Publications, 1987), 29–46. I cite from the latter reprinting, at 34. Also reprinted in *Ariel* 32 (1973): 5–24; *Devarim be-Go*, 541–56; and *OPJM*, 176–190.

61. Elliot R. Wolfson, *Journal of Religion* 73 (1993): 655–657.

62. *MSG*, 6.

63. Biale, *Gershom Scholem*, 68.

64. From a 30 December 1950 letter to Morton Smith:

I am not a psychologist myself, and even in Ascona (where the influence of C. G. Jung is very much felt, he himself being the moving spirit of those congresses called "Eranos") I did refrain from psychological excursions. But I felt that much could be done in this field by somebody with a sound philological training and not given to the more extreme forms of psychoanalytical fantasies for which I cannot arouse much sympathy on my part. I feel that much of the amateurish character of psychological researches into the History of Religion, especially of a book of the Freudian and Jungian brand, is caused by the lack of a sound philological basis for their contentions. (*Briefe I*, 19).

65. Compare Heidegger's comment that "He who thinks greatly must err greatly," cited by James Miller, "Heidegger's Guilt," *Salmagundi*, 109–110 (1996): 178–243, at 178.

66. Letter 63, Jerusalem, 7 May 1963, in *Briefe II*, 95. I thank Werner Brandl for his translation of some of Scholem's letters.

67. It is perhaps useful to recall that all three had interrupted publishing histories: *Gnosis* was written in two parts, the second part largely lost, and it led a long underground existence. *Moses* was written in two parts, before and after his escape. And *Dialectic* bears an American copyright of 1944 but a Dutch first edition of 1947 and did not find its readership until two decades after its publication.

68. The eminent Egyptologist Hans J. Polotsky was a member of the original group. When Freud was writing *Moses and Monotheism*, trans. from the German by Katherine Jones (New York: Vintage Books, 1967), he also was corresponding

with his disciple Arnold Zweig in Palestine. In a letter sent from Haifa in December 1935, Zweig informed Freud that he had conferred with Polotsky concerning Freud's thesis on Moses. In short, Scholem could have heard from Polotsky about Freud's book at a time when he was writing "Redemption through Sin." *The Letters of Sigmund Freud and Arnold Zweig*, ed. Ernst L. Freud, trans. from the German by Elaine and William Robson-Scott (London: Hogarth Press, 1970), 118. Jonas described his participation in the Pilegesh circle with his interviewer Ioan Culianu. See Culianu, *Gnosticismo e pensiero moderno: Hans Jonas* (Rome: L'Erma di Bretschneider, 1985). Poems and other artifacts from this circle are found in the Jewish National Library, Jerusalem.

69. Horkheimer and Adorno *Dialectic of Enlightenment*, 68–209.

70. See the discussion in chapter 11, "The Chiliastic Practice of Islamic Studies According to Henry Corbin," in this book.

71. See the interesting discussion by Philip Rieff in Bruce Mazlish, *Psychohistory*.

72. The key word here, for Scholem, was "daring" (*Verwegenheit.*) For some of his many usages, see *MSG*, 55, 87; *OPJM*, 20, 21, 36, 70, 77, 78; *MIJ*, 106. He also used it in his "Ten Unhistorical Aphorisms." See *Judaica 3: Studien zur jüdischen Mystik*, 268. Eliade employed a related conception. "Tantrism represents an audacious art of interiorisation . . . we live in an epoch when one can no longer disengage oneself from the wheels of History, unless by some audacious act of evasion." *MDM*, 150, 154. And one finds analogies in Corbin. He concluded his 1965 Eranos lecture by citing "the great Swabian mystic, Friedrich Oetinger," whose words, Corbin asserted, "have all the virtue of a motto: 'My God, grant me the boldness to change what is in my power to change, and grant me the modesty to bear what is not within my power to change." *TC*, 262. See the suggestive comments of Scholem on Oetinger in *MTJM*, 238.

73. See Harold Bloom, introduction to *Gershom Scholem* (New York: Chelsea House, 1987).

74. *TC*, 375. By 1915–1916, Scholem had already found that "a number of Schleiermacher's Platonic dialogues moved me." *FBJ*, 66. Corbin also concluded a lecture at the University of Tehran in 1948 with an invocation of Schleiermacher. See *VM*, 31.

75. See chapter 1, "Eranos and the 'History of Religions,'" in this book.

76. *Avicenna*, vii.

77. Scholem, *Walter Benjamin*, 136.

78. Biale, *Gershom Scholem*, 22.

79. In his noble essay on "Franz Rosenzweig and his Book, *The Star of Redemption*," he castigated the human sciences. This essay has been reprinted in *OPJM*, 197–216.

80. David Biale, "Gershom Scholem's Ten Unhistorical Aphorisms on Kabbalah: Text and Commentary," *Modern Judaism* 5 (1985): 67–95, at 79–80. One wonders to what extent Scholem continued to engage in a posthumous dialogue with Benjamin. See Benjamin's contrast between *Erlebnis* and *Erfahrung* in "On Some Motifs in Baudelaire," in *Illuminations*, 165.

81. *JJC*, 151.

82. Scholem, "Opening Address" in *Types of Redemption*, 1–12, at 11, emphasis added.

83. See the discussion in David J. Halperin, *Faces of the Chariot: Early Jewish Responses to Ezekiel's Vision* (Tübingen: J. C. B. Mohr, 1988).

84. In his polemic against Hans Joachim Schoeps, cited in Biale, *Gershom Scholem*, 130.

85. Corbin, "Correspondance," *Revue de métaphysique et de morale* (April 1963): 234–237, at 234.

86. *TO*, 19–78, delivered at Eranos in 1958 and published in German in the first issue of *Antaios*.

87. To what extent this "impersonality" required an "experience" is another matter. In a recent poem Czeslaw Milosz imagines an archaic tribe, without iron or pottery wheel, making an immense granite ball.

> What did it mean to them? The opposite
> Of everything that passes and perishes? Of muscles, skin?
> Of leaves crackling in a fire? A lofty abstraction
> Stronger than anything because it is not alive?

"A Ball," trans. Czeslaw Milosz and Robert Hass, *Partisan Review* 4 (1998): 600.

88. One can find this citation as the epigraph to Friedrich Meinicke's *Historism: The Rise of a New Historical Outlook*, trans. J. E. Anderson (New York: Herder and Herder, 1972). For a discussion of this aphorism, see 393 n. 1. Meinicke confesses himself unable to locate the source of the saying.

89. Leo Baeck, "Individuum ineffabile," *Eranos-Jahrbuch* 15 (1948): 385–436.

90. Corbin, "The Time of Eranos," in *Man and Time*, xv, xvii.

91. Corbin, "Cyclical Time," 164, emphasis in the original.

92. Jung contributed the introduction to Schmid-Guisan's book. For their friendship see Frank McLynn, *Carl Gustav Jung: A Biography* (New York: St. Martin's Press, 1996), 193.

93. In the introduction, Jung notes rather sententiously that "This book is neither for nor of the masses." *The Symbolic Life*, 759.

94. *MLIS*, 57.

95. See Eliade's late remembrances of d'Ors in *OL*, 82–83.

96. *TC*, 253.

97. *OKS*, 195. Peter Schäfer notes the dropping of the "telluric." See Schäfer "The Magic of the Golem: The Early Development of the Golem Legend," *Journal of Jewish Studies* 46 (1995): 249–261, at 249.

98. On these points see chapter 8, "Collective Renovatio," in this book.

99. His most sustained English-language effort along these lines is *Zalmoxis*.

100. *SBCE*, 4.

101. Corbin, "Theologie au bord du lac," *Henry Corbin, Cahiers l'Herne*, 62–63.

102. Ibid., 264–265.

103. For the formative influence on Jung by Nietzsche, see the fine monograph by Paul Bishop, *The Dionysian Self*.

104. Eliezer Schweid, "Prophetic Mysticism," *Modern Judaism* 14, no. 2 (1994): 150.

105. See chapter 6, "Aesthetic Solutions," in this book for a further discussion of this point.

106. The related allegory of the righteous in every generation, it has recently been observed by Kurt Erich Grözinger, was translated into fables by Franz Kafka. On this reinvention of the "Tzaddik ha-dor" motif see Karl Erich Grözinger, *Kafka and Kabbalah*, trans. S. H. Ray (New York: Continuum, 1994), 145–150.

107. An allegory of this chain makes up the final paragraph of Scholem's *MTJM*.

108. On Scholem's friendship with this Swiss-Jewish Jungian analyst Siegmund Hurwitz, see *Briefe II*, 13, 118, 277. See the high praise of Hurwitz by Werblowsky in "Recent Literature on Psychology and the Study of Religions," *Journal of Jewish Studies* 6 (1955): 172–182, at 179–182.

109. Scholem, *Devarim Be-Go* (Tel Aviv: Am 'Oved, 1975), 2:351–360.

110. C. G. Jung, "Religion and Psychology: A Reply to Martin Buber," in *The Collected Works Volume Eighteen: The Symbolic* Life, trans. R. F. C. Hull (London: Routledge and Kegan Paul, 1977), 197.

111. It is worth noting that Eliade published a collection called *Oceanografie (Oceanography)* in Bucharest in 1934.

112. Foreword, dated November 1960, *TO*, 10. Eliade had already used this paragraph, verbatim, in his introduction to an Eranos anthology. Dated November 1959, this introduction, "Encounters at Ascona," was then modified as the introduction to *The Two and the One*. See *Spiritual Disciplines*, ed. Joseph Campbell (New York: Pantheon, 1960), xvii–xxi. The exact same paragraph appears again in a 1964 article: *Q*, 49.

113. Among the many references in Scholem to a kind of group psychology, see *MIJ*, 86, 89, 92, 109, 112, 116; *OKS*, 2, 3, 33, 106, and 204.

114. *MTJM*, 298.

115. *OKS*, 106.

116. Ibid., 2; *Du*, April 1955, 64–65.

117. *CI*, 215, emphasis added.

118. *OKS*, 204.

119. *CI*, 215; *SEI*, 4. In *SBCE*, Corbin invokes the notion of "the psychocosmic center." 75.

120. *FC*, 34.

121. *TO*, 49.

122. *IS*, 36, *Q*, 173–174.

123. *PCR*, 455, emphasis added. For the motif of transformation into symbol, and closely analogous statements by Corbin and Scholem, see chapter 5, "On Symbols and Symbolizing," in this book.

124. Foreword, *IS*, 20–21.

125. *OL*, 163,

126. This is exemplified in Eliade's 1952 lecture at Eranos, "Indian Symbolisms of Time and Eternity." On the one hand, he identifies the Tantric Yoga system with the Jungian system. "The *vasanas* represent also the entire collective memory transmitted by language and tradition: They are, in a sense, the 'collective unconcious' of Professor Jung." *IS* 89. But in the footnote on the same page he insists on the "ignorance of Western scientists concerning the psychological reality of the yogis' experience." Presumably he was excluding Jung from this

generalization. I would also observe that this both/and position mirrors their insistence, in philosophical terms, on *coincidentia oppositorum*. See chapter 4, dedicated to this idea, in this book.

Chapter 13
Uses of the Androgyne in the History of Religions

1. This essay was originally delivered as a lecture at the Ohio State University. I thank Professors Jane Hathaway and Tamar Rudavsky for their invitation and hospitality.

2. The paperback title was changed to *The Two and The One*, trans. J. M. Cohen (New York: Harper and Row, 1969), another allusion to the "mysteries" of androgyny.

3. Ibid., 80. Eliade himself reviewed this publishing history here.

4. *TO*, 78.

5. *TC*, 183–185.

6. Corbin, *En Islam Iranien II*, 324.

7. *J I*, 61–72, describes the intense euphoria Eliade experienced reading Balzac and working on a biographical essay of him. In August 1947, he was considering writing a book on Balzac as Swedenborgian "mystic and visionary" with reference to *Séraphita*: "Probably this project will become one of the numerous books I shall never write!" Ibid., 63. This draft, indeed, seems to have been misplaced. *J II*, 49.

8. *OWCF*, 52.

9. *TO*, 123–124.

10. *TO*, 78.

11. *TO*, 98. In this formulation, one cannot but be reminded of a parallel phrasing expressed by the Italian theorist of fascism and writer, Julius Evola. In *The Metaphysics of Sex* (Rochester, Vt.: Inner Traditions, 1983), a work cited by Eliade and praised by Jung, Evola asserted "the very metaphysics of male and female. This law is the 'reciprocal integration and completion together with *a subordination of the female principle to the male*.' Everything else, as Nietzsche would say, is nonsense." 171, emphasis added. It may also be noted that Eliade's ardent approval of the Swedenborgian themes in *Séraphita* may be compared to Corbin's more extensive treatment in *SEI*.

12. Eliade, "Androgyne," *The Encyclopedia of Religion*, ed. Mircea Eliade with Wendy Doniger O'Flaherty (New York: Macmillan, 1986), 1:276–281, at 280.

13. On this theme in the theosophy of the classical Kabbalah, see the magisterial work of Elliot R. Wolfson, *Through a Speculum That Shines* (Princeton, N.J.: Princeton University Press, 1994).

14. *TO*, 99. Eliade praised Séraphita in the French version of *Yoga*, but I have not been able to locate this statement in the English translation. See the citation in Gaston Bachelard, an admirer both of Corbin and of Eliade, who also studied *Séraphita*. Bachelard, "Séraphîta," in *Le Droit de Rêver* (Paris: PUF, 1970), 125–133.

15. See chapter 2 "Toward the Origins of History of Religions," in this book.

16. *Yoga*, 271.

17. *OWCF*, 111. This phrase is used to describe ostensible "Phibionite sex rituals."

18. *TC*, 183–185. Commenting here on a review of two studies of Balzac in the Parisian journal *Combat* 4 February 4 1965, Corbin prefers the position taken by the fascist ideologue and literary critic Maurice Bardèche. He begins by invoking (without explicit attribution) C. G. Jung's notion of being stuck on the ground floor, in reference to those limited by "sociology, demography and the economy." 185. By constrast, Bardèche's position (according to Corbin) is that Balzac was not a function of the nineteenth century but that the nineteenth century was a function of Balzac: "Balzac is the creator, he who embraces in his work the society of the nineteenth century as well as that of other centuries. Society is his creation. It cannot do without him." 185. *Combat* was the journal in which Eliade published his glowing review of Jung's *Response to Job*, which in turn stimulated Corbin's subsequent review of the same book.

19. The sex or sexlessness of angels has been addressed variously by Stuart Schneiderman, *An Angel Passes* (New York: New York University Press, 1988), and by Lutz Niethammer, *Posthistoire*, 112–116.

20. Corbin, *En Islam Iranien II*, 324, emphasis in original, my translation.

21. A useful discussion can be found in Lynn R. Wilkinson, *The Dream of an Absolute Language: Emmanual Swedenborg and French Literary Culture* (Albany: State University of New York Press, 1996), esp. 171–184. A full study of the influence of *Séraphita* seems to be in order. To take yet another example, there is evidence that Arnold Schoenberg's invention of the twelve-tone system of composition was inspired by his reading of Séraphita. A fascinating reading of this influence is found in Dore Ashton, "Arnold Schoenberg's Ascent," in *A Fable of Modern Art* (London: Thames and Hudson, 1980), 96–120. I found this reference in the illuminating article by Joscelyn Godwin, "Music and the Hermetic Tradition," in *Gnosis and Hermeticism from Antiquity to Modern Times*, ed. Roelof can den Broek and Wouter J. Hanegraaff (Albany: State University of New York, 1997), 183–197, at 190.

22. *SEI*, 79. Corbin further notes that "more precisely, in Swedenborgian terms, the spiritual constiution of the androgyne persists in the celestial *couple*, and that is why it is said that the two members of that couple are a single angel, each being the 'reciprocal' of the other" (emphasis in original). In any case, *Séraphita* did have some other reception, including Baudelaire, many turn-of-the-century Russian mystics, and even the great Soviet filmmaker Sergei Eisenstein. See V. W. Ivanow, "The Semiotic Theory of Carnival as the Inversion of Bipolar Opposites," in *Carnival!* ed. Thomas Seebok (Berlin: Mouton, 1984), 11–35, at 16, for Eisenstein's *Séraphita*, and 24 n. 12, on the popularity of *Séraphita* in Russia. For Baudelaire, see Nicolæ Babuts, "Baudelaire et les anges de Swedenborg," *Romance Notes* 21 (1981): 309–312. Swedenborg was certainly taken up by various friends and associates of the Historians of Religion, including Ernst Jünger. See Martin Meyer, "Afterward," English translation of Ernst Jünger, *Aladdin's Problem* (London: Quartet Encounters, 1992), 129. For more on the influence of Swedenborg on Balzac and his contemporaries see Wilkinson, *The Dream of an Absolute Language*.

23. For the romantic androgyne, one may consult the classic by M. H. Abrams, *Natural Supernaturalism* (London: Oxford University Press, 1971). Extensive discussions of androgyny in the esoteric traditions are provided in Antoine Faivre, *Access to Western Esotericism*, especially the essay, "Love and Androgyny in Franz von Baader," 201–275. Of various exemplary specialized studies in recent years, special notice must be may of Elliot R. Wolfson, "Woman—The Feminine as Other in Theosophic Kabbalah: Some Philosophical Observations on the Divine Androgyne," in *The Other in Jewish Thought and History: Constructions of Jewish Culture and Identity* ed. Lawrence J. Silberstein and Robert L. Cohn (New York: New York University Press, 1994), 166–205.

24. Ivanow, "Carnival as Inversion of Opposites," at 16.

25. Walter Benjamin, "Agesilaus Santander" (second and final version, Ibiza, 13 August 1933), translated in Gershom Scholem, "Walter Benjamin and his Angel," in *OJJC*, 198–236, at 207.

26. Ibid., 216.

27. Ibid., 229.

28. Ibid., 230.

29. The first was in the final sentence of his first Eranos essay, "Kabbalah and Myth," delivered at Ascona in 1949. The second was in the final pages of the final essay of *On the Mystical Shape of the Godhead*, titled "*Tselem*: The Concept of the Astral Body." This was the sole one of the six lectures in this collection which was not originally delivered at Eranos. It was first published in the original German version of *Von der Mystischen Gestalt der Gottheit* in 1962. The use of "perfect nature" there (*MSG*, 256–257, with reference to Corbin), thus long preceded its application to Benjamin in the 1972 essay, "Walter Benjamin und sein Engel."

30. The best discussion of the origins of the Baphomet myth in the writings of Joseph von Purgstall-Hammer is in Peter Partner, *The Murdered Magicians: The Templars and Their Myth* (New York: Barnes and Noble, 1987), 138–145. Hammer's theory, in Partner's words, was that of "an androgynous deity called Baphomet or Achamoth, which had from early times been the patron of a phallic cult requiring orgies for its celebration." 141.

31. Klossowski wrote a letter to Eliade dated 7 June 1952, praising "Andronic," Eliade's novella concerning an androgyne. See *Mircea Eliade*, ed. C. Tacou (Paris: Cahiers l'Herne, 1978), 284. See also Jeffrey Mehlman, "Literature and Hospitality: Klossowski's Hamann," *Studies in Romanticism* 22 (1983): 329–347, at 333, for Klossowski's high praise of Corbin's translation of Hamann's *Aesthetica in Nuce*. This latter text also had a profound effect on Scholem.

32. Their shared themes included orientalism, androgyny, Templarism, gnosis, and antinomianism.

33. Gustav Meyrink, *Der Engel vom westlichen Fenster* (Leipzig and Zürich: Grethlein, 1927), recently translated into English as *The Angel of the West Window*, trans. Mike Mitchell (Riverside, Calif.: Dedalus/Ariadne, 1995). Julius Evola translated this novel into Italian in 1949. Elsewhere Evola suggested that he believed in the Baphomet story, which plays a central role in *The Angel of the West Window*. See Evola, *The Mystery of the Grail*, 135 n. 7. The shared inspiration for Evola and Eliade, René Guénon, wrote to Evola on 13 June 1949, con-

cerning the possible "initiatory" secrets in Meyrink's fiction. See Julius Evola, *René Guenon: A Teacher for Modern Times*, transl. G. Stucco (Edmonds, Wash.: Sure Fire Press, 1994), 32.

34. Scholem's meeting has now been further detailed in the second edition of the German translation of *FBJ*, *Von Berlin nach Jerusalem: Jugenderinnerungen* (Frankfurt am Main: Judischer Verlag, 1994), 163–167, which incorporates late additions he inserted into the Hebrew version. For Eliade's meeting Scholem see *JI*, 111–112. Eliade refers to his pleasure in "rereading" Meyrink twenty-four years later. See *JIII*, 176.

35. He cited *Gustav Meyrink*, ed. Yvonne Caroutch (Paris: Cahier de l'Herne, 1976), in *Paradoxe*, 161 n. 46. This volume includes a piece by Eliade (234).

36. One novel that purported to articulate the Baphomet myth was written by Lawrence Durrell, *Monsieur, or, The Prince of Darkness* (London: Faber, 1976). See *TO*, 98–100, on the literary treatments of the androgyne in the nineteenth century. For the influence of *Séraphita* on occult novelist Sar Péladan (1858–1918), see Christopher McIntosh, *Eliaphas Lévi and the French Occult Revival* (New York: Samuel Weisner, 1972), 165–166.

37. Scholem snubbed Crowley during the latter's lifetime: "No words need be wasted on the subject of Crowley's 'Kabbalistic' writings" *MTJM*, 353 n. 3. The Jerusalem philologist later called the magician's knowledge of Kabbalah "infinitesimal." *Kabbalah*, 203. Eliade associated Crowley with Julius Evola, in terms of their emphasis on "noninhibited sexuality." See *OWCF*, 126 n. 29. The Historian of Religions enthused at some length on reading Crowley's biography. See *JI*, 176–177.

38. *TO*, 78.

39. It will be recalled that Corbin's paean to Jung was titled "Sophia Éternelle," on which see chapter 12, "Psychoanalysis in Reverse," in this book.

40. *SBCE*, 66–67, emphasis in original. See also his "Sufism and Sophia," *VM*, 217–231.

41. *MSG*, 256.

42. *MLIS*, 15. He also also dealt with Prometheus as man of light in *Avicenna*, 232–233.

43. Hans Blumenberg, *Work on Myth*, trans. Robert M. Wallace (Cambridge, Mass.: MIT Press, 1995), 530.

44. The last phrase is Blumenberg's (*Work on Myth*, 529). Compare Goethe's "extraordinary saying" with Shahrastani's Gayomartians, "If I had an adversary, what would he be like?" in Corbin, "Cyclical Time," 135.

45. Corbin, "The Dramatic Element Common to the Gnostic Cosmogonies of the Religions of the Book," originally published in *Cahiers de l'Université Saint Jean de Jérusalem* 5:141–173. I use the unattributed English translation in *Studies in Comparative Religion* 14 (1980): 191–221, at 212.

46. Corbin, "The Dramatic Element."

47. Ibid., 211–212.

48. Jung, *The Portable Jung*, 520.

49. Jung, *Memories, Dreams, Reflections* 341.

50. This dictum forms the basis of the illuminating recent volume by Jaroslav Pelikan, *Faust the Theologian* (New Haven, Conn.: Yale University Press, 1995).

51. Blumenberg, *Work on Myth*, 533.

52. The Androgyne was both a symbol and a *coincidentia oppositorum*. These topics have been addressed in chapters 13 and 4, respectively, of this book.

53. He makes the point both in *OKS* and in *OMSG*. I provide detailed analysis in chapter 12 "Psychoanalysis in Reverse," in this book.

54. *CI*, 215; *SEI*, 4.

55. For a substantial gathering of traditions on this mytheme, see Ernst Benz, *Adam: der Mythos vom Urmenschen* (Munich: O. W. Barth, 1955).

56. Marxism, as Martin Jay has shown exhaustively in his *Marxism and Totality* (Cambridge, Mass.: Polity, 1984), lost its claims on totality. They became, so to speak, up for grabs.

57. See, for details, chapter 2, "Toward the Origins of History of Religions" in this book.

58. Gilbert Durand, "La pensée d'Henry Corbin et le Temple Maçonnique," *Travaux de Villard de Honnecourt* 3 (1981): 173–182: "Au cours d'une conversation, en 1966, sous les Cèdres d'Ascona, alors que je lui demandais si'il n'avait été incliné à entrer dans une *tariqâ* musulmane et ne me répondant pas directement, il me disait : < C'est une chose difficile lorsque tu n'es pas *élève* dans le contexte religieux et culturel, mais sais-tu ce qu'un Shayk m'a répondu à la même question que tu me poses ? Ce serait très facile, m'a-t-il dit, si tu étais déjà initié par les Francs Maçons par exemple >. C'était la première fois que nous prononcions le mot de <Franc-Maçonnerie.>" 175.

59. See the classic study by George Simmel, "The Sociology of Secrecy and Secret Societies," *American Journal of Sociology* 11 (1905–1906): 441–498.

60. Ivanow, "Carnival as Inversion of Opposites," 16.

61. *MIJ*, 126–127.

62. Cited in Ivanow, "Carnival as Inversion of Opposites," 16.

63. Martin Buber, *Eclipse of God* (New York: Harper, 1952), 89.

64. Ibid.

65. Watts, *The Two Hands of God: The Myths of Polarity* (Toronto: Collier Books, 1969), 38.

66. *OL*, 121.

67. Ibid., 187.

68. *MDM*, 174.

69. *J II*, 314, emphasis in original.

70. Jung, *Response to Job*, 561, 566, 611.

71. Benjamin, "Theses on the Philosophy of History," in *Illuminations*, 259. In this famous passage, Benjamin meditates on Klee's "Angelus Novus." The section begins with a quatrain from Scholem's poem on that Angel. For more on this point, see chapter 6 "Aesthetic Solutions," in this book.

72. For important discussions of the seminar, see Aschheim, *The Nietzsche Legacy in Germany* (Berkeley: University of California Press, 1992), 258–262, and Bishop, *The Dionysian Self*, 298–321.

73. For the project of "reversal" see chapter 12, "Psychoanalysis in Reverse," in this book.

74. Corbin, "The Time of Eranos," in *Man and Time*, xiv.

75. To take one example: insofar as they apparently felt empowered to link such disparate phenomena as Faust and Séraphita, Baphomet, and "perfect na-

ture," they seem to have been drawing on an esoteric theory of correspondences. I thank my student Jeremy Walton for this observation and for his acute editing of this essay.

Chapter 14
Defeating Evil from Within: Comparative Perspectives on "Redemption through Sin"

1. The publishing and translation history of this essay are provided in the new edition of the German version, which has appeared as *Judaica V* of the Suhrkamp edition of Scholem, edited and translated by Michael Brocke (Frankfurt am Main: Suhrkamp Verlag, 1992). In the present essay I cite Hillel Halkin's English translation printed in *MIJ*.

2. Nathan Rotenstreich, "Symbolism and Transcendence: On Some Philosophical Aspects of Gershom Scholem's Opus," *Review of Metaphysics* 31 (1977–78): 604–614, at 604.

3. "Redemption through Sin," *MIJ*, 89, 110.

4. Joseph Dan has observed that Scholem "contributed significantly to the integration of Jewish studies into the humanities as a whole as well as of Jewish mysticism into the general fields of religion and mysticism. He did not accomplish this by drawing parallels between Jewish mystics and Christian and Moslem ones; in fact, he very seldom did that." *Gershom Scholem and the Mystical Dimension of Jewish History* (New York: New York University Press, 1988), 27. However much weight one puts on the judgment "seldom" here, it is the case that Scholem suceeded in the "integration" of which Dan properly speaks. He did so by means both of a general conception of religion and an application of comparisons.

5. *OK*, 11. He also refers to this work as intended for historians of religions in his "Author's Preface to the First (German) Edition" (xv) and in the volume's final paragraph (475).

6. Scholem, "Franz Rosenzweig and His Book *The Star of Redemption*," translated in *The Philosophy of Franz Rosenzweig*, ed. Paul Mendes-Flohr (Hanover, N.H.: University Press of New England, 1988), 20–42, at 27. For a more general discussion of their relationship, see Michael Brocke, "Franz Rosenzweig und Gerhard Gershom Scholem," in *Juden in der Weimarer Republik*, ed. Walter Grab and Julius H. Schoeps (Stuttgart: Burg Verlag), 127–153.

7. Scholem, *Walter Benjamin: The Story of a Friendship*, 136. For more on his concept of "experience" see chapter 12, "Psychoanalysis in Reverse," in this book.

8. Scholem was already corresponding with his future Eranos colleagues in the 1930s. For example, he was already in correspondence with Henry Corbin in 1937: see the letter of Scholem reproduced in *Cahier l'Herne: Henry Corbin*, 332. On phenomenology see chapter 1, "Eranos and the 'History of Religions,'" in this book.

9. *MIJ*, 34

10. *OKS*, 89, emphasis in original. See also "Star of David," *MIJ*, 257.

11. *OKS*, 22.

12. Ibid., 31.

13. "Redemption through Sin," *MIJ*, 87

14. Eliade's magnum opus, *Yoga*, was subtitled *Immortality and Freedom*. Its last sentence reads, "Everything depends upon what is meant by freedom" 364.

15. Ibid., 84, emphasis added. Compare this with Benjamin, "Surrealism": "This is the moment to embark on a work." 184.

16. One wonders to what extent this "attraction and *fascination*" pertained to Jacob Frank, whom Scholem called "the most hideous and *uncanny* figure in the whole history of Jewish Messianism." *MTJM*, 308. Scholem retrospectively claimed Frankism as anticipatory of Stalinism. "Irving Howe Interviews Gershom Scholem: 'The Only Thing in My Life I Have Never Doubted Is the Existence of God,'" 53–57, at 56.

17. *MTJM*, 315; *OKS*, 13.

18. Scholem, *Walter Benjamin*, 136. Indeed, in the very final pages of the final version of *OK*, speaking of antinomianism in *Sefer Temuna*, one sees the theme replayed: "One is amazed at the degree of freedom with which Kabbalistic speculation attempted to combine its conception of the deity with a new understanding of the world, not only as a natural or cosmic entity, but also a historical one." 474.

19. "Redemption through Sin," *MIJ*, 136. Scholem saw Benjamin only once more, for five days in Paris, in 1938.

20. Apollinaire is cited in *The Marquis de Sade: The Complete Justine, Philosophy in the Bedroom and other Writings*, comp. and trans. Richard Seaver and Austryn Wainhouse (New York: Grove Press, 1965), xiii.

21. Klossowski, "The Marquis de Sade and the Revolution," Tuesday, 7 February 1939, in *The College of Sociology, 1937–1939*, ed. Denis Hollier and trans. Betsy Wing (Minneapolis: University of Minnesota Press, 1988), 218–233.

22. On Klossowski see chapter 13, "Uses of the Androgyne in the History of Religions," in this book.

23. Scholem, *Du Frankisme au Jacobinisme*, Marc Bloch Lectures (Paris: Seuil, 1981). Jacob Taubes was one of the few to object to this argument: "The death of a Frankist adventurer at the guillotine of the French Revolution does not secure a link between Sabbatian Messianism and the *Aufklärung*" (Jacob Taubes, "Scholem's theses on Messianism reconsidered," *Social Science Information* 21 4/5 [1982]: 665–675, at 672).

24. The connection between Klossowski and Scholem is not so remote as one might imagine. Klossowski knew Benjamin in Paris, and translated his "L'Oeuvre d'art à l'époque de sa reproduction méchanisée," in *Zeitschrift für Sozialforschung* 5 (1936), ed. Horkheimer and Adorno. For a penetrating investigation of the links between Klossowski's reading of Benjamin and his antinomian Sadism, see Mehlman, *Walter Benjamin for Children*. And Horkeimer and Adorno famously linked de Sade to the Enlightenment in "Excursus II. *Juliette* or Enlightment and Morality," *Dialectic of Enlightenment* (New York: Continuum, 1972), 81–120.

25. "The conjecture is that underlying the Revolution, there was a sort of moral conspiracy whose aim would have been to compel a humanity that was at loose ends, having lost its sense of social necessity, to become aware of its guilt. And this conspiracy was well served by two methods: an exoteric method practiced by Joseph de Maistre in his sociology of original sin and an infinitely com-

plex, esoteric method that *consists in disguising itself as atheism in order to combat atheism, in speaking the language of moral skepticism in order to combat moral skepticism, with the sole aim of giving back to reason everything this method can, in order to show its worthlessness.*" Klossowski, "The Marquis de Sade and the Revolution," *The College of Sociology*, 222 and 230, emphasis in the original.

26. *MIJ*, 126–127.

27. Thus, in his essay "Religious Authority and Mysticism," Scholem describes the antinomian character of Frank's heresy as deriving from "man's contact with the primal source of life": "Utterly free, fettered by no law or authority, this 'Life' never ceases to produce forms and to destroy what it has produced. It is the anarchic promiscuity of all living things. Into this bubbling cauldron, this continuum of destruction, the mystic plunges. For Frank, anarchic destruction represented all the Luciferian radiance, all the positive tones and overtones, of the word 'Life.'" *OKS*, 28. Scholem's interest in Frank was clearly part of a larger phenomenon in the 1930s. See Chone Shmeruk, "The Frankist Novels of Isaac Bashevis Singer." 12.

28. Frank appears in the last sentence of the first paragraph of "The Messianic Idea in Kabbalism" (*MIJ*, 37); the last sentence of the last paragraph of "The Crisis of Tradition" (*MIJ*, 77); and throughout the last section of "Redemption through Sin." Finally, as previously noted, at the end of his life Scholem wrote *Du Frankisme au Jacobinisme.*

29. "Prior to the French Revolution the historical conditions were lacking which might have caused this upheaval to break forth in the form of an open struggle for social change . . . but it would be mistaken to conclude from this that Sabbatianism did not permanently affect the outward course of Jewish history . . . beneath the surface of lawlessness, antinomianism, and catastrophic negation, powerful constructive impulses were at work, and these, I maintain, it is the duty of the historian to uncover." "Redemption through Sin," *MIJ*, 84.

30. Ibid., 137.

31. Klossowski, *College of Sociology*, 228; see also 418 n. 14 for his other writings on Fourier. And when Klossowski, years later, wrote a brief memoir on Benjamin, titled "Between Marx and Fourier," he again evoked Benjamin's championing of the Fourier's phalansterian "free play of passions." See *On Walter Benjamin*, ed. Smith, (Cambridge, Mass.: MIT Press, 1988; reprint, 1991), 368.

32. Benjamin, "Fourier, or the Arcades," in "Paris, Capital of the Nineteenth Century," *Reflections*, 148. Note also that Benjamin saw Baudelaire's attempted recuperation of *Erfahrung* as mediated through Fourier: Benjamin, "On Some Motifs in Baudelaire," *Illuminations*, 183.

33. *OKS*, 28.

34. Klossowski, *Sade My Neighbor*, trans. Alphonso Lingis (Evanston, Ill.: Northwestern University Press, 1991), 100.

35. "Redemption through Sin," *MIJ*, 132–133.

36. Mehlman, *Walter Benjamin for Children*, 42, emphasis added. See the critical passages on "historical psychology" in *OKS* (made up exclusively of lectures delivered at Eranos), esp. 2, 3, 33, 106, and 204.

37. *MTJM*, 316 and 420 n. 61; Klossowski, *Sade My Neighbor*, 62. Klossowski bemoans a permanant hiatus of interdictions much like that conjured by the cen-

sorious Philip Rieff: "On various sides, presently in the endless struggle for power, are two apparently opposing cadres: 1) rationalizers of technological reason; 2) orgiasts of revolutionary sensuality; these cadres converge in the cult of violence. By 'cult of violence' I mean that openness to possibility in which nothing remains true; in this original of cults, all oppositions are welcomed as if life could be an endless experience of political, technological or interpretative breakthroughs, against orders recognized only for purposes of disestablishment." In *Fellow Teachers* (New York: Harper and Row, 1973), 20–21.

38. See Michael Richardson, "Sociology on the Razor's Edge: Configurations of the Sacred at the College of Sociology," *Theory, Culture and Society* 9 (1992): 27–44, at 35. While Richardson would seem to suggest that this "sacred of the Left Hand," sacred of transgression, was somehow meant to counteract fascism, it may be noted that the fascist theorist of religion, Julius Evola, used the "Way of the Left Hand" to refer to his own brand of fascist spirituality. See, for example, Evola, *Explorations: Hommes et Problèmes* (Puiseaux: Pardès, 1989), especially the essays "Sur la 'Voie de la main gauche'" (141–146), and "Dionysos et la 'voie de la main gauche'" (97–104).

39. See *The College of Sociology*.

40. Horkheimer and Adorno, *Dialectic of Enlightenment*, 105. The Critical Theorists, in this instance, seem not to have recognized the reactionary implications of festival. See Umberto Eco, "The frames of comic 'freedom'," in *Carnival!* 1–9, at 6: "Carnival can exist only as an *authorized* transgression (which in fact represents a blatant case of *contradictio in adjecto* or of happy *double binding*—capable of curing instead of producing neuroses). If the ancient, religious carnival was limited in time, the modern mass-carnival is limited in space: it is reserved for certain places, certain streeets, or framed by the television screen. In this sense, comedy and carnival are not instances of real transgressions: on the contrary, they represent paramount examples of law reinforcement. They remind us of the existence of the law." Also see Ivanow, "Carnival as Inversion of Opposites," 11–34.

41. I would like to thank Professor Bruce Lincoln for providing me with this information.

42. Details can be found in McGuire, *Bollingen*, 76–78.

43. de Rougemont, *The Devil's Share*, 77. Announced in the first catalogue of the Bollingen Series, that of 1944. For his centrality to Mary Mellon and the origins of Bollingen, see McGuire, *Bollingen*, 76–78.

44. On the hidden saint, see "The Thirty-Six Just Men," *MIJ*, 251–257.

45. Reported by de Rougemont, in *Mélanges offerts à Henry Corbin*. (Tehran: Imperial Iranian Academy of Philosophy, 1977) 539–547. Emil Cioran, with Eliade in mind, drew the following conclusion: "We are all of us, and Eliade in the fore, *would-have-been* believers; we are all religious minds without religion." "Beginnings of a Friendship," in *Myths and Symbols, Studies in Honor of Mircea Eliade*, ed. Charles Long and Joseph Kitagawa (Chicago: University of Chcago, 1969), 413–414—while Scholem said of himself that "my secularism is not secular," *JJC*, 46. In short, the cultural Sabbatianism under discussion may more generally be seen as a shared strategy to "save" tradition in a post-traditional age, *by any means necessary*, so to speak.

46. McGuire accurately characterizes Scholem as "the most independent-spirited of the Eranos regulars." *Bollingen*, p. 152.

47. There was both an elective affinity and a genetic filiation between the Eranos group and the figures discussed by Lutz Niethammer in *Posthistoire*. Figures studied by Niethammer associated with those of the Eranos group include Arnold Gehlen, who strongly influenced Adolf Portmann, a leader at Eranos. Walter Benjamin overlapped both groups, and Martin Heidegger influenced both to a substantial extent. A key figure in the *Posthistoire* discussion is Ernst Jünger, who edited the journal *Antaios* with Eliade. Apposite to the present inquiry, Jünger once asserted the following, in justifying the use of drugs on the part of a certain élite: "But to dabble in drugs you need to be intelligent, if you do not master them, they will dominate you, and destroy you," as cited in Nigel Jones, "The Writer as Warrior. An Encounter with Ernst Jünger," *London Magazine* 23, no. 4 (1983): 62–68, at 67. Here again "forbidden" activities are permitted, but only to "the few."

48. Gerardus Van der Leeuw, "Primordial Time and Final Time," in *Man and Time*, ed. Joseph Campbell (New York: Pantheon, 1957), 327. Delivered at the 1949 Eranos meeting, the occasion on which Scholem and Corbin made their first appearances at Eranos, also the occasion when Scholem delivered his programmatic paper, "Kabbalah and Myth." In the eventual English version of the latter essay, Scholem concluded by citing this paper of van der Leeuw (*OKS*, p. 117).

49. Georges Bataille, *Death and Sensuality: A Study of Eroticism and the Taboo* (New York: publisher 1962), 30–31. Later in the same work Bataille clarifies this theory of religion: "[I]n the Christian system what I call transgression is called sin. . . . Take first the death on the Cross: it is a sacrifice, a sacrifice whose victim is God himself. But although the sacrifice redeems us, although the Church sings its paradoxical Felix Culpa! happy error—to the underlying fault, that which redeems us is also that which ought not to have taken place." 259. Corbin spoke of the " 'transgressive' rigor of symbolism" *CIS*, 90.

50. Hugo Rahner, preface to *Greek Myths and Christian Mystery*, English translation (New York. Harper and Row, 1963), xiii, emphasis added.

51. Corbin's version is closely analogous: "Science the liberator has created an instrument of death. But it is my conviction that this despair conceals within itself the redemption of the West. 'Only the weapon that made it will ever cure the wound' says Parzifal in Wagner's drama." In *The Concept of Comparative Philosophy*, 28–29. Compare this redemptive despair with a remark Adorno borrowed from C. D. Grabbe: "For nothing but despair can save us (*Denn nichts als nur Verzweiflung kann uns retten*)," cited by Martin Jay in *Adorno*, 82.

52. See chapter 4, "Coincidentia oppositorum," in this book.

53. This is on the authority of the Catholic theologian Josef Pieper: "Before the Russian commission he maintained that this allegedly Nazi past would have to be understood after the pattern of von Pettenkofer's experiment. The examining officer, although apparently an educated man, naturally had no idea what he was talking about. Around the beginning of the century Max von Pettenkofer, a German scientist, put forward the thesis that infectious diseases were not caused by the bacillus alone; what was decisive was the human being's susceptibility to

disease. To prove this thesis, he drank a glass of water containing a whole culture of the cholera bacillus—and, indeed, remained in good health. Carl Schmitt's conclusion was this: 'You see, I did the same thing. I have drunk the Nazi bacillus, but it did not infect me!'—which, of course, if it were true, would really and truly have made his conduct inexcusable." Josef Pieper, *No One Could Have Known: An Autobiography: The Early Years 1904–1945* (1979; English translation, San Francisco: Ignatius Press, 1987) 176. In correspondence with Schmitt, Benjamin acknowledged the jurist's influence on him. See the literature discussed in Lutz P. Koepnick, "The Spectacle, the *Trauerspiel*, and the Politics of Resolution: Benjamin Reading the Baroque Reading Weimar," *Critical Inquiry* 22 (1996): 268–291, esp. 280–286. Schmitt also enjoyed, for a time, a profound interaction with another friend of Scholem, Leo Strauss. See Heinrich Meier, *Carl Schmitt and Leo Strauss: The Hidden Dialogue* (Chicago: University of Chicago Press, 1995).

54. "The actual problem of our age is to find the method to carry (the values belonging to Tantrism) into effect. This method, justly compared to the the the 'riding on the back of a tiger,' may be summed up in this principle: 'In order to obtain freedom one must employ those same forces which have led to the downfall." Evola, "What Tantrism Means to Modern Western Civilization," *East and West* (Rome) 1, no. 1 (1950): 28–32, at 29. Similarly: "Tantrism has foretold the phase of the last age [Kali Yuga], whose essential traits—those of an epoch of dissolution—can incontrovertibly be recognized in so many events and trends of our day and age. With this in mind, Tantrism has sanctioned the expiration of traditional spiritual forms that in prvious epochs presupposed a different existential situation and a different human type. Tantrism also sought out new forms and new paths that might prove efficacious even in the 'dark age' and it tried to implement the realization of the same ideal of other epochs, namely, the awakening and the activation of the dimension of transcendence within mankind . . . We may well say that the essence of the way to be followed in the dark age is summed up in the saying 'riding the tiger.'" *The Yoga of Power: Tantra, Shakti and the Secret Way*, trans. Guido Stucco (Rochester, Vt.: Inner Traditions, 1992), 189.

55. "Whoever seeks to avoid betraying the bliss which tradition still promises in some of its images and possibilities buried beneath its ruins must abandon that tradition which turns possibilities and meanings into lies. Only that which inexorably denies tradition may once again retreive it." Adorno, "On Tradition," (1966) translated in *Telos* 74 (1992–1993): 82.

56. *OPJM*, 5.

57. Scholem was speaking here (*OK*, 474) of the medieval tract *Sefer Temunah*, but one may justifiably read this ostensible gloss as an historiosophic confession.

58. Benjamin, "Surrealism," in *Reflections*, 184.

Chapter 15
On the Suspension of the Ethical

1. One of his most explicit statements, perhaps, is his contribution to Eliade's Festschrift, *Myths and Symbols: Studies in Honor of Mircea Eliade*, ed. Joseph Kitagawa and Charles Long (Chicago: University of Chicago Press, 1969), titled

"On Sin and Punishment. Some Remarks Concerning Biblical and Rabbinical Ethics," 163–179. His fullest historical study is "Gut und Böse in der Kabbala," *Eranos-Jahrbuch* 30 (1961): 29–67, translated in *MSG*, 56–88.

2. For his alternative, "the dialectics of continuity and revolt" see Avraham Shapiro, introduction to *OPJM*, trans. Jeffrey M. Green; it bears that title (xi–xix). Scholem's statement is found in *FBJ*, 166.

3. *A Kierkegaard Anthology*, ed. Robert Bretall (Princeton, N.J.: Princeton University Press, 1946), 129 ff. Kierkegaard, one recalls, listened to the late Schelling's lectures in Berlin.

4. Martin Buber, *Eclipse of God* (New York: Harper and Row, 1952; reprint, 1957), 113–121.

5. The title of Baeck's contribution at Eranos, published in *Eranos-Jahrbuch* 15 (1947). For more, see chapter 12, "Psychoanalysis in Reverse," in this book.

6. See the discussion of the anti-existentialist idea" in chapter 3, "Tautegorical Sublime: Gershom Scholem and Henry Corbin in Conversation," in this book.

7. *TC*, 338.

8. Martin Green, *Mountain of Truth* (Hanover, N.H.: University Press of New England, for Tufts University Press, 1986), passim.

9. Ibid.

10. For an excellent analysis of many aspects of this claim, see Bishop, "The Mystic Dionysos: Nietzsche, Jung and the Death of God," in *The Dionysian Self*, 323–363.

11. *MIJ*, 338. On the other hand, Scholem certainly expressed reservations about Nietzsche. "None of the exegetes of religion in the previous century—Feuerbach, Marx, Kierkegaard, and Nietzsche—succeeded in explaining the basic concept of Torah, 'the image of God,' an idea which is simple yet earth-shaking in its profundity." *OPJM*, 164. For more on Scholem's early Nietzscheanism, see Herbert Kopp-Oberstebrink, "Unzeitgemäße Betrachtungen zu Nietzsche contra jüdische Nietzscheanismen. Ein Kapitel aus der intellektuellen Frühgeschichte Gershom Scholems," in *Jüdischer Nietzscheanismus*, ed. Werner Stegmaier and Daniel Krochmalnik (Berlin: Walter de Gruyter, 1997), 90–105.

12. *MLIS*, 128. Compare "Divine Epiphany," 158–159. It is rather remarkable that Corbin was able to, as it were, accommodate the Nietzschean readings both of Jung and Heidegger, surely his two primary sources of inspiration for understanding Nietzsche. Jung's most recent biographer, Frank McLynn, notes that it was "a matter of intellectual pride that he [Jung] alone truly understood Nietzsche," and that he accordingly "detested" Heidegger's "assumption of the mantle of Nietzsche." Frank McLynn, *Carl Gustav Jung: A Biography* (New York: St. Martin's Press, 1997), 453.

13. *MR*, 95.

14. See Harold Bloom, *Omens of the Millennium* (New York: Riverhead Books, 1996). The only fair way to read Bloom, perhaps, is to misread him. In the present context, I read Bloom's latest work—in which Corbin, Eliade, and Scholem are among the most elevated sources—against its intended grain.

15. Corbin, "Divine Epiphany," 159. And see chapter 11 "The Chiliastic Practice of Islamic Studies" in this book, for more examples from the corpus of Corbin.

16. *Q*, 64, emphasis added.

17. Eliade, *Zalmoxis*, 250.

18. "Crisis and Renewal," *Q*, 64.

19. Eliade downplayed his debt to Nietzsche's "eternal recurrence." See *CH*, 146.

20. Possible Nietzschean influences may now be usefully considered in the light of the essays gathered in *Nietzsche and Jewish Culture*, ed. Jacob Golomb (New York: Routledge, 1997).

21. *HRI* 2, 374.

22. *Eranos-Jahrbuch* 43 (1974). His last visit in 1979 was the occasion for a retrospective talk, but not a lecture per se.

23. This was in his 1957 "Religiöse Autorität und Mystik," published in *Eranos-Jahrbuch* 26 (1957).

24. Scholem's footnote: Cf. "Religiöse Autorität und Mystik," *Eranos-Jahrbuch* 26 (1957): 248, and my book *Zur Kabbala und ihrer Symbolik*, 16–17.

25. Emphasis added. *Eranos-Jahrbuch* 43 (1974).

26. For discussion and translation of this letter see Lawrence Rosenwald, "For and Against Gershom Scholem," *Prooftexts* 14 (1994): 285–297, at 296. For a relevant discussion of the category nihilism see Löwith, *Martin Heidegger and European Nihilism*. See also the important comment made by Heidegger against nihilism in a 1936 lecture on Schelling. "The two men who, each in his own way, have introduced a countermovement to nihilism—Mussolini and Hitler—have learned from Nietzsche, each in an essentially different way." Cited by Otto Pöggeler in "Heidegger, Nietzsche, and Politics," in *The Heidegger Case: On Philosophy and Politics*, ed. Tom Rockmore and Joseph Margolis (Philadelphia: Temple University Press, 1992), 132.

27. Eliade, "Martin Heidegger," in *Symposion Heidegger*, ed. George Uscatescu (Madrid: Destin, 1971), 9. This was a Romanian émigré publication.

28. For now, see the discussion of Scholem and Heidegger in chapter 8, "Collective Renovatio," in this book. For Heidegger's thought on nihilism, see Martin Heidegger, *Nietzsche, Volume IV: Nihilism*, trans. Frank A. Capuzzi and ed. David Farrell Krell (San Francisco: Harper San Francisco, 1982; reprint, 1991).

29. Corbin, *Paradoxe*, 177–214.

30. Scholem, "The People of the Book," a lecture delivered in 1975, now translated in *OPJM*, 167–175, at 175.

31. For some intriguing remarks on the intellectual relationship between Puech and Corbin, see Faivre, *Accès de l'ésotérisme occidental II*, 243–245.

32. Corbin, "Pour l'anthropologie philosophique: un traité persan inédit de Suhrawardî d'Alep (d. 1191)," *Recherches philosophiques* 2 (1932–1933): 371 ff.; "La théologie dialectique et l'histoire," *Recherches philosophiques* 3 (1933): 250–284. Corbin also reviewed volumes by Wach, Brentano, Dilthey, and Bultmann in the latter issue (432–440).

33. Corbin, "Post-Scriptum biographique," 44.

34. Henri-Charles Puech, "Der Begriff der Erlösung im Manichäismus," *Eranos-Jahrbuch* 4 (1936); "La Gnose et le Temps," *Eranos-Jahrbuch* 20 (1955).

35. See *A I*, 116, 121, 134, 139, 148, 196, for Eliade's relations with Puech between 1946 and 1960.

36. Eliade, "Le problème du chamanisme" *Revue de l'histoire des religions*

131 (1946) pp. 5–52. See *A I*, 116, for the circumstances of its publication. Corbin cited this article favorably in 1951. See *VM*, 70 n. 74.

37. See Corbin's substantial book reviews in *Revue de l'histoire des religions* 153 (1958): 92–101, 264–66. Eliade published a review of *Das Doppelte Geschlecht* in the same issue.

38. Scholem, "Le mouvement sabbataïste en Pologne," *Revue de l'histoire des religions* 143 (1953): 30–90, 209–232; 144 (1953): 42–77; translated from Hebrew by Georges Vajda.

39. *Mélanges d'histoire des religions offerts à Henri-Charles Puech* (Paris: PUF, 1974). Corbin's contribution has been translated into English by Joseph Rowe as "A Shiite Liturgy of the Grail," *VM*, 173–204.

40. *HRI 2*, 374 n. 18.

41. See more in chapter 14, "Defeating Evil from Within: Comparative Perspectives on 'Redemption through Sin,' " in this book.

42. Carl Schmitt, *Political Theology* (Cambridge, Mass.: MIT Press, 1985), 5.

43. Ibid., 15, cited in John McCormick, *Carl Schmitt's Critique of Liberalism: Against Politics as Technology* (Cambridge: Cambridge University Press, 1997), 227.

44. Richard Wolin, "Carl Schmitt. The Conservative Revolutionary Habitus and the Aesthetics of Horror," *Political Theory* 20 (1992): 424–447, at 434. I thank Professor Wolin for sharing this and others of his articles with me.

45. For a first attempt to relate Scholem's thought to that of Schmitt see the provocative essay by Christoph Schmidt, "Ha-Teologia Ha-Politit shel Gershom Scholem," *Teoryah u-vikoret* 6 (1995): 149–160.

46. This is the thrust of the critique rendered by Phillip Rieff. See especially *The Triumph of the Therapeutic* (Harmondsworth: Penguin, 1966), and *Fellow Teachers* (London: Faber, 1975).

47. See chapter 14, "Defeating Evil from Within."

48. See the collection of his essays, *Magie, Mystik, Messianismus*, ed. Gary Smith (New York: Georg Olms Verlag, 1997).

49. R. J. Zwi Werblowsky, *Lucifer and Prometheus: A Study of Milton's Satan* (London: Routledge and Kegan Paul, 1952).

50. Gary Smith,"Über R. J. Zwi Werblowsky," in Werblowsky, *Magie, Mystik, Messianismus*, 9–10.

51. C. G. Jung, *Answer to Job* (Zurich: Rascher, 1952); first translated into English in London, 1954.

52. Corbin, "De l'Iran à Eranos," in *Cahier de l'Herne Henry Corbin*, 262.

53. Corbin, "Sophia Éternelle," in *La Revue de culture européenne* 3 (1955): 11–45.

54. See Jung, *Letters*, vol. 2, *1951–1961*.

55. Eliade, "Note sur Jung et l'Alchimie," *Le Disque Vert: C. G. Jung*, 95–109. Note also that the 1964 French edition of Jung's *Réponse à Job* (Paris: Buchet-Chastel) was printed with a "postface" by Corbin.

56. Ibid. 104.

57. Eliade, "Note sur Jung," 109.

58. Jung, *Response to Job*, 550.

59. Corbin, "Eranos," *Eranos-Jahrbuch* 31 (1962): 9–12, at 11.

60. Scholem, "Quelques remarques sur le mythe de la peine dans le judaisme," in *Le mythe de la peine*, ed. Enrico Castelli (Paris: Auber-Montaigne, 1967), 135–64 , at 158.

61. Eliade, *A II*, 162.

62. *MSG*, 87.

63. See chapter 12, "Psychoanalysis in Reverse," in this book, for his uses of the idea of "daring."

64. Letter of Gershom Scholem to Walter Benjamin, 1 August 1931, cited in Hans Mayer, "Walter Benjamin and Franz Kafka" in *On Walter Benjamin*, ed. Gary Smith (Cambridge, Mass: MIT Press, 1988), 198. Late in life Scholem spoke of an uncompleted metaphysical commentary on *The Book of Job* that he had written as a teenager. *JJC*, 19. In his contribution to Eliade's *Festschrift*, he asserted that "the Book of Job is not without reason the most provocative Biblical text; it is still extremely relevant today, and without it Judaism would not be what it is in the history of religion." "On Sin and Punishment. Some Remarks concerning Biblical and Rabbinical Ethics," *Myths and Symbols*, 170.

65. Letter of Gershom Scholem to Walter Benjamin, 9 July 1934, *Correspondence*, 122–125. See the poem, "With a Copy of Kafka's 'Trial,'" at 124.

66. *MSG*, 87, 211, 219, 226 on *Gilgul*; and 314 n.21.

67. Scholem wrote the following to George Lichtheim:

That you have never understood my position in regard to this question has only become clear to me from your imputed alternatives between theism and blasphemy. Apparently your interest in these affairs has been small, otherwise you would not have missed a poem of mine about Kafka's trial which was printed on the pages 611 and 612 in the letters of Benjamin, and whose central line refers to the fact that God cannot be defended; herewith my position in regard to blasphemy should be evidently demarcated. Never and nowhere have I held a different position. I grant myself the right to recommend you the reading of these verses, even if it happens a little too late. (*Briefe II*, 217)

68. Jung said that *Response to Job* was the only book of his that he would not rewrite. See Malcolm Welland, "Active Imagination in Jung's *Answer to Job*," *Studies in Religion* 26, no. 3 (1997): 297–308, at 297.

69. Buber, *Eclipse of God* 78–92. Buber replies to Jung's rejoinder is translated in this collection, 133–137 ("Supplement: Reply to C. G. Jung").

70. C. G. Jung, "Religion and Psychology: A Reply to Martin Buber," trans. R. F. C. Hull, *Spring: An Annual of Archetypal Psychology and Jungian Thought* (1973): 196–201.

71. Jung, *The Symbolic Life*, 662.

72. Willi Goetschel has noted the complicated character of Scholem's role here.

Unforgiving of deviation in some, [Scholem] could display patience with others. As Sparr notes, the vehemence with which Scholem fought Buber may well stem from unavowed affinity. The ire spent on Buber bears limp comparison with Scholem's participation at Jung's annual Eranos conference. Aggressive in a petty way with Buber, the complexly indirect, underhanded attitude vis-à-vis Jung and his circle shows the complicated role the personal aspect may have played in the case of what now is mistaken for a purely scholarly project. Willi Goetschel, "Review Essay: Scholem's Diaries, Letters, and New Literature on His Work," *The Germanic Review* 72 (1997): 77–91.

73. At other times, he seemed to blame the Holocaust even more directly on God. See for example *The Symbolic Life*, 665. In 1951, Jung's Israeli follower Erich Neumann responded to a draft version of *Antwort auf Hob* with approbation. "For me personally it is like an accusation sheet against God, who allowed six million of his people to be killed." Cited by his son Micha Neumann, "On the Relationship between Erich Neumann and C. G. Jung and the Question of Anti-Semitism," in *Lingering Shadows: Jungians, Freudians and Anti-Semitism*, ed. Aryeh Maidenbaum and Steven A. Martin (Boston: Shambhala, 1991), 273–289, at 286. Neumann, in contrast to Buber, was not offended by Jung's blaming the Holocaust, in a sense, on the God of the Jews.

74. See, for purposes of comparison, Ernst Jünger, "Rund um den Sinai," in *Essays VI: Fassungen I* (Erstdruck: Klett-Cotta, 1979), 475–502. This mythologization of Sinai, in a cosmic and astrological framework, can be compared to Corbin's notion of multiple Sinais. "Au-dessus de ce Sinaï, s'élèvent eu des hauteurs spirituelles insondables d'autres Sinaïs (ce pluriel ressemble à une insinuation visant le pluriel Élohim!)" *Paradoxe*, 65. Corbin here draws on Suhrawardi.

75. Jung insisted, "I am not a philosopher, merely an empiricist." *The Symbolic Life*, 727. By this he meant that he did no more than observe human experience.

76. Scholem, to be sure, insisted that tradition is by definition mediated. In his view, there can be no direct experience of the sacred after revelation. See his 1962 and 1968 Eranos lectures on "tradition" in *MIJ*, 49–78, 282–304.

77. Émile Durkheim, *Elementary Forms of the Religious Life*, trans. Joseph Swain (New York: Free Press, 1915), 239 n. 6.

78. See Steven M. Wasserstrom, "Sense and Senselessness in Religion: Reflections on Walter Burkert's *Creation of the Sacred*," *Religion* (forthcoming).

79. *OPJM*, 155.

80. Ibid., 37.

81. Ibid.

Conclusion

1. Although Religious Studies, in statistical terms, has boomed in the Postwar academy, one may ask, alas, whether it has played any substantial role in the major theoretical and disciplinary shifts of this dramatic moment in our larger intellectual lives.

2. "Akbar" refers to Al-Shaikh al-Akbar, "the Greatest Master," Ibn al-'Arabi. Seyyed Hossein Nasr has done more than anyone else to enshrine this view in the North American study of Islam.

3. It is usually unsaid that this mystocentric assumption derived from the mystical traditions themselves. This is therefore a traditional presupposition that

seems from the outset to have made its decision about the difficult issue of *identification and distance*. See the address of Scholem, "Identification und Distanz."

4. See the apt polemic of Bernd Radtke, "Between Projection and Suppression. Some Considerations concerning the Study of Sufism," in Fred de Jong, ed., *Shi'a Islam, Sects and Sufism* (Utrecht M. Th. Houtsma Sticting, 1992). We do not possess anything in English like Radtke's *Al-Hakim al-Tirmidi: Ein islamischer Theosoph des 3./9 Jahrhunderts* (Freiburg: K. Schwarz, 1980), Fritz Meier's *Die Fawa'ih al-gamal wa-fawatih al-galal des Nagm ad-din al-Kubra* (Wiesbaden: F. Steiner, 1957), or Richard Gramlich's *Die schiitischen Derwischorden persiens*, 3 vol. (Wiesbaden: F. Steiner, 1965; reprint, 1981), and *Die Wunder der Freunde Gottes* (Wiesbaden: F. Steiner, 1987).

5. I am thinking in particular of Michel de Certeau, *The Sixteenth and Seventeenth Centuries*, vol. 2 of *The Mystic Fable* (Chicago: University of Chicago Press, 1992).

6. For example, Nasr edited the two volumes of *Islamic Spirituality* (New York: Crossroad, 1987), the two volumes of the *History of Islamic Philosophy* (London: Routledge, 1996), and Schimmel sat on the editorial board of the *Encyclopedia of Religion* (New York: Macmillan, 1986).

7. Jonathan Z. Smith, *Imagining Religion* (Chicago: University of Chicago Press, 1988).

8. See especially the signal work of Michel Chodkiewicz, *An Ocean Without Shore*.

9. See chapter 8, "Collective Renovatio," in this book.

10. See chapter 9, "The Idea of Incognito: Authority and Its Occultation According to Henry Corbin," in this book.

11. Perhaps the most serious imbalance of much esotericism is its inevitably aggressively antidemocratic bias, expressed as a narrowly exclusivist elistism.

12. See the collections devoted to secrecy in the History of Religions: *Secrecy in Religions*, ed. Kees Bolle, (Leiden: E. J. Brill, 1987); *Secrecy and Concealment: Studies in the History of Mediterranean and Near Eastern Religions*, ed. Guy G. Stroumsa and Hans G. Kippenberg (Leiden: E. J. Brill, 1995); and *Rending the Veil: Concealment and Secrecy in the History of Religions*, ed. Elliot R. Wolfson (New York: Seven Bridges Press, 1999).

13. Scholem and Corbin both hypothesized spontaneous revival—operating, unlike any other elements in the known world, independent of causation—which hypothesis avoided seeing society in any sense as being causative, as if secrets bubbled up from the depths directly into the souls of seekers.

14. The History of Religions, alas, possesses no parallel to the comprehensive survey of Western Marxist theories of totality undertaken by Martin Jay, *Marxism and Totality: The Adventures of a Concept from Lukács to Habermas* (Berkeley: University of California Press, 1984).

15. To vary a phrase by Alfred North Whitehead.

16. Bruce Lincoln, "Theses on Method," *Method and Theory in the Study of Religion*, 8 (1996): 225–227.

17. This post-Kantian, post-Weberian theory claimed to regain coherence in human history, but could only find it in an Idea outside what we would call human history. Scholem, again, is the exception here, but the exception that makes the rule.

18. This point is excellently analyzed by Hanegraaff, in *New Age Religion and Western Culture*.

19. He returned to this favored metaphor, for example, in *OL*.

20. For a useful discussion, see John Patrick Diggins, *Max Weber: Politics and the Spirit of Tragedy* (New York: Basic Books, 1996), 123–125. Diggins notes that although "Weber had shown the importance of religion in history, his methodological theory of inquiry seemed to eliminate religous values from the historian's work as a scientfic investigator." 123.

21. Jung claimed that the archetypes *precede* metaphysical constructions. He accordingly accused Buber of getting this causation backward: "What I am concerned with are psychic phenomena which can be proved empirically to be the bases of metaphysical concepts. . . . Of which metaphysical deity [Buber] is speaking I do not know." "Reply to Martin Buber," 199–200. In fact, Jung's entire "Reply to Martin Buber" is constructed around an attack on "metaphysics." Other examples make it clear that this dichotomy was fundamental for Jung. "One cannot grasp anything metaphysically, but it can be done psychologically. Therefore I strip things of their metaphysical wrappings in order to make them objects of psychology." "Commentary on The Secret of the Golden Flower," in Jung, *Psyche and Symbol*, 344. In the light of such assertions, Jung's talk of "treasures of Judaeo-Christian ethics grounded in metaphysics" appears both loaded and misleading, since he hardly valued those ethics as treasures. See Jung, *The Undiscovered Self*, trans. R. F. C. Hull (New York: New American Library, 1957), 43. Paul Bishop notes that in *Response to Job* (in Bishop's estimation "arguably the most significant and original [work] of his post-war period"), Jung "still poses ostensibly as a psychologist, not as a metaphysician, although this is patently untrue." *The Dionysian Self*, 355. One reason for this stubborn insistence was Jung's view that the "medieval picture of the world was breaking up and the metaphysical authority that ruled it was fast disappearing, only to reappear in Man." Cited by Bishop in *The Dionysian Self*, 332. This latter claim resembles the well-known "end of metaphysics" discourse of Martin Heidegger. Relevant in the present discussion are Corbin's translation of Heidegger's *Qu'est-ce que la métaphysique?* and Manheim's translation of Heidegger's *Introduction to Metaphysics*.

22. Weber, "Science as a Vocation," 128–156.

23. Martin Heidegger, "Who is Nietzsche's Zarathustra?" trans. Bernd Magnus, in *The New Nietzsche*, ed. David B. Allison (Cambridge Mass.: MIT Press, 1977; reprint, 1986), 64–79, at 77.

24. Especially in Scholem, "Zehn unhistorische Sätze über Kabbala."

25. "[Death] is often only the result of our indifference to immortality." *IS*, 56. This was the last sentence of Eliade's 1950 Eranos lecture, his first lecture at those meetings.

26. For Eliade's conception of a bookish initiation, of "baptism by intellect," see chapter 2, "Toward the Origins of History of Religions: Christian Kabbalah as Inspiration and as Initiation," in this book.

27. Weber, *The Protestant Ethic and the Spirit of Capitalism*, 58.

28. The German provides effective terms for this meaning, including *Aufhebung* and *Umfunktionierung*. Scholem used the term *Umfunktionierung* in his touching tribute to the nonogenarian Ernst Bloch—itself a model of dialectical *Aufhebung*. *OPJM*, 216–225.

29. But not to be a "nation like other nations." On Scholem's rejection of this idea, see Yosef Ben-Shlomo, "The Spiritual Universe of Gershom Scholem," *Modern Judaism* 5 (1985): 21–39, at 37.

30. *OPJM*, 67.

31. *FBJ*, 166.

32. I believe this emphasis on historicality owes much to the (direct or indirect) influence of Heideggerian thought.

33. *OPJM*, 67.

34. Ibid., 210.

35. *MTJM*, 27. One is reminded of the ideas of Kairos and Augenblick, on which see chapter 7, "A Rustling in the Woods: The Turn to Myth in Weimar Jewish Thought," in this book.

36. This shared imperative might also help explain why Corbin and Eliade nominally loathed history yet reveled in it across their long careers.

37. "The chain of transmission will not be broken, because it is the translation of the inexhaustible word of God into the human realm, and to that which may be comprehended by the individual." *OPJM*, 173. Compare, importantly, Eliade remarks on the "chaîne initiatique" at the end of "Initiation et modern moderne," 26.

Index

Abraham, 49, 234
Abulafia, Abraham, 96
academicism, 24–25, 32
Acta Iranica, 150
Adam, 121, 124
Adorno, Theodor: on anti-Semitic propaganda, 76; on defeating evil, 224; on *Ergriffenheit,* 32; influence of Heidegger on, 139; on *Mana,* 121; on myth, culture, and history, 190, 191; psychoanalysis in reverse development by, 183; Scholem and, 55–56, 124, 276n.28; use of philosophical analysis by, 123
Aesthetica in Nuce (Hamann), 54, 101
Ahmad, Shaikh, 28
Ahriman, 177–79, 325n.29
allegory, 91–93
Alter, Robert, 101
Altmann, Alexander, 26, 112, 123, 136, 139
Ammons, A. R., 74
Ancient Discovery of the Unconscious, 196
androgynous angel, 206–7, 211
androgyny, 204–5, 206–8, 211–12, 213–14, 336n.22
Angel of the Earth, 194–95
"Angel of History," 211
Angelic Self, 235
angelology, 148
Angels: androgynous, 206–7; combat for the, 155, 156; symbols and, 236
"Angel Satan," 206–7
Angelus Novus (Klee painting), 85, 206, 207
The Angel in the Western Window (Meyrink), 208
animal symbolicum, 91
Annual Meeting of the American Academy of Religion, 12
Anshen, Ruth Nanda, 4, 72
Antaios (ed. by Eliade and Jünger), 4, 72, 144, 161
anthropocosmic destiny, 198
Anthropos, 133
antimodernism, 147–48

antinomianism, 230–32, 341n.18
anti-Semitism, 76, 190, 262n.72, 326n.45
"The Antithetical Sense of Primal Words" (Freud), 78
apocalypse, 143–44
apocalyptic theology, 173–74
Apollinaire, Guillaume, 218
Ibn al-ʿArabi, 239, 240
"Archetypal Psychology" (Hillman), 8
archetypes of all creation, 189
archetypes theory, 5, 186, 352n.21
"Architect of the Invisible" (Hoyveda), 18
Arendt, Hannah, 123, 136, 139
Aristotle, 177
Arnaldez, Roger, 180
Aryamehr, Shahanshah, 151
Aryanism, 133–35, 309n.52, 315n.39
Ascona, 13, 14, 26, 39, 102, 103, 237, 290n.20
Auerbach, Elias, 6, 7
Auschwitz, 101, 234
Ausnahmezustand (exception), 231–32
authority: hidden authority theory, 145, 148–50; moral, 234–36
Avicenna and the Visionary Recital (Corbin), 128, 137, 187

Baader, Franz von, 39, 49, 54–55, 56, 131, 159, 211
Bacharach, Jakob Elchanan, 33
Baeck, Leo, 54, 193
Ball, Hugo, 119
Balzac, Honoré de, 143, 203–4, 205, 211, 213
The Baphomet (Klossowski), 203, 207–8
Bardèche, Maurice, 146
Barth, Karl, 52, 146, 172, 187
Basilides, 220
Bataille, Georges, 77, 141, 218, 219, 221, 222, 230
Bavarian Academy of Arts, 13, 89
Beauvoir, Simone de, 219
Becker, Carl Heinrich, 116
Being and Time (Heidegger), 117, 122, 136